T0340490

MIRRORS OF GREATNESS

ALSO BY DAVID REYNOLDS

The Creation of the Anglo-American Alliance:
A Study in Competitive Cooperation, 1937–1941

An Ocean Apart: The Relationship between Britain and America
in the Twentieth Century (with David Dimbleby)

Britannia Overruled: British Policy and World Power
in the Twentieth Century

The Origins of the Cold War in Europe (editor)

Allies at War: The Soviet, American and British Experience, 1939–1945
(co-edited with Warren F. Kimball and A. O. Chubarian)

Rich Relations: The American Occupation of Britain, 1942–1945

One World Divisible: A Global History since 1945

From Munich to Pearl Harbor: Roosevelt's America
and the Origins of the Second World War

In Command of History: Churchill Fighting
and Writing the Second World War

From World War to Cold War: Churchill, Roosevelt
and the International History of the 1940s

Summits: Six Meetings that Shaped the Twentieth Century

America, Empire of Liberty: A New History

FDR's World: War, Peace, and Legacies
(co-edited with David B. Woolner and Warren F. Kimball)

The Long Shadow: The Great War and the Twentieth Century

Transcending the Cold War: Summits, Statecraft,
and the Dissolution of Bipolarity in Europe, 1970–1990
(co-edited with Kristina Spohr)

The Kremlin Letters: Stalin's Wartime Correspondence with
Churchill and Roosevelt (with Vladimir Pechatnov)

Island Stories: Britain and Its History in the Age of Brexit

MIRRORS OF GREATNESS

CHURCHILL AND THE LEADERS WHO SHAPED HIM

DAVID REYNOLDS

WILLIAM
COLLINS

William Collins
An imprint of HarperCollins*Publishers*
1 London Bridge Street
London SE1 9GF

WilliamCollinsBooks.com

HarperCollins*Publishers*
Macken House
39/40 Mayor Street Upper
Dublin 1
D01 C9W8, Ireland

First published in Great Britain in 2023 by William Collins

1

A catalogue record for this book is available from the British Library

ISBN 978-0-00-843991-0 (hardback)
ISBN 978-0-00-843992-7 (trade paperback)

Typeset in Minion Pro by Typeset by Jouve (UK), Milton Keynes

Printed and bound in the UK using 100% renewable electricity at CPI Group (UK) Ltd

Be not afraid of greatness: some are born great, some achieve greatness, and some have greatness thrust upon 'em.

William Shakespeare, *Twelfth Night* (1602)

The amount of energy wasted by men and women of first-class quality in arriving at their true degree, before they can play on the world stage, can never be measured. One may say that sixty, perhaps seventy per cent of all they have to give is expended on fights which have no other object than to get to their battlefield.

Winston S. Churchill, *Great Contemporaries* (1937)

Winston Churchill appeared to me, from one end of the drama to the other, as the great champion of a great enterprise and the great artist of a great history.

Charles de Gaulle, *Mémoires de Guerre* (1959)

Jake, Toby and Isla

What's past is prologue

Contents

Introduction

Winston Churchill is 150 years young.

Born on 30 November 1874, he lived past the age of 90, breathing his last on 24 January 1965. Yet his name still burns bright. He remains, for millions across the world in the twenty-first century, the Greatest Briton of all time, and 2024 will trigger a new surge of events, exhibitions and reflections about what made him great. Many accounts depict him as a self-made man, a solitary hero. *Mirrors of Greatness* offers an alternative perspective by showing how Churchill learned from others as he rose to national and global prominence.

The book also explores how posterity's estimate of Churchill has been shaped, as he intended, by his estimate of himself. This was a man who made history and also wrote himself into history, to a degree unique in modern times. His 150th anniversary is a good moment to move out of Churchill's self-imposed shadow and take a twenty-first-century view of the man and his significance. Because, like all commanding figures as they recede into the past, he now polarises opinion – lauded by some, especially as a war leader against Nazism, but criticised by others for perpetuating imperial rule and colonial attitudes.[1]

Winston Churchill was obsessed by 'greatness'. Lacking any belief in an afterlife, and convinced he would die young, he was determined to leave his mark on history, like the leaders of old who had been dubbed 'the Great' – from Alexander of Macedonia to Frederick of

Prussia. For Churchill as for them, personal greatness was tied to the political: the building or consolidation of a great empire. Thanks to the fame gained in his lifetime, he hoped to win immortality. In that ambition he achieved remarkable success. Biographers have described his exceptional array of talents, and also his periodic failures of judgment, leaving the impression of a stand-alone genius with dazzling gifts and jagged flaws who, despite endless struggles, followed his own star to reach eventual apotheosis. A triumph of a great man over lesser mortals.

Yet the story is more complex. Churchill was largely self-taught. He never went to university – probably to his benefit, because a traditional classical education might well have stifled his serendipitous genius. But throughout his life he paid careful attention to others. In 1937, aged 62, he published *Great Contemporaries*, a series of essays on 'Great Men of our age' which was intended to evoke some 'wonderful giants of old', presenting 'not only the actors but the scene'. Most of his cast of characters dated from the late Victorian era and the years around the Great War. He included no contemporary British politicians; there were brief essays on Franklin Roosevelt and Adolf Hitler but these were composed in 1934–5, when neither man's trajectory was clear.[2]

Churchill never wrote a sequel to *Great Contemporaries*, about the leaders with whom he shared the summit of his career when Britain's Prime Minister in 1940–5 and again in 1951–5. Yet it was during those years of the Second World War and the early Cold War that he finally experienced the full magnitude of leadership – learning its real demands and costs – doing so, moreover, at a time of unprecedented global turmoil. This book explores the odyssey of his life through his encounters with other leading figures. Their successes and failures illuminated his Parsifal-like quest for greatness.

Yet he also saw what he wanted to see. His doctor, Lord Moran, once wrote: 'Where people are concerned, Winston Churchill exists in an imaginary world of his own making.'[3] Although Moran exaggerated, this book contains many examples of how he could indeed create his own reality. That capacity was readily apparent to those who worked with him, arousing a range of emotions from incredulity to amusement, anger to admiration. So we shall also see him through their eyes, observing his skills and his flaws, his charm and his insufferability. As a result, each chapter is a kind of two-way mirror. And by putting these twelve encounters together in a loose chronological sequence it is possible to sketch his whole life in revealing new ways.

A few of the cast are men Churchill unquestionably acknowledged as great, notably David Lloyd George and Franklin Delano Roosevelt – each of whom made an enduring impact on his mind and heart. Others proved obstacles on Churchill's path to the greatness of which he dreamed – such as Neville Chamberlain and Adolf Hitler. Some were adversaries who nevertheless intrigued and impressed him: Benito Mussolini, Josef Stalin and Charles de Gaulle fall into that category. But we shall also look at figures who defy his conception of greatness yet who strike us, in our own age, as worthy of admiration. Mohandas Gandhi posed perhaps the most fundamental challenge, because he had deliberately turned his back on the privileges and accoutrements of British civilisation and because his concept of political leadership belied Churchill's soldierly understanding of power – doing so in ways that undermined the British Empire. Clement Attlee – though, like Churchill, ready to fight and die for his country in the Great War – developed an entirely different sense of the values for which it was worth living: a socialist Britain in a progressively post-colonial world. Churchill's interactions with them reveal how his conception of 'greatness' ossified in later life – reminding us that historical interpretation is a constant interplay of past and present. What's more, their outlook and achievements sometimes accord better than his with the values of the twenty-first century.

This is particularly true of his wife, Clementine, whose immense yet costly contribution to his career is more apparent in an age that is finally taking women seriously as political actors. Clementine's contemporary, in time though not in mind, was the author Virginia Woolf, who remarked penetratingly in *A Room of One's Own* (1929) about the male need for female mirrors:

Women have served all these centuries as looking-glasses possessing the magic and delicious power of reflecting the figure of man at twice its natural size. Without that power probably the earth would still be swamp and jungle. The glories of our wars would be unknown ... Whatever may be their use in civilized societies, mirrors are essential to all violent and heroic action. That is why Napoleon and Mussolini both insist so emphatically upon the inferiority of women, for if they were not inferior, they would cease to enlarge ... For if she begins to tell the truth, the figure in the looking-glass shrinks; his fitness for life is diminished. How is he to go on giving judgement, civilizing natives, making laws, writing books, dressing up and speechifying at banquets, unless he can see himself at breakfast and at dinner at least twice the size he really is? ... The looking-glass vision is of supreme importance ... [4]

These observations also apply to relations between men. Males, especially those in the public gaze, are prone to measure themselves against each other. And that was supremely true of Winston Churchill.

Of course, greatness isn't simply about measurable achievements (or false impressions) but whether these are publicly recognised and endorsed. In other words, what matters is reputation. Many have aspired to greatness, but few have had Churchill's relentless determination to burnish his own name. Renowned as a political leader, he was also a prodigious writer – that was how he earned his living – and most of his books dealt with his own family, broadly conceived, including volumes on his own father and his martial ancestor John Churchill, first Duke of Marlborough. Above all, he wrote about himself, whether in the journalistic self-promotions of his youth or in the monumental pair of six-volume memoirs in which he chronicled the two world wars and defined his place within them. He had no intention of leaving the 'verdict of history' to others. For that reason, this book about Churchill's path to greatness, illuminated by his inter-actions with some of his great contemporaries, begins with how he created a father and ends with how he mirrored himself.

Charles de Gaulle remarked that 'Winston Churchill appeared to me, from one end of the drama to the other, as the great champion of a great enterprise and the great artist of a great history.'[5] The reference to artistry was apt – because of Winston's passion for painting, which he took up in his forties after becoming the prime scapegoat for the Gallipoli campaign, a disaster that seemed for a while to be a fatal setback in his quest for greatness. But de Gaulle also captured how Churchill's writing was imbued with a profound historical imagination and a sparkling sense of the dramatic. An avid theatre-goer, he was deeply read in English history, which he understood as a grand, Whiggish progression in which the ascent of 'liberty' was paramount. Centre stage in the theatre of history he placed great men – both good and bad – who were depicted as the prime agents of political change. And into that drama he took infinite pains to inscribe himself.

Thanks to the double impact of his deeds and his words, Churchill became a historical icon: the heroic image that now pervades the public culture of Britain and America. Yet he never took his reputation for granted. On one occasion during his final years, after a moody dinner, he suddenly exclaimed, 'I have worked very hard all my life, and I have achieved a great deal – in the end to achieve NOTHING.'[6] Was he expressing the inevitable self-pity of the old? Or revealing a deeper, existential anxiety about what he had accomplished? With the passage of time, new questions have indeed been asked about his achievements. Did he defeat Hitler's Reich only to help Stalin grab Eastern Europe? Had his triumph over European fascism allowed socialism to entrench itself at home? A prophetic voice for Franco-German rapprochement, did he fail to see its implications for Britain? And was his intoxication with the 'special relationship' mere blindness to the erosion of Britain's empire and its global power?

These are questions to be explored in the looking-glass chapters that follow. Along the way, we should keep in mind Shakespeare's dictum about those who are born great, those who achieve greatness and those who have greatness thrust upon them – because all three apply to Churchill at various stages in his life.[7] We should recall too the observation in his 1937 book about those who become significant actors on the 'world stage', that two-thirds of their lifetime is used up on 'fights which have no other object than to get to their battlefield'.[8] Winston Churchill reached *his* great battlefield on 10 May 1940, aged 65, after a campaign that commenced in childhood. So that observation fits him perfectly. Yet, within a week, the battlefield was a total wreck, and catastrophe stared Churchill, Britain and the Empire in the face, thanks to a man whom he never dignified with the accolade of greatness. Ironically, it was this despised German who gave Churchill his chance for glory.

After May 1940, the rest of Churchill's political life was improvisation. Yet it's a tribute to his abilities as a leader *and* as a writer that this is rarely appreciated. Which is why we need to enter this hall of mirrors. And by doing so, we may discover a novel way both to narrate and also to interrogate this remarkable life.

His Father's Voice: the spirit of Lord Randolph coaching the young
parliamentarian. E.T. Reed in *Punch*, 27 February 1901.

1

Lord Randolph Churchill

Creating a Father

Solitary trees, if they grow at all, grow strong: and a boy deprived of a father's care often develops, if he escape the perils of youth, an independence and a vigour of thought which may restore in after life the heavy loss of early days.

Winston to his mother, 1899[1]

Until the end he worshipped at the altar of his Unknown Father.

Violet Bonham Carter, 1965[2]

The final call came early on Saturday 24 January 1895. Grosvenor Square was still in darkness, with snow on the ground. Winston Churchill had been sleeping in a house nearby. He ran across the square to number 50, his grandmother's London home, and reached his father's bedside just in time. 'His end was quite painless,' Winston wrote in *My Early Life* (1930). 'All my dreams of comradeship with him, of entering Parliament at his side and in his support, were ended. There remained for me only to pursue his aims and vindicate his memory.'[3]

Lord Randolph Churchill – younger son of the Duke of Marlborough, apostle of 'Tory Democracy' and a meteor of British politics in the early 1880s – had been consigned to outer darkness since his ill-judged resignation at Christmas 1886 from the Marquess of Salisbury's government. This was the climax of a power struggle that had been brewing for months. And for Randolph, only 37, there was no way back. Over the following decade, the erratic impetuosity evident since his youth morphed into violent mood swings; physicians diagnosed a form of paralytic dementia. By late 1894 his condition had deteriorated markedly: 'Has been violent and apathetic by turns', noted his doctor on 4 November. 'Gait staggering and uncertain.' On the 16th: 'Voice weak. Takes little interest in things. Face losing its expression.' By the New Year Lord Randolph's illness was clearly terminal. After two bouts of 'acute mania' he sank into a coma and on 24 January 1895 his doctor recorded: 'Lord Randolph died very quietly this morning at 6.15. His lungs began to fill up very quickly yesterday and this evidently was the immediate cause of death.'[4]

Lord Randolph's life ended a few weeks before his forty-sixth birthday. Winston, his elder son, had been spared much of the physical horror of his father's slow degeneration, but the emotional impact of his passing was immense. It was widely rumoured that Randolph had died from the effects of syphilis, contracted in his youth. Although some recent commentators have suggested that a brain tumour also fits the symptoms, Winston had to live with the syphilis stigma for the rest of his life.[5] Worse still, Lord Randolph had never allowed him to come close – instead periodically penning caustic letters about young Winston's laziness and extravagance. The most scorching missive was written in August 1893 after his son finally scraped into Sandhurst. Lord Randolph berated the 'slovenly happy-go-lucky harum scarum style of work for which you have always been distinguished at your different schools'. He warned against any further self-pleading 'because I no longer attach the slightest weight to anything you may say about your own acquirements and exploits'. He told Winston bluntly that if he carried on this 'idle, useless and unprofitable life' he would become 'a mere social wastrel, one of the hundreds of the public school failures', and would 'degenerate into a shabby, unhappy & futile existence'. The letter was signed 'Your aff[ectiona]te father, Randolph S.C.' In 1930, thirty-seven years later, his son could still quote parts of that letter from memory.[6]

In January 1895, the same month that Lord Randolph died, Winston completed his training as an officer cadet at Sandhurst, the Royal Military Academy. He graduated 20th in a class of 130 – having entered ten from the bottom on a list of 102.[7] Thereafter, his trajectory proved spectacular. 'Seldom, if ever,' observed historian Paul Addison, 'has an ambitious young man carried out such a stupendous programme of self-advancement as Churchill between 1895 and 1900.' By the time he took his seat as MP for Oldham in February 1901, aged 26, Winston had fought in four wars, published five books, written more than 200 newspaper articles and earned the equivalent of £1 million in today's money on the lecture circuit.[8]

And over the next five years, he also came to terms with his father. Once in Parliament, he persuaded Lord Randolph's executors to entrust him with the task of writing an official biography, which he later called a work of vindication.[9] In its pages, he presented his opportunist father as a man of consistent principle who had brought about his own downfall because misplaced party loyalty restrained him from taking the values of Tory Democracy to a more appropriate home on the Liberal benches. *Lord Randolph Churchill* appeared in January 1906 just as Winston was elected MP for Manchester North West, now as a Liberal. And so, eleven years after Lord Randolph's death and five since Winston became an MP, he was beginning to break free from his father – or at least from the father he had created. As his cousin Ivor Guest put it, 'Few fathers had done less for their sons. Few sons have done more for their fathers.'[10]

* * *

The decade from 1895 to 1906 set a clear path for what followed. Winston was a man of words as much as a man of action, fighting and writing himself into history. Both were equally important in his path to greatness, even though it suited him in *My Early Life* to hype up his military exploits and play down his experience of formal education. Worst of all was Latin. Forced to learn the first declension, he expressed incredulity at the vocative case.

'Why does mensa mean "O table" as well as "a table"?'

'You would use it in speaking to a table.'

'But I never do.'

'If you are impertinent, you will be punished, and punished, let me tell you, very severely.'[11]

'In all the twelve years I was at school,' he proudly asserted in *My Early Life*, 'no one ever succeeded in making me write a Latin verse or learn any Greek except the alphabet.' Told that Gladstone read Homer for fun, Winston thought it 'served him right'. Freed after two years from a brutal prep school in Ascot, he spent another three in a more congenial institution near Brighton where he did subjects that attracted him: 'French, History, lots of Poetry by heart'. 'Where my reason, imagination or interest were not engaged, I would not or I could not learn.' His was a roving, inquisitive mind, buttressed by a prodigious memory. Throughout these years, contrary to the dunce-like impression conveyed in *My Early Life*, school reports were far from damning: even at Ascot he was in 'the top half or usually the top third of the class'.[12]

His Achilles heel was examinations, especially those *bêtes noires*: Classics and Mathematics. In the entrance exam for Harrow, he said he was 'unable to answer a single question on the Latin paper'. He did write his name on the sheet of paper, together with the number of the first question. 'After much reflection', brackets were inserted around the number. But, apart from 'a blot and several smudges', nothing more was added in two hours. Although scraping into Harrow, he was assigned to the lowest division of the fourth form and lingered there for nearly a year. As a result, he was drilled in 'mere English' so that 'I got into my bones the essential structure of the ordinary British sentence – which is a noble thing.' Spending three years in the 'Army Class' also spared him further Latin and Greek, because such 'splendid things' were reserved only for 'the cleverer boys'.[13]

Adopting this mocking tone in 1930, as a man now famed and successful, Winston was able to send up the exam system and much that passed for education in late Victorian England. Yet *My Early Life* does make very clear that, when interested, he displayed considerable talents. At Harrow, he won a prize for learning and reciting without a mistake 1,200 lines of Macaulay's *Lays of Ancient Rome*, which became one of his most cherished books. And then in 1896–7, as a subaltern in Bangalore with time on his hands, the 22-year-old Churchill was seized by 'a desire for learning' of the sort never generated by Harrow or Sandhurst, especially in history, philosophy, economics and recent politics. And so, during the sweltering afternoons when others snoozed, he sampled Plato and Aristotle, Schopenhauer and Darwin, deepened his acquaintance with Macaulay and worked his way through Gibbon's *Decline and Fall of the Roman Empire*.[14] In more utilitarian vein, Winston studied Bartlett's *Familiar Quotations*, as well as *The Annual Register* – the classic political almanac first edited by Edmund Burke – reading and annotating the volumes since the 1870s, and poring over its record of parliamentary debates. Sometimes he even composed speeches that he would have delivered on issues of the moment and pasted them into the relevant volumes.

Most of these books were sent out to him by his mother, Jennie, daughter of the New York financier, Leonard Jerome. Many of the Commons debates he studied featured his father who also, Winston gathered, had read Gibbon 'with delight' and 'knew whole pages of it by heart'.[15] Yearning for closer relations with both of his parents pervades the opening chapters of *My Early Life*. Equally vivid is the deep affection and support of his nanny, Mrs Everest – a mother-substitute known as 'Woom' or 'Woomany'. Parental distancing was a familiar element of the upbringing of many upper-class Victorians, but Winston seems to have resented it much more than his younger brother, Jack. It has been calculated by one biographer that in the years 1885–92 his parents sent him six letters (mostly in remonstration) and he wrote to them on seventy-six occasions (mostly begging for attention). Some of the messages are truly pathetic. 'Darling Mummy, do attend to my letter. I am so wretched. Even now I weep. Please my darling Mummy be kind to your loving son . . . Let me at least think that you love me.' Even if Winston was trying it on, this is surely a remarkable letter for a seventeen-year-old.[16]

The craving for parental love is a dominant theme of *My Early Life*. 'My mother always seemed to me like a fairy princess . . . She shone for me like the Evening Star. I loved her dearly – but at a distance.' He laments his twelve years in school as 'the only barren and unhappy period' of his life. 'I would far rather have been apprenticed as a bricklayer's mate', he added, 'or helped my father dress the front windows of a grocer's shop.' Such work would have been 'real' and 'natural' and 'I should have got to know my father, which would have been a joy to me.'[17]

Yet relations between child and parent change over time, and Winston's experience was no exception. His 'Evening Star' came much closer to earth after January 1895, the month when he graduated from Sandhurst and Lord Randolph breathed his last. Jennie plunged back into London society. Only 40, and still alluring, she contracted two further marriages with younger men of Winston's age. But she also exploited her contacts to advance his career. 'We worked together on even terms', Winston wrote later in *My Early Life*, 'more like brother and sister than mother and son. At least so it seemed to me.' The supply of books was but one example. She also acted variously as banker, courier, lobbyist and literary agent – not to mention appreciative reader of his frantically self-promoting letters. As Winston put it: 'In my interest she left no wire unpulled, no stone unturned, no cutlet uncooked.'[18]

While the relationship with his mother evolved, that of father and son was frozen in death. 'Had he lived another four or five years', Winston insisted in *My Early Life*, 'he could not have done without me.'[19] Yet that assertion assumed a truly inconceivable transformation of his father's domineering and volatile character. It would be more accurate to say that Lord Randolph's death, though a devastating shock, proved truly liberating for his son, especially given the adult rapport now developing with his mother. Winston was able to create, imaginatively, the relationship with his father for which he had yearned in vain. It proved more advantageous to have a famous father who was dead not alive.

Winston had already set his heart on following Lord Randolph into politics. Yet the Churchill name was a liability as much as an asset. Although Winston had been born at Blenheim – the palace built by his ancestor John Churchill, first Duke of Marlborough, to mark his triumph over the armies of Louis XIV in 1704 – in fact the Churchill clan was notorious to most Victorians for opportunism, profligacy and incompetence. Gladstone, admittedly no family friend, declared in 1882, 'There never was a Churchill from John of Marlborough down that had either morals or principles.'[20] Lord Randolph fitted the bill. Addicted to drink and gambling, he racked up huge debts and his whirlwind courtship of an American heiress was widely regarded as a marriage of financial convenience. The assumption in London society that he had died from the effects of syphilis squared with his dissolute image. In order to campaign successfully under the Churchill banner, Winston therefore had to make his own name and fortune.

The explosive trajectory from 1895 seems astounding, if we take at face value the self-portrait in *My Early Life* of an indolent dunce and all those whining letters home. One Harrow contemporary remembered an 'uncouth' red-haired boy (only five foot six when he left), usually a loner, whose face registered a mix of 'resentment and pride'. The congenital lisp provoked derision; his poor health and lack of physical strength marginalised him from the camaraderie of team sports. When fired up, however, Winston could be 'precocious, bumptious and talkative' – pronouncing assertively as he walked, leaning forward with his neck stuck out.[21] And in 1892 he won the Public Schools Fencing Championship, against taller and stronger boys, a feat which the Harrow magazine attributed to his 'quick and dashing attack which quite took his opponents by surprise.'[22] Fearful of being judged a coward, Winston indulged in daredevil acts, often at the cost of serious injury. Craving attention, he broke rules with impunity and answered back when punished. Once, while being 'swished' in the good old public-school manner for some misdemeanour by the head boy, Nugent Hicks, he exploded: 'I shall be a greater man than you.' Hicks was not impressed – 'You can have two more for that' – but

Winston's prophecy proved correct: Harrow's head boy climbed only to the dizzy heights of Bishop of Lincoln.[23]

A reckless desire to stand out for bravery was a hallmark of the young Churchill. 'Being in many ways a coward, particularly at school,' he told his brother, 'there is no ambition I cherish so keenly as to gain a reputation of personal courage.'[24] Indeed, it became the *raison d'être* of his brief but dramatic military career. By stripping that story down to its highlights, it is possible to see just how manic was his pursuit of fame and his desire for greatness.

* * *

While he was home on leave from Bangalore for the London Season at the end of July 1897, a piece in a newspaper caught Churchill's eye. General Sir Bindon Blood was about to mount a punitive expedition against rebellious tribesmen on the North-West Frontier of India. Blood was an old friend of the family from whom Winston had extracted a promise months before to let him join any such expedition. Cabling the General to remind him of that pledge but not waiting for a reply, Winston rushed back to India – in the haste forgetting his pet dog and his polo sticks. He asked his mother to sort all this out and to settle various outstanding bills. After a two-day journey on the weekly 'Indian Mail' train from London to Calais and then down to the Adriatic port of Brindisi, on the heel of Italy, he embarked on the hot, crowded steamer for Bombay. From there he travelled south to wangle leave from his regiment, before undertaking a five-day train journey of some 2,000 miles up north to join Blood's field force on the Afghan border. He was accredited as a war correspondent, sending reports to the *Daily Telegraph*.[25]

Winston deliberately put himself in the thick of things. On his first day in action, 16 September, he shot at least four of the enemy and saved one wounded colleague from being 'cut up horribly by these wild beasts' – telling his mother, 'My pants are still stained with the man's blood.' Two days later, 'I rode on my grey pony all along the skirmish line where everyone else was lying down under cover. Foolish perhaps but I play for high stakes and, given an audience, there is no act too daring or too noble.' He added tellingly: 'Without the gallery things are very different.' The 'grey pony' was actually a white horse, purchased deliberately so that he would be conspicuous in combat. Later, having learned that he would be mentioned in despatches, Winston told her, 'I am glad my follies have not been altogether unnoticed' – though he had to ride along the skirmish line on three occasions before his white horse was spotted by a senior officer. He declared that 'bullets' were 'not worth considering' because 'I am so conceited that I do not believe the Gods would create so potent a being as myself for so prosaic an ending.'[26]

Winston's larger ambition was 'bringing my personality before the electorate', and he did not care whether that risked trouble with the army authorities: 'if I am to avoid doing "unusual" things it is difficult to see what chance I have of being more than an average person.' He was therefore furious that his mother decided it was prudent to anonymise his reports for the *Telegraph* and substitute 'By a Young Officer'. He set about stamping his name on his exploits by publishing a book entitled *The Story of the Malakand Field Force: An Episode of Frontier War*. 'I have discovered a great power of application which I did not think I possessed,' he proudly told his mother in December. 'For two months I have worked not less than 5 hours a day.' He sent her the manuscript on New Year's Eve, with detailed instructions about maps, proofreading and expected earnings – leaving her to find a publisher. By the following week, his mind was moving on: 'You must make a tremendous effort to get me to Egypt', he insisted, because it was now the 'fashionable theatre of war'. This was 'most important', he told her. 'It would mean another medal – perhaps two.' So 'do stir up all your influence ... have no scruples but worry right and left and take no refusal.'[27]

Even the persuasive powers of 'Mamma' were not, however, suffi-cient to convince General Sir Herbert Kitchener, commander of the force tasked with finishing off the Dervish Empire in the Sudan. Like other senior officers, Kitchener had taken umbrage at the writings of this uppity young subaltern. With Winston's hopes of another campaign apparently blocked, his main consolation was the praise for his first book – despite the appalling typos. (According to one reviewer, it suggested 'in style a volume by Disraeli revised by a mad printer's reader'.) In upbeat moments, Winston now imagined 'a long series of volumes', starting with a life of the Italian nationalist hero Garibaldi, through which he would make his mark in the 'literary sphere of action' and achieve financial independence.[28]

During the first half of 1898, Winston therefore had to cool his heels in Bangalore. It was only after he returned to London on leave that the logjam broke, thanks to a fortuitous interview with the Prime Minister, Lord Salisbury – who had been intrigued by the book and wanted to talk with its precocious author, son of the politician he had destroyed. As a result, strings were pulled to override Kitchener and get the young Churchill to his next war zone, as a 'supernumerary lieutenant' with the 21st Lancers at Cairo. He was to travel at his own expense and on the strict understanding that, if killed or wounded during the Sudan campaign, 'no charge of any kind would fall on British Army funds.'[29]

And so the race for fame was on again. Having arranged terms with the *Morning Post* (this time at £15 per column), Winston did not to wait for leave from his regiment in Bangalore and took the earliest possible train across the Channel to Paris. His odyssey continued down to Marseilles, across the Mediterranean on a 'filthy' tramp steamer, to Cairo and then by train again 1,400 miles up the Nile. The battle he sought took place just outside Khartoum, near the village of Omdurman, on 2 September. The Dervish warriors were shot to pieces by superior British firepower: rifles, artillery and the lethal Maxim machine guns. But in popular memory, Omdurman went down as the last great cavalry charge of the British Army – mounted by the 21st Lancers.

Churchill's men were in the thick of it. Charging what seemed like a thin line of Dervish riflemen, they discovered very late that it concealed thick ranks of 'spearmen' lurking in a steeply sloping gulley. As usual, Winston was mounted on a 'grey', thereby standing out to friend and foe alike. Crashing into the enemy, his troop lost all cohesion. Any soldier toppled from his horse was hacked to pieces in seconds, but Winston stayed in the saddle. During the melee, he emptied his pistol at close range, 'killing several – 3 for certain – 2 doubtful'. Taking in the scene for a moment too long, he became the target of direct fire, but the bullets went 'Heaven knows where' as he spurred his horse forward to join the rest of his squadron, regrouping some 150 yards away. There they dismounted and used their carbines to harry the enemy, much to the disappointment of Lieutenant Churchill. 'I was very anxious for the regiment to charge back – *pour la gloire*', he wrote home. Although admitting that 'the dismounted fire was more practical', he felt that 'British cavalry so seldom get a chance that they must aim at the magnificent rather than the practical – and another fifty or sixty casualties would have made the performance historic.' As it was the losses in his troop were considerable: 5 officers killed or wounded out of 20, and 65 men out of 280, all in a couple of minutes.[30] But Winston emerged unscathed, whereas Col. Frank Rhodes, *The Times* correspondent – already fingered to write his heroic obituary (just in case) – was shot through the shoulder and seriously wounded. Just two days after the battle Winston informed his mother that 'I shall write a history of this war', adding that he had persuaded Rhodes to 'give me all his photographs.'[31]

The book that ensued, *The River War*, was altogether more substantial than *Malakand Field Force* – and about a more significant subject. Indeed, Churchill decided to build his account of Omdurman into a full-scale study of Britain's struggle to control the strategically vital headwaters of the Nile, starting with the revolt of 'the Mahdi' – the charismatic Nubian leader Muhammad Ahmad – in 1881 and the death of Gen. Charles Gordon at the siege of Khartoum in 1885. Gordon had become an icon of late-Victorian England, commemorated almost as a martyr in paintings and postcards. In other words, Churchill's book addressed a topic far closer to British minds and hearts than India's Afghan frontier. As usual, Winston had learnt lessons from his first foray into serious publishing: he researched intensively in Cairo and London and paid close attention to the proofreading of what became two volumes and 950 pages. In writing what was now 'almost a history of the ruin and rescue of the Soudan', he also had the opportunity to indulge his stylistic love of Macaulay and Gibbon – what he called 'the staccato antitheses of the former and the rolling sentences and genitival endings of the latter' – with 'a bit of my own from time to time'.[32]

Winston wrote the book firmly convinced of the rightness of British rule over Egypt and the Sudan – sure that control of the Nile would 'drive civilisation and prosperity to the south' and, conversely, 'bear wealth and commerce to the sea'.[33] But that conviction did not mean denigrating Britain's opponents. Indeed, with his love of the heroic, he sought to build up both Gordon and the Mahdi into tragic figures. Struck that the Mahdi had been orphaned when young, he wrote: 'Solitary trees, if they grow at all, grow strong: and a boy deprived of a father's care often develops, if he escape the perils of youth, an independence and a vigour of thought which may restore in after life the heavy loss of early days.' He made a point of sending that sentence to his mother. Nor did Winston's belief in Britain's cause deter him from caustic criticism of those charged with carrying it out. His private dislike of Kitchener for initially frustrating his ambitions – 'a general but never a gentleman' – carried over into the first edition of the book, where he denounced Kitchener for desecrating the Mahdi's tomb in deliberate retaliation for Mahdist butchery of Gordon's corpse. The book, though praised by most reviewers, went down badly in army circles; it was dubbed 'A Subaltern's Hints to Generals'.[34]

Winston's double life as a serving officer and a war correspondent had become untenable. And his financial situation was also increasingly precarious. So he decided he should resign his commission and live with his mother while finishing *The River War*, now feeling that writing could be the way to earn a living. But then another war broke out on the edge of empire: this time in South Africa.

After the discovery of gold in the Transvaal in the 1880s, tensions escalated between the Boer republics of Dutch settlers and the

'Uitlanders' (outsiders) – many of them British – who wanted to join the gold rush. By the late 1890s, the British government of the Cape Colony, under its Prime Minister Cecil Rhodes, was contemplating annexation of its rich and troublesome northern neighbours. When negotiations broke down, the Boers moved first and invaded Cape Colony. Churchill had seen this coming. When approached to act as the *Daily Mail*'s war correspondent, he used the offer to leverage a better deal from the *Morning Post*: £1,000 for the first four months ('shore to shore') and £200 per month thereafter. This was probably the most lucrative contract to date for a war correspondent. He also had more time than in the past to prepare: in addition to getting his field glasses repaired and buying a new compass, he ordered six assorted cases of champagne, claret, port, whisky and brandy, and twelve bottles of Rose's Lime Cordial. Winston, as his own son Randolph later noted, 'never believed that war should be needlessly uncomfortable'.[35]

On 14 October 1899, three days after fighting began, Winston set out from Southampton on a ship carrying many of the British war correspondents. On board, he struck up a friendship with John Atkins, reporting for the *Manchester Guardian*, who, half a century later, vividly recalled a 'most unusual young man. He was slim, slightly reddish-haired, pale, lively, frequently plunging along the deck "with neck out-thrust," as Browning fancied Napoleon'. Sometimes, though, he was 'sitting in meditation, folding and unfolding his hands' as though 'helping himself to untie mental knots'. To Atkins it seemed 'obvious that he was in love with words' – hesitating before choosing one or changing his mind to insert a word that was better. But this was no mere writer: when talking of a political career like that of his father, 'then such a gleam shot from him that he was almost transfigured'. Atkins had 'not before encountered this sort of ambition, unabashed, frankly egotistical, communicating its excitement, and extorting sympathy'. Young Churchill also showed 'no reverence for his seniors as such and talked about them as though they were his own age, or younger'. Yet 'he could laugh at his dreams of glory', and there were flashes of 'impish fun' which 'suddenly shone out through his eyes' when about to tell a joke or make a 'mischievous remark' so that 'the whole illuminated face grinned'. But there was anxiety, too: 'My father died too young,' he recalled Winston saying. 'I must try to accomplish whatever I can by the time I am forty.'[36]

During the voyage, Winston was afraid that the Boers might be routed before their ship berthed. That definitely proved not to be the case. With British troops forced to retreat to the town of Ladysmith, Winston tried to get there, only to find that the rail line had been cut. After being cooped up for a few days at an army base near Durban, he was suddenly invited by Captain Aylmer Haldane, with whom he had served in India, to join an armoured train that was being sent out on reconnaissance. Keen for a story and, as he admitted, 'eager for trouble', Winston readily agreed. And on 15 November he got much more trouble than he bargained for. The Boers ambushed the train. Despite a tenacious fight, most of the British were captured and packed off to the Boer capital, Pretoria, as prisoners of war.

What followed matched the popular adventure stories in *The Boy's Own Paper* and the novels of G.A. Henty. Winston managed to escape from the converted school in which the British were imprisoned, scrambling over the wall when a sentry's back was turned. Crouching in the garden for a while in case others followed, as planned, he eventually struck out on his own – jumping aboard a coal train to get out of Pretoria and then wandering in the bush until acute hunger drove him to knock on a cottage door. Fortunately, it was opened by an English settler, who hid him in a mine shaft, with rats for company, until the Boer hue and cry died down. Winston was then smuggled onto a freight train going to the port of Lourenço Marques, in Portuguese East Africa. Finally arriving back in Durban, he found he was already a celebrity. Exaggerated stories about his exploits in trying to rescue the armoured train had been followed by news that he had escaped and then, after nine days of suspense, that he was alive and safe.

Capture by the Boers had not proved a disaster, as he gloomily feared at the time, cutting him out of the war. Instead, as he reflected in 1930, 'this misfortune' was to 'lay the foundations of my later life' – making his own name as a Churchill, enabling him to earn his living as an author and speeding him into politics.[37] By the time Winston entered Pretoria with the victorious British troops on 5 June 1900 – helping to liberate his former colleagues, still POWs – he had already turned his despatches for the *Morning Post* into another book, *London to Ladysmith via Pretoria*, which rapidly sold out its first print run of 10,000. On 25 July, five days after docking at Southampton, he was adopted by the Tories of Oldham, a bustling mill town near Manchester. And on 1 October he was elected to the Commons in the 'khaki election' of 1900, which swept the Tories to a substantial majority on a jingoistic tide.

Even so, the voting in Oldham – a constituency with a strong Radical tradition – was close and Winston acknowledged privately that 'nothing but personal popularity arising out of the late South African War carried me in'. With new MPs not taking their seats until the New Year, he cashed in this popularity by undertaking a whirlwind speaking tour of Britain and North America, talking about his wartime experiences. In the course of five weeks, he ranged across the UK – from Brighton to Dundee, from Newcastle to Dublin – in the process earning nearly £4,000. North America proved much less remunerative, and Winston greatly disliked the 'vulgar and offensive advertisements' used by his US agent. But on New Year's Day 1901, totting up his earnings from writing and speaking, he proudly told his mother, 'I am very proud of the fact that there is not one person in a million who at my age could have earned £10,000 without any capital in less than two years.'[38]

His claim about earning £10,000 (around £1.2 million today) 'without any capital' does require a moment's interrogation. Unlike other British contemporaries – prime ministers such as Stanley Baldwin and Neville Chamberlain – Winston did not come from a prosperous business family. He was a child of privilege, rather than wealth, but that privilege was of inestimable value. His double career as a soldier-journalist rested on a firm belief that strict rules should and would be bent in his case. Nor could he have flourished if his mother had not pulled all the wires and cooked all those 'cutlets' at her considerable disposal. And throughout his military career, he exploited his father's friends (Lord Cromer in Egypt, for instance, when writing *The River War*) and even those with whom Lord Randolph had been at odds (such as Lord Salisbury and Joseph Chamberlain). In short, Churchill may not have had much financial capital, but he could draw on an enviable stock of social capital when he set out as 'subaltern of empire and journalist of opportunity' to make his own name.[39]

Yet it had taken a formidable personality to make so much of those opportunities. Deliberately rushing to the world's hotspots and flamboyantly courting danger, he displayed immense courage in battle. He also showed an impressive, and very different, ability to keep a cool head under fire and to command men much older than himself. But heroics alone would not have got him very far. He had also turned his facility with words into a lucrative and self-promoting career as journalist and author. And, despite that lisp, he had become a successful public speaker, much in demand after his exploits in South Africa. Combining the pen and the sword (or the pistol), he had won fame and fortune – enough to embark on the political career, in the mirror of his father, of which he had dreamed.

* * *

Winston delivered his maiden speech on the evening of 18 February 1901. The House was full. This was partly because he followed David Lloyd George and indeed jousted briefly with him – of which more in the next chapter – but also because of a general curiosity to see and hear 'Randolph's boy' in the flesh after all the hullabaloo from South Africa. The speech attracted considerable comment in the papers, though opinion was mixed as to whether it was the equal of his father's maiden speech in 1874, a few months before Winston was born. After making their debut, it was customary for new members of the Commons to keep silent for a while, but young Churchill was not one for either custom or silence. Having prospered during his military career as a subaltern sniping at his superiors, he saw no reason to become House-trained. Like his father, he intended to make a noise, and a nuisance of himself.

His political creed was complicated from the start. He told his mother in 1897 that, if not for his opposition to Home Rule for Ireland – 'to which I will never consent – I would enter Parliament as a Liberal. As it is, Tory Democracy will have to be the standard under which I shall range myself.' Winston was indeed a Liberal in many aspects of domestic policy, favouring the vote for all adult males and universal education. But he was a firm advocate of 'imperialism abroad', insisting that east of Suez, 'democracy was impossible' and 'India must be governed on old principles.' He favoured federalism for settler colonies like those in Australia, but not – at this stage – for the United Kingdom. His attitude to European affairs was one of 'Non-intervention. Keep absolutely unembroiled – Isolated if you like.' And he was adamant that, with a large navy, Britain needed only a tiny army.[40]

Although this seems a strange attitude for a cavalry subaltern, it was a position that Winston maintained for much of his life, and one that would assume particular importance in the 1930s. It was also the issue on which he launched his parliamentary career: as an act of both firm principle and risky pietas – for this was the cause that had sunk his father. And he did so in a speech that already displayed the hallmarks of his rhetorical style: not merely memorable soundbites but also firm structure and lucid argument.

On 13 May 1901 he mounted a vehement attack on the plan of William St John Brodrick, the Secretary of State for War, to increase the peacetime establishment of the Army to six corps. He developed three main concerns. First, he asserted that 'the superiority of the Navy is vital to our national existence.' Without this, 'foreign expeditions or home defence' would be 'utterly vain and futile'. Secondly, he emphasised the distinctive position of Britain as an island nation: 'whereas every European Power has to support a vast Army first of all, we in this fortunate, happy island, relieved by our insular position of a double burden, may turn our undivided efforts and attention to the Fleet. Why should we sacrifice a game in which we are sure to

win to play a game in which we are bound to lose?' Thirdly, he deplored
the huge costs of maintaining a large standing army and the consequent need for the un-British device of conscription, because 'standing
armies' were 'not suited to our national character'. The country, he
argued, 'must avoid a servile imitation of the clanking military empires
of the European continent'.[41]

With striking presentiment in 1901 of the half-century to come, he
also warned: 'A European war cannot be anything but a cruel, heart-
rending struggle, which, if we are ever to enjoy the bitter fruits of
victory, must demand, perhaps for several years, the whole manhood
of the nation, the entire suspension of peaceful industries, and the
concentrating to one end of every vital energy in the community.' He
reminded the Commons that modern warfare was different from the
wars of kings and cabinets, fought by small armies of professional
soldiers during a few summer months. Now, however, 'when mighty
populations are impelled on each other' and 'when the resources of
science and civilisation sweep away everything that might mitigate
their fury, a European war can only end in the ruin of the vanquished
and the scarcely less fatal commercial dislocation and exhaustion of
the conquerors. Democracy is more vindictive than Cabinets. The
wars of peoples will be more terrible than those of kings.'[42]

It was a powerful speech, not just in content but in delivery. Winston,
as usual, had prepared the text meticulously – rewriting the argument
and polishing the rhetoric for six weeks. And he committed the whole
piece to memory, so he could focus all his energy and attention on
performance in the Commons chamber. He also sent his text to the
press in advance, to make sure that his words received extensive attention in the next morning's newspapers. That had also been his father's
practice. Indeed, Lord Randolph was integral to the speech. Early on,
when reminding the House of the relentless increase in Army expenditure over the previous twenty years, Winston alluded to the campaign
mounted against that growth by the Treasury in 1886. 'The controversy
was bitter, the struggle uncertain, but in the end the Government
triumphed, and the Chancellor of the Exchequer went down for ever,

and with him, as it now seems, there fell also the cause of retrenchment and economy.' He quoted at length from the Chancellor's
resignation letter, whose sentiments bore close resemblance to his
own. 'Wise words', he then observed, 'stand the test of time, and I am
very glad that this House has allowed me, after an interval of fifteen
years, to lift again the tattered flag of retrenchment and economy.'
What's more, 'no one has a better right than I have, for this is a cause
I have inherited, and a cause for which the late Lord Randolph
Churchill made the greatest sacrifice of any Minister of modern times.'
The theatrical effect was compelling. Just before midnight, in a darkened Commons, he had summoned his father's ghost.[43]

This dramatic oration put Winston openly at odds with his party.
With the South African war dragging on, backbench Tories were
clamouring for a large standing army and Winston was the only one
to vote against Brodrick's proposal. 'As a speech, it was certainly
successful,' he reflected later in My Early Life, 'but it marked a definite
divergence of thought and sympathy from nearly all those who
thronged the benches around me.'[44] He was, in fact, already becoming
disenchanted with the whole ethos of the Tory party. In 1896, well
before entering Parliament, he described its 'solid remnant' as 'peers,
property, publicans, parsons & turnips'.[45] By October 1902 his professed
ideal was a 'Government of the Middle' – a party 'free at once of the
sordid selfishness and callousness of Toryism on the one hand & the
blind appetites of the Radical masses on the other'. He considered
'Tory-Liberal' to be 'a much better name' than either 'Tory-Democrat'
or 'Liberal Imperialist' but confessed: 'The real difficulty I have to
encounter is the suspicion that I am moved by mere restless ambition.'
Yet, he added, 'if some definite issue – such as Tariff – were to arise –
that difficulty would disappear.'[46]

Joseph Chamberlain, an old political adversary of his father, was
developing a systematic case for protective tariffs against foreign
competition, mitigated by preferential arrangements for the countries
of the Empire in order to consolidate a British bloc in the face of
deepening international rivalries. Winston firmly opposed this project

of 'Imperial Preference'. He told a constituent in Oldham that he was 'a sober admirer of Free Trade principles' who considered it 'a fantastic policy to endeavour to shut the British Empire up in a ringed fence'. He felt it 'very much better that the great nations of the world should be interdependent one upon the other than that they should be independent of each other. That makes powerfully for peace.'[47]

Chamberlain's campaign moved into top gear in late 1903, splitting the Tories between free traders and protectionists. And, as Winston had anticipated, this gave him both licence and freedom to move. In a letter dated 24 October 1903 to his close friend Hugh 'Linky' Cecil – not sent but articulating what was now firm resolution – he declared, 'I am an English Liberal. I hate the Tory party, their men, their words & their methods.' He was now ready for a 'complete and irrevocable' break with the Tories.[48]

When the new session opened in February 1902, Winston started to vote with the Liberal Opposition. In response, the Tories withdrew the party whip. Issues aside, his irreverent manner – intended to attract attention – was riling many Tories. Even Joseph Chamberlain, who enjoyed dishing it out, asked, 'Is it really necessary to be quite as personal in your speeches? You can attack a policy without imputing all sorts of crimes to its author.' Meanwhile, Prime Minister Arthur Balfour kept prevaricating on tariff reform. On 2 February Winston sent a warning letter, phrased with lofty insolence: 'My position is that of a wholehearted opponent of Mr Chamberlain & his policies & it is quite possible that in such a position I may be forced into action which though not necessarily contrary to the permanent interests of the Unionist party may be incidentally hostile to the existing government.' By late March, rumours were circulating that Churchill would soon cross the floor.[49]

Tuesday 29 March was the occasion of the adjournment debate before the Easter recess and the House was full. After exchanges about tariff reform between Balfour and the Liberal front bench, Winston was recognised by the Speaker as the next to speak. As he stood up, Balfour rose at the same time and left the Chamber. Churchill immediately protested to the Speaker that Balfour's exit showed 'lack of deference and respect' to the House. At this, all the Tory ministers rose and departed to the Smoking Room, followed almost immediately by their backbenchers, some of them jeering at Churchill. He stood alone and silent, with only a handful of Tory free traders for company.[50]

Despite regaining his poise as his speech progressed, it was a deeply unsettling experience, even for one with Winston's chutzpah. 'I was the object of a very unpleasant and disconcerting demonstration,' he confessed to Linky Cecil: 'the feeling of the whole audience melting behind one and being left with crowded Liberal benches and an absolutely empty Government side was most disquieting, and it was only by a considerable effort that I forced myself to proceed to the end of my remarks.' He added: 'my whole speech was intended to elicit information' from Balfour 'and of course it lost its whole point in his absence.'[51] Which was presumably why the Prime Minister left the chamber.

The black theatre of 29 March 1904 left a deep impression on Winston, showing that his hatred of the Tories was fully reciprocated. And worse was to follow. He had continued his practice of writing out his parliamentary speeches and then committing them to memory. On 22 April he spoke about the Trades Disputes bill, calling for a clearer definition of union rights. Suddenly, he lost his thread and dried up. After fumbling in vain through his pockets for some notes, he abruptly sat down, head in hands. *Hansard* records: 'The hon. Member here faltered in the conclusion of his speech, and, amid sympathetic cheers, resumed his seat, after thanking the House for having listened to him.' It was not yet a decade since Lord Randolph's final halting performances in the Commons. Was his son now going the same way?[52]

But Winston was not deterred. On 29 April 1904 the Liberal party in Manchester North West adopted him as its parliamentary candidate for the next election. A month later, on 31 May, the first day after the Whitsun recess, he entered the Commons chamber, glanced at both the Government and Opposition benches and then turned sharply to sit with the Liberals. He deliberately took the seat he believed his father had occupied when in opposition – the one on which Lord Randolph had stood waving his handkerchief to cheer the fall of Gladstone in 1885.[53]

Once again, an act of would-be pietas. But Lord Randolph, for all his radical effusions about democracy, never changed parties. Winston had now taken that ultimate step. Pietas also required him to make peace with his father. And that he did – in his own way. Having defied the generals and mocked the grandees, it was now time to rewrite history.

* * *

Winston had approached his father's executors at Christmas 1901 about writing a biography. The response was positive, although it took several rounds of correspondence before they acceded to his request for full independence as an author, except for quotations that concerned living persons or matters of national interest. By August 1902 he had custody of eighteen tin boxes of papers and had recruited his brother Jack to put them in good order. 'There emerges from these dusty records', he told his mother, 'a great and vivid drama', and he felt confident he would be able 'to write what many will care to read'.[54] The publishers Macmillan offered a very good deal for the English-language rights: an £8,000 advance, plus an equal share of the profits once they had made £4,000 on the enterprise. Winston was delighted with a contract that guaranteed him at least £1 million in today's money.[55]

Yet bringing to life this 'great and vivid drama' was no easy task. For a start, there was the enigma of Lord Randolph himself and the abiding sense that his life had been a spectacular failure. This was captured well in an 1895 obituary by George Brodrick, an Oxford don when Lord Randolph was at the University and then in 1874 the defeated opponent at his first parliamentary election:

> His audacity was perfectly natural; . . . it was restrained by few scruples, and by little respect for others . . . In fact, his strength as well as his weakness largely consisted in his combinations of two natures,

both equally genuine, the one prompting a shameless and almost aggressive self-assertion, the other tempered by kindliness, public spirit and patriotism . . . Few have ever enjoyed 'one crowded hour of glorious life' more fully than he; fewer still have atoned for a too reckless enjoyment of it by a swifter Nemesis of political failure and premature decay.[56]

Lord Rosebery, an old friend of his father, admitted that 'to no one could the task of narrating Lord Randolph's career be easy', but he noted problems that only Winston would face:

To write it ten years after his death required no common courage. But to a son bound by all the ties and truth of filial devotion, yet who may be said not to have known his father, politically speaking, at all; who was determined to write as impartially as possible; who has himself taken the step from which his father shrank, and has exchanged Toryism for Liberalism; and who has therefore had to face some hostility on both sides, Liberal antagonism to his father and Tory resentment to himself, the work presented obstacles that might well have been insuperable.[57]

Explaining the human enigma and finding thematic unity in such a kaleidoscopic career would have been challenge enough for a young and already controversial politician. Yet Winston intended to produce no mere biography. Lord Randolph's perplexing story could only be understood against the political circumstances of Britain in the mid-1880s, in the Victorian 'Life and Times' tradition. Beyond that, he intended to make a case for his father and for himself in a book that was biography yet almost autobiography. In the years 1902–5, when writing *Lord Randolph Churchill*, he also seemed 'intent upon re-creating his father's career, in fighting his enemies, battling for his policies, and repeating his errors'. He even emulated Lord Randolph's dress and mannerisms, including the practice of learning speeches by heart, until the debacle of April 1904. One contemporary also noted 'the same gaminerie and contempt for the conventional', delivered with 'engaging plain-spokenness'.[58]

Yet *Lord Randolph Churchill* was more than pietas. Winston was not merely emulating his father and vindicating his memory, he was also explaining the enigma in a way that benefited himself. In the preface, he addressed the challenge head-on: 'Lord Randolph's part in national affairs is not to be measured by long years in office. No great legislation stands in his name upon the statute book. He was a Chancellor of the Exchequer without a Budget, a Leader of the House of Commons for but a single session', and 'no tangible or enduring records – unless it be the Burma province – exist of his labours'.[59] In short, this was a political life lacking all the customary marks of 'greatness' that would have automatically placed him in the same rank as Gladstone, Disraeli or his Nemesis, Salisbury. But these were ultimately party politicians; Winston argued that his father should be judged by different and higher standards – standards that he also wished to be applied to his own career.

Along the way, in writing the book, he cut corners. Quotations were often filleted for enhanced effect. Lord Randolph's flirtations with 'Fair Trade', the Liberals and Parnell were glossed over or denied: on Irish Home Rule, for instance, despite his father's equivocations, Winston insisted: 'No Unionist politician has a clearer record.' And crucial issues were omitted on grounds of sensitivity, including Lord Randolph's chronic dependence on the advice and finance of the banker Nathan Rothschild, to whom he owed the huge sum of £67,900 when he died but whose name does not even appear in the index.[60] The biography also had little to say of the periods before 1880 and after 1890. Half of it was devoted to the dramas of 1885 and 1886, and the fulcrum of the work lay in chapter six, entitled 'Tory Democracy, 1882–5'. Yet, in reality, between 1880 and 1885 Lord Randolph used this Disraelian phrase rarely and vaguely – once in an article and thrice in speeches. Privately he admitted its use was 'chiefly opportunism' and only on 6 November 1885, addressing a huge election rally in Manchester, did he attempt to define what it meant. 'The Tory Democracy is a democracy which has embraced the principles of the Tory party. It is a democracy which believes that an hereditary monarchy and hereditary House of Lords are the strongest fortifications which the wisdom of man, illuminated by the experience of centuries, can possibly provide for the protection – not of Whig privilege – but of democratic freedom.' Although Winston quoted at length from this speech, he did so in a different chapter and there broke off before the sentences set out above.[61]

In the Manchester speech, the weight in the phrase 'Tory Democracy' lies on the adjective: the demos co-opted to the values of Conservatism. But Winston encouraged his readers to place the weight on the noun: the Tory party had been converted to democratic values in the fevered era of parliamentary reform. He used the phrases 'Tory Democracy' and 'the Tory democratic movement' as if they denoted a vast, coherent body of people.[62] And he suggested it was Lord Randolph who, single-handed, had converted those people into a political force. 'All of a sudden, a man arose alone, or almost alone, to do battle on their behalf. They watched him struggling day after day against over-whelming odds, overthrown a score of times, deserted and even tripped up by those who should have sustained him; yet always returning with inexhaustible activity to the attack and gaining from month to month substantial and undoubted success.' Buttressing his argument, Winston quoted some of his father's most extravagant phrases, such as 'Trust the people' and his claim, bowdlerising Abraham Lincoln, that the Tory party's motto was 'of the people, for the people, by the people.'[63]

He ended the book by admitting that Lord Randolph's name would not be 'recorded upon the bead-roll of either party'. But this, he declared, did not matter in the long run. 'There is an England which stretches far beyond the well-drilled masses who are assembled by party machinery . . . an England of wise men who gaze without self-deception at the failings and follies of both political parties . . . It was to that England that Lord Randolph Churchill appealed; it was that England he so nearly won; it is by that England he will be justly judged.'[64]

Here, then, was a politician of rare ability, whose political ascent – we are told – had been excelled in 'swiftness' only by that of the younger Pitt nearly a century before. Here was 'the Grand Young Man' of British politics – 'only a single step from a career of dazzling prosperity and fame'.[65] Having thus bracketed his father with some of the 'greats' of British public life, Winston also showed why Lord Randolph ultimately fell short. He tried to build democracy within the Tory party, instead of taking its liberalising tendencies into a more appropriate party. No one could miss the underlying autobiographical point. As one reviewer put it, 'he has endeavoured throughout his story to persuade his readers that, if Lord Randolph had been guided by the logic of his convictions, he would have deserted the Conservative fold and embraced Liberalism.' But now his son, while resurrecting Tory Democracy, had 'perverted it into a justification for joining the Liberal ranks'.[66]

Winston was in no way abashed by such criticism. 'I admit I have changed my party. I don't deny it. I am proud of it,' he told an election rally. 'When I think of all the labours Lord Randolph Churchill gave to the fortunes of the Conservative Party and the ungrateful way in which he was treated by them when they obtained the power they would never have had but for him, I am delighted that circumstances have enabled me to break with them while I am still young and still have the first energies of my life to give to the popular cause.'[67]

Lord Randolph Churchill was published in two volumes on 2 January 1906. Apart from a couple of vitriolic pieces about the man himself, the work was warmly received – selling over 2,300 copies in the first week and nearly 6,000 by the end of April. It was also published separately in the United States. Even those who saw Lord Randolph as more opportunistic in his politics and less important as a historical figure did not dispute the 'extraordinary interest' of the work itself, both with respect to the man and his times.[68] The veteran newspaperman W.F. Monypenny – then engaged on the official biography of Disraeli and thus, as he said, 'one of the small band of people' who comprehended 'the difficulties of such a task' – told Winston that 'alike in style and architecture and for its spirit, grasp and insight the book seems to me truly admirable.' Another eminent journalist and editor,

J.A. Spender, commented that the book placed its author 'among the literary few – which is a great thing for a politician'.[69]

Less than two weeks later, on 13 January 1906, the author-politician was elected MP for Manchester North West in the Liberal landslide. 'This election is the justification of my father's life and points the moral of my book,' he told a family friend. 'The one crowning irretrievable catastrophe which he always dreaded has now overtaken the old gang, and with them, the great party they misruled.'[70] Winston changed parties before the Tories were overtaken by what seemed like terminal disaster. He had the courage of his convictions, unlike his father – or at least the man depicted in his book.

And so the New Year of 1906 – with the publication of Lord Randolph Churchill and Winston's election as Liberal MP – marked a triumphant caesura in his life. The war journalist was now established as a noted author, setting a path for his future profession as a man of letters. And the ambitious politician had made his mark as a parliamentarian, while also successfully negotiating the hazards of 'crossing the floor'. Above all, Winston was finally coming to terms with his father – in print, if not in person – and would indeed surge on to surpass him. Yet Lord Randolph remained an abiding presence. 'Until the end,' wrote Asquith's daughter in 1965, Winston 'worshipped at the altar of his Unknown Father'.[71]

The Welsh Wizard and his Wary Apprentice, 1907.

2

David Lloyd George

Master and Servant

His steering gear is too weak for his horse-power.
David Lloyd George on Winston S. Churchill, March 1916[1]

The relationship between Master and Servant. And I was the Servant.
Winston S. Churchill, in the late 1920s[2]

During Winston Churchill's years as a Liberal, David Lloyd George – widely known as LG – was his closest associate and the most powerful influence on his career. Winston's senior by eleven years, Lloyd George proved a kind of father figure who gave Churchill's restless ambition a sense of direction. When Winston crossed the Commons floor in May 1904, he took his seat on the Liberal benches next to LG and within a few years they became inseparable political colleagues – despite the gulf in social backgrounds between the son of an aristocrat, at the heart of the English establishment, and the product of a strict Baptist upbringing in rural North Wales. Regarded by their (many) critics as little men in a big hurry, neither concealed his appetite for power. It was sometimes said that 'L.G. was born a cad and never forgot it; Winston was born a gentleman and never remembered it.'[3]

Yet theirs was an unequal relationship. Violet Asquith – daughter of the Liberal Prime Minister, who became a close and enduring friend of Churchill – wrote of LG: 'His was the only personal leadership I have ever known Winston to accept unquestioningly in his whole political career.' Churchill, she said, 'was fascinated by a mind more swift and agile than his own, by its fertility and resource, by its uncanny intuition and gymnastic nimbleness, and by a political sophistication which he lacked' – at least at that stage in his career.[4]

Winston's Liberal years spanned two decades from 1904: a period that encompassed the foundations of the modern welfare state and Britain's hard-won and almost pyrrhic victory in the Great War. Although labelled a Radical in his early years, Winston was essentially a Liberal imperialist – his motto captured in this line from a letter written in 1901: 'I see little glory in an Empire which can rule the waves and is unable to flush its sewers.'[5] Up to 1911, both men focused mostly on domestic reform. From LG, wrote Violet, Winston learned 'the language of Radicalism. It was Lloyd George's native tongue, but it was not his own, and despite his efforts he spoke it "with a difference".'[6] Churchill's attitude to social reform, as befitted a scion of the landed elite, was more paternalistic – looking down, as it were, from above. But being more of a public intellectual than LG, Winston wrote important commentaries on the 'New Liberalism'. From 1911 both men began to concentrate on the mounting threat of war with Germany and, as First Lord of the Admiralty, Winston – the former soldier – became intoxicated with building and running the navy. For a time, his closest associate was Admiral 'Jackie' Fisher, the First Sea Lord, a mesmeric influence until his resignation in 1915 over the Dardanelles campaign. That unfolding disaster eventually forced Winston, too, out of office. Though devastated, he gradually rebuilt his career in a series of war-related posts – all of them under Lloyd George, Prime Minister of a coalition government.

During this third and last phase of his Liberal years, after 1918, Winston became obsessed with the threat from the Left: Bolshevik Russia abroad and the rise of Labour at home. Throughout, however, he never lost his belief in 'Tory Democracy' as a force that transcended parties, and that belief would eventually ease his way back into the Conservative ranks in 1924. But although LG, after 1922, had lost power and party, Winston could not shake off his sense of subordination. Later in the 1920s, when Chancellor of the Exchequer, he wanted to discuss with LG some episodes from the Great War about which he was writing in his memoirs. LG duly came round to the Treasury, and they talked for an hour. 'He answered all my questions,' Winston told his parliamentary private secretary afterwards. Then his eyes hardened. 'Within five minutes the relationship between us was completely re-established. The relationship between Master and Servant. And I was the Servant.'[7]

* * *

David George was born in Manchester in 1863 but, after the death of his father, he was adopted by his Welsh mother's brother, Richard Lloyd, and took 'Lloyd' as his middle name. 'Uncle Lloyd' was a shoemaker and Baptist pastor – a prominent figure in the little town of Llanystumdwy, on the Llŷn peninsula near Criccieth. Although the mythology surrounding LG played up his humble roots, the family was not poor and the house was full of books, which the young boy devoured. He lost his Christian faith as a teenager but, similarly to Winston, religious feeling was transmuted into a potent sense of his providential destiny, and he was captivated by the Commons chamber during a visit in 1881. Three years later, while in London again, he attended a Commons debate and witnessed Lord Randolph Churchill battling with Gladstone over the Reform Bill.[8]

While establishing himself in the legal profession, Lloyd George threw himself into Liberal politics, becoming a champion of Welsh Nonconformity against the Anglican landed establishment. In 1890 he squeaked into Parliament after a by-election for Carnarvon Boroughs, the seat he would hold until just before his death in 1945. During the 1890s he sat in the Commons with a group of Welsh Liberals, all committed to trademark causes of temperance, Welsh Home Rule and disestablishment of the Anglican Church in Wales. LG's fiery polemics attracted attention, but he needed to move out of the purely Welsh orbit in order to make his name, and the Boer War proved his chance. Though not an anti-imperialist, he spoke out against the Government's inept and costly conduct of the war and the Army's cruel treatment of the Boers. And it was over the war that the two men first met on 18 February 1901, the occasion of Winston's maiden speech. After crossing swords briefly in the Commons chamber, they were introduced to each other. LG offered the obligatory compliments on the maiden speech but added, 'Judging from your remarks you are standing against the Light.' Winston replied: 'You take a singularly detached view of the British Empire.' Reporting this exchange in 1930, he added delphically: 'Thus began an association which has persisted through many vicissitudes.'[9]

In 1901, Winston privately referred to LG as 'a vulgar, chattering little cad' because of his Boer War agitation.[10] But after the war was over and Winston crossed the floor, he and LG became notorious for their irreverent criticism of senior Tories – a party now riven by the issue of tariff reform. On 18 April 1905 a cartoon in the *Pall Mall Gazette* showed the two of them as street urchins, with mud on their hands, being rebuked from his porticoed doorstep by Prime Minister Balfour: 'I'm afraid, gentlemen, that in this persistent mud-throwing you only waste your time.' To which they reply: 'Not a bit of it, we're qualifying for "high positions" in the next Liberal Government.'[11] Balfour limped on until December but then resigned. Eventually the new Liberal premier, Sir Henry Campbell-Bannerman, appointed LG to be President of the Board of Trade, with a seat in the Cabinet. Winston was offered only the post of Under-Secretary for the Colonies, but since the Colonial Secretary, the Earl of Elgin, sat in the Lords, Winston expected to enjoy freedom and visibility in the Commons.

For a while, thereafter, the dynamic duo went their separate ways. Winston, as usual, threw himself into the job at hand, determined to master his brief and advance his career. Already we can see what became Winston's typical approach to all his ministerial posts: the passion and capacity for ambitious strategic thinking. He loved to get his head around a role and reduce it to an eye-catching project. In this case, a tour of Africa in the autumn of 1907 – unusual for a

Colonial Office minister but emulating Lord Randolph's direct engagement with India – resulted in a stream of Churchillian memoranda
about reorganising colonial government, which ruffled feathers in
Whitehall. Sir Francis Hopwood, the senior civil servant at the Colonial
Office and prime target of Winston's documentary barrage, commented
to Lord Elgin: 'He is most tiresome to deal with & will I fear give
great trouble – as his Father did – in any position to which he may
be called. The restless energy, the uncontrollable desire for notoriety
& the lack of moral perception make him an anxiety indeed!' Such
anxiety would follow Winston in the decades to come.[12]

In October 1906, Winston told a Manchester audience that the
Liberals' priority should be to play down colonial and foreign affairs
as far as possible, 'so that the lines may be kept clear for the express
trains of social reform'.[13] Developing this theme in Glasgow he alluded
to the situation in Germany, where no Liberal party now existed and
'a great social democratic party' stood 'bluntly and squarely' against
'a capitalist and military confederation'. In Britain, however, Liberalism
proceeded 'by courses of moderation' and 'gradual steps', enlisting
'hundreds of thousands upon the side of progress and democratic
reform' whom otherwise 'militant Socialism would drive into violent
Tory reaction'. Declaring that 'the cause of the Liberal Party is the
cause of the left-out millions', he sought a middle way between the
ideologies of collectivism and individualism because both were parts
of man's 'dual nature'. 'No view of society can possibly be complete
which does not comprise within its scope both collective organisation
and individual initiative.' Winston insisted he did not wish to impair
'the vigour of competition' but to help 'mitigate the consequences of
failure'. In other words, 'we want to have free competition upwards;
we decline to allow free competition to run downwards.'[14]

In these pithy phrases, Winston captured the essence of what
became known as the 'New Liberalism'. The opportunity for both men
came when Campbell-Bannerman – a traditional Liberal committed
to free trade and a minimal state – was forced by ill health to relin-
quish the premiership in April 1908. His successor was Herbert Henry

Asquith (Violet's father), who rebalanced the Cabinet by giving top jobs to the party's two leading Radicals: LG became Chancellor of the Exchequer, in succession to Asquith, and Winston was appointed President of the Board of Trade, bringing him into the Cabinet at only 33 – now as one of the MPs for Dundee. This Scottish city, a centre of the jute industry, gave him wider exposure to the human realities of Britain's industrial economy and also to the problems of holding the United Kingdom together.

One evening early in 1908 Winston regaled Charles Masterman, a fellow Liberal MP, with his hopes and ambitions, marching up and down the room with animated gestures. 'He is full of the poor whom he has just discovered', Masterman noted in his diary. 'He thinks he is called by Providence – to do something for them. "Why have I always been kept safe within a hair's breadth of death," he asked, "except to do something like this? I'm not going to live long." ' Masterman pushed back: 'You can't deny that you enjoy it all immensely – the speeches – the crowds – the sense of increasing power.' Winston was unabashed: 'Of course I do.' Masterman, only a year older than Winston, wrote, 'I always feel of immense age when I am with him.' He seemed 'just an extraordinarily gifted boy, with genius and astonishing energy'. One other Churchillism from that evening stuck in Masterman's mind: 'Sometimes I feel as if I could lift the whole world on my shoulders.'[15]

Lloyd George, Winston's predecessor as President of the Board of Trade, made headlines in November 1907 when his skill as a conciliator averted a national rail strike. He also reformed the UK's patents law and passed a Merchant Shipping Act to improve conditions for seamen. Indeed, such was his record at the Board of Trade that Winston supposedly said, soon after his appointment: 'there is nothing to do here: LG has taken all the plums.'[16] But he did find ways to make his own mark. His Trade Boards Act, for instance, established minimum pay and conditions in the 'sweated trades', particularly the garment industry where most workers were female. And, drawing on ideas from the Fabian socialist Sidney Webb, he set up a system of Labour Exchanges across the country, to put those out of work in touch with potential employers, thereby bringing Britain in line with most continental countries.[17]

He had informed Asquith of this idea on Boxing Day, 26 December 1908, talking of 'an impressive social policy to be unfolded' which would 'leave an abiding mark on national history'. Three days later he sent the PM a six-point plan for legislation – ranging from unemployment insurance to compulsory education until the age of 17. This was intended to put 'a big slice of Bismarckianism' over the 'underside of our industrial system'. He noted that Germany 'is organised not only for war, but for peace. We are organised for nothing except party politics.' And he assured Asquith that the plan could be 'carried out triumphantly' and 'not only benefit the state but fortify the party'.[18]

Asquith did not reply – he had other things to do over the New Year (such as golf) – but Winston's Christmas manifesto of 1908 set a pattern for many similar grand designs in the future. And he was also ready to work in collaboration with LG – because both of them recognised that much more could be achieved if dynamic ministers operated in tandem. This was a strategy that Winston would try again when he was Chancellor in the 1920s and Neville Chamberlain was Minister of Health.

The expensive ideas for national insurance he and LG articulated would require cuts elsewhere, and in 1908 they targeted defence spending. Reprising Winston's Randolphian assault on the War Office in 1901, they tried to trim plans for an expeditionary force to the Continent in the event of a European war, but the War Office successfully rallied its supporters. Opening a new front, both ministers called publicly for an Anglo-German détente to slow the arms race, only to be slapped down by Asquith for straying outside their departmental briefs. Unabashed, in the winter of 1908–9 they turned their attention to naval spending, as public agitation grew for more of the new 'Dreadnought' battleships, a clamour expressed in the slogan 'We want eight and we won't wait.' Asquith was irritated by their 'combined machinations', but eventually LG helped broker a '4 + 4' compromise: half the Dreadnoughts would be laid down at once, and preparations made for the other four to be built quickly if needed. Some blamed the new political turbulence squarely on young Churchill. 'My idea is that Winston wanted to push to the front of the Cabinet,' opined the Court insider, Viscount Esher. 'He thinks himself Napoleon.' Esher was becoming allergic to Churchill, but the reference to Napoleon was not pure malice. Winston had started to acquire what became a very large collection of books (some 300) about the French emperor, intending to write a major biography. The book never materialised, but the fascination proved enduring.[19]

Lloyd George introduced his new budget on 29 April 1909, calling it 'a war budget' for 'raising money to wage implacable war against poverty and squalidness'. It included increased income tax, higher death duties and a new 'Super-Tax' on annual incomes over £5,000. The Tories denounced the Budget as nothing less than a revolutionary 'attack on property' and used their massive majority in the Lords to reject the Finance Bill in November 1909. So LG's budget became a battle over the constitutional powers of the House of Lords: 'the peers versus the people', to quote the famous Liberal slogan of 1910. The Parliament Act of 1911 eventually removed the Lords' power to reject money bills, and replaced their veto over public bills with the power merely to delay.

Yet this was a pyrrhic victory for the Liberals. In the bitter elections of January and December 1910, their majority over the Tories in the Commons was cut to almost nothing, and they only continued in power with the support of Irish Nationalists. The atmosphere of class warfare poisoned political and social life, a situation eased only briefly by the sudden death of Edward VII in May 1910 and the temporary party truce that followed. Lloyd George and Churchill were at the centre of the storm. Whether or not LG intended to pick a fight with the Lords, he relished the conflict when it arose. He singled out 'expensive dukes' by name, telling a delighted audience in Newcastle in October 1901 that 'a fully-equipped duke costs as much to keep up as two Dreadnoughts – and they are just as great a terror – and they last longer.' The essential question, he argued, was 'whether five hundred men, chosen accidentally from the ranks of the unemployed, should override the judgment – the deliberate judgment – of millions of people who are engaged in the industry which makes the wealth of this country.'[20]

Winston did not match such sparkle, but he blasted the Lords as 'one-sided, hereditary, unpurged, unrepresentative, irresponsible, absentee' and vilified the Tories as the 'forces of reaction': 'old doddering peers . . . cute financial magnates . . . clever wirepullers . . . big brewers with bulbous noses.'[21] Yet LG had been born into radicalism and sounded authentic, whereas Winston was denouncing his own caste – indeed some of his relatives. His stance was seen as having been contrived for political purposes, and this compounded the sense of betrayal after he had deserted the Tory party. But together the two of them had become celebrities.

Most contemporary observers judged that Winston in the end deferred to LG. Sometimes he said as much himself. In 1908, while on a walk together, he suddenly burst out, 'You are much stronger than I: I have noticed you go about things quietly and calmly, you do not excite yourself too much, but what you wish happens as you desire it. I am too excitable, I tear about and make too much noise.' Indeed, it was often remarked that Winston tended to talk too much, whereas LG was a much better listener. Also that one left an encounter with Winston certain that Winston was the most interesting person alive; whereas one left a meeting with LG convinced of oneself being the most interesting person alive.[22]

After the first election of 1910, Asquith asked Winston to consider 'one of our most delicate & difficult posts – the Irish Office'. But Winston had the nerve to decline (politely), proposing instead the Admiralty or the Home Office. He asserted that 'it is fitting, if you will allow me to say so, that Ministers should occupy positions in the Government which correspond to some extent with their position in the country.'[23] His presumption paid off. Asquith made him Home Secretary – alongside the Treasury and the Foreign Office one of the top three offices of state – at the age of 35. Of his predecessors only Sir Robert Peel in 1822 had been younger. As usual, Winston promptly looked for a big project: in this case 'The Abatement of Imprisonment' to reduce the number of working-class people put away for petty offences. 'I am quite sure', he told his Cabinet colleagues, 'that an extensive field of activity is open here in which the Government may gain in a minor way a great deal of commendation from all parties.'[24]

This typically ambitious plan was crowded out of the parliamentary timetable by the battle with the House of Lords but, as historian Paul Addison observed, it showed again Winston's distance from traditional Liberal men of business. 'Unlike them he suffered from a hyperactive imagination and a histrionic urge. He was captivated by ideas and longed to dramatise them on the democratic stage.'[25] One striking example occurred on 3 January 1911, when a gang of Baltic anarchists, who had killed three policemen during a burglary, were cornered at a house in Sidney Street in London's East End. The gang opened fire on police, who requested army assistance. Winston agreed to the use of a platoon of the Scots Guards, who were nearby at the Tower of London, guarding the Crown Jewels. Breaking off from writing a review of the political situation for Asquith, he was driven to Sidney Street to watch events unfold. When the house went up in flames during the fighting, he approved the decision not to risk the lives of the fire brigade. Returning home, he finished his letter to the PM with a vivid account of 'firing from every window, bullets chipping the brickwork, police and Scots Guards armed with loaded weapons, artillery brought up, etc.' He told Asquith, 'I thought it better to let the House burn down rather than spend good British lives in rescuing those ferocious rascals.'[26]

The bodies of two anarchists were found in the smoking ruins. Afterwards, images of Winston at the 'Siege of Sidney Street' – incongruous in top hat and fur-lined coat amid the policemen and soldiers – circulated widely in photographs and newsreels. The journalist A.G. Gardiner cited Sidney Street as an example of how 'he is always unconsciously playing a part – an heroic part. And he is himself his most astonished spectator . . . He thinks of Napoleon; he thinks of his great ancestor', the first Duke of Marlborough. Hence, said Gardiner, 'that tendency to exaggerate a situation which is so characteristic of him'. Charles Masterman was furious when he heard about Sidney Street: 'What the hell have you been doing now, Winston?' Back came the reply, in that inimitable Churchillian lisp: 'Now Charlie. Don't be so croth. It was such fun.'[27]

The law-and-order issue also created strains between the Home Secretary and the Chancellor. Winston would gain lasting notoriety in Labour circles for using soldiers against strikers with loss of life. The charge was not justified in the most celebrated case – Tonypandy in South Wales in November 1910 – when he took pains to hold English troops in reserve as support for the police. But their intimidating presence in the Rhondda Valley for another year enabled the owners to resist the miners' demands. During the national rail strike of August 1911, which threatened to bring the country to a standstill, Winston overrode Army Regulations. These required the local civil power to decide when to request military support where order had broken down. Instead, he simply deployed armed troops to key points, in order to help the rail companies keep trains moving with non-union labour, believing that national security was at stake. By contrast, LG threw himself into round-the-clock negotiations – opening talks with union leaders, persuading the employers to reinstate the strikers who had been locked out and wrapping up a vague agreement in slippery words. In forty-eight hours, he brought the strike to an end. 'I'm very sorry to hear it,' Winston told LG. 'It would have been better to have gone on and given these men a good thrashing.'[28]

The most interesting tension between Winston and LG was over women. As Home Secretary, Winston had to deal with the law-and-order problems raised by militant suffragettes, whose campaign for the vote had escalated into violence against property and persons, and to hunger strikes in prison. In fact, every parliament since 1870 had given approval to the principle of female suffrage, but the political parties were unable to agree about how many women should be enfranchised and on what terms. LG was more alert than Winston to the larger implications of women's suffrage for the political balance. Traditionally the right to vote had depended on ownership of property – a sign that someone had a stake in society. But any plan for women's rights based simply on extending the householder franchise was likely to benefit the Tories, since it would give the vote to wealthier women. The 'extended franchise' plan that LG preferred would give the vote to all adult males, thus addressing the 'democratic' deficit and also enfranchising working-class voters likely to be anti-Tory. He would then add to that bill a provision for an amendment in favour of women's suffrage.[29]

By late 1911, Winston was incensed about the idea of extending the franchise. He warned that if LG continued this 'mawkish frenzy' about large-scale female enfranchisement, 'I could not find any good foothold for common action.' Winston's alternative was to hold two national referenda on female suffrage: 'first to find out if they want it, and then to the men to know if they will give it'. He added, 'I am quite willing to abide by the result' – which, of course, in the second case was likely to be overwhelmingly negative. He told the Liberal chief whip, 'What a ridiculous tragedy it will be if this strong Government & party which has made its mark on history were to go down on Petticoat politics!'[30]

Yet there was another dimension to 'petticoat politics' – and one much closer to home. On April Fool's Day 1912, The Times published a letter in response to a statement by a distinguished pathologist questioning women's 'fitness' to vote. The letter suggested that his statement in effect shifted the question from 'should women have votes?' to 'ought women not to be abolished altogether?', and asked whether science could offer 'some assurance, or at least some ground for hope, that we are now on the eve of the greatest discovery of all – i.e. how to maintain a race of males by purely scientific means'. Asquith declared the letter, signed only 'CSC', to be 'much the best thing that I have read on the Woman question for a long time'. Po-faced, he asked Winston: 'Have you any clue to the identity of the writer?'[31]

CSC, as Asquith well knew, was Clementine Spencer Churchill, Winston's wife for two and a half years. After a whirlwind courtship in the spring of 1908, they were married in St Margaret's, Westminster, on

12 September. LG was among those present; he and Winston talked politics while the marriage registers were being signed, and Winston kept up with departmental papers while on honeymoon in Italy. Clementine quickly saw that family came second to his work and she would have to live with that. 'I am so much centred in my politics, that I often feel I must be a dull companion to anyone who is not in the trade, too,' he admitted in September 1909. Here was the same message, albeit less bluntly expressed, as that conveyed by LG some twenty years before to the young Margaret Owen, his future wife, when he warned that his 'supreme Idea' was 'to get on' and that he was 'prepared to thrust even love itself' under the wheels of his political 'Juggernaut'.[32]

Clementine had no doubt that she had married an obsessive politician and recognised that her best chance to engage with Winston was by taking an interest in his work. This came naturally to her; indeed, she was more radical than him, as shown by her letter to *The Times*. Despite some serious ups and downs, theirs was a marriage that would last the rest of his life, becoming an especially effective double-act during his wartime premiership. Margaret Lloyd George, by contrast, preferred to stay at home in North Wales and raise the family. She spent much less time in London, leaving LG – lonely and highly sexed – to his own devices. He had a series of affairs while Chancellor, and from 1911 formed a special liaison with Frances Stevenson, twenty-five years his junior. As cover, he made her his shorthand secretary and just after his fiftieth birthday in 1913 the relationship was formalised in what they called their unofficial 'marriage'. But not only was this relationship on the same politics-first terms which Maggie Owen had been offered, LG also made clear that he would not divorce his wife, who still mattered to him.

Frances was thus 'condemning herself to a life of secrecy, giving up her youth to a much older man who could never publicly acknowledge her' and probably abandoning any 'realistic hope of having children'. She was, however, captivated by LG and, like Clemmie, willing to sacrifice her youthful feminism for a man in whose star she believed. Yet there was a stark difference between the two women. LG was effectively

a bigamist: 'In different ways he needed both women, and with characteristic nerve and resourcefulness he got what he wanted.' Winston
also got what he wanted: Mrs Churchill. Whatever his failings as a
husband and father, he was openly proud of Clementine and of their
marriage, and would remain so throughout his life.[33]

* * *

The partnership between Churchill and Lloyd George took a new turn
in July 1911, as their attention shifted towards international affairs. The
catalyst was what might now seem a comic-opera crisis in French-
controlled Morocco. Seeking to leverage territory in Africa for Germany,
the Kaiser's government sent a gunboat, the *Panther*, to Agadir on
Morocco's Atlantic coast, triggering a major international incident.
Germany demanded the whole of the French Congo in return for
conceding French control of Morocco, and there were fears in Whitehall
that the situation could rapidly escalate into hostilities.[34]

The Agadir crisis was settled by negotiation a few months later. But
it had a dramatic effect on LG and especially Winston. It was as if
the war scare had suddenly made him think about defence matters,
and then, as usual, his racing mind and vivid imagination took hold –
even though these issues had little to do with his official position as
Home Secretary. During July, he penned a memo about how the crisis
might escalate, urging that, if negotiations failed, the Government
should 'propose to France and Russia a triple alliance to safeguard
(*inter alia*) the independence of Belgium, Holland and Denmark' –
North Sea neighbours of Britain. In early September he feared a
surprise attack by the Kaiser through Belgium, noting rumours of '12
regiments of German cavalry' near the border.[35] He even composed
a memo about how a future war with Germany might develop. This
assumed that the German army would break through the French
defences along the Meuse river on day twenty, but that thereafter its
momentum would falter because of mounting casualties, extended
supply lines, the arrival of 100,000 British troops and growing Russian
pressure on the Eastern Front. By the fortieth day, Winston predicted,

the allies should be able to hold the Germans or, 'if desirable, to assume the offensive in concert'.[36]

This memo of 13 August 1911 has been described as 'one of the most prescient strategic documents that Churchill ever wrote'.[37] Its scenario proved accurate, almost to the day, when war did break out in 1914. The paper, together with the fact that he was one of only two members of the Cabinet with any military experience, secured Winston a seat at a special meeting of the Committee of Imperial Defence (CID) on 23 August. The Army stated that Britain would have to send troops to the Continent if Germany attacked France. The Navy resisted any such idea and insisted that Britain should simply maintain naval supremacy and blockade Germany. Churchill and LG were furious at what Winston called the Navy's 'cocksure, *insouciant* and apathetic' attitude and Asquith concluded that changes would have to be made. Churchill became First Lord of the Admiralty, swapping jobs with a resentful Reginald McKenna. The PM may have also decided, after Winston's tirades about the rail strikers, that it was time for 'a calm-down at the Home Office' as well as 'a shake-up at the Admiralty'.[38]

Winston was jubilant about his new job. 'Look at the people I have had to deal with so far – judges and convicts!' he exclaimed to Violet Asquith. 'This is a big thing – the biggest thing that has ever come my way.' She wrote in 1965: 'Never, before or since, have I seen him more completely and profoundly happy'.[39] The First Lord of the Admiralty was traditionally responsible for presenting the annual naval estimates to Parliament and generally representing the Admiralty to the Government, leaving the admirals to decide policy and operations. But Winston had no intention of being fettered, and the position of First Lord proved probably his most productive departmental appointment. Not only did he create, as agreed with Asquith, a naval general staff which then prepared the contingency plans to move six British divisions across the Channel in the event of war, he also updated the Royal Navy's 'blue water' capability. Crucially, he oversaw development of the new 'Super-Dreadnoughts' with unprecedented 15-inch guns and a range of nearly eleven miles, and masterminded the conversion of the Royal Navy from coal to oil, which enabled ships to stay at sea for much longer. To safe-guard oil supplies, Winston negotiated long-term contracts with Shell Oil and Anglo-Persian, and arranged the British Government's purchase of a controlling interest in the latter company. He also created a signals intelligence unit (Room 40) – harbinger of a lifelong interest in this field, whose importance he grasped more acutely than most politicians. And he created the Royal Naval Air Service. Indeed, he took up flying himself, with typical passion and indifference to danger, until Clemmie finally put her foot down in 1914.

'Winston is Navy mad', LG complained in February 1912. 'As usual he regards the office he presides over for the time being as the pivot upon which the Universe attends.' In fact, Winston's obsession with naval rearmament was to provoke one of the worst rows between the two men. After the Moroccan crisis was resolved, LG sought to mend fences with critics of his apparent jingoism by reasserting his Radical credentials, at least rhetorically. His reputation had also been tainted by the 1912 Marconi share scandal, when he was accused of profitable insider trading. Seeking to regain political momentum, he embarked on a campaign of land reform, to address various social ills including unemployment and housing shortages. This touched on Winston's own sensitivities – 'he hates inflicting any hurt upon the aristocracy', LG observed tartly. The Chancellor claimed he had managed to strike 'a bargain' with the First Lord: 'He will support my land policy with which he is not in sympathy, and I have agreed to give him more money for the Navy.' But in the winter of 1913–14 this 'bargain' became unstuck, with almost disastrous consequences for them both.[40]

In December 1913 Winston presented the naval estimates for 1914–15 to the Cabinet, calling for an increase in expenditure of nearly £3 million over the previous year, to bring the total to over £50 million. These proposals, backed by several Churchillian orations about the inexorable growth of the German navy, provoked a revolt from trad-itional Gladstonian Liberals, including the still aggrieved McKenna. Trying to appease them, LG felt obliged to accept cuts – prompting a bitter note across the Cabinet table from Winston: 'I consider you are going back on your word.'[41] Looking to swing public opinion, LG gave a newspaper interview, published on New Year's Day 1914, in which he depicted Anglo-German relations as far more relaxed than during the Agadir crisis, thanks to Foreign Secretary Edward Grey's 'wise and patient diplomacy', and deprecated 'feverish efforts' to increase Britain's already clear naval superiority. He even recalled the protest by Winston's own father against profligate naval spending when he was Chancellor – which, as everyone knew, had precipitated Lord Randolph's downfall.[42] Winston was predictably furious at the intervention, though Asquith and, privately, King George V weighed in on Winston's side and eventually a deal was reached on his terms, sugared with the promise of likely reductions for 1915–16 (a promise which, of course, was never fulfilled).[43]

Winston finally presented the estimates to the Commons on 17 March 1914. His exposition, lasting over two hours, displayed the logical argument and mastery of detail that characterised his very best speeches. And he ended with a geopolitical statement about why Britain needed a navy second to none: to defend its island borders, to protect its global supply lines, and to make its voice heard in world affairs in the absence of a large conscript army like those of the continental powers. These were familiar assertions, going back to his invective against 'Mr Brodrick's Army' in 1901. But there was also a new note of anxiety, because the island empire now seemed dangerously exposed:

We have won for ourselves, in times when other powerful nations were paralysed by barbarism or internal war, an exceptional share of the wealth and traffic of the world. We have got all we want in territory, but our claims to be left in undisputed enjoyment of vast and splendid possessions, largely acquired by war and largely maintained by force, is often one which seems less reasonable to others than to us.[44]

What we have, we hold – or will try to. That would be his motto for the rest of his political life.

Winston's victory in the matter of the naval estimates was not as decisive as it seemed. There was talk around Whitehall that many in the Cabinet were getting fed up with him and were looking for ways to force him out. His apparent indifference to traditional Liberal principles of peace and retrenchment was one bone of contention. He was also criticised for deviating from the other Gladstonian verity of complete Home Rule for Ireland – now even more important given the party's reliance on Irish Nationalist votes for its majority. Sir John Simon, a leading Cabinet critic, told Asquith that 'the loss of WC, though regrettable' would help strengthen the party ahead of the next election: 'the feeling that the Cabinet *fights for economy* but pursues Home Rule inflinchingly [sic] is just what is wanted.'[45] Winston supported Home Rule but with the crucial qualification that he wanted to exclude the largely Protestant countries of Ulster, in the north-east. That was a firm *Tory* commitment – indeed, it was one of his father's passions – and he aroused deep hostility in Liberal circles by speaking out on the issue and even dining with leading Tories to seek a compromise. But then Winston compounded his difficulties, alienating Tory Unionists in March 1914 when he helped mobilise naval and army units amid the shadowy attempted 'mutiny' against Home Rule by some diehard officers in Ulster. All in all, Churchill seemed impulsive, unreliable and trigger-happy. On this, though on little else in the spring of 1914, there was cross-party agreement.[46]

In July 1914, the Irish crisis looked to be boiling up into civil war. On 20 July, the King convened an inter-party conference to try to agree the terms of Ulster's exclusion, but it broke up without agreement. Then the escalating Balkan crisis suddenly transformed the agenda and also redeemed Winston's fortunes. Germany sided with Austria-Hungary in its strike on Serbia; Britain was drawn into support of France when the Kaiser's forces violated Belgian neutrality. As Big Ben struck 11 p.m. on 4 August, British warships across the world received a coded cable: 'Commence hostilities against Germany.' In the chaotic slide to war, what stood out clearly was that, as Winston had intended and planned, the Navy was ready. The problem was that it wasn't ready for the war that actually developed.

Churchill, like Grey, was clear from the start of the July crisis that Britain had to fight if France and Belgium were threatened: the whole European balance of power was at stake. His excitement at being a war leader was unconcealed. Indeed, on the night of 3 October he rushed across to Antwerp to help defend the vital port until French help arrived. He also deployed there two brigades from his newly formed Royal Naval Division (of spare naval reservists). 'The man must have been mad,' exclaimed Admiral David Beatty, to think he could relieve Antwerp 'by putting 8,000 half-trained troops into it'.[47] On the 5th the Cabinet burst out laughing when told that Winston wanted to resign his office and be given military rank to take command at Antwerp. Asquith ordered him to return immediately, but found Winston now yearning for one of the 'glittering commands' and declaring that 'a political career was nothing to him in comparison with military glory'. His 'cataract' of rhetoric was bewitching. 'He is a wonderful creature, with a curious dash of schoolboy simplicity,' the PM reflected, 'and what someone said about genius – "a zigzag streak of lightning in the brain." '[48] Antwerp held out until 10 October, but nearly three thousand British troops were killed, wounded or captured, and press comment – though sometimes ill-informed – was largely critical. The Tory *Morning Post* hoped the 'costly blunder' of Antwerp would teach Churchill he was 'a Minister of the Crown' and not 'a Napoleon'.[49]

Yet Churchill was not deflected by the Antwerp fiasco. Throughout the autumn he made regular trips across the Channel to sniff out the military situation and talk strategy and operations with Sir John French, the British Army commander. Eventually Lord Kitchener, Winston's old foe from East Africa days and now Secretary of State for War, threatened resignation if this practice did not cease. At the same time that Winston seemed to be meddling elsewhere, several naval disasters suggested that he wasn't doing his own job very well. On 22 September the Germans sank three British cruisers, with the loss of 1,500 men, off the Dogger Bank – just after the First Lord had warned that if the German navy didn't come out and fight, they would be 'dug out like rats in a hole' – and on 1 November two more cruisers were lost in the Battle of Coronel, off the coast of Chile. LG was among those sniping privately at Winston, telling Frances Stevenson that he was 'too busy trying to get a flashy success to attend to the real business of the Admiralty'.[50]

In order to shore up the Navy's credibility, Admiral Lord Fisher was recalled to the Admiralty at the age of 73, and Winston, a great fan, made him First Sea Lord. Some critics of Churchill hoped that Fisher would act as a restraining influence, but Admiral Beatty was more prescient. Here were 'two very strong and clever men, one old, wily, and of vast experience, one young, self-assertive, with a great self-satisfaction but unstable. They cannot work together, they cannot both run the show'.[51]

By October the war in France had sunk into stalemate. Thanks in large measure to the plans which Winston had developed and implemented after his move to the Admiralty, four regular divisions had been rapidly transported across the Channel, helping the French delay the German thrust towards Paris until the Russians advanced into Prussia. On the Eastern Front, the war then oscillated to and fro. In the west, however, the conflict became bogged down in two lines of opposing trenches stretching from the Swiss border to the sea. LG and Churchill turned their fertile minds to breaking the deadlock.

Both used the Christmas break to compose weighty memos for Asquith. 'Are there not alternatives than sending our armies to chew barbed wire in Flanders?' Winston asked caustically. 'Further, cannot the power of the Navy be brought more directly to bear upon the enemy?' He urged Fisher's (half-baked) idea of seizing Borkum – one of the East Frisian islands – as a base for amphibious operations. His hyper-fluent pen then transported Asquith from Borkum to Berlin and the brink of victory in just three sentences: 'The invasion of Schleswig-Holstein from the sea would threaten the Kiel Canal and enable Denmark to join us. The accession of Denmark would throw open the Baltic. British naval command of the Baltic would enable the Russian armies to land within 90 miles of Berlin . . .'[52]

The idea was ludicrous, but a succession of smoothly falling dominoes was to be the hallmark of many Churchillian strategic scenarios.

In this case, consider just the first domino: Borkum, that small island just off the German coast at the estuary of the Ems River, a mere 100 miles by sea from the great German naval base of Wilhelmshaven. As one historian has observed, 'Borkum in British hands would have been a hostage to fortune.' The Germans would have thrown everything into evicting the British. Winston, like most of his admirals, yearned for a titanic sea battle between the two fleets – a twentieth-century version of Trafalgar – but that would be risking 'the Royal Navy's command of the North Sea' and perhaps the Royal Navy itself.[53]

LG's Christmas present to Asquith was equally glittering, but less fantastic because he targeted weaker members of Germany's coalition, the Central Powers. He proposed either fighting the Austrians on the southern flank by joining forces with Britain's Balkan allies, especially Serbia, or else mounting a campaign in the Levant, close to the sea, against the Ottoman Turks. Another memo was submitted by Colonel Maurice Hankey, Secretary to the Committee of Imperial Defence. After rejecting other options, he asked whether it was 'impossible now to weave a web around Turkey which shall end her career as a European power'. Like LG, Hankey looked to the Balkans, but also suggested that a campaign there could lead on to 'the occupation of Constantinople, the Dardanelles, and Bosphorus'. This would also open up sea communications via the Black Sea with Britain's hard-pressed Russian ally.[54]

It was Hankey who, at the end of 1914, broached the idea of forcing the Dardanelles – taking control of the narrow straits, some forty miles long, that connected the Mediterranean to the Sea of Marmara, 175 miles wide, on the other side of which lay the Ottoman capital. Winston assumed that forcing the Dardanelles would require both naval and military forces and initially stuck to his Borkum plan. But the naval commander in the eastern Mediterranean advised that it might be possible to do so with ships alone, and on 13 January 1915 the weary War Council seized on this as a way out of their strategic deadlock. At the Council on the 24th Winston made clear that it was not his intention to use the Army as well, though he said he could 'conceive a case where the Navy had almost succeeded, but where a military force would just make the difference between success and failure'. LG took a different view. According to the minutes, he 'hoped that the Army would not be expected or required to pull the chestnuts out of the fire for the Navy. If we failed at the Dardanelles we ought to be immediately ready to try something else' – for example the Levant.[55] Dining with Clementine and Violet on the 22nd, Winston was full of the operation. He wanted the naval units he had commanded at Antwerp to be among the troops marching into Constantinople, to take possession of the Turkish capital. 'That will make them sit up – the swine who snarled at the Naval Division!' In full flood, he suddenly broke off: 'I think a curse should rest on me because I am so happy. I know this war is smashing and shattering the lives of thousands every moment – and yet – I cannot help it – I enjoy every second I live.'[56]

On 19 February the Navy commenced bombardment of the outer forts on the Dardanelles. The main assault began on 18 March, with a fleet of eighteen British and French warships trying to break through the heavily mined Straits. But the losses were severe – three battleships sunk and three others seriously damaged – and the action was suspended. It was at this point that the strategic emphasis shifted to an amphibious landing on the Gallipoli peninsula, at the far end of the Straits, in order to seize the key forts and protect the Navy. The landings did not commence until 25 April, allowing the underestimated Turks yet more time to prepare. Footholds were gained, but little more. The botched campaign sucked in troops and supplies from elsewhere. By this stage Churchill was not directly responsible – the Navy was simply providing transport and gunfire – but his name was now inextricably tied up with the Dardanelles at a moment when frustrations with the war effort reached boiling point.

On 14 May *The Times* published a despatch from its military correspondent on the Western Front stating that 'the want of an unlimited supply of high explosive was a fatal bar to our success.' This triggered what became known as the shells scandal. The following day Fisher resigned as First Sea Lord. The main cause was his anger at the way the Dardanelles campaign was drawing ships and resources away from what he judged the vital naval battle against the Germans, together with his frustration about working with Winston. 'At every turn he will be thinking of the military and not the naval side,' Fisher complained to McKenna: 'His heart is ashore, not afloat!' Fisher's whispering campaign drew in the Tory leader, Andrew Bonar Law, whom he told: '*a great national disaster is very near us in the Dardanelles!* . . . W.C. is a bigger danger than the Germans by a long way.'[57] Fisher was now mentally unbalanced, but his resignation as First Sea Lord caused a press furore and undermined the Liberal government. Bonar Law told Asquith and Lloyd George that a key condition for any coalition was that Churchill must resign as well.

The crisis had given vengeful Tories the chance finally to settle old scores with Winston. And the cocky young turncoat had few friends among the Liberals. The wholesale animosity he had generated seems to have surprised Winston. Initially he tried to bargain with Asquith for another 'fitting' post, namely 'a military department', but when he realised that the furore was not just 'mere uninformed newspaper hostility', he ended up grovelling to the PM: 'I will accept any office – the lowest if you like – that you care to offer me.'[58] And it *was* the lowest: Chancellor of the Duchy of Lancaster, a sinecure with no department, whose main responsibility was to appoint county magistrates.[59]

In anguish, Winston lashed out in every direction. 'You don't care what becomes of me,' he shouted at LG. 'You don't care whether I am trampled under foot by my enemies. You don't care for my personal reputation.' The reply was blunt. 'No, I don't care for my own at the present moment. The only thing I care about now is that we win the war.'[60] LG could see that Winston had become a political liability and that the new coalition desperately needed to get a grip on the war. To deal with the shells scandal, he accepted the post of Minister of Munitions and threw himself into that role. During thirteen feverish months of 'creative improvisation' Lloyd George transformed relation-ships between state, industry and labour in ways that helped win the war and also had lasting impact on Britain.[61] Meanwhile Winston, who had been in his element at the Admiralty, was now spinning his wheels, fretting about the Dardanelles and the whole war. He told a friend bitterly, 'Between me and Ll G tout est fini.'[62]

Yet, with typical resolve, Winston pulled himself out of the pit of despair. Encouraged by his sister-in-law, he became captivated by painting – finding that total absorption in canvas and paint could take his mind off the Dardanelles. Weekends that summer at a rented cottage in Surrey not only provided solace and sanity; they also began a lifelong passion for painting which revealed the creative diversity of this politics junkie. And when Gallipoli was about to be evacuated and he finally recognised the futility of his Duchy post, Winston decided to seek a military position. His new grand ambition was to command the British forces in East Africa, but that was ruled out as too politically controversial. So, again, he had to put up with something more lowly, and went off to the Western Front. Turning down a cosy job at headquarters, he hoped for command of a brigade but, when news leaked out in London, questions in the House showed that Churchill was still politically toxic and Asquith personally vetoed the rank of brigadier-general. 'Altogether I am inclined to think that his conduct reached the limits of meanness & ungenerousness', Winston scribbled to Clementine. But he accepted the sop offered instead – command of the 6th Battalion, Royal Scots Fusiliers.[63]

* * *

Soldiering, like painting, helped Winston cope to some degree with his humiliation over the Admiralty. In typical style, he threw himself into his new position, taking a solicitous interest in his men – mostly workers from Clydeside – and leading from the front with frequent night raids into no-man's-land. But a battalion command at Ploegsteert in Belgium, a relatively quiet sector of the Western Front, was hardly enough for a man chafing to lead. Returning to London on 2 March 1916, Winston learned that Balfour – his successor at the Admiralty – was to introduce his own naval estimates on the 7th. Abandoning the idea of a few days of leisurely painting, Winston worked frantically on his speech – apparently persuading himself that a parliamentary *tour de force* could catapult him from a dugout on the Western Front to de facto leader of the opposition against Asquith's lethargic coalition and even perhaps to supreme power. It was just the kind of challenge he relished, telling one friendly journalist that this speech 'needed more courage than the war in the trenches'.[64]

On the afternoon of 7 March, as soon as Balfour sat down, Winston rose. His speech was somewhat contrived – picking holes in actual British naval programmes while conjuring up the worst possible scenarios for what the Germans might perhaps be up to. But he was playing on fears widely shared in Westminster, and doing so with his usual panache and vigour. 'You must continually drive the vast machine forward at its utmost speed,' he enjoined the House, adding a flying metaphor that he often used: 'To lose momentum is not merely to stop, but to fall.' But then came his crash-landing. In the peroration, offering his own remedy for the problems he'd outlined, he called for the immediate return of Jackie Fisher as First Sea Lord.[65]

Apparently, Winston imagined that this proposal would show he had moved on from the rancour of May 1915. Instead, his punchline turned a powerful oration, cleverly conjuring up fears that Britain might lose the war, into an object of derision. Lloyd George called the speech 'a great error', adding that 'he should have stopped after criticising the Administration.' Asquith was dumbstruck at such a 'suicidal' idea, privately urging Winston not to repeat the folly of his father.[66] The Tory press drove in the knife and next day Balfour wiped the floor with him in the Commons. It was Winston's greatest parliamentary debacle between the time he dried up in 1904 and his quixotic defence of the King during the Abdication crisis of 1936, and it confirmed all the worst mutterings about his judgment and balance. Deeply shaken, Colonel Churchill returned to his Belgian dugout.

In May 1916 the amalgamation of his battalion with another gave him a pretext to return to London and renew his bid for a central role in running the war. But Tory animosity had, if anything, been strengthened by Winston's attack on Balfour, and this was Asquith's main justification for keeping him out of the coalition. With his speeches often interrupted by the mocking question 'What about the Dardanelles?', Winston decided he must clear his name with regard to the disaster that had ensued. But the planned parliamentary inquest in public, backed by documentary evidence, turned into a commission of inquiry, meeting in secret. Winston was incensed. 'Is it not damnable that I should be denied all real scope to serve this country in this tremendous hour?' he asked his brother on 15 July. 'Jack my dear, I am learning to hate.'[67]

On 1 July 1916 the long-awaited offensive on the Somme opened. Resulting in the death of nearly 20,000 soldiers, this was the worst day in the history of the British Army. Weeks before, Winston – one of the few MPs who had first-hand experience of life and death in the trenches – had lamented how 'this war proceeds along its terrible path by the slaughter of infantry.' In a broad survey of army manpower for the Commons on 23 May, he criticised any further premature offensives, even if they seemed diplomatically imperative to support the French.[68] But his opinion counted for little at Westminster. So Winston pinned his hopes on the displacement of Asquith by Lloyd George, with whom he was in regular touch, and who – he was confident – would give him a big role in a new government. Asquith's coalition finally collapsed in early December. But although the Tories agreed to serve under Lloyd George in his new coalition government, which included Labour as well, they vetoed Winston's inclusion. On 7 December 1916 LG posed the Churchill question directly to Andrew Bonar Law, the Tory leader: 'Is he more dangerous when he is FOR you than when he is AGAINST you?' Law's reply was categorical: 'I would rather have him against us every time.' The British public 'learn with relief and satisfaction', declared *The Times* smugly, 'that Mr. Churchill will not be offered any post in the new Administration.'[69]

Winston was beside himself, convinced, as he had told Clemmie in January 1916, that he could use power 'better than any other living Englishman to determine the war policy of Britain.'[70] But not only was Lloyd George swayed by Tory hatred; he had his own doubts. 'A brilliant fellow without judgement which is adequate to his fiery impulse', LG observed in March 1916. 'His steering gear is too weak for his horse-power.' How should one deal with a man like that? LG's instinctive answer, unlike Bonar Law's, remained what he had told Winston himself in November 1912: 'I regard you as one might a leading barrister that you don't want your opponent in a case to get, so you retain him your-self. I think your fees rather excessive but I am willing to go with you as far as I can in reason.' This remained his default position throughout their political relationship. It was similar in sentiment, if not tone, to US President Lyndon Johnson's notorious comment about FBI Director J. Edgar Hoover: 'It's probably better to have him inside the tent pissing out, than outside the tent pissing in.'[71]

Winston therefore decided to keep showing what a nuisance he could be if left outside the tent. On 10 May 1917, he delivered a commanding *tour d'horizon* of the war. The occasion was a secret session of the Commons, from which press and visitors were barred so that the Government could take MPs into its confidence. Asquith was still in a sulk, so Winston opened for the Opposition. No record of the debate was kept, but he summarised his argument in his war memoirs.

The speech showed Winston at his clear and compelling best. He began by stressing the huge significance of two recent events: the collapse of Tsarist Russia and American entry into the war. 'If time is given,' he assured the House, 'nothing can stand against Great Britain and the United States together', even if 'every other Ally fails', because of America's vast wealth and manpower. But such was US unreadiness for war, it might take months or even years before 'this mighty force can be brought to bear'. Meanwhile, Germany's all-out U-boat war threatened to sever Britain's crucial Atlantic lifeline. Winston's conclu-sion was therefore clear: 'Master the U-boat attack. Bring over the American millions. And meanwhile maintain an active defensive on the Western Front, so as to economize French and British lives', in preparation for what he called 'a decisive effort in a later year'. He implored the Prime Minister to use all his personal and political authority to 'prevent the French and British High Commands from dragging each other into fresh, bloody and disastrous adventures'.[72]

This strategy of the slow but remorseless application of British and American might was a foretaste of Winston's 'closing the ring' scenario for the next war. In both conflicts, however, it was easier said than done, because of the political pressures for a quick victory. After Winston sat down, LG expressed general agreement with the Churchillian scenario while declining to commit himself against a new offensive. As in 1916 over the Somme, so in 1917 French demands for help were proving impossible to resist – and the ensuing offensive to seize Passchendaele ridge near Ypres predictably turned into another British bloodbath, lasting from the end of July to mid-November. Yet Winston's speech did demonstrate again his intellectual firepower and political presence. When the two men huddled afterwards behind the Speaker's Chair, according to Winston, LG offered new assurances of 'his desire to have me at his side'.[73]

In private the PM continued to make snide remarks about Winston – accusing him for example of having 'spoilt himself by reading about Napoleon'[74] – but by mid-1917 he felt sufficiently established as premier to override continued Tory protests and appoint Winston as Minister of Munitions. According to Hankey – the new Cabinet Secretary in LG's shake-up of Whitehall – Winston confessed that he had 'no idea of the depth of public opinion against his return to public life, until his appointment was made'. A few days later LG crossed the Channel to discuss strategy with the French. 'Don't get torpedoed,' Winston told him; 'for if I am left alone your colleagues will eat me'.[75]

July 1917 was the first of Winston's four appointments in the Lloyd George coalition: Munitions, War, Air and the Colonies. Collectively they gave him an unrivalled feel for the sinews of Britain's global power. And working for the next five years with Tory colleagues also helped to soften some of their vitriolic hatred, dating back to his defection in 1904. Yet his personal relations with Lloyd George remained as complex as ever.

Moving into Munitions, accompanied by his now notorious bust of

Napoleon, Winston quickly stamped his mark on a department of 12,000 staff overseeing 2½ million factory workers. Following in the pioneering footsteps of LG in 1915–16, his brief was to maintain the soaring momentum of production as the Allies built up their strength for eventual victory. He streamlined the ministry, reducing its fifty divisions to ten and creating a Munitions Council that met daily to coordinate policy. He also dealt with the rash of strikes by addressing key grievances but also by buying off skilled workers with bonus payments that fuelled inflation. And as usual, despite not having a seat in Cabinet, he interpreted his brief expansively – promoting the development of tanks, for instance, and travelling regularly across the Channel, using meetings with French counterparts to foster good relations with Field Marshal Sir Douglas Haig, the Commander of the BEF, despite being deeply critical of his strategy.

The morning of 21 March 1918 saw the first of five great German onslaughts along the Western Front, taking desperate advantage of the Bolshevik revolution and Lenin's decision to sign a separate peace with Germany, bringing to an end the Eastern Front. Winston had seen this coming and – adhering to the strategy of attrition he had outlined to the Commons in May 1916 – he positively welcomed such a shift in the war's dynamics. 'Thank God our offensives are at an end.' Now it was the Germans' turn to waste themselves in futile attacks. 'Let them rejoice in the occasional capture of placeless names & sterile ridges,' he crowed; gradually the Allies' superior firepower would 'break their hearts & leave them bankrupt in resources'. The Americans were now coming into the line. He also saw the tank as a winning weapon. The 'cavalry myth' had been 'exploded at last' by the 'modern science of war'. So, 'embark in the chariots of war', he urged Archie Sinclair, his former deputy at Ploegsteert, 'and slay the malignants with arms of precision.'[76]

Winston expected that the Allies would absorb the punches throughout 1918, while the American build-up continued, and then they would all take the offensive in 1919. 'His schemes are all timed for completion in *next June!*' Haig fumed in his diary on 21 August. 'I told him we ought to do our utmost to get a decision this autumn.' And that was indeed what transpired. An attack near Amiens on 8 August broke through the enemy line and the momentum was maintained over the next couple of months as the German army, hungry and exhausted, surrendered or deserted en masse. Haig's 'Hundred Days' were lauded as the greatest ever triumph of a British imperial army, now numbering some sixty divisions. Meanwhile, Germany's allies crumbled – starting with Bulgaria at the end of September, followed by Ottoman Turkey, Austria-Hungary and then the Kaiserreich itself. Winston was amazed at the sudden collapse of the Central Powers, calling it 'a drizzle of empires falling through the air'.[77] This miraculous denouement became a precedent to which he would cling in the dark days of 1940.

* * *

In the December 1918 election, Lloyd George's coalition won a landslide victory – virtually wiping Asquith's Liberals off the political map. Yet the PM was now in an exposed position. 'George thinks he has won the election,' remarked Walter Long, a Tory right-winger. 'But he didn't. It was the Tories that won the election, *and he will soon begin to find that out.*'[78] Winston himself remained beholden to LG. He lobbied hard for the Admiralty, which the Prime Minister apparently thought was still too sensitive after Gallipoli, but he did at last return to the Cabinet in January 1919, as Secretary of State for War and Air.

His early months in that post were taken up with troop protests and mutinies about the chaotic process of demobilisation, which Winston helped defuse with a policy of 'first in, first out'. But at times he clashed with the PM, who wanted more rapid shrinkage of the Army to appease popular sentiment and slash the massive costs. Presenting the army estimates on 3 March, he offered the House 'two maxims' from history that 'should always be acted upon in the hour of victory'. First: 'Do not be carried away by success into demanding or taking more than is right or prudent.' Second: 'Do not disband your army until you have got your terms.' He was anxious to maintain 'a strong armed Power' in these 'times of trouble', in order to 'preserve for long and splendid years the position which our country has attained'.[79]

Winston's view of the post-war world was bleak. 'The greater part of Europe and the greater part of Asia are plunged in varying degrees of disorder and anarchy', he told the Commons in March 1919. The revolutionary force that troubled him most was 'the Bolshevist pestilence'. His crusading zeal to eradicate that 'foul combination of criminality and animalism', which he considered 'far worse than German militarism', provoked his most serious clash with Lloyd George. It also set a course for much of Winston's subsequent political career.[80]

During 1918 the Lloyd George coalition, and other Allied governments, had provided supplies and troops to support the anti-Bolshevik forces in Russia, in the hope of re-creating an Eastern Front and thereby reducing German pressure in the west. Once Germany signed an armistice on 11 November 1918 that imperative no longer applied. Winston insisted that the Allies should 'use force to restore the situation and set up a democratic government' in Russia. In his view, 'Bolshevism in Russia represented only a mere fraction of the population and would be exposed and swept away by a General Election held under Allied auspices.' LG regarded such talk as fantasy. He pointed out that 'the Allies were on the mere fringe of Russia, with fewer than 100,000 troops.' Calling that country 'a jungle in which one could not say what was within a few yards of him', the PM made clear that he was 'definitely opposed to military intervention in any shape'.[81] That was the line he took at the Paris peace conference.

When Winston went to Paris to lobby the Allies, LG ensured that his own opposition was made known to the Americans. Winston was furious at being outflanked, and told LG so, but there was nothing he could do. An unsent letter of complaint laid bare his basic difference of approach to the current Russian anarchy:

There will be no peace in Europe until Russia is restored. There can be no League of Nations without Russia. If we abandon Russia, Germany and Japan will not . . . Germany will regain by her influence

over Russia far more than she has lost in colonies overseas or provinces in the West. Japan will no doubt arrive at a somewhat similar
conclusion . . . In five years, or even less, it will be apparent that the
whole fruits of our victories have been lost.[82]

Churchill's blend of hyperbole and prescience did not deflect LG
and the Cabinet, who agreed on 6 March to evacuate all British forces
from Russia. But on 23 March Hungarian communists seized power
in Budapest, fortifying Winston's conviction about the spreading
Bolshevik menace. He foresaw a replay of the French revolution, with
'all civil society being destroyed' until a military regime took power
in Bonapartist style. His favoured policy at the peace conference, he
told LG on 9 April, was 'Feed Germany; fight Bolshevism; make
Germany fight Bolshevism.' Or, stated more colloquially to Violet: 'Kill
the Bolshie, Kiss the Hun.'[83]

The PM repeatedly begged him to focus on cutting military
spending at a time of economic crisis. On 22 September, he asked
Winston to 'throw off this obsession which, if you will forgive me for
saying so, is upsetting your balance'. Privately, Lloyd George repeated
his bon mot that Winston was like a barrister employed by a solicitor
not because he was the best man but because 'he would be dangerous
on the other side.'[84] On 6 November Winston delivered another bravura
defence of his policy in the Commons: 'Lenin was sent into Russia by
the Germans in the same way that you might put a phial containing
a culture of typhoid or of cholera to be poured into water supply of
a great city.' Churchill's long-time sparring partner A.J. Balfour told
him afterwards, 'I admire the exaggerated way you tell the truth.'[85]

But, with Bolshevik victory now in sight, Lloyd George was determined to move on from perpetual war. He told the Commons on 10
February that trade would 'bring an end to the ferocity, the rapine,
and the crudities of Bolshevism surer than any other method. Europe
needs what Russia can give', especially its grain, and this would also
help to reduce discontent at home. He told the House, 'We must fight
anarchy with abundance.'[86] Here was the Cobdenite vision of classical

Liberalism: trade as a pacifying force. But LG's hopes were dashed in the spring by the dangerous escalation of the border war between Russia and newly independent Poland. This allowed Winston to open a new front against the Bolsheviks (and Lloyd George) – calling for aid to the Poles to help contain what he called 'plague-bearing Russia', bent on spreading 'world revolution'.[87]

LG was still determined to open trade negotiations with the Bolsheviks, but Winston led the opposition every step of the way. When the vote in Cabinet went against him on 18 November 1920, according to Hankey, 'he was so upset by the decision that he declared himself unequal to the task of discussing other items on the agenda. He was quite pale and did not speak again during the meeting.' Having requested that the Cabinet minutes should leave all ministers free to make anti-Bolshevist speeches, he availed himself of the freedom that very evening, telling the Oxford Union, 'The policy I will always advocate is the overthrow and destruction of that criminal regime.'[88]

The Anglo-Soviet trade treaty was eventually concluded in March 1921, leaving relations between Churchill and LG severely strained. Winston accepted a move from the War Office to the Colonial Office, but was then furious when passed over for the Chancellorship during a Cabinet reshuffle in favour of Sir Robert Horne, who had been a minister for just two years. Correspondence turned frosty, with 'Dear Ll.G' or even 'My Dear David' being replaced by 'Dear Prime Minister'.[89]

Yet, apparently against the grain, the last months of 1921 saw a renewal of their partnership. Lloyd George brought Winston on to his ministerial team of negotiators trying to agree an Anglo-Irish treaty to end Ireland's bloody war of independence. In part his reasoning was that, as usual, it seemed safer to have Winston inside the tent, but also he still valued his old friend's formidable energy and sharpness. In January 1922, Winston told Clemmie: 'The PM is singularly tame. I have never seen him quite like this. Very pleased to have me with him again. He is piling a great deal on to me now.'[90]

But the coalition was now on its last legs. The Tories, its bedrock, were increasingly restless, and a meeting of their MPs at the Carlton

Club on 19 October was hijacked by the rebels. The majority voted to withdraw from the coalition, and Lloyd George resigned four days later.

Bonar Law was asked to form a Tory government, and he immediately called an election. But Winston missed most of the action, having been operated on suddenly for chronic appendicitis the day before the Carlton Club meeting. He was unable to travel to Dundee until just before polling day on 15 November. Amid large-scale unemployment and strident accusations of being a 'War Monger', he went down to defeat – as did most of the coalition Liberals. 'In the twinkling of an eye', he wrote later, 'I found myself without an office, without a seat, without a party, and without an appendix.'[91]

* * *

Never again would Winston Churchill and David Lloyd George be members of the same Cabinet. But this was not evident at the time. Both still hankered after a new centre party. During the Slump and the Great Depression LG tried to reinvent Liberalism, toying with Keynesian ideas about expanding government spending and public works. By contrast, Winston turned his fire on the rising Labour Party, which he damned in 1922 as 'unfit to govern'. Not only were its doctrines 'as hateful to the principles of Liberalism as they are pernicious to the general interests of the British Empire' but also, behind British socialism, he claimed, 'crouch the shadows of Communist folly and Bolshevik crimes'.[92] His argument reflected a deeper reading of British history, namely that the Great War had 'closed a political epoch'. He claimed that there was 'scarcely any great or worthy objective which either the Conservative or Liberal Parties have set before themselves in the last 20 years which has either not been achieved or is not now conceded'. So, he insisted, it was essential to deal with 'the living questions of the day' and 'group ourselves according to the view which we take of these realities'.[93]

Winston had advanced this reading of history before – for instance, in his 1906 biography of Lord Randolph – but the dual challenge from Bolshevism abroad and socialism at home gave it new force. His convictions were genuine. Yet, as Paul Addison observed, 'there was something histrionic about his appeals to the nation' because 'Churchill needed the Labour party for career reasons.'[94] As the Liberals crumbled, split between Asquith and Lloyd George, anti-socialism proved his ticket back into the Tory fold. It would form his political creed for the rest of his life.

Yet Winston never wrote off LG – especially in the summer of 1940, when he made several efforts to bring 'the Wizard' into the coalition government. His reasoning was rather like LG's towards him during the Great War: better onside than offside. But Lloyd George was much more sceptical than Winston about Britain's prospects in 1940, and he refused to be drawn in. He told his private secretary in October, 'I shall wait until Winston is bust.'[95]

That wasn't to be. Instead, Churchill led Britain to total victory over Nazi Germany. Although LG did not quite live to see it, dying of cancer in March 1945, by then the outcome of the war was clear. And their relationship achieved a new equilibrium. In May 1944 LG and Frances (finally, his wife, after Margaret's death in 1941) discussed the historian Lord Acton's remark, 'I have never had any contemporaries' – in other words, that there was no one else alive of his stature. She told Lloyd George that the same might be said of him. The reply surprised her: 'I regard Winston as my only contemporary.'[96]

Leader in Waiting: The new War Cabinet (November 1939)
with Winston looking over the PM's shoulder.

3

Neville Chamberlain

The Temptation of Grand Designs

Each year it is necessary for a modern British Government to place some large issue or measure before the country, or to be engaged in some struggle which holds the public mind.
Winston S. Churchill, 6 June 1927[1]

His part is to brush in broad splashes of paint with highlights and deep shadows. Accuracy of drawing is beyond his ken.
Neville Chamberlain, 25 January 1928[2]

On Friday 13 November 1939 the Churchills invited the Chamberlains to dinner. Neville had been Prime Minister for two and a half years; Winston was his new First Lord of the Admiralty, appointed at the start of the war in September. Theirs was not an easy relationship: Churchill had been the leading critic of appeasement, and Chamberlain worked hard to keep him of out of government for most of the 1930s. In fact, the couples had never before dined socially. Staying off politics that evening, their conversation ranged widely and at one stage Chamberlain – loosening up as the meal progressed – reminisced about his time during the 1890s on Andros, a barren island in the Bahamas. He had been given the task of trying to grow sisal there by his domineering father, 'Radical Joe', and tried for five years to make it a success – in vain.

Writing about the dinner in 1947 for his memoirs, Churchill said he had been fascinated by this tale of 'gallant endeavour', thinking to himself, 'What a pity Hitler did not know when he met this sober English politician at Berchtesgaden, Godesberg and Munich, that he was actually talking to a hard-bitten pioneer from the outer marches of the British Empire!' Reading the passage in draft, his wife Clementine disagreed – 'Three months annual holiday & access to a gay little town like Nassau is not a very lonely, arduous existence' – but Winston clearly found the anecdote revealing.[3] It showed how little he had known on a human level about a man who was his colleague and rival for nearly twenty years. Theirs was a 'frenemy' relationship, rooted in the contest between two great political dynasties. But it also reflected two different conceptions of what mattered in political leadership: bold ideas or attention to detail. Their animosities would peak in 1938 over appeasement but would then mellow into mutual respect in 1940 – Winston's finest hour and Neville's last.

∗ ∗ ∗

Between 1886 and 1940 two Churchills and three Chamberlains yearned to become Prime Minister of the United Kingdom, and two of them eventually managed to do so. During that time four served as Chancellor of the Exchequer and three were leaders of the Conservative Party. Two were also awarded the Nobel Prize: one for Peace, the other for Literature. It has been said that 'British politics in the last quarter of the nineteenth century and the first half of the twentieth century were fundamentally shaped by the rival dynasties of the Churchill and Chamberlain families, in a way that has no equal in Britain since the War.'[4]

The two patriarchs seemed very different. Whereas Lord Randolph Churchill was a rakish aristocrat, educated at Eton and Oxford and a natural Tory, Joseph Chamberlain (1836–1914) was self-made – a successful screw manufacturer of Nonconformist background and Liberal politics, who became a dynamic reforming mayor of Birmingham in the 1870s. What they had in common was opportunistic brilliance – adroitly exploiting the expansion of the franchise in the Reform Acts of 1867 and 1884 by appealing to working men and the new constituency organisations against the party establishments. Yet a consuming appetite for power eventually consumed both of them. Each ended his days a wasted wreck of expected greatness.

'Radical Joe' did not become a Liberal MP until the age of 39, but then made up for lost time. In *Great Contemporaries* Winston Churchill depicted him as the 'robust, virile, aggressive champion of change and overturn, marching forward into battle against almost all the venerable, accepted institutions of the Victorian epoch' – monarchy, Church, aristocracy and eventually the 'Grand Old Man' of British politics himself: his own party leader and premier, William Ewart Gladstone. In their 1886 'duel' over Gladstone's plan for Home Rule for Ireland, Churchill wrote, the PM 'beat him' and 'broke him' – in fact 'drove him into the wilderness'.[5] But Joe, in turn, broke the party, taking with him a large minority of 'Liberal Unionists' who eventually joined with the Tories to form a 'Unionist' coalition (1895–1905) in which Chamberlain served for eight years as Colonial Secretary. Having helped splinter the Liberals, he then did the same to the Unionists by espousing tariff reform in 1903. This rejection of the 'free trade' to which Victorian Britain had been wedded since the 1830s split the Government, contributed to the Tories' rout in 1906 and precipitated a stroke that left him partially paralysed. Chamberlain died in July 1914, a month before the Great War began.

The era of Lord Randolph and Radical Joe was the crucible of Winston's political career, and he was deeply affected by both men – in a strange way, he brought them together in death. In *Great Contemporaries* he recalled how Chamberlain warmly assisted his research on his father, inviting Winston to stay overnight at his country house near Birmingham in September 1904 and staying up till 2 a.m. as they pored over old documents from the 1880s and polished off an 1834 port. In that same essay Winston recalled his youthful admiration for Joe – the stand-out political figure of that late Victorian era, 'the one who made the weather', and also a man who later showed Winston considerable kindness.

Although Churchill had left the Tories and joined the Liberals in reaction to tariff reform, Chamberlain bore no ill will, saying 'you are quite right, feeling as you do'. Winston remarked poignantly, 'I must have had a great many more real talks with him than I ever had with my own father.'[6]

Joseph Chamberlain had two sons – Austen (1863–1937) and his half-brother Neville (1869–1940). Joe also had four talented and forthright daughters with political interests of their own, but in such an intensely patriarchal family they took second place. Ida and Hilda were recipients of Neville's weekly diary letters, acting as confidantes and mirrors to his growing aspirations. As for the half-brothers, Austen, groomed from the start for politics, was educated at Trinity College, Cambridge, and Sciences Po in Paris; while Neville, intended for business, endured Mason Science College in Birmingham and then his ill-fated sojourn on the island of Andros.

Austen's rise was rapid – becoming Chancellor before the age of 40 – but he remained his father's son, right down to the monocle in his eye and the orchid in his buttonhole. Even when Joe was debilitated, Austen failed to become his own man. And in 1922, by then party leader, he stayed loyal for too long to David Lloyd George's wartime coalition, which was toppled by rebellious Tory MPs in that notorious Carlton Club coup of October 1922. Austen's brief moment of glory came in 1925 when, as Foreign Secretary, he helped broker the Locarno Treaty in which Britain and Italy offered mutual guarantees of the frontiers between France, Belgium and Germany. This seemed to herald a new era of peace in Western Europe and won him the Nobel Peace Prize. But after 1931, Austen languished in the political wilderness and, unlike Winston, never came back. In part this was because he lacked his father's ruthless ambition – 'poor man', Winston once remarked, 'he always plays the game and never wins it'[7] – but also because he again got caught in the family shadow, this time by his younger brother.

Andros made Neville – after that financial disaster he was determined to redeem himself – but it also marked him, accentuating the solitariness and rigidity of his character. This would only be partly softened in his forties by a late but very happy marriage to Anne Cole. Back in Birmingham in the 1900s Neville threw himself into business life and civic issues. In 1915 he became Lord Mayor of Birmingham and then an MP in 1918, fully blossoming with the fall of the Lloyd George coalition that blighted Austen.

The Carlton Club revolt produced a government of what Winston later derisively called 'The Second Eleven'. The most significant among them was Stanley Baldwin, who was premier briefly in 1923 and then for two lengthier spells in 1924–9 and 1935–7. As Tory leader for fourteen years between 1923 and 1937, he decisively shaped the careers of both Winston and Neville. The latter became Baldwin's right-hand man and eventually his designated successor. Their backgrounds were similar – both being scions of prosperous industrial families from the Midlands – but their temperaments were not. Neville's energy and decisiveness stood in marked contrast to his leader's frequent lethargy and dithering, but he lacked – in the end fatally – Baldwin's emollient manner and 'feel' for people. For his part, Winston never had much time for Baldwin and eventually felt deep anger about his defence policy in the 1930s. His reply, when asked to compose a tribute for Baldwin's eightieth birthday in 1947, was that 'it would have been much better for our country if he had never lived.'[8] Yet in 1924 Winston, even more than Neville, was the beneficiary of Baldwin's patronage – in fact quite astoundingly.

When Baldwin formed his Cabinet after the Tory landslide of October 1924, he first offered the Chancellorship to Chamberlain, but the latter preferred the Ministry of Health. Baldwin consented. Social reform had been Neville's passion when in Birmingham. 'I ought to be a great Minister of Health', he confided to his sisters, 'but am not likely to be more than a second-rate Chancellor.'[9] Baldwin then called in Churchill, now vehemently anti-socialist but currently belonging to no party. Winston was stunned to be offered the Chancellorship and recalled the interview vividly in 1947 in a long passage dictated and then amended in draft for his memoirs.

'Will you go to the Treasury?' Baldwin asked.

'I should have liked to have answered, "Will the bloody duck swim?" but as it was a formal and important occasion I replied, "This far exceeds fulfils my ambition. I still have my father's robe as Chancellor. I shall be proud to serve you in this splendid office."

'The Conservative Party was dumbfounded. There must have been fury commotion in the Chamberlain camp.'

When the new ministers met the King at Buckingham Palace, 'the Chamberlain brothers would hardly speak to me.'[10]

The remark about filial piety was genuine. On his first day at the Treasury, Winston arrived with a one-page summary, in Lord Randolph's handwriting, of the Budget he had never introduced in 1886.[11] But Winston's comments about the Chamberlains give a misleading impression – certainly of his relationship with Neville. During the Baldwin Government of 1924–9 the two men worked closely together – and in large measure productively, though not without serious friction later in the 1920s. The whole story offers revealing glimpses into their distinctive approaches to political leadership.

Both were responding to the dramatic expansion of the electorate in the decade after the Great War – even more massive than the enlargements their fathers had faced in the late Victorian era. Franchise reform in 1918 almost tripled the number of voters to over 21 million. It also gave two-thirds of women the vote – a revolution completed by the Equal Suffrage Act of 1928, which established a common voting age of 21 and helped swell the electorate to over 28 million. Within a decade British politics had therefore been transformed by the quadrupling of the electorate and by the fact that suddenly over half the potential voters were women. Dealing with mass democracy required huge adaptations by politicians raised in the pre-war era. Reversing President Woodrow Wilson's famous slogan of 1917 – 'the world must be made safe for democracy' – in 1928 Baldwin warned, 'we have got to make democracy safe for the world.'[12] That's why both Churchill and Chamberlain had no doubt that social reform was now a key issue. In fact, Winston had gone into his momentous meeting with Baldwin intending to bid for the Ministry of Health.[13]

Each man set about his task with fierce intensity. The Ministry of Health had only been created in 1919, with a mish-mash of responsibilities that needed to be clarified, coordinated and updated for an age when the old machinery of district and county government had become ill-suited to the new suburban sprawl. Chamberlain swiftly prepared a 'provisional programme of legislation' to take advantage of the 'prospect of a continuous administration for a few years ahead'. On 19 November – less than two weeks after taking up his post – he laid before the Cabinet a list of twenty-five measures which he wanted to have passed by Parliament. (Of these, twenty-one became law before he left the Ministry and the remaining four were incorporated in later legislation.) Winston was equally energetic in examining the files and interrogating his civil servants. On 26 November, explaining his priorities to the Cabinet, he urged the Government to 'concentrate on a few great issues in the social sphere' such as housing, health insurance and pensions.[14]

Churchill and Chamberlain were therefore eyeing the same ground as each sought to make his mark, but in 1924–5 their relationship was fruitful and generally harmonious. Winston – evidently seeking to update his double act with Lloyd George in the 1900s – offered to help finance Chamberlain's pension scheme but wanted it brought forward to 1925. Neville agreed. To find the money Winston managed to curb naval expenditure and impose a large increase in death duties (inheritance tax), while cutting income tax by sixpence in the pound – naturally a politically popular move. He announced these measures in his first Budget speech on 18 April 1925 – now mostly remembered for the statement that Britain would return to the Gold Standard – and also outlined the new contributory insurance pensions for which, he said, he and the Minister of Health had 'done our best to frame a scheme'.[15] Chamberlain then introduced the bill. The Widows, Orphans and Old Age Pensions Act of 1925 was a landmark piece of social legislation – the UK's first contributory scheme of state pensions, covering some

15 million people – and it was not superseded for twenty years. Several of Chamberlain's staff were indignant that Churchill seemed to be reaping some of the credit, but he had spent much time on the small print and the whole project would never have been realised so quickly without his support. Neville acknowledged as much in his diary: 'We were pledged to something of the kind, but I don't think we should have done it this year if he had not made it part of his Budget scheme.' On a personal level, there also seemed much to admire. 'I like him. I like his humour and his vitality. I admire his courage,' Neville told his sisters. And yet, he added, 'there is somehow a great gulf fixed between us which I don't think I shall ever cross.'[16]

That personal gulf became more apparent in 1927. At a crucial stage in Chamberlain's reform programme, he had to deal with Churchill at full throttle again just when also locked in bitter political arguments with Labour over his plan to sweep away the old Poor Law Unions, last reformed in the 1830s, as part of a wholesale reform of local government – its competences, structure and finance. In the process, Chamberlain developed a real animus to some of the Labour MPs who fought against his reforms and denigrated his motives. His speeches in the Commons were distinguished by cold clarity and mastery of detail – one critic called him 'more of a machine than a man' – and, in debate, his tone often became sarcastic and scathing. After one such exchange in June 1927, Baldwin 'begged me to remember that I was addressing a meeting of gentlemen. I always gave the impression, he said, that when I spoke in the House of Commons, that I looked on the Labour party as dirt.' Reporting this to his sister, Neville added, 'The fact is that intellectually, with few exceptions, they *are* dirt.'[17]

This mutual animosity was to cost Chamberlain dear in 1940. And his Commons demeanour contrasted sharply with Churchill at his best. 'It is admitted on all sides', Neville wrote in August 1927, 'that he has no equal in the House of Commons. His manner with the opposition is so good-humoured that although they often interrupt him, they look forward to his speeches as the finest entertainment the House can offer.' As an example, Neville instanced Winston's response when Labour MPs repeatedly interrupted him during a speech on trades union reform. 'Of course it is perfectly possible for Honourable members to prevent my speaking, and indeed I do not want to cast my pearls before . . .' Loaded pause, as the anger opposite mounted, and then his punchline: '. . . before those who do not want them.' This provoked what Chamberlain called 'a roar of delight that lasted several minutes'.[18]

Yet this showman aspect of Churchill also infuriated Chamberlain, especially when it seemed to jeopardise his tenacious work on local government reform. On 6 June 1927 Winston sent an agenda-setting letter to Baldwin, akin to his Christmas manifesto to Asquith in 1908. 'Each year it is necessary for a modern British Government to place some large issue or measure before the country, or to be engaged in some struggle which holds the public mind.' He set out how this had been done in the recent past – the Widows' Pension in 1925, for instance, or the General Strike in 1926 – but warned that there was nothing comparable on the stocks for 1928. 'It is for these reasons that I have been casting about for some large new constructive measure which, by its importance and scope, by its antagonisms as well as its appeal, will lift us above the ruck of current affairs.' His big idea was a substantial reduction of the rates – a local property tax – to the tune of £30 million, paid for by naval cuts and a new tax on petrol. All this would benefit 'every town and every part of the country, as well as every class', alongside hard-pressed industries such as coal, ship-building and railways. Wholesale 'de-rating', he told Baldwin, could be the centrepiece of the 1928 budget.[19]

Winston's strategy was similar to the one he adopted in 1925. And he explicitly intended de-rating to complement Neville's own work; as he told the PM, '£30 million applied to the Rates would enable us to make Neville Chamberlain's Bill the greatest measure of the Parliament. It would be a steam roller flattening out all the petty interests' that were seeking to obstruct rating reform. The following day he shared his ideas with Chamberlain, only to receive a cautious response questioning the need for £30 million and suggesting that 'the disposal of so large a sum would provoke quite as much criticism as approval.' In reply, Churchill insisted the scale of his proposal was 'fundamental', adding, 'I should take no interest in a petty handling of this subject.' They would argue about it, with growing passion, over the next nine months.[20]

Historian Paul Addison neatly portrayed this as 'a contest, by proxy, between Birmingham Town Hall and Blenheim Palace' – pitting a man whose tendency was to 'reduce politics' to questions of 'economic and efficient administration' against one who 'regarded administrative problems as the raw material from which great political themes were constructed'.[21] But even more was at issue. Chamberlain detected deeper character flaws. 'As usual,' Neville told his sisters in October, 'he looks not at the merits but at the electioneering value of any project that I put up to him and he seems to want to draw me into some new mad idea which is at present simmering in that volatile and turbulent brain of his.' In December Neville fumed: 'He has nothing worked out but gets so enamoured with his ideas that he won't listen to difficulties or wait until plans have been made to get over them. It's like Gallipoli again.'[22]

That last sentence is a reminder of how the fiasco of 1915 had left a lasting stigma – prompting knee-jerk suspicion towards any of Winston's schemes. But Chamberlain was wrong to say he had 'nothing worked out'. Treasury staff had been going over the matter for months. Likewise, Winston's critique of Neville's 'most obstinate' and 'tyrannical' resistance as largely 'a matter of *amour propre*' was also unfair:[23] one of Chamberlain's core objections to comprehensive de-rating was that this could sever the responsible involvement of business in local government. Churchill eventually conceded that industry would be relieved of only 75 per cent of the rates. But he got his own way that railway companies would also be excluded from the rates.

This was a struggle for territory between the two 'big beasts' of the Baldwin government, both of whom were spoken of as the next Prime Minister. On 2 April 1928, according to the deliberately dry Cabinet minutes, 'the whole of the morning meeting was taken up by explanations by the Chancellor of the Exchequer and the Minister of Health of their respective points of view.' The meeting reconvened that afternoon but since the differences were still not resolved, next day both men were excluded from further discussion so that the Cabinet could thrash out the basis of a compromise.[24]

As Churchill had intended, he was able to make de-rating the headline issue of his 1928 Budget. For his part, Chamberlain eventually got his Rating and Valuation (Apportionment) Bill through Parliament that summer. Reflecting at leisure on his battles with Winston, Neville observed: 'One doesn't often come across a real man of genius or, perhaps, appreciate him when one does. Winston is such a man and he has *les defauts de ses qualités*. To listen to him on the platform or in the House is sheer delight.' But, Chamberlain added, 'he seeks instinctively for the large and preferably the novel idea such as is capable of representation by the broadest brush'. (This was Neville's frequent complaint – as in his comment about Winston's love for vivid 'splashes of paint', used as an epigraph to this chapter.) By 1928 the 'gulf' Chamberlain detected between them in 1925 had become almost a chasm. 'There is too deep a difference between our natures for me to feel at home with him or to regard him with affection. He is like a wayward child who compels admiration but who wears out his guardians with the constant strain he puts upon them.'[25]

After the general election of May 1929, Labour was able to form a government with Liberal support. Out of a job, both Churchill and Chamberlain had time to take stock of where they were and where they hoped to go. Winston, needing to maintain his expensive lifestyle, immediately resumed his career as an author and speaker, spending three months on a lecture tour of North America. He found himself 'greatly attracted' by Canada – where, he told his wife, there were 'fortunes to be made in many directions'. He added: 'I have made up my mind that if N. Ch. is made leader of the C[onservative] P[arty] or anyone else of that kind, I clear out of politics & see if I cannot make you & the kittens a little more comfortable before I die. Only one goal still attracts me, & if that were barred I shd quit the dreary field for pastures new.' This scribbled letter lays bare both his ambition – to become Prime Minister – and his sense that Neville Chamberlain was now his main rival.[26]

While Neville stayed within the Tory fold, continuing to work closely with Baldwin, Winston took a different course, which also reflected a touch of pietas. Frustrated in his idea of a new alliance with the Lloyd George Liberals, he placed himself at the head of right-wing opposition to Baldwin, who was supporting the Labour Government's plan to turn the Raj into another Dominion of the British Commonwealth of Nations. The details must await a later chapter; it's important here to comment on Churchill's motives. Fellow Tory Leo Amery noted in early 1931, 'I imagine his game is to be a lonely and formidable figure available as a possible Prime Minister in a confused situation later on.' Shades of Lord Randolph in 1886! Winston was sure that this bipartisan policy on India was a derogation of Britain's greatness and showed a disastrous loss of national willpower. Reflecting in September 1930 on how Britain 'poured out blood and money' in the Great War, he fumed, 'I cannot understand why it is that we now throw away our conquests and our inheritance with both hands, through helplessness and pusillanimity.' Churchill was angry with Baldwin for going along with Labour on India, telling his old friend Max Beaverbrook, the Canadian-British newspaper magnate, 'my only interest in politics is to see this position retrieved.'[27]

In early 1931 Baldwin seemed acutely vulnerable over India, but he weathered the storm and then found his position transformed by the collapse of Ramsay MacDonald's Labour ministry amid the financial crash that summer. In the new National Government of August 1931, MacDonald remained Prime Minister, but he was now a figurehead while Baldwin, the power behind the throne, was Lord President of the Council. After the National Government won a landslide election victory in October, Neville Chamberlain was made Chancellor of the Exchequer. Churchill, having rebelled against his party leader over India, was out. 'Winston is very weak these days,' commented a friendly journalist, 'like a schoolboy trying to get into the team.'

He also observed that Churchill was 'nearly always slightly the worse for drink'.[28]

Over the next few years, Churchill utilised various issues on which he felt passionately as tools to attack the Government, apparently hoping that by making sufficient noise he could force his way back into office. From his earliest days in politics, Winston had believed that 'wild extravagance of language' was a hallmark of compelling rhetoric. Such hyperbole, he wrote in 1897, 'usually embodies in an extreme form the principles' the speaker was genuinely espousing. He believed this could have a 'tremendous' effect on politics, even becoming 'the watchwords of parties and the creed of nationalities'. As biographer Andrew Roberts notes, this rhetorical style was also 'designed to win him fame and attention' and 'keep him at the centre of debate', but during the 1930s his repeated controversies aroused deep distrust in many quarters. He had played Cassandra too often.[29] Baldwin put it picturesquely, suggesting that 'when Winston was born lots of fairies swooped down on his cradle' and lavished on him a glittering array of gifts – 'imagination, eloquence, industry, ability', and so on. But then, said Baldwin, one fairy declared that 'no one person has the right to so many gifts', and gave him such a shake that he was denied 'judgment and wisdom'.[30]

The crucial period was 1935–6. By this time Churchill had lost his long and bitter battle against the India bill but still hoped, despite all the vitriol, that he could work his way back into the Government. At the Tory conference on 3 October 1935, he offered a warm, though carefully phrased tribute to Baldwin as 'a statesman who has gathered to himself a greater volume of confidence and goodwill than any public man I recollect in my long career'. After the election Churchill spent six days at Chartwell waiting for a letter or phone call. But Baldwin now had a crushing majority of more than 250, and he saw no need to include a man who had been the principal thorn in his side over India and was constantly challenging his policy on Germany. Yet, intriguingly, Baldwin also remarked privately that 'if there is going to be a war – and who can say there is not – we must keep him fresh to be our war Prime Minister.'[31]

Another opportunity for Churchill seemed to open up in March 1936, when Baldwin was under pressure to appoint a defence minister – the kind of post for which Churchill seemed outstandingly suited. So keen was he for the job that he privately approached Chamberlain for a tip-off about Baldwin's intentions. According to Chamberlain's diary on 8 March, Churchill 'wanted to make a "telling" speech' – by which Chamberlain understood 'a fierce attack' on Baldwin – 'if he were ruled out from the post, but not if there were any chance of it being offered to him'. Chamberlain told Churchill that Baldwin had not yet made up his mind, but noted in his diary, 'I thought it an audacious piece of impertinence to ask me such a question with such a motive.' This meeting took place the day after Hitler marched into the Rhineland. Baldwin's eventual choice as the new 'Minister for the Coordination of Defence' was Sir Thomas Inskip – a lawyer with no special defence experience. *The Times*, following a lead from Downing Street, commented that others had been ruled out as 'ill-adapted to teamwork or (what is equally important) to work with this particular team', especially because 'their appointment at this particular moment in the world's affairs might be misunderstood or misrepresented.' Whatever Churchill's potential as a war leader, Baldwin had not given up on appeasement – far from it.[32]

Looking back, Churchill felt grateful that he had not been entangled in government during the 1930s. 'Over me beat invisible wings,' he wrote in 1948. But at the time he was hurt, angry and often demoralised.[33] While Winston's star faded, Neville's was rising. Exploiting his position as Chancellor, at a time when the verities of Victorian finance had been blown away by Britain's abandonment of the Gold Standard, he was finally able to push through tariff reform and Imperial Preference, to strengthen the British Empire as a trading bloc. Winston's act of pietas in 1925, when delivering his first Budget dressed in his father's robes, was trumped by Neville's performance in the Commons on 4 February 1932 as he brought down the curtain on decades of free trade, with Austen sitting on the Tory benches and

Joseph Chamberlain's widow and family watching from the gallery. It was a bravura performance.

Although Neville could never rival Winston in rhetorical style and range, he was clearly developing his own public persona – as many politicians do when gaining self-confidence as they near the top of the 'greasy pole'. His confidence and theatricality were on full display when he finally took over the premiership from Baldwin in May 1937.

Chamberlain did not deny the need for rearmament, especially against the threat from Hitler's Luftwaffe. But he did not share Churchill's sense of existential urgency, his fear being that too rapid rearmament could damage the civilian economy and weaken foreign confidence in Britain's financial position. As in the 1920s, he felt that he was seeing the context as a whole, whereas Winston was latching on to a single aspect in hyperbolic language. 'I am thankful', he told his sisters in April 1936, 'that we do not have Winston as a colleague. He is in his usual excited condition that comes on him when he smells war and if he were in the Cabinet we should be spending all our time in holding him down instead of getting on with our business.'[34]

On issues of diplomacy rather than defence, however, their positions were almost reversed. Churchill was not demanding big gestures, only firmness in standing up to Hitler: by 1938 he had abandoned any hope of a general settlement with Nazi Germany. Chamberlain, by contrast, not only believed it was still possible to defuse the mounting tension but also that it was his personal mission to be the peacemaker of Europe. In August 1937, soon after moving into 10 Downing Street, Neville expressed his delight at 'the wonderful power that the Premiership gives you'. When Chancellor, he told his sisters, 'I could hardly have moved a pebble: now I have only to raise a finger & the whole face of Europe is changed!'[35]

One obstacle was Anthony Eden, the Foreign Secretary whom Neville had inherited from Baldwin and now began to bypass. In early 1938, he took advantage of the presence in Rome of Ivy Chamberlain, Austen's widow and confidante of Benito Mussolini, to convey messages to and from him. He also tried to divert and delay a sudden 'bombshell' message from Washington that US President Franklin D. Roosevelt was minded to call an international conference about arms reduction, equal access to raw materials, and other problems. He saw this vague presidential idea as a direct threat to his own diplomacy, whereas Eden insisted that 'Anglo-American cooperation in an attempt to ensure world peace' was far more important than 'a piece-meal settlement approached by way of a problematical agreement with Mussolini'. But Roosevelt backed off when informed of the PM's plans for talks with Italy. These policy differences over Italy and America were the ostensible grounds for Eden's resignation on 20 February 1938, but the basic issue was Chamberlain's determination to be his own Foreign Secretary.[36]

Ultimately Chamberlain's biggest foreign policy battle – as in the 1920s over socio-economic policy – was with Churchill himself. This emerged starkly in March 1938 after Hitler's *Anschluss* uniting Austria with the German Reich. On 14 March, two days later, Winston told the Commons that Europe was now 'confronted with a programme of aggression, nicely calculated and timed, unfolding stage by stage'. The only wise course was to 'take effective measures while time remains', either to 'preserve the peace of Europe' or at least to 'preserve the freedom of the nations of Europe'. He called for Britain and France to conclude 'a solemn treaty for mutual defence against aggression', backed by 'staff arrangements' between their armed forces – either as an act of deterrence or as preparation for possible war.[37]

In March 1938 Chamberlain headed off this challenge from Churchill, stressing London's solidarity with Paris over any threat to France and Belgium and promising to make rearmament the 'first priority in the nation's effort', despite the 'consequent interference with normal commercial work'.[38] But during August, amid Hitler's mounting agitation over the position of the Sudeten Germans in Czechoslovakia, Chamberlain decided he must make a dramatic personal effort to bring peace to Europe. Truly 'broad splashes' on a grand canvas. His three visits to Hitler in a couple of weeks caught the imagination of the world. They are worth particular attention here because they established modern summitry in patterns that Winston would mirror after he took over in Number 10.

* * *

At 9 p.m. on the evening of 14 September, London journalists were summoned to a special briefing at Number 10 and informed that the PM would fly to see Hitler in his Alpine lair at Berchtesgaden. Next morning this was the main story in British newspapers, almost all the editorial comment being favourable. Even the *News Chronicle* – a Liberal paper generally critical of the Government – credited Chamberlain with 'one of the boldest and most dramatic strokes' in modern diplomacy. Whatever the outcome, it stated, 'Neville Chamberlain is now assured of a place in history.'[39]

Chamberlain had come up with the idea at the end of August. He believed 'you could say more to a man face to face than you could in a letter' and thought that 'doubts about the British attitude would be better removed by discussion than by any other means.'[40] After all, Hitler was clearly not normal. Chamberlain's repeated belief that he might be dealing with some kind of 'lunatic' underpinned his wish to see the reclusive dictator for himself.[41]

Yet the PM also viewed the visit in PR terms, as a grand gesture to wrest the initiative from Hitler. That's why he decided to fly – an idea that 'rather took Halifax's breath away' when Chamberlain broached the idea to his Foreign Secretary.[42] And to have invited the Führer to London 'would have deprived my coup of much of its dramatic force'.[43] The world media was riveted by the idea of this sedate-looking 69-year-old, who had never flown before apart from one brief spin around Birmingham airfield, undertaking a four-hour flight to Munich. Chamberlain must also have hoped that diplomatic success would deliver domestic dividends – with an election likely in 1939. And pietas also figured. After the flight to Berchtesgaden, Neville's sister Hilda wrote to express 'immense pride' at his brilliant coup: 'our father was the only other man whom I could imagine either conceiving it or carrying it out!' Hilda was 'quite right,' Neville replied. 'It was an idea after Father's own heart.'[44]

The gesture was indeed dramatic and bold, but its execution was spectacularly inept. Contemptuous of the cautious Foreign Office and anxious to build trust, the PM decided to meet the Führer alone at Berchtesgaden, without even his own translator or note-taker – relying simply on a German interpreter. Hitler quickly took control and, with customary histrionics, upped his demands from autonomy for the Sudeten Germans within Czechoslovakia to the secession of their territory into the Third Reich. Chamberlain said he was personally inclined to the same solution but would have to consult the Cabinet.

Back in London, Chamberlain tried to accentuate the positives, telling Cabinet colleagues that he no longer feared Hitler was mad and judged his aims to be 'strictly limited' – his intention was simply to bring all Germans within the Reich. He also made much of 'information from other sources' (actually it came from German diplomats seeking to play on his vanity) that Hitler had been 'most favourably impressed' with the PM. This showed, said Chamberlain, the wisdom of his 'new technique of diplomacy relying on personal contacts' rather than ponderous exchanges of documents. Even some Chamberlain loyalists found the whole story 'a little painful' – it 'was plain that Hitler had made all the running' and 'had in fact blackmailed the PM', one of them noted in his diary.[45] The Cabinet made clear that any deal had to include concessions from Hitler as well.

Chamberlain tried again on 22–23 September at Bad Godesberg, a spa town on the Rhine. This time he travelled with more professional diplomats, including a fluent German speaker from the British Embassy in Berlin who would act as interpreter and note-taker. And he outlined his proposal, agreed with Paris and Prague for a phased transfer of Czech territory to Germany, overseen by an international commission. But once again Hitler upped the ante, demanding during a series of fraught exchanges that the transfer had to be completed by 1 October. Tired and angry, Chamberlain returned home and again tried to put the best face on events – aware that he had now placed Britain's prestige (and his own) on the line.

According to the Cabinet minutes, Chamberlain accepted the Führer's assurance that 'once the present question had been settled, he had no more territorial ambitions in Europe', and said he was confident that such a settlement 'might be a turning-point in Anglo-German relations'. But his ministers were not persuaded. Foreign Secretary Lord Halifax, who was close to Chamberlain, aired his unease about Hitler having 'given us nothing' and 'dictating terms, just as though he had won a war', and stated that his own 'ultimate aim' was 'the destruction of Nazi-ism' because 'so long as Nazi-ism lasted, peace would be uncertain'.[46] There was considerable support for Halifax within a now divided Cabinet, and his firmer line was stiffened by the French and by Prague's rejection of Hitler's ultimatum. On 27 September the Führer was warned that Britain would stand with France and go to war if Germany attacked Czechoslovakia. At 11.30 a.m. on the 28th, Chamberlain sent a last-ditch message telling Hitler he was still ready for another meeting to achieve a peaceful settlement, but then set about finalising his statement that afternoon to the Commons. Although intending to show how hard he had worked for peace, Chamberlain knew that, with German troops massing on the Czech border, he might have to announce a declaration of war.

The Commons chamber was packed. Anne Chamberlain was in the gallery, together with several members of the royal family, while the ambassadors of all the interested powers were crammed into the diplomatic seats. At 2.54 p.m. Chamberlain rose. He embarked on a long and detailed account of the Czechoslovak crisis, of his visits to Hitler and of their correspondence. The House listened in attentive silence, the PM's relentless chronology increasing the tension. At key moments in the narrative, he removed his pince-nez and looked up to the skylight. It was compelling theatre, but Chamberlain must have been painfully aware that he lacked a punchline. The sudden denouement was, Chamberlain wrote later, 'a piece of drama that no work of fiction ever surpassed'.[47]

Around 4.15 p.m. the audience was distracted by mutterings and movement around the Speaker's Chair. A piece of paper was passed along the Government front bench. Everyone could sense its importance. Chamberlain was given the note during a burst of applause. Having just reached the final passage about his appeals that morning to Hitler and Mussolini, he broke off, adjusted his pince-nez, and scrutinised the paper. Then, observed MP Harold Nicolson, 'his whole face, his whole body, seemed to change . . . he appeared ten years younger and triumphant.'[48] Raising his face to the sunlight, Chamberlain went on: 'I have now been informed by Herr Hitler that he invites me to meet him at Munich tomorrow morning.' As the Commons erupted, he smiled: 'I need not say what my answer will be.' Many MPs stood on the benches, throwing their order papers in the air. Amid the cheering, the PM proposed an adjournment for a few days, after which 'perhaps we may meet in happier circumstances.' It was an amazing piece of brinksmanship, what he later called 'the last desperate snatch at the last tuft on the very verge of the precipice.'[49]

At the eleventh hour, it was Hitler who had blinked – a point often forgotten in accounts of the crisis. The firm British-French stance, the mobilisation of the Royal Navy and Mussolini's refusal to join in any war were all probably factors, together with the evident lack of enthusiasm among the German people for another war. The Führer invited Chamberlain, Mussolini and the French premier Edouard Daladier to meet him in Munich. But at their conference on the 29th, the British and French gave him the transfer of territory he wanted – over ten days rather than on 1 October. For Chamberlain, however, what mattered was not Czechoslovakia – long seen as an unviable relic of the Versailles peace in 1919 – but Hitler's signature on a document next day in which together they pledged 'the desire of our two peoples never to go to war with one another.' This was the famous 'piece of paper' that the PM took back to London, waving it at the airport. Despite pouring rain, he was greeted by euphoric crowds, and invited by the King onto the balcony of Buckingham Palace. At 10 Downing Street, he was urged by aides to repeat Benjamin Disraeli's triumphant words on returning from the Congress of Berlin sixty years before. 'No,' he retorted, 'I do not do that sort of thing.' But when he went upstairs to acknowledge the throng in the street below, he was conscious of standing at the very window from which Disraeli had spoken. Emotionally exhausted, perhaps impelled by that ingrained desire to eclipse his father and his brother, Neville let his emotions get the better of his reason. 'My good friends,' he said. 'This is the second time in our history there has come back from Germany to Downing Street peace with honour. I believe it is peace for our time.' This was an extravagance too far. 'He knew at once that it was a mistake, and that he could not justify the claim,' the PM's parliamentary private secretary Alec Douglas Home commented later. 'It haunted him for the rest of his life.'[50]

Throughout the September crisis, Chamberlain had made sure to keep in touch with Churchill. But in public their differences were now stark, as Winston repeatedly urged a firm Anglo-French front, ideally with Russian support. On 15 September, the morning the PM flew to Berchtesgaden, the *Daily Telegraph* carried on page 12 an article by Winston headlined 'Can Europe Stave Off War? Joint Warning By Powers The Strongest Hope'.[51] Neville was convinced that no democratic state should 'make a threat of war unless it was both ready to carry it out and prepared to do so', whereas Winston believed the PM should have toughed it out and called Hitler's bluff. He pronounced Chamberlain's visit to the Berghof 'the stupidest thing that has ever been done' and was one of the few MPs to remain seated when the Commons exploded in delight on 28 September at news of a third conference in Munich. Eventually he did walk over to wish Chamberlain 'God speed' but added, to the PM's irritation, 'You were very lucky.'[52]

During the debate on Munich in the Commons on 5 October Winston damned the settlement as 'a total and unmitigated defeat' and cut through all the casuistry about the different terms offered at Berchtesgaden, Godesberg and Munich: '£1 was demanded at the pistol's point. When it was given, £2 were demanded at the pistol's point. Finally, the dictator consented to take £1 17s 6d and the rest in promises of goodwill for the future.' In other words, summitry

Chamberlain-style was not diplomatic negotiation but highway robbery. Churchill predicted that the rump state of Czechoslovakia would soon be 'engulfed in the Nazi regime', perhaps within months, and warned that 'if the Nazi dictator should choose to look westward, as he may', France and England would 'bitterly' regret the loss of the Czech army.[53]

In the Munich debate Chamberlain was already trying to distance himself from 'peace for our time' – calling the claim 'words used in a moment of some emotion, after a long and exhausting day' – but he remained defiant. 'I say, by my action I did avert war. I feel equally sure that I was right in doing so.' After the debate there was a tart exchange of letters between the two men, trading epithets such as 'unworthy' and 'offensive'. Chamberlain accused Churchill of being 'singularly sensitive for a man who so constantly attacks others'.[54]

Over the next few months, however, Winston's warnings seemed increasingly prescient. Despite the Nazi *Kristallnacht* pogroms against the Jews in November, Chamberlain maintained his search for a settlement with Germany until Hitler's takeover of the rest of Czechoslovakia in March 1939. This panicked the PM into a belated effort to form a Churchillian deterrent front by guarantees to countries in east and south-east Europe, notably Poland. Hitler was not deterred, especially after his bombshell pact with Stalin in August eliminated the danger of war with the USSR, and he gobbled up Poland in September.

Chamberlain reluctantly accepted that he would have to honour the Polish guarantee and Britain, with France, declared war on 3 September. At long last, he brought Churchill into his government, joining the new War Cabinet as First Lord of the Admiralty, the post Winston had held when war broke out in 1914. 'How I do hate and loathe this war,' Neville told his sisters in October, lamenting the death and destruction. 'I was never meant to be a War Minister.' Winston, he added, was 'enjoying every moment of the war'.[55]

From the start, Churchill was determined to take the initiative. 'I could never become responsible for a naval strategy which excluded the offensive principle and relegated us to keeping open the lines of communication and maintaining the blockade,' he told the First Sea

Lord, Admiral Sir Dudley Pound.[56] Historically, blockade had been a key weapon of Britain's wars – in 1914–18, for instance, or against Napoleon – and in 1939 it was crucial to the war of attrition Britain planned to wage against Hitler. But Churchill, who idolised Napoleon, believed that wars were won by audacity. Through the autumn of 1939, he kept pressing Operation Catherine – intended to force a passage into the Baltic and maintain a naval force there in order to swing the Scandinavian neutrals to the Allies and block German iron-ore supplies from Sweden. This was a highly risky idea given the threat from aircraft and U-boats within a narrow and largely enclosed waterway, as Pound and senior naval staff kept arguing.

Churchill's passion for broad splashes of paint also made him acutely conscious about publicity. He was always on the lookout for positive stories and did not scruple about manipulating them. He initiated a weekly radio broadcast in which, recalled his Director of Naval Intelligence, Admiral John Godfrey, 'good news was made to seem better; bad news was toned down, delayed or sometimes suppressed. Any particularly spicey bit of news might be held up for three or four days until it could be included in the First Lord's broadcast.' Churchill regularly exaggerated U-boat losses. In February 1940, he claimed that twenty-eight U-boats had been sunk – actually half the number with which Germany entered the war – while Godfrey at the time estimated nine. (The correct figure was ten.) One particularly diligent fact-checker at the Admiralty paid a high price for questioning fake news. In April 1940 Churchill told Pound, 'It might be a good thing if Captain Talbot went to sea as soon as possible.'[57]

As Admiral Godfrey drily observed, 'no one was more conscious than Mr. Churchill of the popularity of the bringer of good tidings.' A classic example was his first speech to the Commons as First Lord, on 26 September 1939 – vividly documented by the diarist Harold Nicolson. Churchill followed Chamberlain, who was 'dressed in deep mourning relieved only by a white handkerchief and gold watch chain'. During the PM's lugubrious statement, wrote Nicolson, one felt 'the confidence and spirits of the House dropping inch by inch'. Beside

Chamberlain sat the hunched figure of Churchill, 'looking like the Chinese god of plenty suffering from acute indigestion'. When he rose, the effect of his speech was 'infinitely greater than could be derived from any reading of the text'. Churchill 'sounded every note from deep preoccupation to flippancy, from resolution to sheer boyishness'. Not only could one feel 'the spirits of the House rising with every word', observed Nicolson, in those twenty minutes 'Churchill brought himself nearer the post of Prime Minister than he has ever been before.'[58]

Being Winston, however, he didn't always get the details right. Although blocked over Operation Catherine, he did eventually persuade the Cabinet to mine Norway's territorial waters, hoping to force German iron-ore shipments from Sweden into open sea where they could be attacked by the Royal Navy. The mining took place on the night of 8 April, but at dawn next day the Nazis invaded Norway and Denmark. Churchill compounded Government embarrassment by treating the ensuing war in Norway as a grand opportunity to take the initiative, even though he lacked a clear plan and oscillated between various operational targets. There was also scant coordination between the three services. Exhausted by the pressure, on 11 April Winston turned in one of his worst parliamentary performances. 'He was pale, couldn't find the right words, stumbled and kept getting mixed up', noted the Soviet ambassador, watching from the gallery. Grabbing at silly historical analogies, Churchill blustered that 'Herr Hitler has committed a grave strategic error in spreading the war so far to the North' – indeed 'as great a strategic and political error as that which was committed by Napoleon in 1807 or 1808, when he invaded Spain.'[59]

By the end of April, it was being whispered that Churchill would be made the scapegoat, Gallipoli-style. Eventually Chamberlain appointed him head of the 'Military Coordination Committee', effectively Minister of Defence, against the wish of several senior ministers – a revealing sign that, in a war situation, Winston seemed impossible but indispensable. As the PM remarked, the friction with officials and ministers that Churchill generated in trying to push through his ideas was 'the price we have to pay for the asset we have in his personality and popularity'. But, he added, 'I do wish we could have the latter without the former.'[60]

By early May, most of the British troops had been evacuated. An acrimonious Norway debate in the Commons on 7–8 May turned into a vote of confidence in the Government. It was striking that several speakers, not all of them Winston's natural allies, sought to distance him from Chamberlain. Lloyd George, in a rare Commons intervention, advised the First Lord not to let himself 'be converted into an air-raid shelter to keep the splinters from hitting his colleagues'. At ten o'clock, it was Winston's difficult task to wind up for the Government. Harold Nicolson felt that he managed to 'defend the Services' and be 'loyal to the Prime Minister' while demonstrating 'that he really has nothing to do with this confused and timid gang'.[61]

The vote was 281 to 200 – a devastating blow for Chamberlain, whose majority was normally around two hundred. Next morning, he discussed the situation with Halifax and agreed that Labour and the Liberals must be brought into the Government – something the Foreign Secretary had been urging since Munich. Aware of the hatred on the Opposition benches, after years under his stinging tongue, Chamberlain said that, if Labour refused, he would be ready to serve in a government under Halifax. But the Foreign Secretary made it clear that he had no wish to be Prime Minister, citing the constitutional problem that, as a peer, he did not sit in the House of Commons. This was not an insuperable obstacle; the real issue was that the prospect of being PM made him feel physically sick. At 4.30 p.m. Chamberlain and Halifax met with Churchill and the Government chief whip. No record was kept, and several somewhat conflicting *post facto* accounts exist. In his memoirs, Churchill claimed he kept (a rare) silence while Halifax talked himself out of the job; other versions suggest that Winston made clear he felt better qualified than Halifax. But the question of whether, on 9 May, Churchill 'seized the premiership' or 'had it handed to him'[62] should not obscure the essential point. Neither Chamberlain nor Halifax had what it took to be a war leader – and they knew it. Whatever the continued doubts about Churchill's balance and judgment – doubts which Norway had inevitably fanned – he was clearly the only man for the job. In a sense, this had always been a hidden assumption behind the politics of exclusion during the 1930s.[63]

On 10 May Hitler launched his long-delayed offensive on the Western Front. Chamberlain thought of trying to avoid resignation, and loyalists tried to change Halifax's mind – only to find he had chosen to slip out to the dentist. So Chamberlain went to the Palace to hand in his resignation. Like Chamberlain, King George VI would have preferred Halifax, who was close to the royal family, and he had not forgotten Churchill's passionate defence of his brother, Edward VIII, during the Abdication crisis. But, accepting that there was no alternative, at 6 p.m. he invited Churchill to form a government. He would never have any regrets.

This was not the end of the Churchill–Chamberlain saga. Their relations warmed during the long summer of 1940 when Winston found his predecessor to be a loyal and industrious colleague and admired his dignified fortitude in struggling with bowel cancer. 'What shall I do without poor Neville?' Winston lamented after Chamberlain died in November 1940. 'I was relying on him to look after the Home Front for me.' By now the arch-appeaser's reputation lay in ruins and 'Munich' had already become a term of abuse. 'Few men can have known such a tremendous reverse of fortune in so short a time,' Chamberlain reflected just before he died.[64]

Nemesis was born of hubris – or, if you like, of the egotistical idealism of a man who was sure he could bring peace to Europe. He had also been fired up by the ambition of a marginalised younger son determined to fly higher than his father and his brother. But, having risen so far, Neville had much further to fall. There was also, perhaps, too, the fatal attraction of what he had learned from Winston in the 1920s about the political value of a 'broad splash of paint'. Ironically, Neville's trademark 'accuracy of drawing' deserted him when he ventured abroad to practise the dark arts of personal diplomacy. Whereas Winston – the man so often accused of lacking judgment – got it right on the issue that really mattered in the late 1930s.

Yet, whatever Churchill's private feelings about Chamberlain, he did not drive in the knife. The valedictory tribute he delivered in the Commons on 12 November 1940 was one of his noblest orations, partly because of that new-found respect for Chamberlain but also because he, too, knew the fickleness of fame, having been stretched out on fortune's wheel. 'In one phase men seem to have been right, in another they seem to have been wrong. Then again, a few years later, when the perspective of time has lengthened, all stands in a different setting.' Throughout, Churchill continued, 'the only guide to a man is his conscience; the only shield to his memory is the rectitude and sincerity of his actions.' And 'whatever else history may or may not say about these terrible, tremendous years, we can be sure that Neville Chamberlain acted with perfect sincerity according to his lights and strove to the utmost of his capacity and authority, which were powerful, to save the world from the awful, devastating struggle in which we are now engaged ... Herr Hitler protests with frantic words and gestures that he has only desired peace. What do these ravings and outpourings count before the silence of Neville Chamberlain's tomb?'[65]

At the empty tomb: Winston amid the ruins of Hitler's Chancellery in Berlin (16 July 1945). Daughter Mary is in the centre.

4

Adolf Hitler

The 'Thirty Years War'

As a prophet I now proclaim: A great world empire will be destroyed . . . the continuation of this war will end only in the complete shattering of one of the two warring parties. Mr. Churchill may believe this to be Germany. I know it to be England.

Adolf Hitler, July 1940[1]

Great Britain could have no other object but to use her whole influence and resources consistently over a long period of years to weave France and Germany so closely together economically, socially and morally, as to prevent the occasion of quarrels and make their causes die in a realization of mutual prosperity and interdependence.

Winston S. Churchill, March 1929[2]

On 16 May 1940, Churchill flew to Paris for a crisis meeting at the Quai d'Orsay, France's Foreign Ministry. There General Maurice Gamelin, the French army commander, explained that German tanks had made a surprise breakthrough across the Meuse river at Sedan and were thrusting towards the Channel, around the back of the French and British armies in Belgium. '*Ou est la masse de manoeuvre?*' demanded Churchill in his best French. With a Gallic shrug, Gamelin uttered just one word: '*Aucune*'. No strategic reserve! Churchill was dumbfounded. Struggling to think, he walked over to the windows.

Looking down into the gardens below, he saw 'venerable functionaries' pushing wheelbarrows full of archives onto great bonfires. Already, the evacuation of Paris was being prepared. In his memoirs, Churchill called this 'one of the greatest surprises I have had in my life'.[3]

The German offensive had begun only six days earlier, on 10 May. That was also the day Churchill was appointed Prime Minister, finally gaining the prize for which he had yearned. Yet, within less than a week, Adolf Hitler had shattered Britain's whole strategy for waging the war. What we now know as Churchill's 'finest hour' was largely frantic improvisation. Indeed, he would have to keep improvising throughout the war, arguably for the rest of his political life.

Just as he had written in 1937 of earlier leaders,[4] so it was for Winston: by 1940 it had taken him two-thirds of his life to reach his chosen 'battlefield'. But having arrived, he had to fight on ground that was definitely not of his own choosing and alongside allies to whom he was very much the junior partner. That predicament was his tragedy. How he dealt with it was his triumph.

Yet, throughout the long and dark tunnel of the war, Churchill never lost sight of a visionary aim he had held for years. Eventually Germany must shake hands with France and make peace. Hitler's war was part of that thirty-year struggle.

* * *

On one occasion the two men nearly met – before Hitler became Chancellor. In August 1932 Churchill, at work on a biography of his ancestor John Churchill, first Duke of Marlborough, visited southern Germany to tour the battlefield of Blenheim. Afterwards he spent a week in Munich. At his hotel, the Regina, he got chatting with Ernst 'Putzi' Hanfstaengel, a crony of Hitler, who, said Putzi, came to the Regina every afternoon around 5 p.m. So 'nothing would be easier' than to arrange a meeting. Churchill was willing: he knew little about Hitler at this stage but admired men who were ready to 'stand up for their country'. Hitler, however, got cold feet. He seems to have taken offence at a comment Churchill made about the Jewish question. 'Why

is your chief so violent about the Jews?' Winston recalled asking Putzi.
'How can a man help how he was born?' But Putzi remembered a
sharper stab from the British politician: 'Tell your boss from me that
anti-Semitism may be a good starter, but it is a bad sticker.' When
Putzi made one last overture to Hitler about a meeting, he was rebuffed.
'What part does Churchill play?' Hitler scoffed. 'He's in opposition
and no one pays any attention to him.' Putzi muttered: 'People say the
same thing about you.'[5]

Churchill's trip to Munich in 1932, at the age of 57, was only his
third visit to Germany; the previous two (both brief) had been in 1906
and 1909 to view military manoeuvres. He called the German army 'a
terrible engine' and said he was 'very thankful that there is a sea between
that army and England'.[6] Churchill evinced little interest in the country
or its culture – literature, philosophy, art or music – and his knowledge
of German was non-existent. 'I'll never learn the beastly language', he
exclaimed on the eve of the Great War, 'until the Kaiser marches on
London.' Historian Gordon Craig observes that 'nothing he ever said
or wrote indicated that he had any real understanding of the nature of
the political process' during either the *Kaiserreich* or the Weimar
Republic. What gripped Churchill's attention was Germany's role as a
great power – its geopolitical relations with neighbours and rivals.[7]

All very different from Churchill's attitude to France. Biographer
Martin Gilbert estimated that by the time war broke out in September
1939, Churchill had already crossed the Channel over a hundred times.
Many of those visits had been on political and military business, especially during the Great War, but Churchill also travelled to France for
pleasure – to paint, write books or gamble in the casinos. He was well
connected with French politicians and had numerous Parisian friends,
through his mother's contacts and his own. He knew the French language
better than he pretended and was well read in French history, entertaining particular respect for Joan of Arc as well as for Napoleon (another
small man in a big hurry), whose biography he longed to write.[8]

Churchill's approach to Franco-German relations in the 1930s owed
much to his considered judgments on the Great War, set out in six

volumes of memoirs. Essentially, he believed that Germany had lost the war but the Allies had lost the peace. The Treaty of Versailles in 1919 left 'the central problem' of Europe 'quite untouched', above all France's fear of likely German revenge. It had taken the combined efforts of Britain, France, Italy and America, as well as Tsarist Russia until 1917, to bring Germany to its knees. 'But would those conditions ever return?' Without the resurrection of such an unlikely alliance, what in time could stop Germany with its 60 million people and advanced technology from overcoming 40 million French? Otherwise, Churchill feared that 'a future generation' would see Europe 'laid in dust and ashes' once more.[9]

This assessment did not turn on Churchill's knowledge, or otherwise, of Germany. It derived from his analysis of Europe's imbalance of power and from his underlying philosophy of history: 'The story of the human race is War. Except for brief and precarious interludes there has never been peace in the world.' Yet he offered a revolutionary answer to the German problem, namely for Britain to gradually 'weave France and Germany' into a relationship of 'mutual prosperity and interdependence'.[10] Henceforth, Churchill's European policy had two prongs: determination in the long run to foster a lasting Franco-German rapprochement, but vigilance in the short term about the revival of German military power. The short term turned out to be much longer and more catastrophic than he had imagined.

His warnings about a revival of German militarism were clear from the early 1930s. In May 1932 he asked those in the Commons 'who would like to see Germany and France on an equal footing in armaments: "Do you wish for war?"'[11] A few months later, he offered the 'general principle' that 'the removal of the just grievances of the vanquished ought to precede the disarmament of the victors'.[12] Hitler's appointment as German Chancellor in January 1933 and his ruthless purge of opponents served as further justification of these arguments. 'I daresay,' Churchill told the House on 23 March, that during these 'anxious' times there were 'a good many people who have said to themselves, as I have been saying for several years: "Thank God for the French army." When we read about Germany, when we watch with surprise and distress the tumultuous insurgence, the pitiless ill-treatment of minorities, the denial of the normal protections of civilised society to large numbers of individuals solely on the ground of race' – one could not help 'feeling glad that the fierce passions that are raging in Germany have not found, as yet, any other outlet but upon themselves'.[13] But such national self-absorption could not be taken for granted once Hitler began to break free of the shackles imposed on German military power by the Treaty of Versailles.

Today, Churchill is renowned for his prophetic speeches in the 1930s about the imperative need for British rearmament. Yet it's important to be clear about what kind of rearmament Churchill wanted. He focused above all on the need to strengthen the Royal Air Force, rather than the Navy or the Army. And the reason was clear. Back in 1914, he told MPs in February 1934, the Navy had been 'the "sure shield" of Britain', but now the 'cursed, hellish invention and development of war from the air has revolutionised our position'. He went so far as to say, 'We are not the same kind of country we used to be when we were an island, only 20 years ago.'[14]

Winston was not alone in highlighting the air-power revolution. Many others also did so – in office, officialdom, the military and Parliament. Yet, as usual, Winston's warnings were melodramatic, designed to capture attention. A striking example is the amendment he put down on 28 November 1934, during the annual debate on the King's Speech, expressing concern about Britain's air defences. He flatly stated that 'no one can doubt' that after 'a week or 10 days' intensive bombing attack upon London ... at least 30,000 or 40,000 people would be killed or maimed'. And in the course of 'continuous air attack upon London at least 3,000,000 or 4,000,000 people would be driven out into the open country around the Metropolis ... without shelter and without food, without sanitation and without special provision for the maintenance of order'. Nor would the chaos be confined to London. Other great manufacturing centres such as Birmingham and Sheffield would be targeted as well.[15]

The impact was certainly what he wanted, eliciting a public commitment from Baldwin that, henceforth, Britain would maintain air parity with Germany. Yet Churchill's predictions were excessive. During the whole of the Second World War, aerial bombing caused 147,000 casualties in the UK, of which 61,000 were fatal. As for German front-line air strength, Winston was also prone to overstate his case, for instance asserting in October 1935 that within a year the Germans could have 2,000 front-line aircraft and would 'have it in their power' to reach at least 3,000 by October 1937. In fact, the actual figure was less than 3,000 even in September 1939.[16] But he was using statistics not as precision instruments but as shock weapons to provoke action. He admitted as much in his war memoirs: 'I strove my utmost to galvanise the Government into vehemence and extraordinary preparation, even at the cost of world alarm. In these endeavours no doubt I painted the picture even darker than it was.'[17]

Of course, Winston was not alone in such exaggeration. Writing in the mid-1960s, politician Harold Macmillan recalled that 'we thought of air warfare in 1938 rather as people think of nuclear warfare today.'[18] For much of the decade, Winston shared the widespread belief in official circles that, as Baldwin had put it in 1932, 'the bomber will always get through'. In 1934 he insisted that, 'pending some new discovery, the only direct measure of defence upon a great scale is the certainty of being able to inflict simultaneously upon the enemy as great damage as he can inflict upon ourselves', through 'the most hideous reciprocal injuries'. In other words, by building up a substantial bomber force as a deterrent to that of the Luftwaffe.[19] Until this could be done, the prospect of going to war seemed in Westminster and Whitehall to be literally suicidal. The development of radar – in which Churchill took a keen interest – offered an alternative to reciprocal bombing, but only when linked into a modern telephone network and a sophisticated command and control system. It also had to be backed by new fast monoplane fighters, the Hurricane and the Spitfire, which could counter German bombers with speed and firepower. This system of air defence was not operational till 1939.

Moreover, Winston's preoccupation with airpower diverted his attention from the other two armed services. In the case of the navy, initially he wanted 'freedom of design', enabling Britain to break free from the restraints imposed by the international arms control treaties of the 1920s, so as to build the warships it wanted, in the quantities needed. As the 1930s progressed, he focused on the need for destroyers to combat the likely U-boat threat to the country's oceanic supply lines. The Army came bottom of his list of priorities, especially any thought of sending another British Expeditionary Force to France and Belgium, as in 1914. And he wrote in a newspaper article in May 1938 that, 'if our Fleet and our Air Force are adequate, there is no need for conscription in time of peace. No one has ever been able to give a satisfactory answer to the question: "What do you want conscription for?" '[20]

Churchill's rearmament campaign, as the historian Donald Cameron Watt observed, 'never focused on the issues that might have made an impact on German military opinion – military arms production, conscription, a Continental commitment'.[21] Air rearmament had a bias towards isolationism – the defence of the United Kingdom – whereas greater resources for the Army would have implied projecting British power across the Channel. Such were the ghosts of the Somme and Passchendaele that in 1934 the Government banned use of the term 'Expeditionary Force' in public statements and even internal documents.[22] On this, Churchill was broadly at one with Chamberlain, public opinion and most politicians.

'Isolation is, I believe, utterly impossible,' Churchill declared in 1933, 'but we should nevertheless practise a certain degree of sober detachment from the European scene' – resisting what he called the 'natural' desire of British leaders 'to play a great part on the European stage, and to bestride Europe in the cause of peace, to be as it were the saviours of Europe'. Those words were aimed specifically at Prime Minister Ramsay MacDonald, whom he mocked as a 'modern Don Quixote', tilting at windmills in his campaign for international arms reduction at the Geneva Disarmament Conference. But grandstanding on the European stage was also the charge that he levelled in 1938 at

Neville Chamberlain's personal diplomacy. Rather than displays of solo virtuosity, he argued that 'we shall find our greatest safety in co-operating with the other Powers of Europe' by 'recreating the Concert of Europe through the League of Nations'.[23]

The reference to the League was largely tactical. What mattered to him was a Franco-British treaty of 'mutual defence against aggression', backed by 'arrangements' between their military staffs, which he spoke of as a 'Grand Alliance'.[24] This had been the name of the coalition against an earlier European despot, Louis XIV, and it was in Churchill's mind because in 1938 he was completing the fourth and final volume of *Marlborough: His Life and Times*. What he meant by the Grand Alliance had been expressed in 1936: 'the union of the British Fleet and the French Army, together with their combined Air Forces oper-ating from behind the French and Belgian frontiers'.[25] The fundamental division of labour, in essence, was that Britain would provide the seapower and the French the land power. That's why in May 1940 there were only 10 British divisions alongside 104 French on the Western Front.

'Thank God for the French Army' remained Churchill's refrain throughout the 1930s. He made the same point repeatedly in the early chapters of Volume I of *The Second World War* – despite an apparent exception on page 56 when he stated that the French army was the 'poop of the life of France'. (An errata slip inserted in the book stated: 'For "poop" read "prop."')[26] Churchill was not naively optimistic about the French army. In February 1938 he warned the Commons that 'with every month that passes its strength is being outmatched by the ceaseless development of the new forms into which the vastly superior manhood of Germany is being formed.'[27] What worried him was power not strategy: the shifting overall balance between France and Germany rather than any fear that Hitler had a brilliant plan that would turn the tables dramatically. In short, Winston's 1930s rearmament campaign played a part in winning the Battle of Britain, but it did little or nothing to prevent the disaster of the Battle of France. By probing what might seem the familiar story of 1940, we can see more clearly Churchill's conception of leadership and why he could not concede to Hitler the appellation 'great'.

* * *

Like most British politicians and generals, who assumed the situation was an updated version of August 1914, Churchill totally failed to anticipate Hitler's offensive in May 1940 – in two respects. First, it entailed not a massive encounter battle in Belgium but a lightning German thrust around the south flank of the main Allied army, over the Meuse and then to the Channel at Dunkirk. Secondly, that thrust used most of Hitler's armoured divisions, closely supported by tactical airpower, especially the terrifying Stuka dive-bombers – what became known as Blitzkrieg warfare.

The first misplaced assumption was not entirely wrong. A thrust through Belgium, akin to the Schlieffen Plan of 1914, was indeed the original German intention. But on 10 January 1940 a Luftwaffe plane crashed on Belgian soil carrying a copy of Berlin's plan to attack through Belgium on the 14th. After a radical strategic reassessment, the Germans shifted their main thrust south to the Ardennes. But neither the French nor the British reviewed their strategy. And so they moved rapidly into Belgium on 10 May, while the Germans moved even more swiftly around their right flank.[28]

That speed exposed Winston's second misplaced assumption: about Blitzkrieg warfare. His fame as a pioneer of the tank during the Great War and his prophetic warnings about airpower in the 1930s should not obscure his blind spots in 1940. Despite his alarm about strategic bombing, he was little troubled by *tactical* airpower. Writing for *Collier's* magazine in January 1939, he did express alarm about 'mass terror applied to crowded cities' but cited the Spanish Civil War as evidence that, 'so far as fighting troops are concerned, it would seem that aircraft are an additional complication rather than a decisive weapon'. In parallel, he played down the modern potential of the tank. In an article entitled 'How Wars of the Future Will be Waged' in April 1938, Winston extolled the tank and its 'glorious part in the victory' of 1918 but doubted that tanks would 'play as decisive a part in the next war as they did in the last . . . Nowadays, the anti-tank rifle and the anti-tank gun have made such great strides that the poor tank cannot carry a thick enough skin to stand up to them.'[29]

Gunpower not air power. The supremacy of defence over offence. These were Churchill's conceptions of land warfare in the late 1930s. And he acknowledged his error briefly in *The Gathering Storm* – 'in the war of armies I was under the thrall of defensive fire-power'.[30] An earlier draft was more candid: 'In my conscience I reproach myself for having allowed my concentration upon the Air and the Navy to have absorbed all my thought and Parliamentary activities.'[31]

Winston saw what he wanted to see. But his judgment was clear and sharp on the question of leadership. As PM he immediately made himself Minister of Defence, thereby acting on all the sobering lessons he had learnt over many years from Gallipoli to Norway. There was no institutional Ministry of Defence – nor would there be until the 1960s – though the minister had a small but high-powered secretariat headed by General Hastings 'Pug' Ismay. What Churchill wanted above all was the authority to engage directly with the three Chiefs of Staff, bypassing their ministers, in order to plan and implement wartime strategy. Appointing himself Minister of Defence was one of his key innovations in May 1940 and it would prove essential to waging war against Hitler.[32]

Winston did offer a vision of the future when addressing the Commons for the first time on 13 May: 'You ask, what is our aim? I can answer in one word: It is victory, victory at all costs, victory in spite of all terror, victory, however long and hard the road may be; for without victory, there is no survival.' As historian Richard Toye observes, 'the repetition of that single word "victory" five times within one sentence created an impressive sense of Churchill's single-mindedness and determination.'

But at this stage his political position was far from secure. On 13 May, when he addressed the Commons for the first time as Prime Minister, it was obvious that the Tory benches cheered Chamberlain much more loudly.[33] Despite Winston's role as military supremo,

Chamberlain remained Tory leader, and there was a backwash of Chamberlainite feeling when emotions cooled after the Norway debate. 'To a large extent I am in y[ou]r hands', Winston scribbled to Chamberlain on 10 May.[34] Both Chamberlain and Halifax (still Foreign Secretary) were in his new inner War Cabinet. The other two members, apart from Churchill, were Clement Attlee and his deputy Arthur Greenwood. This reflected the importance of Labour in the war effort as well as in the parliamentary revolt against Chamberlain on 8 May.

Immersed in building his coalition, Churchill omitted to pay close attention to news from the Western Front. He was aware on the evening of 14 May that the Germans had crossed the Meuse at Sedan, but it was not until the next morning that the full gravity of the crisis hit him. At 7.30 a.m. (a profoundly un-Churchillian hour) he was awakened by a phone call from Paul Reynaud, the French premier, who shouted in English, 'we are beaten; we have lost the battle.' That's why Churchill flew to Paris on the 16th, to hear Gamelin reveal the magnitude of the Nazi breakthrough. Cabinet colleagues were equally shocked, as their diary entries make clear. Chamberlain described the disintegration of the French front as 'incredible news'. Halifax noted: 'The one firm rock on which everybody had been willing to build for the last two years was the French Army, and the Germans walked through it like they did through the Poles.'[35]

On 25 May the Chiefs of Staff submitted an assessment entitled 'British Strategy in a Certain Eventuality' – an official euphemism for the fall of France. And the following day the War Cabinet began to discuss what should happen if the bulk of the British Expeditionary Force – the core of the country's trained army – could not be extricated from Dunkirk and the surrounding beaches. These debates are crucial for understanding the relationship between Churchill and Hitler, and also how Winston was seen by his closest colleagues.

When the evacuation began, it was expected that, at best, only 50,000 troops could be rescued – hardly the basis for a successful defence against invasion. Moreover, intelligence estimates suggested that Hitler might curtail operations in France in order to mount an immediate air assault on Britain – Whitehall's nightmare scenario throughout the 1930s. Halifax, deeply shaken by the French collapse and appalled at the prospect of saturation bombing of British cities, began to look for some way out. He insisted he would fight to the end if Britain's integrity and independence were endangered – if, for instance, Hitler demanded surrender of the British fleet or the RAF. But if terms could be secured to guarantee British independence – even by surrendering parts of the Empire – then, Halifax said, 'we should be foolish if we did not accept them' in order to 'save the country from an avoidable disaster'.[36]

The argument rumbled across five crucial meetings of the War Cabinet on 26, 27 and 28 May. Pressed by Halifax, Churchill conceded some ground. On 26 May he is recorded as saying that 'if we could get out of this jam by giving up Malta and Gibraltar and some African colonies he would jump at it'. On the 27th he indicated that if Hitler 'were prepared to make peace on the terms of the restoration of German colonies and the overlordship of Central Europe', that would be an acceptable basis for negotiation. But the PM was emphatic that such scenarios were 'most unlikely' – given Hitler's current position he would surely set terms that 'would put us completely at his mercy' – and insisted that 'we should get no worse terms if we went on fighting, even if we were beaten, than were open to us now . . . A time might come when we felt we had to put an end to the struggle, but the terms would not then be more mortal than those offered to us now'.[37]

The two Labour members of the War Cabinet, Attlee and Greenwood, said little but they sided with Churchill, and Chamberlain came round firmly to the PM's view. This left Halifax completely isolated. The idea of sounding out the Italians was dropped and a consensus formed in Cabinet around Churchill's position that no question of peace terms could even be raised until the Battle of Britain had been won. However, the War Cabinet debate had revolved around the idea of eventually securing a negotiated peace rather than total victory. Halifax and his parliamentary under-secretary R.A. Butler were particularly emphatic on this point. The message from Halifax reported by the Swedish ambassador on 17 June was that 'common sense not bravado would dictate the British Government's policy.'[38]

In his book *Five Days in London, May 1940*, the American historian John Lukacs depicted these discussions as a fundamental clash between Churchill and Halifax, the 'visionary' and the 'pragmatist', on which 'the fate of Britain' and even 'the outcome of the Second World War' largely hinged.[39] This exaggerates the drama. For one thing, timing matters. On 28 May Churchill was saying that 'we should certainly be able to get 50,000 away' from the beaches and that 'if we could get 100,000 away, that would be a magnificent performance.'[40] But that was hardly an army. By the time the evacuation from Dunkirk (Operation Dynamo) ended on 4 June, however, 337,000 Allied troops had been evacuated, two-thirds of them British, and Britain's prospects were thereby transformed.

It's also clear that emotion exacerbated the Cabinet arguments. Halifax's diary for May is full of comments on the new premier – praising Churchill's courage and inspiration, yet lamenting his impulsiveness and lack of judgment. During the decisive War Cabinet discussion on the afternoon of 27 May the Foreign Secretary's pent-up feelings exploded. 'I thought Winston talked the most frightful rot, also Greenwood', he noted in his diary, 'and after bearing it for some time I said exactly what I thought of them, adding that if that was really their view, and if it came to the point, our ways must separate.' Chastened by this hint of resignation, Churchill was 'full of apologies and affection' afterwards in the garden of Number 10. But, wrote Halifax, 'it does drive me to despair when he works himself up into a passion of emotion when he ought to make his brain think and reason'. Hence the reference on 17 June to 'common sense not bravado'.[41]

Halifax was no traitor, but he was naïve when talking about terms that guaranteed Britain's independence and integrity. And Churchill was surely right that even to broach negotiation at this stage would start the country down a slippery slope. In a shrewd tactical move, he also widened the discussion by explaining the situation to a meeting of all government ministers on 28 May. At the end he said, 'I have thought carefully in these last days whether it was part of my duty to consider entering into negotiations with That Man,' but he then reiterated the view he had expressed to the War Cabinet that 'it was idle to think that, if we tried to make peace now, we should get better terms than if we fought it out.' Hitler would demand the fleet, 'our naval bases, and much else. We should become a slave state.' In any case, Churchill concluded, 'I am convinced that every man of you would rise up and tear me down from my place if I were for one moment to contemplate parley or surrender. If this long island story of ours is to end at last, let it end only when each one of us lies choking in his own blood.' At the end of Winston's oration, there was 'a murmur of approval round the table' and not 'the faintest flicker of dissent'. Several ministers congratulated him afterwards. 'He was quite magnificent,' remarked the Labour politician Hugh Dalton. 'The man, and the only man we have, for this hour.'[42]

None of this is unfamiliar. Indeed, it fits with the public image Churchill projected – 'victory at all costs' (13 May), 'we shall fight them on the beaches . . . we shall never surrender' (4 June), and so on. But in private, the PM's mood was at times much more sombre. In July 1946 General Ismay recalled for Roosevelt's former speechwriter Robert Sherwood a talk he had with Churchill on 12 June 1940, after meeting the demoralised French leaders at Briare. According to Sherwood's notes, 'When Churchill went to the airport to return to England, he said to Ismay that, it seems, "we fight alone." Ismay said he was glad of it, that "we'll win the Battle of Britain." Winston gave him a look and remarked, "You and I will be dead in three months' time." '[43] Yet on 18 June, six days after this exchange with Ismay, when France had asked Hitler for an armistice, the PM told the Commons and the country to 'brace ourselves to our duties and so bear ourselves that, if the British Empire and its Commonwealth last for a thousand years, men will still say "This was their finest hour." '[44] No mere bravado, indeed. Far from being an unthinkingly pugnacious bulldog, this was a man who had stared into the abyss and could still look up, smiling, to declaim words of inspiration.

But we should notice that Winston was no longer talking about 'victory at all costs'. On 28 May he issued a general injunction to ministers and officials about the need to maintain high morale, 'showing confidence in our ability and inflexible resolve to continue the war till we have broken the will of the enemy to bring all Europe under his domination'. And on 3 August he told the Foreign Office that a 'firm reply' to Hitler's current peace overtures was 'the only chance of extorting from Germany any offers which are not fantastic'.[45] To understand this we should remember that 'unconditional surrender' was only promulgated as an Allied war aim in January 1943, when America and Russia had added their combined might to Britain's cause. In the summer of 1940 it was inconceivable that the British Empire alone could impose total victory on Germany, now that Hitler bestrode continental Europe. After the fall of France, the most favourable outcome seemed to be a negotiated peace at some point with an alternative post-Nazi German government.

In the meantime, Winston needed to offer not just rhetoric but also reasons – or, more exactly, rationalisations – for his gut instinct to fight on. The most substantial, stated as the prime assumption of the Chiefs of Staff's 'Certain Eventuality' paper on 25 May, was that the United States were 'willing to give us full economic and financial support, *without which we do not think we could continue the war with any chance of success*'. Given the USA's firm neutrality in 1940, a presidential election year, this was quite an assumption to make.[46]

In addition, Churchill and the Chiefs of Staff did not accept that they must fight another continental land to defeat Hitler's Germany. It remained an *idée fixe* of British intelligence that the German war economy was already overstretched and that underlying shortages of food and raw materials, especially oil, would soon make themselves felt. Winston seems to have shared these assumptions. In Cabinet on 26 May 1940, he (like Attlee and Chamberlain) took the line that 'if only we could stick things out for another three months, the position would be entirely different'. He had never forgotten the abruptness with which the Central Powers had collapsed in 1918, alluding to it publicly in his 'finest hour' speech on 18 June 1940. 'During the first four years of the last war the Allies experienced nothing but disaster and disappointment. During that war we repeatedly asked ourselves the question: "How are we going to win?" and no one was able ever to answer it with much precision, until, at the end, quite suddenly, quite unexpectedly, our terrible foe collapsed before us.' And then, Winston told MPs, 'we were so glutted with victory that in our folly we threw it away.'[47]

The hope was therefore that, against this daunting but hopefully brittle enemy, a major land war might not prove necessary. In a strategy paper on 4 September, the Chiefs of Staff insisted that 'it is not our policy to attempt to raise, and land on the continent, an army comparable in size to that of Germany.' Rather, the professed aim was to wear down the enemy and secure 'conditions when numerically inferior forces can be employed with good chance of success'. At that point Britain should 're-establish a striking force on the Continent with which we can enter Germany and impose our terms.'[48]

How exactly could the enemy be worn down? Planning papers in 1939 had cited Britain's traditional weapon, naval blockade, plus the new policy of aerial bombing. In the summer of 1940, with Nazism rampant across continental Europe, Winston admitted that the blockade had been 'blunted' as a weapon. But he claimed that Hitler's vast new empire was a liability as much as an asset. In July he created the Special Operations Executive (SOE), mandated to work with local resistance movements and 'set Europe ablaze'. According to the Chiefs of Staff, SOE would assist the economic degradation of the enemy by sabotaging industrial plant, and would help partisans prepare 'a general uprising' against Hitler which, 'coinciding with major operations by our forces, may finally assist to bring about his defeat.'[49] The 'general uprising' scenario was grossly optimistic: despite the courage of continental resistance movements, 'setting Europe ablaze' would prove a damp squib. But the hope of some fireworks helped boost official morale in 1940.

Greater confidence was placed in the effect on Hitler of strategic bombing. On 8 July Winston noted that the 'one thing' that would 'bring him down' was 'an absolutely devastating exterminating attack by very heavy bombers from this country on the Nazi homeland'. So the PM gave priority, even in the summer of 1940, to bomber production. 'The Fighters are our salvation', he wrote in a memorandum of 3 September at the height of the Battle of Britain, 'but the Bombers alone provide the means of victory.' The RAF must 'pulverize the entire industry and scientific structure on which the war effort and economic life of the enemy depend, while holding him at arm's length from our Island. In no other way at present visible can we hope to overcome the immense military power of Germany.'[50]

Though much more devastating than SOE, strategic bombing similarly proved not to be a decisive weapon. Yet faith in its offensive power was the obverse of the fear of the bomber during the 1930s. In fact, it reminds us that strategy is often dictated by logistics, rather than the other way round – reasoning from what capacities one has to what one tries to do. The RAF was the great legacy of Thirties rearmament, and the Army the Cinderella service. As Prime Minister, Churchill had to make the best of the armed forces he had helped to will into existence when he was in the political wilderness. Despite all the strategising, his policy after the fall of France was essentially that, as he told ministers on 28 May, 'it was idle to think that if we made peace now, we should get better terms from Germany than if we went on and fought it out.' In other words (in private) – KBO, Keep Buggering On.[51]

Grand rhetoric, breathing defiance and replete with rationalisations: this is what Churchill offered in the summer of 1940. But what mattered beyond everything were actions. The great lines spoken in June 1940 now take on their significance from the victory achieved in May 1945. At the time they were easily dismissed as last-ditch bombast from a country on the skids.

That is why what happened on 3–4 July was so important.

On 22 June the French signed an armistice with Germany, which took direct control of the north and west of the country and stipulated that the French fleet would be 'demobilised' under German or Italian control. Winston did not place much faith in private assurances from French admirals that their fleet would never be surrendered or allowed to fall under German control. He was particularly concerned about the French capital ships. 'If these fell into the hands of the Germans,' he told the War Cabinet, they would have a very formidable line of battle when the *Bismarck* was commissioned in August 1940. Rather than running 'the mortal risk of allowing these ships to fall into the hands of the enemy,' he declared, 'we should have to fight and sink them.'[52] That is, indeed, what happened on 3 July. After abortive negotiations at Mers-el-Kebir, near Oran in French North Africa, a British task force opened fire, sinking one battleship and damaging two others. Another, the *Jean Bart*, escaped from France to Casablanca, but the *Richelieu* was badly damaged in Dakar by British torpedo bombers. In all, nearly 1,300 French sailors were killed – men who had been Britain's allies less than two weeks before.

The precise outcome was still unclear when Churchill rose to address the House on 4 July, but his speech had immense impact. This was not so much thanks to any purple passages, but from the way he unfolded the story. The US military attaché, listening to the PM from the gallery, was struck by how, 'with the most dramatic effect and yet with the most superb composure, he narrated as a historian this vivid passage of history'. This performance was no one-off. As Richard Toye has noted, the power of many of Winston's speeches derived from the revelation of 'new information' within a 'compelling narrative'.[53]

First, Churchill described the Cabinet debates. This was 'a decision to which, with aching hearts but with clear vision, we unitedly came'. He next detailed the capture of French vessels in British and Egyptian ports, before building up to 'the most serious part of the story' at Mers-el-Kebir. He read out the ultimatum, discussed the negotiations, and then recounted the 'melancholy action' that ensued. Glossing over the escape of the *Richelieu* and *Jean Bart*, he summed up the outcome: 'A large proportion of the French Fleet has, therefore, passed into our hands or has been put out of action or otherwise withheld from Germany by yesterday's events.' He told the House, 'I leave the judgment of our action, with confidence, to Parliament. I leave it to the nation, and I leave it to the United States. I leave it to the world and to history.' No lengthy perorations, no grand phrases – just a brisk description of sad necessity. Winston reminded the Commons that before very long 'we must, of course, expect to be attacked, or even invaded, if that proves to be possible'. But, he concluded, the action just taken against the French fleet should be 'sufficient to dispose once and for all of the lies and rumours' spread by Nazi propaganda 'that we have the slightest intention of entering into negotiations in any form and through any channel . . . We shall, on the contrary, prosecute the war with the utmost vigour by all the means that are open to us until the righteous purposes for which we entered upon it have been fulfilled.'[54]

The speech, lasting less than half an hour, was heard in tense silence. But at the end, the *Illustrated London News* recorded, 'Parliament stood and demonstrated its approval', while 'Mr Churchill sat with his elbows on his knees, visibly moved.'[55] He was, in fact, in tears. Partly because he was the greatest Francophile in the Cabinet. 'This is heartbreaking for me,' he told one MP.[56] His mantra was no longer 'Thank God for the French army' – more like, 'Adieu to the French fleet'. The emotion was also personal. As he wrote in his memoirs: 'Up till this moment the Conservative Party had treated me with some reserve, and it was from the Labour benches that I received the warmest welcome . . . But now all joined in solemn stentorian accord.' Above all, the events of 3–4 July showed the world, as Churchill wrote later, that Britain 'feared nothing and would stop at nothing.'[57] Ringing rhetoric had been followed by ruthless action – which was then explained in simple confident narrative. That Churchillian combination of words and deeds: his signature of leadership.

Hitler was certainly taken aback. Early July 1940, rather than the Dunkirk days of late May, was the high point in the struggle between Churchill and Hitler – the moment when, briefly, the two men really engaged with each other in a contest for greatness.

The Führer periodically described Churchill as a 'warmonger' (*Kriegshetzer*) but generally saw him as an agent of the Jewish 'plutocracy', rather than as a great man like himself. Addressing his generals on 23 November 1939, Hitler called himself 'irreplaceable', adding that 'Neither a military man nor a civilian could replace me.' It was the

Führer who drove his doubting generals into an early attack on France, arguing that, overall, 'time is working for our adversaries. Now there is a relationship of forces which can never be more propitious for us, but which can only deteriorate.'[58] Although the detailed planning was done by others, Hitler played a decisive role in reorienting the main thrust of the German offensive from Belgium, as with the Schlieffen Plan of 1914, to the supposedly impenetrable Ardennes and thence to a weak part of the French front along the Meuse. That was where most of Germany's armoured divisions – discounted by Winston, like most Allied leaders – were deployed in a 'sickle cut' (*Sichelschnitt*) around the back of the French and British forces in Belgium and on to the Channel. Churchill never really acknowledged the audacity of Hitler's gamble or the historical magnitude of his victory. Although, in his memoirs, he briefly compared the sickle cut to Napoleon's famous surprise assault on the Pratzen Heights during the Battle of Austerlitz in 1805, the latter move was tactical not strategic. Overall, Churchill attributed the breakthrough in May 1940 to French complacency rather than German brilliance.[59]

As Hitler's writings in the 1920s indicated, he did not see 'England' as a necessary enemy of Germany. Aryan racial solidarity and complementary geopolitical interests both pointed towards collaboration. In March 1940 he reiterated his familiar line that France had to be smashed, as an 'act of historical justice' in retribution for 1918 and in order to give Germany a free hand on the continent of Europe. But, he added, 'England can have peace if it keeps out of Europe and gives us back our colonies and a bit more besides.' That peace could come only when England had been dealt what he kept calling a 'knock-out blow' in the form of France's defeat. Once France agreed to an armistice, Hitler assumed that Churchill would see sense. He claimed that the British Empire was 'an important factor in world equilibrium' and that he did not want it to fall into the hands of 'foreign great powers' – a reference particularly to America and Japan. But, as Winston was grimly aware, there was no reason to believe, given Hitler's record on keeping promises, that Europe would be the Führer's limit if opportunity knocked.[60]

Hitler returned home from Paris on 6 July 1940. Berliners waited for hours at the Anhalter Bahnhof to welcome his train. The streets were strewn with flowers and 'the greatest warlord of all time' was called time and again onto the balcony of the Reich Chancellery to acknowledge the applause. Little wonder. It had cost the lives of fewer than 30,000 Germans to vanquish France in four weeks, compared with more than two million dead in 1914–18 as Germany plunged to disaster.[61]

For a few days after Mers-el-Kebir Hitler reviewed his options. Eventually he decided to give the British one last chance. If this were rejected, propaganda minister Josef Goebbels noted, they would immediately be dealt 'an annihilatory blow'. The Führer had already ordered contingency planning for an invasion, but he was warned by the Navy that this would depend on gaining and maintaining air superiority – no easy tasks, since heavy losses had been sustained by the Kriegsmarine in Norway and by the Luftwaffe in the battle for France. Therefore, Hitler still hoped that the British would be sensible.[62]

The Führer made his last-chance offer on 19 July, during a speech to celebrate the 'historic uniqueness' of Germany's recent victory. Surveying the recent past, he portrayed himself as a man of peace who had been driven to war because of British and French refusal to concede the German people their rights. His cast of villains included the usual characters – 'Jews and Freemasons, armament industrialists and war profiteers' – plus the Allied leaders, not least Churchill, whom he accused of 'bloody dilettantism'. Yet even now, he declared, he was making one last 'appeal to reason in England', to avoid future 'nameless suffering'. 'Naturally,' he added, 'this does not apply to Herr Churchill himself since by then he will surely be secure in Canada, where the money and the children of the most distinguished of war profiteers have already been brought.' But there would be 'great tragedy for millions' of the less fortunate if this appeal were not heeded: 'A great world empire will be destroyed. A world empire which I never had the ambition to destroy or as much as harm. Alas, I am fully aware that the continuation of this war will end only in the complete shattering of one of the two warring parties. Mister Churchill may believe this to be Germany. I know it to be England.'[63]

'I do not propose to say anything in reply to Herr Hitler's speech,' the PM told the Foreign Office – 'not being on speaking terms with him.'[64] Instead, Halifax, due to deliver a routine broadcast speech as Foreign Secretary on 22 July, used the occasion to dismiss Hitler's appeal. On the previous weekend, Winston had taken pains to invite Halifax and his wife to Chequers, the PM's official country residence. During their visit the two men discussed Halifax's draft and the PM added some muscular monosyllables to the Foreign Secretary's customary circumlocutions. Some in London felt the speech was too much of a 'sermon' – referring to 'God' seventeen times – but Goebbels denounced it as a 'war crime', and there was an ironical aptness about the ditherer of Dunkirk telling Hitler where to get off.[65]

'The Führer is greatly puzzled by England's persistent unwillingness to make peace,' noted General Franz Halder, the Army Chief of Staff, on 13 July. 'He sees (as we do) the answer in England's hope in Russia.' Churchill did indeed tell his private secretary, Jock Colville, next day that 'Hitler must invade or fail. If he fails, he is bound to go East, and fail he will.' Lurking in his mind was presumably the historical analogy of Napoleon in 1812. But in 1940 Russia was not at the centre of British thinking. The main hope was for growing support from the US – a design stated categorically by the Chiefs of Staff in their 'Certain Eventuality' paper on 25 May, which made only passing reference to Russia. On 31 July – told by the navy that the earliest possible date for an invasion of Britain was 15 September, when the Channel would probably be increasingly stormy – the Führer indicated that his gaze was turning east. According to Halder's notes: 'With Russia smashed, England's last hope would be shattered. Germany then will be master of Europe ... If we start in May 1941, we would have five months to finish the job.'[66]

Reading this today, the whole scenario seems fantastic. With Britain still not defeated, Hitler was planning to invade the USSR – despite all he had written in the past about the folly of Germany, in the centre of Europe, trying to wage war on two fronts. But Berlin was in euphoric mood: greatness had gone to Hitler's head. The Third Reich had needed little more than a month to rout the French, supposedly the best army in Europe. He told his generals that 'a campaign against Russia would be child's play' (*Sandkastenspiel*). Once the Battle of Britain turned against Germany, in mid-September, the invasion was postponed indefinitely. On 18 December the Führer issued a directive that the Wehrmacht must be prepared, 'before the end of the war with England *to crush Soviet Russia in a rapid campaign*' the following spring. He told his staff, 'we must solve all continental European problems in 1941 since the US would be in a position to intervene from 1942 onwards.' Waging war on two fronts was an act of hubris by Hitler. It would prove his Nemesis.[67]

* * *

The rest of the conflict will be traced in the next three chapters. But, first, let's follow the Churchill–Hitler saga to its endgame. Doing so underlines their strange non-relationship. And it also sheds further light on what Winston meant by that crucial word 'victory', which he had proclaimed as his overriding war aim three days after becoming Prime Minister.

Winston's rhetoric about the Führer did become more emotional over time. During his valedictory for Neville Chamberlain in November 1940, he had spoken of 'Herr Hitler' and his 'ravings'.[68] By the time Germany invaded Russia, after the British people had endured a winter of Blitz and blockade, his language was considerably less restrained. In the PM's radio broadcast on 22 June 1941, the 'Herr' was dropped – clearly it was inappropriate for someone he called 'a monster of wickedness, insatiable in his lust for blood and plunder . . . a blood-thirsty guttersnipe' who, 'not content with having all Europe under his heel . . . must now carry his work of butchery and desolation' to Russia and Asia. Yet Winston's prime focus in that speech remained German militarism: that 'vast military machine' with its 'heel-clicking, dandified Prussian officers' and the 'brutish masses of the Hun soldiery', which Britain and the rest of 'the civilised world' had so foolishly allowed 'the Nazi gangsters' to keep building up year by year. The juggernaut could not 'stand idle lest it rust or fall to pieces' but 'must be in continual motion, grinding up human lives and trampling down the homes and the rights of hundreds of millions'. [69] It was the 'machine' which had to be smashed; the 'monster' perched on top was almost secondary.

Hitler on Churchill was similarly vitriolic, calling him in October 1941 'that puppet of the Jewry that pulls the strings'. A few weeks after Pearl Harbor he said, 'I like an Englishman a thousand times better than an American,' but added that Churchill was an Englishman who had been 'bought' by America – a society 'half Judaised' and 'half negrified' for which the Führer felt only 'hatred and deep repugnance'. As for America's paraplegic leader, 'he's a sick brain.' The secretary who took the Führer's dictation could still recall, years later, how 'emotion would take possession of him' when speaking of Churchill or Roosevelt.[70] Stalin, however, was judged indubitably great. Despite Hitler's ideological and racist hatred of Soviet Russia, he declared in July 1941 that 'Stalin is one of the most extraordinary figures in world history. He began as a small clerk, and he has never stopped being a clerk. Stalin owes nothing to rhetoric. He governs from his office, thanks to a bureaucracy that obeys his every nod and gesture.' A year later Hitler could still say of Stalin, 'In his own way he is a hell of a fellow!', likening him at the same time to Genghis Khan.[71]

Through the looking glass, Churchill and Hitler each saw a man who was essentially the agent of greater forces. For Winston, 'victory' was about destroying the machine not vanquishing the leader. But during 1941 his essential policy remained 'KBO'. He did not want to state explicit war aims or be pinned down on how the war could and should end. On 5 July, two weeks after Barbarossa began, Anthony Eden, who had replaced Halifax as Foreign Secretary, publicly announced that Britain was 'not prepared to negotiate with Hitler at any time and on any subject'. Drawing the War Cabinet's attention to these precise words, Churchill explained that it had been felt necessary to forestall any peace offensive by the Führer, which might damage Russian morale. But on 27 November 1941 – when the US was still neutral and the Wehrmacht could see the golden domes of the Kremlin gleaming in the winter sun – the PM recalled the July statement that 'we would not negotiate with Hitler or with the Nazi *régime*'. He then added that 'it would be going too far to say that we should not nego-tiate with a Germany controlled by the Army.' It was 'impossible to forecast what form of Government there might be in Germany at a time when their resistance weakened and they wished to negotiate'.[72]

Within a couple of weeks, however, Britain's strategic situation was totally transformed. On 5 December, the Red Army's winter offensive – using divisions redeployed from Siberia – drove the Germans back in disarray from the outskirts of Moscow. Hitler's hopes of a quick victory evaporated. And then on the 7th Japan's devastating air assault on the US fleet at Pearl Harbor pitchforked the United States into a Pacific war. Four days later, Hitler – long convinced that war with the Americans was inevitable and confident that this 'mongrel' race would never get its act together – seized the initiative and declared war on the United States. In six months from June to December 1941, the Führer had enlarged the war against Churchill's Britain into a global war against two other great powers. Hubris indeed.

Whatever Winston had implied on 13 May 1940, winning a crushing victory over Hitler was implausible for Britain and France in tandem, and inconceivable for Britain alone. After December 1941, however, it became a possibility because of the immensity of America's 'arsenal of democracy'. And it's no accident that the slogan 'Unconditional Surrender' was coined by the President of the United States in January 1943. This time, unlike 1918, Roosevelt insisted Germany's armed forces must be utterly defeated and the country occupied by the victorious Allies, who would then oversee a root and branch process of demilitarisation, denazification, democratisation and, perhaps, even deindustrialisation. These three (or four) Ds would transform the country.

Winston was never keen on such a radical policy. Although in no doubt about the first three Ds, except for a brief flurry in the autumn of 1944, he opposed deindustrialisation and also rejected the dismemberment of Bismarckian Germany into a number of small states. He feared that a truly punitive policy would only fuel revanchism, as had happened after 1918, and thereby vitiate the chances of Europe's economic recovery – which depended on a rebuilt Germany. For similar reasons he and the Cabinet opposed a lengthy process of war crimes trials, similar to that which had descended into farce in the 1920s after the Kaiser had escaped to neutral Holland. In 1945–6, the British were unable to resist the American desire for a full international legal process to prove to the world that Nazi Germany had committed 'crimes against the peace' and 'crimes against humanity'. But they were sure it would have been better to deal with the Nazi ringleaders through summary trial and execution administered by firing squad. For Hitler, 'the mainspring of evil', Churchill proposed the 'electric chair', as used for 'gangsters' in the United States. 'No doubt', he joked, one such chair could be obtained via Lend-Lease.[73]

Hitler, of course, avoided any such fate, taking his own life on 30 April 1945. To the very end he insisted that Churchill was a 'senile clown' who, far from being the 'second Pitt' he imagined, failed to see Britain's true interests. Instead of negotiating a peace in 1940–1 and thereby salvaging the British Empire, Churchill's Britain preferred to 'obey the orders of her Jewish and American allies'. After Germany's downfall, he predicted a few weeks before his death, 'there will remain in the world only two powers capable of confronting each other: the United States and Soviet Russia', claiming that 'the laws of both history and geography will compel these two Powers to a trial of strength'.[74]

Winston, too, was already setting the war in historical perspective. Addressing the Commons in February 1945, after the Yalta conference, he described the conflict as part of a modern Thirty Years War, dating back to 1914.[75] And the following year he developed an argument previously stated in *The Aftermath* (1929), that the way out of this cyclical nightmare was to 'weave France and Germany so closely together' that war would become unimaginable.[76] Speaking in Zurich in September 1946, he lamented 'the tragedy of Europe', a continent ravaged in a 'series of frightful nationalistic quarrels, originated by the Teutonic nations in their rise to power'. Of course, he said, 'the guilty must be punished' and Germany 'deprived of the power to rearm and make another aggressive war'. But then 'there must be an end to retribution.' And, he added, 'I am now going to say something that will astonish you. The first step in the re-creation of the European family must be a partnership between France and Germany.' What he envisioned was 'a kind of United States of Europe . . . in this urgent work France and Germany must take the lead together.'[77]

In 1945–6, as before, Winston was focusing on the German problem rather than on the monstrosity of Hitler. It's striking that when the British delegation visited Berlin in July 1945, just before the Potsdam conference, Churchill's companions were profoundly affected by the detritus of the Thousand Year Reich that had nearly overwhelmed the British Empire – the upturned marble-topped desk and the litter of papers and Iron Crosses in Hitler's office, the Berliners on the Reichstag steps bartering clothes and household goods for food from Russian soldiers. To Lord Moran, Winston's physician, the 'evisceration' of the bombed-out houses reminded him of the first time he watched a surgeon open a belly and the intestines gushed out. But Churchill was not much interested in the ruins of the Reichstag and the Chancellery, or even the bunker where the Führer died. He offered little comment beyond observing that, 'if *they* had won the war, we would have been the bunker.'[78]

Germany had not won the war – thanks, crucially, to British defiance in 1940–1 under Churchill's leadership. But victory over Germany depended largely on Britain's two great allies, the United States and Soviet Russia. As Hitler had foreseen, they would then engage in their own 'trial of strength'. Before exploring Winston's dealings with Roosevelt and Stalin, however, let us look at his relationship with the Führer's accomplice in crime, Benito Mussolini – a story that offers a strange contrast with that of Churchill and Hitler.

'Where There's Smoke . . .': As the Allies extinguish Mussolini's
empire in North Africa, cartoonist George Butterworth
in *Empire News*, 6 December 1942, anticipates the Duce's demise.

5

Benito Mussolini

Strong Leader, Fake Empire

Assuming Italy is hostile, which we may perhaps hope will not be the case, England's first battlefield is the Mediterranean . . . On no account must anything which threatens in the Far East divert us from this prime objective.

Winston S. Churchill, 25 March 1939[1]

If you strip the Englishman of the clothes he wears for his tea at 5 o'clock, you will find the old primitive barbarian Briton, with his skin painted in various colours, who was tamed by the veritable square legions of Caesar and Claudius.

Benito Mussolini, 2 December 1942[2]

'Today,' wrote Churchill in October 1938, 'Herr Hitler is dictator of Germany and Signor Mussolini is dictator of Italy.' But, he added, 'there is between them one vital difference: had there been no war and no aftermath, Signor Mussolini would still have been great.' He also discerned 'a difference equally vital between the two nations over which these two men ruled' – because 'under any government Germany would still be formidable.' From this, he concluded: 'It is, perhaps, just as well for the world that Signor Mussolini was not born a German.'[3]

Cryptic observations, but clear. Although Benito Mussolini became

Britain's enemy in the Second World War, he was a leader for whom Churchill entertained a lingering respect throughout his life – in marked contrast with his attitude to Adolf Hitler. In part this was rooted in Churchillian fascination with imperial Rome, dating back to youthful days in India immersed in Gibbon's *Decline and Fall* and Macaulay's *Lays of Ancient Rome*. What's more, during most of the Great War, Italy had been Britain's ally against Germany, throwing in its lot with the Entente powers in May 1915. And on a personal level, Mussolini commended himself to Churchill as a decisive anti-Bolshevist, turning back the 'Red Tide' in Europe after 1918 and quelling Italy's civil strife.

Churchill's words from 1938 also remind us that his assessment of great international contemporaries was usually intertwined with estimates of their countries' geopolitical importance. In the case of Italy in the 1930s, his judgment was finely balanced. On the one hand, the Duce dreamed of a new Roman empire in the Mediterranean, challenging Britain's position in Egypt. Yet Mussolini also considered himself the senior fascist and Hitler a potential rival. Therefore, in the early 1930s, Winston – prioritising the German threat – was ready to appease Mussolini, seeing Italy as a bulwark against Hitler's expansion into Austria and southern Europe. In 1938 and 1939 the Duce stood back, but the fall of France in June 1940 seemed to him an unmissable opportunity. Once Italy joined Hitler, Churchill and Mussolini became locked in a long battle for the Mediterranean, a theatre of operations which Winston considered far more important in 1939–41 than any possible threat from Japan. The struggle drew in both Hitler and Roosevelt and helped delay the Second Front. Churchill's policy saved Britain's position in Egypt, but the consequent damage in Asia was severe and lasting.

* * *

Winston's view of Mussolini was shaped by deeper attitudes to the Roman empire, and to empire in general. In May 1897, en route home on leave from India, he paid his first visit to 'the Imperial city around which my reading for so many months has centred'.[4] For him, what always mattered was 'Ancient Rome': he told his wife three decades later that 'the Middle Ages and the Renaissance are v[er]y small topics beside the long Imperial splendour.'[5] That splendour gripped him throughout his life. When Berlin failed to 'touch his imagination' in 1945, his doctor was struck by the contrast with Churchill's speech to soldiers of the Eighth Army two years before, in the remains of the Roman amphitheatre at Carthage. 'When he was about to speak to them, the associations of the place suddenly gripped him and for some time he dared not trust himself to speak.'[6] Addressing soldiers of the British Empire in the theatre of another great empire, now extinct, built on the ruins of the empire it had erased from the face of the earth, Winston was overcome by emotion.

The 'associations of the place' were not merely historical. Would the British Empire also go the way of Rome? That question lurked in Winston's mind. 'I was a child of the Victorian age,' he told readers of *My Early Life* in 1930. 'In those days the dominant forces in Great Britain were very sure of themselves and of their doctrines . . . They were sure they were supreme at sea and consequently safe at home. They rested therefore sedately under the convictions of power and security.' But, he added: 'Very different is the aspect of these anxious times.'[7] So, in the Thirties and Forties, when he considered modern Italy and modern Britain, the grandeur that was Rome always lurked in the background and, with it, the haunting question of whether the British Empire could defy the Gibbonian Nemesis.

He also approached Thirties Italy with memories of the Great War alliance. During the first winter of that conflict, Italy had sat on the fence. Churchill, at the Admiralty, was impatient, telling the Foreign Secretary that if Italy could be 'induced to join with us the Austrian fleet w[oul]d be powerless & the Mediterranean as safe as an English lake'.[8] (This image of the Mediterranean as 'an English lake' was a persistent mirage for Churchill.) Italy finally joined Britain, France and Russia at the end of May 1915, ironically just as the war was turning against the Entente powers, both in the Dardanelles and on the Russian front. In *The World Crisis* Winston observed that Italian Liberal leaders had sold belligerency to the country as 'an easy war of limited liability and great material gains'. Instead, he noted, at great cost in 'blood' and 'treasure' Italy had to 'struggle on to a victory which was to bring no complete satisfaction to her ambitions'. But he paid tribute to 'the generous heart of the Italian nation', which in 1915–18 'proved not unequal to the long trials and disappointments of the struggle, nor unworthy to sustain amid its mocking fortunes the ancient fame of Rome'. And, he added, this mattered because 'the falling away of Italy' from the Allied cause at this time 'would have been an event more pregnant with consequences than all the triumphs of March 21, 1918', when the Germans nearly broke the British line on the Somme.[9]

The allure of ancient Rome and the positive memories of a Great War ally both coloured Churchill's attitude to post-1918 Italy. So did the allowances he was ready to make for *Il Duce* himself, as a strong leader turning back the Bolshevist tide. In the autumn of 1914, Mussolini, a radical journalist, had broken with fellow socialists over his support for intervention, setting up his own newspaper *Il Populo d'Italia* in Milan (largely supported by secret French and British funds). In 1919 he founded a radical right movement, the *Fasci di Combattimento*, whose paramilitary 'squads' battled with socialist labour leagues in the 'red provinces' of Tuscany and the Po valley. In October 1921 the fascists gained some respectability and wider support when Mussolini formed a political party (*Partito Nazionale Fascista*) and built up his position in parliament. The combination of a polemical newspaper, armed thuggery and political presence proved irresistible, especially when the unions called a disastrous general strike in July 1922 – allowing the Fascists to pose as saviours of the nation. With weak Liberal governments coming and going and the squads seizing control in many provinces, Mussolini pressured the politicians and the King into making him Prime Minister on 28 October. He arrived in the capital next morning on the night sleeper from Milan; the 'March on Rome' of Fascist mythology came after the fact, when hundreds of his 'blackshirts' rampaged through the city.

One of the big grievances in Italy after 1918 was the so-called 'mutilated victory' (*vittoria mutilata*). Italy's leaders had overplayed their hand at the Paris peace conference and the Allies – especially President Woodrow Wilson – were blamed for denying them the port of Fiume and the whole of Dalmatia along the Adriatic coast. Mussolini was ready to use foreign policy, as well as domestic repression, to help strengthen his power, playing on frustrated nationalism. In August 1923, in defiance of the new League of Nations, he bombed and occupied the island of Corfu in a dispute between Greece and Italy, using as pretext the assassination of an Italian general on Greek territory. 'What a swine this Mussolini is,' Winston complained to his wife.[10] But the dispute was settled by international arbitration, and Italy withdrew after Greek apologies and compensation. Having flexed his muscles, Mussolini spent much of the 1920s trying to build up a reputation for international citizenship, not least through his role in the Locarno pact of 1925 as co-guarantor, with Britain, of the post-war borders of France, Germany and Belgium.

The British architect of Locarno, Foreign Secretary Austen Chamberlain, considered Mussolini 'a remarkable man' who had 'given a new life and a new standing to Italy', whatever one thought of his methods. Judging that Italy wanted 'above all things now to be treated as a great power on a position of equality with France, Germany and ourselves', Chamberlain favoured a generous settlement of the country's outstanding war debts to Britain, and he asked Churchill as Chancellor to help maintain the spirit of Locarno. This Churchill did – overruling his own officials – and Italy agreed in January 1926 to fully repay its debt of £592 million by 1988. When the agreement was signed, Winston commented that the 'considerable offers' of territory made to Italy in 1915 to induce its declaration of war had not all been fulfilled in 1919 and paid tribute to the 'loyal and manly attitude' that the Italians had adopted. He also commended its government 'under the commanding leadership of Signor Mussolini' which had shown 'the courage to impose the financial remedies required to stabilise the national recovery'.[11]

Over the next year, the Churchills also developed warm personal relations with Mussolini, at least in public. When Clementine stayed at the British Embassy in Rome a couple of months after the debt agreement was signed, Mussolini turned on the charm, presenting her with a signed photograph inscribed *Devotamente*. It seems to have worked. 'He is most impressive,' she wrote to Winston,

> quite simple and <u>natural</u>, very dignified, has a charming smile & the most beautiful golden brown piercing eyes which you see but can't look at . . . He fills you with the most pleasurable awe – You feel at once you would like to do something for him, or at least quickly carry out his wishes . . . I am sure he is a very great person.

Churchill wrote back teasingly from London: 'What a picture you draw of Mussolini! I feel sure you are right in regarding him as a prodigy.' But he recalled an aphorism of the Victorian politician Augustine Birrell: 'It is better to read about a world figure, than to live under his rule.'[12]

In January 1927 Winston visited Rome and had a couple of meetings with Mussolini, who seems to have given him much of the credit for the debt settlement. Speaking to the press, Winston recalled warmly the wartime alliance between their two countries and said of Mussolini, 'I could not help being charmed, like so many people have been, by his gentle and simple bearing and by his calm, detached poise in spite of so many burdens and dangers.' As for ideology, his comments were both positive and politic:

> If I had been an Italian, I am sure I should have been whole-heartedly with you from the start to finish in your triumphant struggle against the bestial appetites and passions of Leninism. But in England we have not yet had to face this danger in the same deadly form. We have our own way of doing things. But that we shall succeed in grappling with Communism and choking the life out of it – of that I am absolutely sure.

He added that 'externally, your movement has rendered service to the entire world.'

Back home the Labour and Liberal press accused him of endorsing Fascism. Clemmie wrote to her husband with amusement that the *Manchester Guardian* was 'vexed over your partiality to "Pussolini".[13]

The moral outrage of the British left about fascism intensified in 1933 when Hitler came to power, but, for conservatives like Churchill, Mussolini became increasingly important as a bulwark against German expansion in Europe. Yet the Duce was now embarking on his own empire-building in Africa. Churchill was out of office but his interwoven commentaries on the crises over Austria and Abyssinia reveal his own balancing act with respect to appeasement. He was much readier to appease Mussolini's Italy than Hitler's Germany.

* * *

On the first page of chapter one of *Mein Kampf* Hitler made clear his determination to annex Austria; if that happened it would bring German power right up to Italy's Alpine border. Mussolini therefore issued a guarantee of Austrian independence against 'Prussian barbarism'. In July 1934, when the country's Fascist leader Engelbert Dollfuss – Mussolini's protégé – was murdered by Austrian Nazis in an attempted putsch, the Duce mobilised Italian troops on the border and helped suppress the coup. Not only did the putsch fail, Hitler also wound down his campaign of propaganda and subversion against Austria. It was a big personal success for Mussolini, strengthening his contempt for the Führer. When they met for the first time in Venice on 14 June – only six weeks before the putsch – Mussolini, in an elegant military uniform, had upstaged his guest who was wearing a civilian suit, soft hat and yellow mackintosh for what he understood to be a private meeting. He looked like a shady commercial traveller. Mussolini dismissed Hitler as 'a clown' who was 'quite mad' and droned on 'like a gramophone with only seven tunes'.[14]

It would prove a costly underestimation. The man hailed by fellow Nazis in 1922 as 'the German Mussolini' would quickly become master not follower once he gained power in Berlin. The Duce's search for living space (*spazio vitale*) did not collide directly with the Fuhrer's vision of *Lebensraum* in Eastern Europe and Russia, directed as it was at the French and British dominance along the African littoral, where Italy's sole major colony was Libya. In the longer term, Mussolini had his eyes fixed on a new Roman empire – 'the Mediterranean shall once again be ours' – insisting that Italy must not be 'encircled' by a 'chain of hostility' in 'its own sea'.[15] But the Austrian crisis of July 1934 and Hitler's announcement of military conscription in March 1935, breaching the Treaty of Versailles, underlined the fragility of Italy's northeast border. The following month Mussolini invited the French and British leaders to Stresa, on Lake Maggiore, where on 14 April they affirmed their determination to maintain 'the independence and integrity of Austria' and their opposition to any 'unilateral repudiation of treaties which may endanger the peace of Europe'.[16]

The words 'of Europe' were added at Mussolini's insistence because he was now planning an invasion of the ancient East African empire of Abyssinia in October. He was confident that 'no one will raise any difficulties in Europe if the conduct of military operations results rapidly in a *fait accompli*. It will suffice to let England and France know that their interests will be safeguarded.'[17] Up to a point, the Duce was right. Neither power objected to Italian control of Abyssinia: the British did not perceive any real threat to their interests in Egypt and the Sudan, and France hoped to turn the Stresa agreement into a proper military alliance. They wanted moreover to avoid a diplomatic crisis and, above all, a war. But their backstage attempts at deal-making were complicated in the New Year of 1935 when Emperor Haile Selassie took the dispute to the League of Nations. Over the next few months, the British press was full of reports about the Italian military build-up in neighbouring Eritrea.

During 1935 the League became a totemic issue in Britain. Half a million volunteers from the League of Nations Union (LNU) had gone door-to-door to gauge public support for the League. On 27 June 1935 the results of the 'Peace Ballot' were announced at a mass meeting at the Albert Hall. Some 11.6 million people answered the LNU questionnaire – 38 per cent of the adult population and over half the number of people who voted in the 1935 general election. There was overwhelming approval (87 per cent) for economic and non-military sanctions against an aggressor state and a majority (59 per cent) for the use of force. Although the ballot was not a real opinion poll, no politician could ignore such an expression of public feeling. The National Government, now headed by Stanley Baldwin, moved more warships to the Mediterranean and, after the Italian invasion of Abyssinia began on 3 October, it led the League's imposition of limited economic sanctions. Such actions proved extremely popular and prompted Baldwin to call an early general election on 18 November, at which he won a huge majority.

Behind the scenes, however, Paris and London – fearful that the crisis could escalate into war with their erstwhile friend – were still intent on brokering a territorial deal with Mussolini. On 7–8 December Sir Samuel Hoare, Britain's Foreign Secretary, met secretly with his French counterpart Pierre Laval (also France's Prime Minister) in Paris. The 'Hoare-Laval plan' envisaged giving Italy roughly two-thirds of Abyssinia and consoling the rump kingdom with a corridor to the Red Sea. Hoare was acting with Cabinet knowledge and approval but, when the deal was leaked – provoking a public outcry – he became the scapegoat and was sacked. Historian Zara Steiner called the abandonment of the Hoare-Laval pact 'one of the very few inter-war examples of the government in London giving way to public pressure, at least as it was filtered through Parliament.'[18]

Like all British politicians, Churchill found it hard to keep his footing amid the twists and turns of 1935. On 2 May he had welcomed the Stresa accord in the Commons. His sole criticism was that it should have been done 'two or three years ago'. He declared that 'we are bound to act in concert with France and Italy and other Powers, great and small, who are anxious to preserve peace' – indeed with any government that was 'willing to work under the authority and sanction of the League of Nations'. References to the League were now becoming more frequent in his speeches, as in those of other MPs as the Peace Ballot neared its climax.[19]

Even though Mussolini was clearly preparing to invade Abyssinia, Winston remained keen to distinguish Italy from Germany. Writing in *Collier's* magazine on 4 May about 'Nations on the Loose', he said that it was 'in Germany that nationalism presents itself in its most repulsive form. The bitterness of defeat has produced a monstrous reaction. A whole people, the most educated, the most scientific and one of the most gifted in the world . . . has plunged back into the Middle Ages with Jew-baiting and official murder as the accepted, nay, the vaunted features of national life' – all in the name of 'racial purity'. Churchill made no explicit mention of Hitler or Nazism, vaguely ascribing this 'terrible reversion' to some kind of national 'inferiority complex'. By contrast, he said, 'the Italian story is different. Here there was no bitterness of defeat; here there was a really great man.' Nevertheless, Italy was now gripped by 'a nationalism so intense as to absorb the whole energies of the nation'. He noted how gratifying it must be for Italian national pride that 'Signor Mussolini should be so largely instrumental in maintaining the precarious independence of Austria' – especially when northern Italy had once been the puppet of Habsburg Austria.[20]

As the crisis unfolded that autumn, Churchill became increasingly unhappy about British policy. 'It would be a terrible thing to smash up Italy,' he told Austen Chamberlain on 1 October, 'and it will cost us dear'. The Government 'should not have taken the lead in such a vehement way'.[21] Publicly, however, Winston backed Baldwin, declaring on 26 September that he had been 'absolutely right' in 'strengthening our naval power in the Mediterranean' but insisting that the quarrel was between Italy and the League, not Italy and Britain. And he expressed surprise that 'so great a man and so wise a ruler as Signor Mussolini should be willing and even eager to put his gallant nation in such an uncomfortable military and financial position' by following a course which 'seems to remove our Italian comrades and old allies from the group of great powers striving to rebuild harmony in the

European family in which the greatness of the revivified Italian nation must play a noble part'.[22]

In short, a tone of sorrow not anger – all very different from Winston's diatribes about German expansion. But, of course, he saw the two cases as totally different in geopolitical terms. Germany, he told the Commons on 24 October, was 'well on her way' to becoming 'the most heavily armed nation in the world and the nation most completely ready for war. There is the dominant factor; there is the factor which dwarfs all others.' By comparison, 'this war between Italy and Abyssinia, of which the newspapers are so full' was 'a very small matter'. Trying to keep the House focused on what for him was the big issue – rearmament against Germany – he argued that the reason why the League was 'now a reality' was not 'the moral force of public opinion' but 'because there has been behind it, as there was behind so many causes vital to human progress and freedom, the Royal Navy'. He went on to claim that there was 'no antagonism' between passionate advocates of the League and staunch defenders of the British Empire: 'I believe these two ideas are at present the only practical counterparts of one another.'[23]

When he ended his speech, the Labour MP Arthur Greenwood jumped up to say that Churchill was 'trying to have it both ways' – at once pro-League and pro-British Empire – adding sarcastically that Churchill now had 'probably succeeded in justifying his appointment to high office' if the Government won next month's election.[24] But although Baldwin did win, Winston did not. His hopes of returning to the Cabinet dashed, he left England on 10 December for a writing vacation in the Mediterranean; even after returning at the end of January 1936, he delivered no major speech in the Commons until 10 March. Meanwhile, Mussolini gradually neared his victory while London argued with Paris (now with a caretaker government after the fall of Laval) about whether to impose oil sanctions and what to do if such an action triggered war with Italy. Their dithering encouraged Hitler on 7 March to occupy the Rhineland.

On 5 May 1936 the Abyssinian capital, Addis Ababa, capitulated and four days later the Duce proclaimed the new fascist empire, evoking the grandeur of imperial Rome. He now began to tilt towards Berlin. On 11 July, urged on by the Duce, Austria and Germany signed a new accord, which affirmed Austrian sovereignty but as a 'German state'. At the end of July, Mussolini and Hitler sent planes and pilots to assist General Francisco Franco in Spain, after his coup against the Popular Front government started a civil war. They did so once confident that France and Britain would not intervene. And on 25 October Mussolini's foreign minister (and son-in-law) Galeazzo Ciano signed an accord with Germany affirming their common struggle against Bolshevism and recognising Italy's annexation of Abyssinia. The agreement was trumpeted by Mussolini on 1 November as 'an axis round which all those European States which are animated by a desire for collaboration and peace can revolve'. The term 'Axis' caught the international imagination and reinforced the impression of 'dictators' on the march, but the Rome-Berlin Axis was myth-making rather than hard reality. Although both leaders saw France and Britain as major obstacles to their goals, Mussolini remained wary of being yoked to Hitler, as the rest of the 1930s would show.[25]

The crisis of 1935–6 proved the tipping point in Winston's hopes of maintaining a diplomatic friendship with Mussolini. After the summer of 1936 his goal shifted from cultivating Mussolini as a potential wartime ally against Hitler to the more limited aim of keeping the Duce on the sidelines in any future conflict. Yet he found that the tangles in which he had got himself over Abyssinia – between the moral simplicities of supporting the League and the pragmatic pursuit of British interests – would continue to vitiate his policy towards Italy.

His attempts to use the League as a cause around which to mobilise a strong foreign policy for Britain was seriously strained by the Spanish Civil War. Whereas centre and left opinion discerned there a struggle between fascism and democracy, in his view 'Fascism confronts Communism. The spirit and prowess of Mussolini and Hitler strive with those of Trotsky and Bela Kun.'[26] Churchill's main concern was to avoid the involvement of Britain and France in the conflict, which would thereby distract them from the German challenge. On 14 April 1937 he adopted a detached, almost jocular tone, telling the Commons that 'quite frankly, I have not been able to work up the same state of passionate indignation or enthusiasm about either side in Spain that I see is so sincerely present in the breasts of many Members.' It did not help his image with pro-League opinion when he added: 'I will not pretend that, if I had to choose between Communism and Nazism, I would choose Communism.' Twelve days later, a historic Basque town behind the battle lines was bombed by German and Italian planes and a dramatic report in *The Times* announced to the world 'The Tragedy of Guernica.'[27]

On Spain, Churchill supported the Government's policy of non-intervention, going out of his way to compliment the new Foreign Secretary, Anthony Eden.[28] But he and Eden did not see eye-to-eye on the bigger issues of Hitler and Mussolini. Churchill wanted toughness towards Germany and conciliation of Italy. Eden's emphasis was the opposite. He doubted that much would come from negotiations with the Duce and strongly objected to Britain conceding formal diplomatic recognition of Italy's conquests. He felt by 1937 that Neville Chamberlain, Baldwin's successor as PM, 'really believed it would be possible to get an agreement with Mussolini by running after him.'[29]

What Eden called 'Facing the Dictators' was therefore a complicated business: it mattered which dictator you were looking at.[30] This was evident during a Commons debate on 5 November 1936. Eden was at pains to rebut Mussolini's recent remark that, whereas the Mediterranean was for Italy 'our very life', for Britain it was only 'a short cut' to its 'outlying territories'. No, replied Eden, for the British Empire and Commonwealth 'the Mediterranean is not a short cut but a main arterial road.' Winston entirely agreed, but saw no need to play word games. British policy towards Italy should not be one of 'nagging'. While reaffirming the 'special amity' between the two countries, he asserted that 'for more than 200 years we have held naval command of the Mediterranean' and observed bluntly that any attempt to limit Britain's presence there would be irrelevant. 'Nothing can possibly prevent the stronger navy from, in a few days, placing any force it may desire and which it can spare from home waters in the Mediterranean.' In short: no need to nag because power would always trump bluster.[31]

In his speeches and writings in 1936–9, Winston continued to make laudatory asides about Mussolini the leader – this 'extraordinary man', Italy's 'spirited and successful chief'[32] – while downplaying the Duce's damaging successes in Abyssinia, Spain and the Mediterranean; in the larger context Churchill portrayed the possibility of an ever-closer British-French front towards Germany within which there was still space for Italy. This balancing act required a good deal of fancy footwork. In an article in May 1938, he made the best of Hitler's *Anschluss* with Austria – which confirmed the marked shift in the German-Italian balance since 1934 – by trying to offset it against Chamberlain's Anglo-Italian Agreement: 'France and Britain, more closely associated than ever, are both entering into arrangements with Italy, designed if possible, and if they are kept, to make the Mediterranean an area excluded from a possible war.' Even more extravagant special pleading was required after Mussolini's invasion of Albania in April 1939. Winston admitted that the Anglo-Italian Agreement had been 'violated in the most barefaced manner', but speculated that this might not be 'a final test' of Mussolini's intentions in any future European war because the Duce could represent Albania as 'a mere local incident' which gave him something imperialistic to show his people while not bringing them into direct conflict with Britain and France. Although admitting the hazards of prophecy, he concluded, 'we may at least feel at the time of writing that the Berlin-Rome Axis stands upon no more sacred foundation than does the Anglo-Italian Pact.'[33]

Churchill was not a bad prophet. The Albanian invasion was intended by Mussolini and Ciano to show that they were not Hitler's lackeys. The Führer had not told them in advance of his takeover of Czechoslovakia in March 1939; likewise, they did not warn him of their imminent seizure of a country already largely under Italian control. Similarly, the so-called Pact of Steel signed by the two Axis powers in May 1939 proved of very pliable metal. Although Italy pledged its aid if Germany were involved in a war, Mussolini insisted on a grace period of three years, to allow time for Italian rearmament. Surprised and shocked by the Nazi-Soviet Pact, he used this get-out clause to stay neutral (or as he put it 'non-belligerent') in September 1939.[34]

So Churchill was proved right in 1939 about the limits of the Rome-Berlin axis. But why did he keep bending over backwards to make the best case for Mussolini? Largely as a consequence of his contrasting view of the two men and their two states, which he expressed in the 1938 article quoted at start of this chapter. Notes for that essay read, 'Mussolini is the greater man who is on a small moke [mule], while the other is on an elephant or a tiger.'[35] In other words, Germany was far more formidable for Britain as a foe, and perhaps the Duce might still be persuaded to act in a statesmanlike manner according to Italian interests. Yet the contrast between mule and tiger also pointed to another scenario. If Fascist Italy did eventually throw in its lot with Nazi Germany, then it would be the weaker of Britain's two enemies and an easier target for offensive action.[36]

On 27 March 1939 Churchill sent Neville Chamberlain a lengthy paper entitled 'Memorandum on Sea-Power, 1939'. Three points stand out, each of which would shape his thinking for most of the war. First, although still hoping that Italy might remain neutral in a future war, he argued that – assuming Italy joined Germany – 'England's first battlefield is the Mediterranean ... Our forces alone should be sufficient to drive the Italian ships from the sea, and secure complete command of the Mediterranean, certainly within two months, possibly sooner.' Winston's second major point followed from this. 'On no account must anything which threatens in the Far East divert us from this prime objective.' Should Japan join Germany and Italy, Britain would have to accept temporary losses, including Hong Kong and Shanghai, and aim to hold on to Singapore. But 'this should be easy,' he insisted. 'A fortress of this character with cannon which can hold any fleet at arm's length only requires an adequate garrison and supplies of food and ammunition, preferably for a year; but even six months would probably do. Singapore must hold out until the Mediterranean is safe, and the Italian fleet liquidated.' In any case, he dismissed the idea that Japan would send a fleet and army to conquer Singapore – 'it is as far from Japan as Southampton is from New York', some 'two thousand miles of salt water' (actually 3,000). 'One can take it as quite certain that Japan would not run such a risk,' he assured Chamberlain. 'They are an extremely sensible people.'[37]

Churchill's arguments reflected what was by then axiomatic: that Britain did not have a sufficiently large navy to fight three enemies simultaneously. The home fleet had to be ready to resist a German thrust across the North Sea, while the Mediterranean fleet, based mainly at Alexandria, would deal with Italy or move to Singapore to confront Japan, depending on the international situation. But whereas the balance of naval opinion judged that Britain's second priority after home defence must be Japan, and that Italy should be neutered by blocking up the Mediterranean, Churchill, always keen to take the offensive in any conflict, favoured a rapid knockout blow against Italy – accepting the possibility of short-term losses in the Far East. Henceforth he never wavered in his belief that Britain's second naval theatre after home waters must be the Mediterranean.[38]

Churchill was, however, at one with Royal Navy orthodoxy on the third big point of his memo: the supremacy of the battleship. 'The submarine has been mastered,' he asserted confidently. 'It should be controllable in the outer seas, and certainly in the Mediterranean.' And in his opinion, 'given with great humility (because these things are very difficult to judge), an air attack upon British warships, armed and protected as they now are, will not prevent full exercise of their superior seapower'. He also made the same point publicly, airing in Collier's magazine in January 1939 his 'general view that aircraft will not be a mortal danger to properly equipped modern war fleets'.[39] This scepticism paralleled Churchill's dismissal in the 1930s of tactical airpower on land, discussed in the previous chapter. He would pay a high price in December 1941 for his faith in seapower over airpower.

* * *

For the moment, however, the arguments posed in Churchill's memorandum proved academic. In September 1939, choices between the Mediterranean and the Far East were deferred by Italian non-belligerency. Churchill optimistically told his Cabinet colleagues in November that now 'Italy is neutral, and may even become a friend, the British Fleet has become again entirely mobile' – free to move to Singapore, and thereby shield Australia and New Zealand, if Japan caused trouble.[40]

In the spring of 1940 Mussolini continued to flutter between London and Berlin, aggrieved whenever either capital dented his *amour-propre*. As late as 16 May, with France crumbling, the Cabinet still hoped to keep the Duce non-belligerent and Winston sent him a personal message, in language redolent of the past: 'Now that I have taken up my office as Prime Minister and Minister of Defence, I look back to our meetings in Rome and feel a desire to speak words of goodwill to you as Chief of the Italian Nation across what seems to be a swiftly widening gulf. Is it too late to stop a river of blood from flowing between the British and Italian peoples?' He assured Mussolini, 'I have never been the enemy of Italian greatness, nor ever at heart the foe of the Italian lawgiver.' The Duce brusquely reminded Churchill of the 'grave reasons' that had 'ranged our two countries in opposite camps', dwelling particularly on 'the initiative taken in 1935 by your Government to organise at Geneva sanctions against Italy, engaged in securing for herself a small space in the African sun without causing the slightest injury to your interests and territories or those of others'. He also mentioned 'the real and actual sense of servitude in which Italy finds herself in her own sea' and ended by assuring the PM that Italy would honour its 1939 treaty with Germany. Quoting this message in his memoirs, Winston added, 'From this moment we could have no doubt of Mussolini's intention to enter the war at his most favourable moment.'[41]

Speaking to his ministers in January 1940, Mussolini said Britain and France could 'no longer win the war' and insisted that Italy must not remain neutral until the end of the conflict because that 'would bring us down to second rate among the European powers'. Ideally, he preferred to wait until 1941, when the army would be in better shape, but the surprise collapse of France in May 1940 and what appeared the likelihood that Britain would sign a negotiated peace obliged him to act – overriding all contrary advice from the military. 'Rarely have I seen Mussolini so happy,' Ciano noted on 29 May. 'He has realized his real dream: that of becoming the military leader of the country at war.'[42]

Even then, after declaring war on France and Britain on 10 June, the Duce wanted to stay on the defensive. But the amazing turn of events necessitated some improvised offensives in order to justify his claim for a share of the spoils at the peace table. Mussolini sent thirty air squadrons (a quarter of his effective air force) to assist in the Blitz, but when the planes reached Belgium it become clear that they lacked the range and equipment to bomb Churchill's capital – a prospect that the Duce had been relishing. At the end of October, he lost face very publicly when his invasion of Greece was swiftly driven back into Albania by smaller but well-organised Greek forces. A long and debilitating struggle ensued. On 11–12 November British aircraft took out half the Italian battle fleet in its anchorage at Taranto. And in early December a cautious probe by the Italian army into Egypt from Libya was pre-empted by a surprise attack by British tanks and Indian infantry. This resulted in 38,000 Italian casualties, at a cost to the British of only 634. Far from taking Egypt from Britain, Italy was now in danger of losing its own colony of Libya when the British advanced further in the New Year of 1941.[43]

These humiliating reverses underlined what Mussolini's generals had been saying, sotto voce, for months – that Italy was ill-prepared for modern war, at every level from equipment and training right up to the lack of a proper planning staff. The dictator was making the decisions, and then changing them, without proper knowledge of strategy, command and logistics – mainly to express his own ego. Winston stressed Mussolini's personal culpability in a radio broadcast to the Italian people on 23 December 1940. He celebrated the past history of British-Italian friendship, including the Risorgimento and 'the last war against the barbarous Huns', but now 'your aviators have tried to cast their bombs upon London' and 'our armies are tearing and will tear your African Empire to shreds and tatters.' This is 'all because of one man', he told Italians, 'and one man alone', who had 'arrayed the trustees and inheritors of ancient Rome upon the side of the ferocious, pagan barbarians. *There* lies the tragedy of Italian history, and *there* stands the criminal who has wrought the deed of folly and shame.' Churchill did not deny that Mussolini was 'a great man', but declared it undeniable that 'after eighteen years of unbridled power he has led your country to the horrid verge of ruin'. And he warned that the failed Duce would soon have no choice but to 'call in Attila over the Brenner Pass with his hordes of ravenous soldiery and his gangs of Gestapo policemen'. The PM ended with an invitation to rise up against the regime, by looking forward to the day when 'the Italian nation will once more take a hand in shaping its own fortunes.'[44]

With those Gibbonian flourishes and his depiction of Mussolini as a great man gone wrong, the broadcast was characteristic of Churchill's take on Italy – but, as the MP Harold Nicolson observed, the Prime Minister was also using the war against Italy to address Britain and the world, in what some US correspondents felt was one of his best speeches.[45] Not least because Churchill could narrate 1940 in the Mediterranean as a success story. Today, amid the now conventional preoccupation with Britain's 'finest hour' in the same year – when Hitler's Europe was defied from 'our island fortress' – it is rarely noted how important 1940 was for the country's whole global position. In the summer, even when Britain feared imminent invasion, Churchill's Cabinet committed itself to a major reinforcement of the Mediterranean and the Middle East. Not only would this define British strategy against the Axis for the rest of the war but, in the process, it would also help determine the fate of Britain's Asian empire. It was during 1940 that the priorities outlined in Churchill's 1939 memorandum on seapower were implemented, to historic effect.

The 1930s debate about how the Royal Navy should cope with three potential enemies had been intense but hypothetical. But in June 1940, after France fell and Italy entered the war, the debate became all too urgent. The Admiralty's response was to reiterate the pre-war orthodoxy, temporarily conceding control of the Mediterranean by withdrawing the fleet from Alexandria to Gibraltar and, if necessary, sealing up the other exit by blocking the Suez Canal. Churchill, however, would have none of this. On 3 July a telegram was sent to British posts abroad confirming the Government's determination to hold the Middle East – especially Iraq with its oil, Palestine, Egypt and the Canal – and stating: 'It is intended to retain the fleet in the Eastern Mediterranean as long as possible.'[46] As historian Correlli Barnett observed, 'this grand-strategic choice' effectively 'reversed the pre-war order of global priorities, and opened the way for the Mediterranean and Middle East to become the main focus of the British Empire's war-making for nearly four years'. The strategy sucked in 'an ever-swelling military and logistic investment', on which it became politically imperative to show massive returns.[47]

The most spectacular investment in 1940 was to send to Egypt an armoured brigade of three regiments – with 154 tanks, nearly half of the available strength, as well as substantial artillery – just when Britain was gearing up for possible invasion. This has gone down as one of the country's biggest gambles of the war. They arrived just in time. In December, after the debacles in Greece and Libya, Mussolini accepted the advice of key generals that the only course was to 'put everything in the hands of the Führer because we can do no more.'[48]

General Erwin Rommel arrived in Tripoli on 12 February 1941. Rommel had won his spurs as a daring platoon commander in 1917, when his unit was attached to the Habsburg army that routed the Italians at Caporetto. In May 1940 his armoured division had been in the vanguard of the German thrust across the Meuse. Now, in 1941, his Deutsche Afrika Korps, initially consisting of two divisions, was technically under Italian command, with strict instructions to stay on the defensive and simply prevent further retreats, but Rommel sought every chance to take the initiative. His limited offensive at the end of March proved successful and so he kept advancing. He benefited from Churchill and Eden's decision, supported by General Sir Archibald Wavell, the British commander in Egypt, to divert three divisions (British, Australian and New Zealand) to help the Greeks – on the assumption, gleaned from Ultra and other intelligence, that Rommel was not going to attack. Instead, on 6 April, the Germans invaded both Yugoslavia and Greece, forcing out the British Expeditionary Force within a few weeks. That same day Wavell, outflanked by Rommel's armour, had to pull back 300 miles to the port of Tobruk, whose Australian garrison was now besieged.[49]

Like Mussolini in 1940, Churchill tried to do too much in the Mediterranean in the spring of 1941 – and he paid a high price. The debacles in North Africa and Greece triggered the first bout of serious parliamentary criticism. As usual on such occasions, Winston turned the Commons debate on 6–7 May into a vote of confidence in his government, which he won by 447 to 3. But during it he uttered a significant qualification of his 'victory at all costs' pledge a year before: 'I have never promised anything or offered anything but blood, tears, toil and sweat, to which I will now add our fair share of mistakes, shortcomings and disappointments and also that this may go on for a very long time, at the end of which I firmly believe – though it is not a promise or a guarantee, only a profession of faith – that there will be complete, absolute and final victory.'[50]

The grumbles intensified at the end of May, when German paratroopers overwhelmed the island of Crete. 'On all sides one hears increasing criticism of Churchill,' Tory MP 'Chips' Channon noted. 'He is undergoing a notable slump in popularity.'[51] The criticism was not confined to Britain. From 20 February until 3 May the Australian premier Robert Menzies was in Britain, asking pointed questions in War Cabinet meetings. In his diary he fumed that Churchill was 'acting as the master strategist' but 'without qualification' or often 'knowledge'.[52] After Menzies left, on 21 June the New Zealand premier Peter Fraser arrived in Britain for a visit of two months, taking up Menzies' role, albeit less bluntly. In the wake of the various setbacks around the Mediterranean, these Commonwealth leaders were keen to exert more control over operations in which their troops were being used and, it seemed, misused. Both were worried about Japan's increasingly expansionist policy in the Far East – which for them, as Menzies famously declared in 1939, was actually 'the Near North'.[53]

In July 1941, after Wavell's attempt to relieve Tobruk had failed, Winston replaced him with General Sir Claude Auchinleck. 'The Auk' mounted his own offensive, Operation Crusader, in mid-November. This not only ended the siege of Tobruk after nearly eight months but also drove the Axis forces, short of supplies, 500 miles back along the Libyan coast road to El Agheila. The relief in London was, however, spoiled in late January 1942 when another 'reconnaissance' probe by Rommel failed to encounter serious resistance, and so he pushed on all the way to Gazala, less than 50 miles west of Tobruk. There Rommel and Auchinleck regrouped for a new round in this yo-yo struggle along the North African coast, in which a successful advance by either side was automatically jeopardised by the consequent over-extension of supply lines. A massive logistical build-up was therefore crucial to ensure a decisive breakthrough in 1942.

By this time, Britain was at war with Japan – a profound geopolitical upheaval dramatised by two events: the sinking of the *Prince of Wales* and *Repulse* off the coast of Malaya on 10 December 1941 and the surrender of Singapore on 15 February 1942. These were military disasters of a magnitude that nothing in Mediterranean could match. Yet events in the two theatres were directly related.

The backstory is revealing. At the end of April 1941 Churchill learned by chance that contingency plans existed for the evacuation of Egypt if the desert war went wrong. Incensed at such 'pure defeatism', he issued a directive calling in such plans and insisting that to lose Egypt and the Middle East 'would be a disaster of the first magnitude to Great Britain, second only to successful invasion and final conquest'. He also asserted bluntly that Japan was 'unlikely to enter the war' unless the

Germans had triumphed, or if Tokyo anticipated US belligerency.[54] His arguments were contested by Field Marshal Sir John Dill, Chief of the Imperial General Staff, who stated that 'it has been an accepted principle of our strategy that in the last resort the security of Singapore comes before that of Egypt' and that 'the defences of Singapore are still considerably below standard.' Whereupon Churchill told the man he privately nicknamed 'Dilly-Dally' that the defence of Singapore would necessitate 'only a very small fraction of the troops required to defend the Nile Valley' – to which Britain had committed half a million men. In any case, he assured Dill, even if Japan did declare war, it was 'not likely to besiege Singapore at the outset' because of the magnitude of such an operation.[55]

This exchange shows that the premises of Churchill's global strategy had not altered since his memo on seapower in 1939. And he acted on them in the summer of 1941 when intelligence evidence indicated that Tokyo was gearing up for war. The PM assumed that the damage it could inflict was limited, perhaps the loss of Hong Kong and a threat to Thailand, and he even dismissed the Japanese as 'the Wops of the Pacific' – derogatory British slang for the Italians.[56] Confident that a token display of British force could deter them, Churchill wanted to send two modern battleships of the King George V (KGV) class and an aircraft carrier straight to Singapore, because this could prove 'a decisive deterrent'. He argued that a KGV in the Indian Ocean would have the same effect as the German battleship *Tirpitz* in the Atlantic: 'It exercises a vague, general fear and menaces all parts at once.'[57] Eventually a compromise was reached in October. To satisfy Churchill and the War Cabinet, the *Prince of Wales* – a KGV battleship – together with the battlecruiser *Repulse* and the new aircraft carrier *Indomitable* would converge on Singapore in the next few weeks, under the command of Admiral Sir Tom Phillips. But it was also agreed that older battleships would follow later in the year, followed in 1942 by other capital ships, cruisers and destroyers. In view of the deterrent strategy, extensive publicity was given to the movements of the *Prince of Wales*.[58]

Phillips on the *Prince of Wales* reached Cape Town on 16 November. By this time it was clear that *Indomitable*, damaged during sea trials, could not join her, thereby eliminating almost all air cover. He sailed on to meet the *Repulse* and they reached Singapore on 2 December. On the evening of the 7th, Churchill heard news of the Japanese attack on Pearl Harbor and the destruction of much of the US Pacific fleet. With America now finally a belligerent, he immediately started to plan a trip to Washington, only to receive news that the two great battleships had both been sunk by Japanese planes in a few hours on 10 December. He wrote later, 'In all the war I never received a more direct shock.'[59] It had been on his personal insistence that the *Prince of Wales* was sent to Singapore. Of course, he intended this as a 'deterrent', not a war-fighting operation, but that in turn exposes his underestimation of naval airpower and, even more, of the 'Wops of the Pacific'.[60]

The debacle was followed by the surrender of Singapore on 15 February 1942, which Winston called in his memoirs 'the worst disaster and largest capitulation in British history'.[61] London's strategy for a Far Eastern war had always been based on sending the Mediterranean fleet to Singapore if Japan became hostile. But that policy had been undermined in mid-1940 by the fall of France, Mussolini's entry into the war and Winston's insistence that the Mediterranean was Britain's second priority after the home islands. *Faute de mieux*, airpower was supposed to hold at bay any Japanese force coming down the Malay peninsula – but the RAF's strength there in December 1941 was under half the acceptable minimum and troops in Singapore were at three-quarter strength, most of them deficient in training and supplies. And it was only in mid-January 1942, less than a month before the surrender, that Winston belatedly appreciated that all Singapore's fortifications faced seaward. It had never been intended to resist an attack on the northern side, from Malaya. 'I ought to have known,' he admitted in his memoirs. 'I ought to have been told, and I ought to have asked.' But he added hyperbolically, 'the possibility of Singapore having no landward defences no more entered into my mind than that of a battleship being launched without a bottom.' In unpublished notes, he mused more candidly, 'I have no defence for it either, except that I had not the life and strength to light up the field of interest with the same intensity after I had done all I could in the West and in Africa.' On the big strategic question of the Middle East versus the Far East, about which he had wrestled with Dill in 1941, Winston was unrepentant: 'The major dispositions were right.'[62] But everything had been unhinged by the Japan's Pacific-wide Blitzkrieg. Churchill had assumed that any deficiencies in strategy and dispositions could be redressed once the US was in the war.[63] That assumption went up in smoke at Pearl Harbor. The Australian government, moreover, reviewed its commitment to the desert war now that its own national security seemed in danger. After the loss of the two battleships, John Curtin – Menzies' Labor successor as premier – bluntly announced that in the present crisis 'Australia looks to America, free of any pangs as to our traditional links or kinship with the United Kingdom.' In January 1942 he damned any talk of surrendering Singapore as an 'inexcusable betrayal'. Churchill agreed that two of the three Australian divisions in North Africa should return to the Pacific theatre.[64]

Seizing the opportunities opened up by Britain's distractions in Asia, Rommel mounted a new offensive on 26 May, which outflanked the British forces and surrounded Tobruk. Under sustained tank and air attack, and short of water, its garrison surrendered on 21 June. Churchill was devastated. At Tobruk, as at Singapore, troops of the British Empire had capitulated to a far smaller enemy force. 'Defeat is one thing', he wrote in his memoirs; 'disgrace is another.'[65]

* * *

The fall of Tobruk had a decisive impact on both parties in the conflict. The long siege in 1941 and now the Germans' dramatic success made it a centre of international attention, far beyond the military importance of its small port. To a lesser degree, Tobruk was similar to Stalingrad later in the year – a huge political symbol for both sides. After its fall, the Führer promoted Rommel to field marshal at the age of 50, and urged Mussolini to seize this 'historic turning point' and 'exploit it as quickly and ruthlessly as possible' because 'the goddess of success in battle passes generals only once.' The Duce agreed, overruling his own military, and on 29 June he flew to Libya with an entourage of journalists and politicians to prepare his triumphal entry into Cairo. Imagining himself as a modern Octavian or Napoleon, he would enter Egypt's capital on a white horse.[66]

The problem for both the Allies and the Axis was that there was no quick fix in North Africa. Neither Mussolini nor Churchill had been able to win a rapid victory in 1940. In 1941–2 the 'desert pendulum' had gradually swung towards the Axis, once Italian forces were bolstered by Rommel and his Afrika Korps. But the summer of 1942 proved to be Rommel's high-water mark. In July he was checked by Auchinleck at El Alamein, less than 200 miles from Cairo. A disappointed Duce returned to Rome while the two armies prepared for their decisive encounter.

It was in the second half of 1942 that the desert war reached its turning point, on a personal level, for Mussolini and Churchill. In July, while in Libya, the Duce was stricken with acute internal pains, beginning months of rapid weight loss, long spells in bed, severe oscillations of mood and often a lack of mental grip. The cause is not clear – among those touted were amoebic dysentery or a peptic ulcer – but desperation about his Mediterranean empire must have been a factor.[67] For Winston, too, this was a time of trial. Although his own health held up, younger men were being bruited as possible leaders. Winston later told his doctor that September and October 1942 were the 'two most anxious months of the war'. He had persuaded the Americans to mount landings in Algeria and Morocco (codenamed Operation Torch) – yet feared that this might prove another Gallipoli – and he fretted about plans and dispositions for the forthcoming battle at Alamein. He told Eden, 'if Torch fails, then I'm done for and must hand over to one of you.'[68]

The climactic battle of Alamein ran from 23 October to 4 November 1942. Winston's explanation for the British victory reflected the value he placed on individual leaders. On several occasions in 1942 the PM had paid public tribute to Rommel's skills as a commander, for instance to the Commons in January: 'We have a very daring and skilful opponent against us and, may I say across the havoc of war, a great General.' The audacity and constant aggression of the 'Desert Fox' exemplified what Churchill prized in a soldier; his indifference to logistics was equally Churchillian. In July 1942 Hitler mused that 'not a little' of Rommel's 'world-wide reputation' was 'due to Churchill's speeches in the House of Commons, in which, for tactical reasons of policy, the British Prime Minister always portrays Rommel as a military genius. Churchill's reason for doing so, of course,' said Hitler, 'is that he does not wish to admit that the British are getting a damned good hiding from the Italians in Egypt and Libya.' In the Führer's view, it was stupid of Churchill to build up his opponent in this way: 'The mere name suddenly begins to acquire a value equal to several divisions.'[69]

When Churchill visited Cairo and the desert front in early August 1942, en route to Moscow, he had only one thing on his mind. 'Rommel, Rommel, Rommel, Rommel,' he declaimed, pacing up and down in the British Embassy. 'What else matters but beating him!'[70] Obsessed with leaders, the PM sacked Auchinleck, replacing him as overall commander with Sir Harold Alexander, a handsome and urbane Guards officer, and appointed General Bernard Montgomery as commander of the Eighth Army. He described 'Monty' to his wife as 'a highly competent daring and energetic soldier, well-acquainted with Desert warfare. If he is disagreeable to those about him, he is also disagreeable to the enemy.'[71]

Returning to the desert a couple of weeks later, after visiting Stalin, the PM discerned a dramatic change, telling the War Cabinet on 21 August: 'I am sure we were heading for disaster under the former regime ... Apparently it was intended in the face of heavy attack to retire eastwards to the Delta. Many were looking over their shoulders to make sure of their seat in the lorry, and no plain plan of battle or dominating will-power had reached the units.' But, he went on, 'since then, from what I could see myself of the troops and hear from their Commanders, a complete change of atmosphere has taken place.'[72]

Leaders remained central to Churchill's understanding of the eventual desert victory. Sketching out this part of his memoirs in 1948, he noted, 'I consider Rommel a very great commander, beating us up at heavy odds, hurling us back hundreds of miles in 1941 . . . It was only after we got fine generals like Alexander and Montgomery, and they also got better weapons and equipment, that defeat turns into victory.'[73] Yet Monty benefited from many other developments outside his control. Unlike his predecessors he was now receiving a significant amount of high-grade intelligence about Rommel's supplies and dispositions thanks to intercepts of Italian cable traffic. Just as vital, Monty had time – a commodity neither Wavell nor Auchinleck had enjoyed as they lurched to and fro on the desert pendulum. Not much of a respite – just a couple of months – but enough to reorganise units, boost their morale, and train them for their various tasks in the set-piece battle he was preparing. Meanwhile, Alexander used all his finesse to block Churchill's demands for a premature offensive.

Even so, the battle did not go according to plan. The tanks failed to make a decisive breakthrough or to encircle the shattered enemy forces. Nor was this struggle one of the real epics of the Second World War. The Eighth Army lost 2,350 dead; the Axis death toll has been estimated at 2,120 killed, plus around 30,000 prisoners. These figures were eclipsed by the five-month battle for Stalingrad in 1942–3 which claimed the lives of perhaps a million men on both sides and proved the turning point of the land war in Europe. But, measured on the desert pendulum, the outcome of Alamein was clear and dramatic. After 4 November Rommel was withdrawing along the coast road, pursued by the Eighth Army which covered nearly 800 miles over the next twenty days.[74] This was the big headline, militarily and politically. After two and a half years of defeats and retreats – since Norway and Dunkirk in 1940 – the British Army had now routed the German Army. (No matter that 60 per cent of the 'German' infantry and over 50 per cent of the tanks were Italian, while on the 'British' side nearly 60 per cent of the infantry came from the Empire and 40 per cent of the tanks were American.[75]) Equally important, on the level of personalities, the apparently invincible Desert

Fox had been vanquished by Monty, who now became a national hero. Churchill had finally given Hitler a bloody nose. Never again was his war premiership in doubt.

On 10 November the PM spoke ebulliently in London about this 'new experience' called 'victory', in what he called the 'Battle of Egypt'. He cautioned that 'this is not the end. It is not even the beginning of the end', but predicted, 'it is, perhaps, the end of the beginning.' Churchill also stated pugnaciously: 'We mean to hold our own. I have not become the King's First Minister in order to preside over the liquidation of the British Empire.' And on the 29th, he used a 'world broadcast' to rub it in to Mussolini, declaring that North Africa would be 'no halting-place: it is not a seat but a springboard.' Once the enemy (a first draft referred to 'the Huns and the Wops') had been 'blasted from the Tunisian tip', the Allies would 'bring the weight of the war home to the Italian Fascist state'. He told Italians:

> One man, and one man alone, has brought them to this pass ... Mussolini could not resist the temptation of stabbing prostrate France, and what he thought was helpless Britain, in the back. Mad dreams of imperial glory, the lust of conquest and of booty, the arrogance of long-unbridled tyranny, led him to his fatal, shameful act ... The hyena in his nature broke all bounds of decency. Today his Empire is gone ... Agony grips the fair land of Italy ... How long must this endure?[76]

This was too much for the Duce. Raising himself from his sick bed, he addressed the Italian parliament for the first time in eighteen months. Stung in particular by the 'hyena' gibe, he exclaimed: 'It is said that this gentleman is the descendant of a ducal family and that he has a great deal of blue blood in his veins. In my veins, on the other hand, flows the pure and healthy blood of a blacksmith, and at this moment I feel myself to be infinitely more of a gentleman than this man from whose mouth, fetid with alcohol and tobacco, comes forth such vile baseness.' As for the claim that his empire had gone, the Duce blustered that 'we are the people in whose veins flows the greatest portion of that blood which flowed in the veins of the ancient Romans. And we shall prove it.' He told his countrymen:

> If you strip the Englishman of the clothes he wears for his tea at 5 o'clock, you will find the old primitive barbarian Briton, with his skin painted in various colours, who was tamed by the veritable square legions of Caesar and Claudius. Fifty generations are not enough to change profoundly the inner structure of a people. To a large extent, they have spread over this primitive sediment only a varnish – hypocritical in their hands – from the Old and the New Testaments.[77]

The last gasp of a declining empire is, of course, to play the history card against the upstart that has eclipsed it.

This was Mussolini's last speech to the parliament. During 1943 – in acute pain, subsisting on sedatives and liquids, barely able to get out of bed – he continued to pretend that victory was in sight. But he had no proper plan to defend the country against the invasion that was inevitable once the Allies had cleared North Africa, and he did not resist in July when a majority of the Fascist Grand Council passed a vote of no confidence and the King had him arrested. On 12 September – as Hitler ruthlessly occupied central and northern Italy – a daring rescue mission by German commandos spirited him away to preside over a Nazi puppet regime. Italy's final agony was eighteen months of war and strife, far worse than when Mussolini had made his entry onto the political stage.[78]

Even to the very end, Winston remained ambivalent towards Mussolini. As the Germans retreated, the former Duce and his mistress Clara Petacci were caught by a Partisan patrol. Next day, 28 April 1945, they were summarily shot. Winston saw photos of their corpses hanging, upside down, from a girder in a service station outside Milan. To quote his memoirs, he was 'profoundly shocked', but added, 'at least the world was spared an Italian Nuremberg.'[79]

Offering a final verdict on the Duce, Winston still credited him with more than a whiff of greatness: 'Thus ended Mussolini's twenty-one years of dictatorship during which he had raised the Italian people from the Bolshevism into which they might have sunk in 1919 to a position in Europe such as Italy had never held before. A new impulse had been given to the national life. The Italian Empire in North Africa was built. Many important public works were completed.' But then the Duce took 'the wrong turning' in June 1940 by going to war on the side of Hitler. Fatally, 'he never understood the strength of Britain, nor the long-enduring qualities of Island resistance and sea-power. Thus he marched to ruin.' Then came the final putdown: 'His great roads will remain a monument to his personal power and long reign.'[80]

Not what Winston Churchill envisaged for himself as a memorial to greatness.

SAILORS DO CARE

"The more we get together
The merrier we shall be."

Churchill and Roosevelt celebrate their Destroyers for Bases deal.
Like all cartoonists, Bernard Partridge in *Punch* (11 Sept. 1940)
ignores the Wheelchair President's infirmity.

6

Franklin D. Roosevelt

'Special Relationship'

It is fun to be in the same decade with you.
Franklin D. Roosevelt to Winston S. Churchill, January 1942[1]

How I loved that man.
Winston S. Churchill, 1947[2]

Winston Churchill liked to say, 'There is only one thing worse than fighting with allies, and that is fighting without them.'[3] After France collapsed in 1940, Britain and its empire fought on but they had no hope of winning the war alone. So Winston bent all his efforts to creating what he called 'the Grand Alliance'. Yet operating as 'a small lion' between a 'huge Russian bear' and a 'great American elephant' was a difficult task, requiring constant vigilance.[4] The two emerging 'superpowers' threatened Britain's imperial interests, and each was led by a man who fascinated Churchill – albeit in very different ways.

'Courage is rightly esteemed the first of human qualities,' he wrote in 1937, because 'it is the quality which guarantees all the others.' By that he meant courage both 'physical and moral'.[5] His daughter Mary never forgot Winston suddenly saluting an usher when they were at a London theatre. Noting her puzzlement, he explained that one of the medals the man was wearing was the Victoria Cross. Nor did she forget her first sight of Franklin Delano Roosevelt at the Quebec conference in August 1943. Watching the paraplegic President being brought into the meeting room, then heaved out of the wheelchair, dumped on his seat and his legs arranged by an aide, she realised why her father considered FDR to be indubitably a man of courage.[6]

Winston also respected Roosevelt as the leader of 'the Great Republic' which, after the fall of France, seemed Britain's sole hope for defeating Hitler. More than that: through close cooperation among those he called 'the English-Speaking Peoples', the PM hoped to draw the Americans permanently out of isolationism and, in the process, help maintain Britain's world role. While Franco-German amity was his answer to the problem of Europe after 1945, Churchill's global grand strategy revolved around the 'special relationship'.

Roosevelt's attitudes to Churchill were more complicated. The day after the Japanese bombing of Pearl Harbor, he cabled the PM: 'Today all of us are in the same boat with you and the people of the Empire and it is a ship which will not and cannot be sunk.'[7] But that was the enthusiasm of the moment. The President's attitude to imperial Britain was more equivocal. United in war, yes; and two essential 'policemen' of the post-war peace that FDR was determined to build; yet espousing significantly different political principles. The New Deal president envisioned almost a social democratic future and the sunset of the European empires, in sharp contrast with what he saw as the PM's 'Victorian' values about politics and colonialism. He and Winston were in the same fleet, but were definitely captaining separate vessels. Roosevelt's life was cut short in 1945, but the half-decade that he and Churchill shared as world leaders marked a turning point in America's rise to greatness and in Britain's almost mirror-image decline as a great power.

*   *   *

It might be assumed that, being half-American, Winston always saw the United States as Britain's closest and most natural partner. The reality is more complex.

From an early age, he took a lively interest in his mother's country pestering her in June 1887 to get him off school so he could see William Cody's celebrated Wild West circus. 'I want to see Buffalo Bill,' he told her fervently. 'Don't disappoint me.' Otherwise, 'I shall never trust your promises again.' When reminding her of his impending thirteenth birthday, the message was equally direct: 'I should rather like "Gen Grant's History of the American War" (*Illustrated*).' In November 1895 Winston paid his first visit to New York, en route to Cuba to observe the Spanish army fighting nationalist insurgents, and in the winter of 1900–1 he spent a couple of lucrative months lecturing across the northern United States and Canada before taking up his seat in the Commons.[8]

During the Great War era, Winston became a passionate enthusiast for transatlantic cooperation. He told a meeting of the Anglo-Saxon Fellowship on the Fourth of July 1918 that the Declaration of Independence in 1776 'follows on the Magna Charta and the Bill of Rights as the third great title deed on which the liberties of the English-speaking peoples are founded'. After the current war, he declared, Britain's reward for victory would not be territory or commerce but the 'supreme reconciliation' of the two countries after the 'reproaches' and 'blunders' of the last century and a half: 'That is the reward of Britain: that is the lion's share.' He told a friend: 'If all goes well, England and [the] US may act permanently together. We are living 50 years in one at this rate.'[9]

It was during those heady days in 1918 that Winston first met Franklin Roosevelt, at a banquet for Allied ministers of war in London on 29 July. In his memoirs of the Second World War, published in 1948, Winston wrote vividly of their brief encounter, claiming that, although 'there had been no opportunity for anything but salutations . . . I had been struck by his magnificent presence in all his youth and strength.' In fact, Winston entirely forgot the occasion, while FDR nursed a lasting grudge. In December 1939 the President said, 'I have always disliked him since the time I went over to England in 1918. He acted like a stinker at a dinner I attended, lording it all over us.'

A year later FDR remarked that Churchill was 'one of the few men in public life who was rude to me'.[10]

Winston's grandiose vision of transatlantic amity faded fast after the end of the Great War. He was appalled when the US Senate refused to ratify the Treaty of Versailles and with it the League of Nations. On 30 November 1919, in an article entitled 'Will America Fail Us?', he told readers that 'a more melancholy page in human history could hardly be conceived. We cannot believe it would be written by American hands.'[11] He did not abandon hope, accepting election as President of the English-Speaking Union in 1921, but his term as Chancellor of the Exchequer in 1924–9 was dogged by transatlantic wrangles over the US demand for rapid British repayment of its war debts and about taxation of American profits from movies shown in Britain, estimated at £25 million a year. But the most fractious issue was America's determination to build a 'navy second to none'. Winston even told the Cabinet in July 1927 that although it was doubtless 'quite right in the interests of peace' to keep saying that war with America was 'unthinkable', in fact 'everyone knows this is not true.' However 'foolish and disastrous such a war would be, we do not wish to put ourselves in the power of the United States. We cannot tell what they might do if at some future date they were in a position to give us orders about our policy, say, in India, or Egypt, or Canada, or on any other matter behind which their electioneering forces were marshalled.' That November, one of Clementine's letters to Winston even mentioned 'your known hostility' to America.[12]

It was therefore in a positive but wary mood that Winston took advantage of the Tory defeat in 1929 to make an extended trip around North America – his first since 1901. 'I have never been west of Winnipeg or Milwaukee,' he told one American tycoon. He ended up spending much of October in New York, where he witnessed first-hand the Wall Street Crash in the company of bankers, financiers and 'former' millionaires. Winston himself suffered severe financial losses but offset them by writing twenty-four lucrative articles for the British and American press. In these he extolled the marvels of modern technological America and shrugged off the Crash – 'cruel as it is to thousands' – as 'only a passing episode in the march of a valiant and serviceable people who by fierce experiment are hewing new paths for man'. For him, the North American grand tour was a huge tonic.[13]

While in Manhattan he had hoped to meet Roosevelt, now Governor of New York state, but their diaries did not coincide. FDR was now very different from the man Winston had met in London a decade before. In the election campaign of 1920, he was chosen by the Democrats as their vice-presidential candidate and, although unsuccessful, was widely seen as a coming man – handsome, imposing, articulate, and bearing a famous name. (Former President Teddy Roosevelt, though a Republican, was a distant cousin and FDR had married his niece, Eleanor.) But in August 1921, nearing forty, FDR contracted polio, losing all power in his legs. The next year or so was such acute agony that his doting mother begged him to accept living out his days as a crippled country gentleman on the family estate in the Hudson Valley. Yet FDR persuaded himself that somehow he would walk again and spent most of the 1920s trying to do so. His efforts were in vain but he did develop his upper body immensely, giving him the strength to manoeuvre around on cane and leg-braces, usually supported by a strong but discreet male arm. Remarkably, the extent of his disability remained a closely guarded secret. No photos or film showed him in a wheelchair or being heaved out of a car. Such secrecy was vital because FDR never abandoned his political ambitions. When he walked up to the platform at the Democratic National Convention in June 1928, leaning on the arm of his son Elliott, to formally nominate Al Smith for the presidency, those watching concluded, to quote one biographer, that FDR had recovered from polio and was not 'crippled' but merely 'lame'.[14]

The 1928 presidential election turned into a disaster for the Democrats. The Republican Herbert Hoover surged into the White House, picking up all but eight of the forty-eight states. Yet, bucking the trend, FDR won the governorship of New York and assiduously exploited it as a platform for a presidential bid in 1932. This was presumably why Winston had sought a meeting in 1929: apart from his desire to 'see the country', he wished to 'meet the leaders of its fortune' and FDR was clearly someone to watch.[15]

After Roosevelt was inaugurated as America's thirty-second President in March 1933, Winston sent him the first instalment of what became a four-volume biography of his martial ancestor, John Churchill, first Duke of Marlborough. The inscription read: 'With earnest best wishes for the success of the greatest crusade of modern times.'[16] But where was that crusade going? Winston was not sure. His various comments on FDR's New Deal were laudatory about the man but wary about his policies.

In an essay published on 29 December 1934, Winston described Roosevelt as 'an explorer who has embarked on a voyage as uncertain as that of Columbus, and upon a quest which might conceivably be as important as the discovery of the New World'. Warning notes then followed thick and fast. About the extent of presidential power amid a national emergency: 'Although the Dictatorship is veiled by constitutional forms, it is none the less effective.' And about the growing 'mood to hunt down rich men as if they were noxious beasts' – observing that 'this money-gathering, credit-producing animal can not only walk – he can run', taking capitalism with him. Summing up the dangers lurking in the Roosevelt era, Winston wrote: 'it seems that forces are gathering under his shield which at a certain stage may thrust him into the background and take the lead themselves.' But when in October 1937 he included the essay in *Great Contemporaries*, he added a further paragraph saying that, however this presidency was viewed, 'it is certain that Franklin Roosevelt will rank among the greatest of men who have occupied that proud position.'[17]

By now FDR had turned his mind to foreign affairs. His animosity to Hitler's Germany was more personal and ideological than that of Churchill, who focused on historic Prussian traits of aggressive militarism. On 4 January 1939 the President devoted his annual State of the Union address to 'storms from abroad'. He warned that 'God-fearing democracies of the world' could not 'safely be indifferent to international lawlessness anywhere' and that the days of isolationism were numbered. 'Events abroad have made it increasingly clear to the American people that dangers within are less to be feared than dangers from without . . . Once I prophesied that this generation of Americans had a rendezvous with destiny. That prophecy comes true. To us much is given; more is expected.'[18]

No names were mentioned, but to an American audience mindful of the Sudetenland and of the *Kristallnacht* pogroms against the Jews, FDR's meaning was clear. It was certainly not lost on the Führer, who responded directly in his address to the Reichstag on 30 January 1939, the sixth anniversary of taking power. Professing, as usual, his peaceful intentions in seeking living space (*Lebensraum*) for Germany, he warned that if the 'Jewish media' in the USA, and their allies in British and American politics, were obstructive, then National Socialism was ready for battle. And he replied to the President's 'prophecy' with one of his own: 'Once again I will be a prophet: should international finance-Jewry (*Finanzjudentum*), inside and outside Europe, succeed in plunging mankind into yet another world war, then the result will not be a Bolshevisation of the earth and the victory of Jewry, but the annihilation (*Vernichtung*) of the Jewish race in Europe.'[19]

January 1939 drew crucial ideological battle lines. Hitler's prophecy is the more famous – prefiguring his war of extermination against the Jews – but Roosevelt's is equally important for the contest that followed. It signalled the globalism, both geopolitical and ideological, that would underpin his subsequent foreign policy in ways that would affect not only his enemies but also his allies.

The President's aim in 1938–9 was to bolster British determination to stand up to Hitler and to halt continued appeasement, which he attributed to the corrosive effects of 'too much Eton and Oxford'. In February 1939 he remarked (in a letter intended to get back to London), 'What the British need today is a good stiff grog, inducing not only the desire to save civilization but the continued belief that they can do it. In such an event they will have a lot more support from their American cousins.'[20] Given this outlook, it's not surprising that FDR kept his eye open for British politicians with plenty of 'grog'. Or that, when Britain finally went to war with Germany, he reached out directly to Winston in a personal letter dated 11 September 1939, deftly hung on his earlier enjoyment of 'the Marlboro volumes' and pleasure that Churchill was now 'back again at the Admiralty' after the two of them had 'occupied similar positions' in the previous war. 'What I want you and the Prime Minister to know is that I shall at all times welcome it if you will keep me in touch personally with anything you want me to know about.'[21] FDR – always eager to circumvent the 'striped pants set' in the State Department – wrote in similar vein to Chamberlain, but it was Winston who took up the invitation. During the Phoney War of 1939–40 he sent the President periodic titbits of war news, using the hardly opaque codename 'Naval Person'.

Winston's suspicions of America during the 1920s were now ancient history. 'Everyone', he wrote in 1935, 'can see the arguments against the English-speaking peoples becoming the policemen of the world. The only thing that could be said upon the other side is that if they did so none of us would ever live to see another war.'[22] Despite such rhetoric, Winston still acknowledged in 1937 (as in the 1920s) that, while 'the ideals of the countries are similar, their interests are in many ways divergent', and he had no intention of surrendering Britain's position as a world power: 'I want to see the British Empire preserved for a few more generations in its strength and splendour.'[23] Roosevelt did not.

* * *

These underlying tensions did not disappear when Winston became Prime Minister. On 12 May 1940 – according to Harold Ickes, FDR's Interior Secretary – 'the President said that he supposed Churchill was the best man England had, even if he was drunk half of his time.'[24] Winston's taste for liquor was common gossip in Administration circles, lubricated from London by US Ambassador Joseph Kennedy who warned FDR during 1939 that Churchill had 'developed into a fine two-handed drinker', that his judgment had 'never been proven to be good' and that his rich American friends, mostly Republican critics of the New Deal, were 'definitely . . . not on our team'.[25]

Whether or not he was aware of his reputation in the White House, Winston – now writing as 'Former Naval Person' – intensified his wooing of FDR as France collapsed and the US emerged as Britain's only serious hope of eventual victory, perhaps even survival. But there was an interesting contrast between his postures in public and in private. His hortatory speeches depicted US entry into the war as inevitable and probably imminent. Notes for his address to the Commons on 20 June read: 'All depends upon our resolute bearing and holding out until Election issues are settled there. If we can do so, I cannot doubt the whole English-speaking world will be in line together.' He also frequently insisted that the bombing of Britain would have a profound emotional effect in the US, 'especially in those many towns in the New World which bore the same names as towns in the British Isles'. Years later Charles de Gaulle could still vividly recall Winston at Chequers that summer, raising his fists to the sky and shouting 'So they won't come!' The Free French leader asked why he was in 'such a hurry' to see his towns 'smashed to bits', only to be told that 'the bombing of Oxford, Coventry, Canterbury will cause such a wave of indignation in the United States that they'll come into the war'.[26]

That outburst is a reminder that Winston's acquaintance with America, though intense, was also limited. He had mixed mostly with the Republican elite – WASP or Jewish – on the east and west coasts, and had little feel for the ethnic diversity of the country's heartland or its big cities. Convinced of the ties of kinship and language among 'the English-speaking peoples', he told the Commons on 20 August that henceforth the British Empire and the United States would 'have to be somewhat mixed up in some of their affairs for mutual and general advantage'. This, he declared, was a process no one could stop:

'Like the Mississippi, it just keeps rolling along. Let it roll. Let it roll on full flood, inexorable, irresistible, benignant, to broader lands and better days.'[27]

Despite such grandiloquence in public, the private Winston was more cautious. In May and June, FDR dragged his feet on Churchill's repeated requests for 'the loan of forty or fifty of your older destroyers'. This would, of course, be not at all a neutral act – and would therefore probably require Congressional consent – but in any case, FDR was far from confident that Britain could avoid France's fate. Trying to exploit Britain's limited leverage, Winston warned on 20 May that, although he personally would fight to the end, if 'others came to parley amid the ruins, you must not be blind to the fact that the sole remaining bargaining counter would be the fleet, and if this country was left by the United States to its fate no one would have the right to blame those then responsible if they made the best terms they could for the surviving inhabitants.'[28] These words had no effect. In June the PM was slow to take up FDR's offer of secret military staff talks, noting initially, 'I think they would turn almost entirely on the American side upon the transfer of the British fleet to transatlantic bases.'[29]

During August, FDR agreed to provide the destroyers, once persuaded that he might be able to avoid Congress by using an executive agreement. He was also more confident about Britain's chances, which on 7 July he had rated as 'about one in three'. But the US army and navy could not legally give away weapons and equipment (even if obsolescent) without guaranteeing that to do so would enhance the defence of the United States. So FDR decided he needed some 'molasses' to sweeten the pill: first, a public assurance that the British fleet would never be allowed to fall into German hands; second, leases of land on some British possessions in the Caribbean and Western Atlantic where the US could build air and naval bases. His intent was to demonstrate that the arrangements strengthened the defence of the western hemisphere rather than, as Winston wanted, signalling a move into the British camp. The PM kept trying to play hardball, telling the

FO firmly, 'It doesn't do to give way like this to the Americans. One must strike a balance with them.' But FDR not only stuck to his guns about the fleet, he also upped his demand for base leases from three to eight – all for ninety-nine years. The Colonial Office was furious, and some fifty MPs protested about what seemed likely to prove a perpetual transfer of British territory.[30]

Churchill knew there was no choice. His consolation was that the President had clearly taken a huge step towards aligning his country with the British cause. In concrete terms, however, the bases were clearly worth much more than the old destroyers – only nine of which had entered service with the Royal Navy by the end of 1940.[31] Nor did Roosevelt's third-term victory on 5 November prove as decisive as Winston and many in London had predicted. After sorting out his new team, the exhausted President went off for a fishing cruise in the Caribbean, and Winston told the Cabinet on 2 December that he had been 'rather chilled' by the American attitude since the election.[32] It was Lord Lothian, the British ambassador in Washington, who broke the transatlantic logjam. He and the Foreign Office persuaded the PM to put 'all our cards on the table' in a lengthy, 4,000-word letter setting out Britain's looming shortages of shipping, munitions and finance and spelling out in detail what was needed from the US. This remarkably candid state paper went through several iterations. Winston signed off by asking the President to regard it 'not as an appeal for aid, but as a statement of the minimum action necessary to the achievement of our common purpose.'[33]

The letter, which Winston later called 'one of the most important I ever wrote',[34] forced Roosevelt to consider Britain's predicament as a whole. When he came back, refreshed, from the Caribbean, FDR told the press on 17 December that it was in the interests of US rearmament to take over 'a very large number' of future British war orders to galvanise US production and then arrange for 'their use by the British' on the understanding that 'when the show was over, we would get repaid sometime in kind'. This would avoid 'a dollar debt' (as after the Great War) by substituting 'a gentleman's obligation to repay in kind'. These studiously chatty remarks raised more questions than they answered, but their underlying dynamic was clear. As Treasury Secretary Henry Morgenthau bluntly informed one emissary from Whitehall: 'It gets down to a question of Mr Churchill putting himself in Mr Roosevelt's hands with complete confidence. Then it is up to Mr Roosevelt to say what he will do.'[35]

After FDR's dramatic press conference, Winston got that message loud and clear. A few weeks later he suppressed his private fury on learning that the President had unilaterally sent a US warship to Cape Town to commandeer £50 million of British-owned gold as cover for some of London's immediate purchases. Instead of his draft likening the action to 'a sheriff collecting the last assets of a helpless debtor', he was persuaded to send Roosevelt an 'unclouded' message of praise for a recent radio 'fireside chat' about foreign policy. When his old crony Lord Beaverbrook enjoined him to 'Stand Up to the Democrats' and not sell off the rest of Britain's US assets at knock-down prices, Winston told the Cabinet that 'a few weeks ago' he would have agreed but 'no longer did so, since it was clear that we should receive from America far more than we could possibly give'. Nor did he fuss about the extensive sites and generous rights demanded by the US on the Caribbean leases in return for the destroyers – ignoring Lord Lloyd, the Colonial Secretary, who privately described the Americans as 'gangsters'. The PM and the Cabinet were adamant that the Lend-Lease bill was of 'overriding importance' and 'other matters must give way before it.'[36]

When FDR finally signed the Lend-Lease Act into law on 11 March 1941, after a bruising two-month battle on Capitol Hill, Winston lauded this 'new Magna Carta' and declared that 'the most powerful democracy' in the world had effectively 'declared in solemn Statute that they will devote their overwhelming industrial and financial strength to ensuring the defeat of Nazism'.[37] But it would be months before Lend-Lease aid made a difference, and meanwhile the British Army were beaten in Libya by Rommel and then driven out of Greece. Depressed, on 4 May Churchill sent FDR a new appeal to enter the war – his first since June 1940 – arguing that only this act could counter 'the growing pessimism' internationally about Britain.[38]

In retrospect, Hitler's invasion of the USSR on 22 June proved a turning point in the conflict, but at the time Soviet belligerency was seen in London and Washington as a temporary respite because of deep doubts about the Red Army. The lull did, however, enable the two leaders finally to meet in person. Their long-awaited rendezvous took place on 9–12 August, in a secluded bay off the coast of Newfoundland. The optics were enormously important, especially photos and footage of Prime Minister and President, surrounded by their top brass and the crews of British and US warships, sharing in a worship service on the deck of HMS *Prince of Wales* and singing familiar hymns such as 'Onward, Christian Soldiers'. On a personal level, however, things got off to a bad start during their first lunch, because Winston was still sure he had 'never had the pleasure of meeting President Roosevelt' – reviving FDR's bad memories of that dinner in 1918.[39] But the two men soon hit it off, working and social-ising together intensely. 'He is a tremendously vital person,' FDR told his cousin Daisy Suckley. 'I like him – & lunching alone broke the ice both ways.' The rapport was mutual. The PM 'was greatly taken with him', King George VI noted, 'and has come back feeling that he knows him'.[40] For the first time, too, Winston began to appreciate the extent of the President's disability, and also the grace and courage with which he coped, every waking hour.

Nevertheless, Winston did not get what he came for. 'I must say', he had written to the Queen before leaving London, 'I do not think our friend would have asked me to go so far for what must be a meeting of world-wide importance, unless he had in mind some further forward step.' What Winston clearly anticipated was a pledge that the US would soon become a full belligerent. But instead of a declaration of war, he was given a declaration of war aims.[41] What's more, this was sprung on him without prior notice. FDR proposed the idea over dinner on the first evening, and Sir Alexander Cadogan of the FO, accompanying the PM, had to work up a first draft next morning over his bacon and eggs. Redrafts followed from both sides as the Americans tried to advance their goal of eroding the British Empire, both as a commercial bloc (protected by Imperial Preference) and as a colonial system. Indeed, point three of what became known as the 'Atlantic Charter' started causing problems within days. It stated that Britain and America 'respect the right of all peoples to choose the form of government under which they will live; and they wish to see sovereign rights and self-government restored to those who have been forcibly deprived of them'. Winston insisted that this applied primarily to Nazi-occupied Europe, but in colonial Asia and Africa it was promptly hailed as having global applicability, not least for subjects of a British Empire that had been largely created by force. It is likely that this was always FDR's intention. On 2 January 1942, he told the press that the Charter 'referred to the whole world'. Leo Amery, Secretary of State for India, moaned in his diary: 'We shall no doubt pay dearly in the end for all the fluffy flapdoodle.'[42]

Seeking to counter the feeling in London that the meeting had been something of a 'flop', Winston told his Cabinet that the fact of the US, 'still technically a neutral, joining with a belligerent power in making such a Declaration is astonishing'. He also stressed FDR's problems on Capitol Hill, quoting him to say that 'if he were to put the issue of peace and war to Congress, they would debate it for three months.' The President had therefore 'said he would wage war, but not declare it, and that he would become more provocative. If the Germans did not like it, they could attack American forces.' According to Winston, FDR said that 'he would look for an "incident" which would justify him in opening hostilities.'[43]

In the end, it was the Axis powers which forced the issue. First, Japan's devastating surprise attack on the US fleet at Pearl Harbor on 7 December left Congress no choice but to accept that a state of war now existed in the Pacific. And then on the 11th, Hitler cut through the Atlantic deadlock by declaring war on the United States. The PM was, of course, delighted. Not only had his lengthy court-ship finally paid off, but he now anticipated a more equal relationship with America and its delphic President. When a senior officer proposed a deferential response to some US proposal, he answered – with what Sir Alan Brooke, Chief of the Imperial General Staff, called 'a wicked leer' in his eye – 'Oh! That is the way we talked to her while we were wooing her; now that she is in the harem, we talk to her quite differently!'[44]

* * *

Up to a point Winston was right: after Pearl Harbor, his relationship with Roosevelt did prove more equal. During 1942 and through the summer of 1943 he was able to shape Allied strategy in the direction he wanted, by drawing the US into Britain's imperial war in the Mediterranean as an aspect of 'closing the ring' from all sides on Hitler's Reich. This was also a period of particular closeness with Roosevelt. But the balance would shift significantly in 1944–5, and with it much of the personal intimacy: their first meeting with Stalin, at Tehran in November 1943, was a turning point.

Japan's entry into the war did not take the two leaders by surprise. But its impact certainly did. The air strike on Pearl Harbor sank or badly damaged eight US battleships and killed more than 2,400 personnel. What's more, it was just one of eight separate assaults across the Pacific on 7–8 December, timed in close sequence over thousands of miles of ocean from Hawaii and Guam to Thailand and Singapore. On the 9th, Churchill cabled Roosevelt, effectively inviting himself to Washington in order to 'review the whole war plan in the light of reality and new facts'. He argued that this was a matter which 'best be settled at the highest executive level', adding that 'it would also be a very great pleasure to meet you again, and the sooner the better.' [45] Unspoken was Winston's fear that, left to itself, the US might pivot towards the Pacific in a war of revenge against Japan, thereby diverting vital supplies away from Britain and Russia. He had expected to stay in the British Embassy in Washington, but the President invited him to the White House, where he resided on and off for three weeks in the second-floor Rose Suite, converting the nearby Monroe Room into his Map Room. During that time the two leaders got to know each other much better, spending hours in well-lubricated conversation often into the early hours. On one occasion, FDR was wheeled into Churchill's suite, only to find the PM emerging from the bathroom, naked apart from a large towel. Roosevelt began to withdraw but Winston beckoned him back: 'The Prime Minister of Great Britain has nothing to conceal from the President of the United States.'[46]

During the sea crossing, he spent much time preparing three major strategy papers, determined to get his oar in first.[47] The German war had to be won on terms that benefited the British Empire. Hence his insistence in a paper entitled 'The Atlantic Front' that 'a campaign must be fought in 1942 to gain possession of, or conquer, the whole of the North African shore', including Vichy French territories. This would be a prelude to 'the Campaign of 1943' against occupied Europe. Winston's scenario for this campaign was significantly different from what transpired on D-Day. His paper envisaged 'the liberation of the countries of Western and Southern Europe' by 'the landing at suitable points, successively or simultaneously, of British and American armies strong enough to enable the conquered peoples to revolt'. He did not anticipate that 'great numbers of men would be required', proposing a total strike force equivalent to forty armoured divisions, backed up by a million support troops. 'If the incursion of armoured forces is successful, the uprising of the local population, for whom weapons must be brought, would supply the corpus of the liberating offensive.' If the Allies held to this course, he predicted, 'we might hope, even if no German collapse occurs beforehand, to win the war at the end of 1943 or [in] 1944.'[48]

Armoured landings at several points around the coast of occupied Europe, designed to trigger revolts by the subjugated population – this was a far cry from Operation Overlord, the D-Day invasion of Normandy. Nor, in 1941, did the PM offer a clear scenario for ending the war. Summing up the vision he delivered to the British Chiefs of Staff, Winston spoke of three phases: 'closing the ring', then 'liberating the populations', followed by 'final assault on the German citadel'.[49] The first phase corresponds to his paper on 'The Atlantic Front'; the second to 'The Campaign of 1943'. But nowhere did he explain how the German citadel itself would be subdued (as distinct from liberating the occupied territories), perhaps entertaining hazy hopes of replicating the precipitous collapse of German willpower in 1918 – starting with Bulgaria and the Balkans – that he had recalled to the Commons in June 1940.

Of course, it was impossible, amid the chaotic global kaleidoscope in December 1941, to foresee how the war might end. And it's hard to think of anyone else, on the Allied side or the Axis, who could have authored documents of such range and force: as an essayist on grand strategy, Winston had no peers. But it's important to understand that his aim in the winter of 1941–2 was not to predict the course of the war with strategic clairvoyance but to win immediate diplomatic battles through rhetorical power. And that, in large measure, he did. For a while. 'Closing the ring' would indeed become the British and American strategy for 1942–3. But the 'campaign of 1943' did not start until June 1944; and thereafter, unlike 1918, the German citadel did not crumble – far from it. In that final battle to overcome Hitler's Reich, Winston would no longer call the shots.

This was down the road, however. In 1942, relations between the two leaders were cordial. Thanking the PM for birthday greetings on 30 January, FDR cabled, 'It is fun to be in the same decade as you.' When news came through in mid-February of the surrender of Singapore, the President encouraged Winston not to take too seriously the 'back seat drivers' because he enjoyed 'the great of confidence of the masses of the British people'. FDR added: 'I think of you often and I know you will not hesitate to ask me if there is anything you think I can do.' In March he advised Winston 'to take a leaf out of my notebook. Once a month I go to Hyde Park for four days, crawl into a hole and pull the hole in after me. I am called on the telephone only if something of really great importance occurs. I wish you would try it, and I wish you would lay a few bricks or paint another picture.'

Sage advice, but unlike FDR's family home, in the Hudson Valley, Winston's country retreat of Chartwell was closed up – and in any case Winston was not Franklin.[50]

A flash of Rooseveltian generosity that year, which Winston never forgot, occurred on 21 June 1942. During his second visit to Washington, he was sitting in the President's study when a telegram arrived. After a glance, FDR passed it, without comment, to the PM. 'Tobruk has surrendered, with 25,000 men taken prisoners.' This was the second time in four months that troops of the British Empire had capitulated to much smaller forces. 'I did not attempt to hide from the President the shock I had received,' Winston wrote later. But what he remembered almost as much as this humiliating news was the 'sympathy and chivalry' of FDR's response. 'There were no reproaches; not an unkind word was spoken.' The President simply asked, 'What can we do to help?' The PM immediately requested as many Sherman tanks as possible to help defend Egypt. General George C. Marshall, the Army Chief of Staff, agreed to send 300 tanks to the Mediterranean theatre, taking them away from his own under-equipped armoured divisions. 'A friend in need is a friend indeed,' Winston observed.[51]

During this transatlantic visit Winston was invited to stop over at Hyde Park. As the President drove them around the family estate, Winston gained a new glimpse of how FDR had mastered his infirmity. Because Roosevelt could not use his feet on the pedals, 'an ingenious arrangement enabled him to do everything with his arms, which were amazingly strong and muscular. He invited me to feel his biceps, saying that a famous prize fighter had envied them. This was reassuring; but I confess that when on several occasions the car poised and backed on the grass verges of the precipes over the Hudson, I hoped the mechanical devices would show no defects.'[52]

Despite the two men's growing intimacy, however, Singapore and Tobruk took a heavy toll on the transatlantic relationship. British power was clearly waning – the lion was losing its teeth – and once the shock of Pearl Harbor had passed and US mobilisation was underway, Roosevelt began to assert himself diplomatically against Churchill. During March 1942 he made three major moves. One was to flag up his growing interest in Stalin. In a chatty letter to the PM on 18 March, he wrote, 'I know you will not mind my being brutally frank when I tell you that I think I can personally handle Stalin better than either your Foreign Office or my State Department. Stalin hates the guts of all your top people. He thinks he likes me better, and I hope he will continue to do so.' Considering that FDR had never met Stalin and had exchanged little more than a dozen messages, this was pretty rich – but the breezy tone and brash self-confidence were typical of Roosevelt. And the conviction that he could 'personally handle Stalin' would soon become the President's mantra.[53]

A second issue was India. Not sharing Winston's devotion to the British Empire and anxious to galvanise the Indian war effort against Japan, already deep into neighbouring Burma, on 10 March FDR offered – with 'much diffidence' – some historical advice. Why not emulate the Articles of Confederation that the independent American colonies had adopted in 1783–9, until able to agree a Federal Constitution? In this way 'a temporary Dominion government' might be established in India, charged with preparing the way for 'a more permanent govern-ment' after the war. But Winston was totally opposed to conceding Dominion status to India, which would have put it on the same footing as 'White Dominions' such as Australia and Canada. Nor would he tolerate crude history lessons from a foreigner, even the leader of the Great Republic. When the president's aide Harry Hopkins, visiting London in April, tried to press the issue, he claimed that 'the string of cuss words lasted for two hours in the middle of the night.' Indeed, Winston warned that, if pressed, this would be a resignation issue: 'I could not be responsible for a policy which would throw the whole sub-continent of India into utter confusion while the Japanese invader is at its gates.' Roosevelt never raised the matter directly again.[54]

Third, and most immediately important of his March initiatives, Roosevelt tried to assert himself with respect to Allied strategy. Concerned to head off 'Pacific First' sentiment and to relieve the Red

Army by getting US troops into action against Germans as soon as possible, the President threw his weight behind the War Department's plan to concentrate resources for an early cross-Channel invasion of occupied France, ideally in 1942. This was a deliberate riposte to Winston's conception of gradually 'closing the ring' on Nazi Europe, based on two simple principles: that the shortest route to Germany ran through France and that Britain offered a secure and well-fortified base only twenty-one miles from the French coast. In April 1942 FDR told Winston this plan had 'my heart and *mind* in it' and sent over Marshall, backed by Hopkins, as his emissaries.[55]

The US War Department wanted an immediate and massive build-up of forces in Britain prior to an invasion of France in the spring of 1943 (codenamed Operation Roundup), involving thirty US and eighteen British divisions. It also floated the possibility of a limited 'emergency' landing of five divisions in the autumn of 1942 (Operation Sledgehammer) if the Germans had been 'critically weakened', or if the Soviet position had become desperate. In April, Winston and his advisers did their best to sound enthusiastic, fearful lest any coolness and questioning might push the US towards the Pacific and weaken Soviet morale. Having read 'your masterly document', Winston cabled FDR, 'I am in entire agreement in principle with all you propose, and so are the Chiefs of Staff.' Despite those words 'in principle', the British were full of doubt about the practicalities. Mere 'castles in the air' was the private opinion of General Sir Alan Brooke, Chief of the Imperial General Staff.[56]

The Achilles heel of Marshall's plan was the phrase that Sledgehammer 'should be considered a sacrifice for the common good'.[57] But whose 'good'? And whose 'sacrifice'? By May 1942 it was clear that the British would have to make the sacrifice: only one combat-ready US division would have reached the UK by the summer because of the crisis in the Pacific. Effectively holding a power of veto over any European operation in 1942, Winston pressed his advantage when the two leaders and their staffs met again in Washington in mid-June, urging his 'closing the ring' plan for landings in French North Africa to advance the desert war to a successful conclusion. Marshall opposed a new Mediterranean operation. But Roosevelt wanted to ensure US troops went into battle against the Germans in 1942, in order to divert US public opinion from its fixation with Japan. Since the British could not be convinced to cross the Channel in 1942, he swung behind Winston's plan for landings in North Africa, Operation Torch. It was a signal success for the PM and the only time that Roosevelt, as Commander-in-Chief, overruled his own Joint Chiefs of Staff. Yet it would turn out that 'the president had made the most profound American strategic decision of the European war' – locking the US into the Mediterranean conflict for nearly two years.[58]

That was not FDR's intention. Like Churchill, he asserted that North Africa in 1942 would not prejudice the chances of invading France in 1943. Marshall, however, flatly disagreed – better understanding the logistical consequences of Operation Torch as a 'suction pump', drawing resources away from the build-up in Britain. Afterwards he said, with some bitterness, that 'we failed to see that the leader in a democracy has to keep the people entertained. That may not be the right word, but it conveys the thought . . . People demand action.' His recognition that politicians must keep doing 'something' in order to sustain popular interest and attention is an uncanny echo of Winston's refrain when Chancellor of the Exchequer in the 1920s.[59]

At first all went well. The landings on 8 November around Algiers, Oran and Casablanca were successful and Vichy forces soon surrendered. The following day Winston told his Chiefs of Staff: 'In a month French North Africa should be comfortably and securely in Allied hands.' On 3 December he remained optimistic that 'by the end of the year we may be masters of the whole of French North Africa including Tunisia.' He began to draw up plans for an invasion of France in July 1943 involving thirty-five divisions.[60] Such hopes evaporated, however, as the winter rains turned North Africa's roads and airfields into mud. And Allied intelligence never expected Hitler to reinforce Tunisia with such strength and speed – even at the expense of his vital battle at Stalingrad. As a result, Tunis did not fall until May 1943, making it impossible to move troops and resources back to Britain in time to attack occupied France before the autumnal Channel storms. The new target date for an invasion (codenamed Operation Overlord) was May 1944.

What, then, to do in 1943? With the US Navy obsessed with the Pacific, and the army determined to resume the build-up in Britain, American strategic planning was gridlocked. As a result the British, united and well organised, ran rings around them when Churchill and Roosevelt met for their next strategic conference in Casablanca in January 1943. The fact that Winston now had his eye on Italy greatly dismayed Marshall, still worried about the Mediterranean 'suction pump'. But, given the need to show Stalin that his Western Allies were doing some fighting against the Germans, it was hard to deny the logic of British arguments that the Allies should at least move from Tunisia to Sicily. This would give them the air and naval bases to ensure full control of the Mediterranean. But when the invasion of Sicily on 10 July precipitated the downfall of Mussolini, the Allies crossed to the toe of Italy on 3 September and the new Italian government sought an armistice. Intelligence intercepts from Ultra suggested that the Germans were likely to pull out of Rome and try to hold a line along the River Po in the mountainous north. This would give the Allies a network of airfields from which to pound the industrial centres of southern Germany. Winston also believed that, if the Allies moved quickly, before the Germans, they could take over from surrendering Italian troops on key Mediterranean islands such as Rhodes, and in the Balkans. He hoped this abrupt shift of power in the region might trigger a 1918-style disintegration of the German 'citadel' from within.[61]

But the PM's optimism about German morale was proved wrong. Hitler decided to fight for Rome and his troops also seized Italy's Mediterranean islands, committing numerous atrocities on the inhabitants. As in North Africa in late 1942, the Führer's obduracy ensured that there would be no cheap victories in the Mediterranean. And so, after a year in which Winston had managed – against the odds – to call the shots, FDR shifted back towards his military planners. He resisted the PM's pleas in early October to divert troops and landing craft to seize the islands of Rhodes, Leros and Cos, stating firmly, 'It is my opinion that no diversion of forces or equipment should prejudice OVERLORD as planned. The American Chiefs of Staff agree.'[62] In his memoirs Winston called this rebuttal 'one of the sharpest pangs I suffered in the war', but said he accepted it rather than 'risk any jar in my personal relations with the President'. (An early draft called this 'the only ungenerous act which I experienced in our long military partnership' – one for which he blamed the 'prejudice' of FDR's advisers.)[63]

In fact, Winston's own military were close to despair about the PM's obsession with Rhodes. On the importance of Italy, however, there was unanimity. Summing up a highly charged meeting in London on 19 October, Winston said 'it was clear that if we were in a position to decide the future strategy of the war', the top priorities would be to 'reinforce the Italian theatre to the full' and 'enter the Balkans'. Overlord came fifth and last. As Cadogan of the Foreign Office put it: 'all this "Overlord" folly must be thrown "Overboard." '[64]

Winston did not conceal his lurking fears from the President. 'Unless there is a German collapse', he wrote on 17 October, 'the campaign of 1944 will be far the most dangerous we have undertaken and personally I am more anxious about its success than I was about 1941, 1942 and 1943.' By implication, this put 1944 on a par with 1940: indeed, that was Winston's darkest nightmare about Overlord. Although telling the Chiefs of Staff that he 'felt we should probably effect a lodgement and in the first instance we might make progress', he feared that the Germans would be able to shift troops across the Continent and 'inflict on us a military disaster greater than that of Dunkirk', which would lead to 'the resuscitation of Hitler and the Nazi regime'.[65]

The issue was finally thrashed out when the Big Three – Churchill, Roosevelt and Josef Stalin – met at Tehran at the end of November. Opening the conference, Roosevelt indicated that 'in his opinion the large cross-channel operation should not be delayed by secondary operations.' Stalin agreed. He reckoned that 'Hitler was endeavoring to retain as many allied divisions as possible in Italy where no decision could be reached, and that the best method in the Soviet opinion was getting at Germany through an attack through northern or northwestern France and even through southern France.'[66] Two against one: at Tehran Churchill was outnumbered. After the conference he was laid low by pneumonia and heart complications, from which it took time to recover. His lassitude and despondency, noted by many of the inner circle, also stemmed from trepidation about Overlord. On 19 April he told Cadogan: 'This battle has been forced upon us by the Russians and the United States military authorities. We have gone in wholeheartedly, and I would not raise a timorous cry before a decision in the field has been taken.'[67]

Characteristically, as D-Day neared, the adrenalin began to flow and Winston decided he would watch the landings in Normandy from HMS *Belfast*, one of the bombarding destroyers and therefore a likely target of enemy fire. Only what was effectively an order from King George VI, as Commander-in-Chief of Britain's armed forces, obliged the PM grumpily to desist. Shared anxiety about D-Day brought him and Roosevelt close again, with an exchange of especially cordial messages just before the landings. FDR sent a warm personal letter, thanking Winston for a picture of him that was now on the President's bedroom wall. The PM responded that 'our friendship is my greatest stand-by amid the ever-increasing complications of this exacting war.'[68]

* * *

After D-Day, however, the 'exacting war' became yet more complicated, and personal 'friendship' counted for less and less. In the last year of his life FDR sided nearly all the time with his Joint Chiefs, while Winston chafed at being the junior partner in the transatlantic alliance. Yet, indefatigable as ever, he talked up the 'fraternal association' of their two peoples, proclaiming this as an essential bulwark against the storms of the post-war world.

Despite being outvoted by his allies over Normandy, the PM was determined to 'nourish' the Italian campaign as far as possible. Unlike France, Italy was a theatre in which Britain remained dominant. Winston told Stalin at Tehran that 'there were three or four times more British troops than American' in the Mediterranean, and that roughly ten of the fourteen divisions in Italy were British. This was reflected in the command structure. Winston said he had accepted a US commander for Normandy – General Dwight D. Eisenhower – because the Americans 'would soon have a preponderance in "Overlord" and their stake would be greater after the first few months'. On the other hand, this gesture allowed Britain to nominate its own commander in the Mediterranean, where its forces were more numerous and, the PM added – doubtless with a twinkle in his eye – he 'had his own ideas about the war'. Not surprisingly, he resisted FDR's efforts to make Marshall overall supremo for the whole European theatre. After the war, Alanbrooke recalled Churchill's deep 'desire to form a purely British theatre when the laurels would be all ours'. As historian Sir Michael Howard observed, this 'element of sheer chauvinism' became 'an ever stronger factor in his strategic thinking as time went on' and America's vast mobilisation took full effect.[69]

Even in Italy, US troops, supplies and shipping mattered. In January the PM was able to hang on to a number of landing craft – 90 per cent of which had been built in the US – long enough to mount an amphibious landing behind enemy lines at Anzio, in the hope that this would permit a dash for Rome and break the Italian deadlock. But instead of landing 'a wild cat that would tear out the bowels' of the Germans, Winston lamented, the result was 'a vast whale' stranded on the beach 'with its tail flopping about in the water'. In February 1944 a German counterattack nearly drove the Allies back into the sea, and Rome was not liberated until 4 June – on the eve of D-Day – with the US taking most of the credit.[70]

The progress of Overlord also seemed underwhelming. The failure throughout June to break out of Normandy intensified American determination to divert resources from the Italian campaign. The US Joint

Chiefs stuck to the decision made at Tehran, and backed by Stalin, to mount a supporting invasion of southern France (then codenamed Anvil) using troops from Italy, whereas their British counterparts were now talking up the new prospects in Italy after the fall of Rome. With their military advisers deadlocked, the issue was thrashed out by FDR and Churchill, as had happened in the summer of 1942 during the clash over whether to invade France or North Africa. But by 1944 two things had changed: the balance of the alliance had shifted to the US, and FDR no longer sided with Winston. 'My interest and hopes center on defeating the Germans in front of Eisenhower and driving on to Germany,' the President cabled on 29 June, 'rather than on limiting this action for the purposes of staging a full major effort in Italy.' A furious Winston drafted a cable to FDR threatening to resign at this 'absolutely perverse strategy' – but, like other such threats in the past, the message was never sent. Instead, he eventually fired off a 'we are deeply grieved' reply, informing FDR that 'the splitting up of the campaign in the Mediterranean into two operations, neither of which can do anything decisive, is in my humble and respectful opinion, the first major strategic and political error for which we two have to be responsible.'[71]

That phrase – 'neither of which can do anything decisive' – is a revealing aside. In a lengthy note for the Cabinet on 28 June, copied to Roosevelt, Winston pointed out that Marseilles was 600 miles 'as the crow flies' from Cherbourg and 400 miles from Paris. The terrain was 'most formidable' and, without Hitler 'withdrawing a single division' from Normandy, 'we could be confronted with superior forces at every step we advance up the Rhone valley.' He doubted that the Anvil operation 'would have any tactical relation to the battle we have to fight now and throughout this summer and autumn for Overlord'.[72]

Underpinning his analysis was an essentially dated view of warfare. Winston's experience of combat had stood him in good stead during the Great War, but he was slow to grasp the new American conception of mobile warfare. Repeatedly in 1944 he mocked the US Army's use of motor transport to move troops and supplies. Told in February that there were 18,000 vehicles in the Anzio beachhead, he scoffed, 'We must have a great superiority of chauffeurs.' In June he got into a similar argument with Brooke about Normandy, insisting that what was needed were 'combatants and fighting men instead of a mass of non-combatants'. Brooke observed that 'fighting men without food, ammunition and petrol were useless', but Winston could not be persuaded. What mattered, he asserted, were 'bayonets'.[73] One senses here an essentially foot-slogging conception of war, going back to 1914–18 and perhaps even to the battles of his ancestor the Duke of Marlborough, which he had researched in the 1930s.

The object of Overlord was to gain a 'lodgement' on the continent of Europe, for which the main need was secure supply lines through Cherbourg and the Brittany ports to the *west* of Normandy. What would happen thereafter was left unclear. The official scenario among Allied planners was to push the Germans back to the Seine and the Loire within ninety days, and then regroup in September. Winston was more pessimistic. In July he opined that crossing the Seine would be 'next season's campaign' – in other words a target for 1945. This takes us back to his sweeping planning papers of December 1941, which addressed in detail 'liberating the populations' of captive Europe but never explained the 'final assault on the German citadel'. Winston seems to have imagined a similar slugging match to that of 1917–18 – unless, as he always hoped, Germany once again suddenly crumbled from within. His was a still a policy of KBO, rather than KO.[74]

The PM was therefore astounded at the end of July 1944 by the speed of the American-led breakout from Normandy. 'Good heavens, how do you feed them?' he asked. General Omar Bradley replied that they were running trucks up to the front 'bumper to bumper, twenty-four hours a day'. So much for 'chauffeurs'! When the Americans and French landed in southern France on 15 August, they captured the ports of Marseilles and Toulon in a couple of weeks, greatly easing Eisenhower's supply crisis. And, contrary to Churchill's fears, the

Rhône Valley proved a highway not a cul-de-sac: by 3 September Allied troops had surged 150 miles to Lyon. That was also the day a British armoured division liberated Brussels, because Eisenhower's forces had not paused for logistical breath at the Seine but raced onward, reaching the German border in nineteen days instead of the 260 days anticipated by the planners. Consequently, on 12 September 1944 Allied troops occupied positions they were not 'supposed' to take until 21 May 1945.[75]

What to do next opened up a major row in August and September between Eisenhower and the senior British commander, General Sir Bernard Montgomery, a national icon since his victory at Alamein in 1942. 'Monty' argued that they should exploit the German collapse by mounting a narrow-front advance into the Ruhr and on towards Berlin. There was strategic sense behind the idea, but also national pride because Monty's 21st British Army Group would take the lead. His problem was that British forces alone were insufficient and no US commander would have surrendered to 'the Brits' the necessary forces. The narrow-front idea was abandoned, but only after considerable acrimony.

What's interesting is Churchill's lack of involvement in this debate, considering that it raised such fundamental issues about Allied strategy and national status. But the PM appears not to have seen it as vital. Given his assumptions about a long slogging match in France and Germany in 1944–5, he did not believe the Third Reich was close to defeat. In any case, his attention at this time was mostly elsewhere. He spent much of August in Italy, willing on British troops to a victory beyond their grasp – though he did observe the landings in southern France from offshore in order, he told Clementine, to publicly 'associate myself with this well-conducted but irrelevant and unrelated operation'.[76] Trying to reassert his influence over FDR, he then passed most of September in the US and Canada. Further trips to Italy were arranged in October, sandwiched around a flying visit to Moscow to haggle with Stalin about spheres of influence in the Balkans. As biographer Roy Jenkins observed, in the last weary and frustrating months of Churchill's wartime premiership, it was 'movement and summitry as such which attracted him'.[77]

To round off 1944, the PM spent Christmas in Greece, supervising British troops as they tried to defeat a communist insurrection in a country of particular strategic interest to Britain. A cable from him instructing the British commander to treat Athens as if it were 'a conquered city' was leaked to the *Washington Post*, provoking an outcry in America. 'It grieves me', Churchill cabled Hopkins on 9 December, 'to see signs of our drifting apart at a time when unity becomes ever more important.'[78]

Underlying all the friction was a growing disparity in power. 'You will have the greatest navy in the world,' he told FDR on 28 November. 'You will have, I hope, the greatest air force. You will have the greatest trade. You have all the gold.' He was acutely aware of Britain's diminished leverage. 'Our armies are only about one-half the size of the American and will soon be little more one-third,' he told Jan Smuts in December, so 'it is not so easy as it used to be for me to get things done.' When failing to get his own way, he blamed the President's advisers rather than Roosevelt himself. After the blunt exchanges over Anvil, he called the US Joint Chiefs 'one of the stupidest strategic teams ever seen' – though he added that 'they are good fellows and there is no need to tell them this.'[79]

Winston also noted the effect of FDR's declining health. Although not aware of the grave diagnosis – hypertension, heart disease and anaemia – when the President finally agreed to a proper check-up in March 1944, the PM told Brooke in May that 'Roosevelt was not well' and 'was no longer the man he had been'. Winston added that the same also applied to himself. Brooke noted in his diary: 'He said he could always sleep well, eat well and especially drink well! but that he no longer jumped out of bed the way he used to, and felt as if he would be quite content to spend the whole day in bed.' Brooke had never heard such talk before.[80] Yet what most concerned Winston was the health and strength of his bond with Roosevelt. He had spent enough time with FDR over the last couple of years to see how things had changed. Keeping this relationship alive would become his preoccupation in the final months of the war.

* * *

Winston always used official conferences to contrive such moments of personal intimacy. For instance, after Casablanca in January 1943 he persuaded FDR to spend a night at Marrakech to see the Atlas Mountains – a spectacle that had first captivated him eight years before. After a 150-mile road journey taking five hours they arrived just in time to catch the sunset tinting the snow-capped peaks. 'It was so beautiful that he insisted the President must see it,' Winston's doctor noted in a long diary entry. 'Two of his servants, by holding hands, made a chair with their arms, and in this fashion he was carried up the winding stairs to the roof-top, his paralysed legs dangling like the limbs of a ventriloquist's dummy, limp and flaccid.' As they marvelled in silence at the view, Churchill whispered, 'It's the most lovely spot in the whole world.' Later, during dinner, 'the President and the PM made little affectionate speeches to each other' and sang choruses 'which grew in gusto as the night went on'. After seeing Roosevelt off the next morning, Winston climbed back to the roof of the villa, gazed again for a long time at the city of Marrakech with the purple peaks behind, and then painted the only picture he produced during the whole of his wartime premiership. He presented it to Roosevelt 'as a memento of this short interlude in the crash of war'.[81]

Similarly, when in Cairo in November 1943 before going on to Tehran, he was determined to take FDR to see the Sphinx. This was another sight close to Winston's heart, but he probably also knew that in December 1939 the Washington press corps – trying to intuit whether FDR would run for an unprecedented third term – had presented him with an eight-foot papier-mâché model of the Sphinx, the face adorned with FDR's glasses and trademark cigar holder. Greatly amused, Roosevelt acquired the model as the centrepiece of the presidential museum he opened at Hyde Park in 1941. Whatever was in Winston's mind in Cairo, he was delighted when his daughter Sarah – who accompanied him on this trip – confirmed that a journey by car was possible. Whereupon, she recalled, he 'bounded' into Roosevelt's room and declared, 'Mr. President, you simply must come to see the Sphinx and the Pyramids. I've arranged it all.' Eagerly Roosevelt leaned forward on the arms of his chair, trying for an instant to pull himself up, only to sink back again. Winston turned away, saying, 'We'll wait for you in the car.' Outside in the sunlight, Sarah could see that her father's eyes were bright with tears. 'I love that man,' he murmured.[82]

Such warmth of affection was never entirely reciprocated. Indeed, the image of the Sphinx had significance far beyond the 1940 election. Roosevelt, despite his bonhomie, was a deeply secretive man who opened himself up to very few. As he told Henry Morgenthau, one of his (relative) intimates, in 1942: 'I am a juggler, and I never let my right hand know what my left hand does ... I may have one policy for Europe and one diametrically opposite for North and South America. I may be entirely inconsistent, and furthermore I am perfectly willing to mislead and tell untruths if it will help win the war.'[83]

Nor did FDR share Winston's passion for policy and politics. At Tehran in November 1943, Eden recorded this appraisal by the PM of the President: 'FDR was "a charming country gentleman," but business methods were almost non-existent, so Winston had to play the role of courtier and seize opportunities as and when they arose.' Eden added: 'I am amazed at [the] patience with which he does this.' When asked by his doctor whether the Quebec conference with FDR in September 1944 had tired him, the PM was dismissive: 'What is this conference? Two talks with the Chiefs of Staff; the rest was waiting for the chance to put in a word with the President. One has to seize the occasion.' That he did during two days at Hyde Park, when the two men finally had a long discussion about the atomic bomb.[84]

In 1944 and 1945 Winston felt Franklin gradually slipping away from him. Their correspondence had lost much of its personal touch.

'I cannot believe any of these telegrams come from the President,' he complained to Eden in March 1944. 'They are merely put before him when he is fatigued and pushed upon us by those who are pulling him about.'[85] Hence the PM's desperate desire to break through the cocoon of FDR's advisers by way of more personal meetings – requests for which were now ignored or brushed aside. He was particularly chagrined not to be allowed quality time with the President in Malta before their conference with Stalin at Yalta. The reason became apparent when the USS *Quincy* finally docked in Valletta harbour on the morning of 2 February. 'What a change in the President since we saw him at Hyde Park,' exclaimed Winston's secretary Marian Holmes in her diary. 'He seems to have lost so much weight, has dark circles under his eyes, looks altogether frail and as if he is hardly in this world at all.' After the first session at Yalta, Eden noted in his diary: 'President vague and loose and ineffective.' Hopkins, also present, told the British later that he doubted whether FDR 'had heard more than half of what went on round the table'.[86]

Yalta was the last time they met. After the conference, Winston kept up a barrage of policy telegrams to the White House, but few of them received an answer. Learning in mid-March from Samuel Rosenman, a close friend of the President, of the full gravity of FDR's medical condition, he changed tack, sending a chatty missive of family news and reminiscences about some high points of their partnership: FDR's announcement of Lend-Lease, their Atlantic meeting in 1941, and 'when you comforted me for the loss of Tobruk by giving me the 300 Shermans of subsequent Alamein fame'. He told Roosevelt on 18 March 1945: 'Our friendship is the rock on which I build for the future of the world so long as I am one of the builders.'[87]

Here we come to the heart of what FDR meant to him. It was clear that the war, while weakening Britain, had accelerated the rise of America to what was already being called 'superpower' status. Winston hoped the relationship he had forged with the intrepid wheelchair President would ensure that Britain and its empire could continue to play a leading role in world affairs. At Harvard in

September 1943, he preached what he called 'the doctrine of fraternal association of our two peoples' for the sake of 'service to mankind' – rooted in shared values of justice and freedom and in the 'priceless inheritance' of a 'common tongue'. He told his audience: 'If we are together, nothing is impossible. If we are divided, all will fail.' He told the Foreign Office in February 1944, in the genesis of a portentous phrase: 'It is my deepest conviction that unless Britain and the United States are joined in a special relationship, including Combined Staff organisation and a wide measure of reciprocity in the use of bases – all within the ambit of a world organisation – another destructive war will come to pass.'[88]

The most urgent lesson of this war, he believed, was to avoid the mistakes made after the last – above all America's retreat into isolationism. This time the sceptre was being passed, and it was his role – as a son of both countries – to smooth and manage the transition. What particularly distressed him were FDR's periodic warnings that Congress would not tolerate a US military presence in Europe after the war was over. 'You know, of course,' the President cabled on 18 November 1944, 'that after Germany's collapse I must bring American troops home as rapidly as transportation problems will permit.' Expressing 'alarm' at this message, Winston asked how it would 'be possible to hold down Western Germany beyond the present Russian occupation line? We certainly could not undertake the task without your aid and that of the French. All would therefore rapidly disintegrate as it did last time.' At Yalta FDR did agree to give the French a full role in the occupation of Germany, but he continued to insist that he could not 'keep an army in Europe for a long time. Two years would be the limit.'[89]

In Winston's mind, therefore, a huge amount hung on what he deemed the two special relationships: those of Britain with America, and of himself with Roosevelt. The news of the President's fatal stroke on 12 April 1945, though not entirely surprising, was a devastating blow. Winston's first thought was to fly across the Atlantic to attend the funeral and talk with the new president, Harry S. Truman, but he dropped the idea at the last minute. His main reason was that Eden and other ministers were in San Francisco for the founding conference of the United Nations Organisation, but he was also conscious that his wartime coalition was near to breaking point. At any event, though often in tears, he threw himself into the memorial service at St Paul's Cathedral on the morning of 17 April and his valedictory tribute in the Commons that afternoon. Indeed, this may well have been another compelling reason for staying in London. Because – being Winston – he understood the power of words and the need to compose the first draft of history.

Passages in his valediction were deeply personal. 'I conceived an admiration for him as a statesman, a man of affairs, and a war leader. I felt the utmost confidence in his upright, inspiring character and outlook and a personal regard – affection I must say – for him beyond my power to express to-day.' Winston paid tribute to the fortitude of FDR in his personal odyssey, 'stricken and crippled as he was', calling it an 'extraordinary effort of the spirit over the flesh, the will-power over physical infirmity'. Also striking was the line that the President 'died in harness and we may well say in battle harness, like his soldiers, sailors and airmen' – after which the weary Prime Minister added, 'What an enviable death was his.' This was a thought to which Winston would often return over the next twenty years. He benchmarked Roosevelt's legacy: 'In war he had raised the strength, might and glory of the great Republic to a height never attained by any nation in history.' And he ended by calling FDR 'the greatest American friend we have ever known and the greatest champion of freedom who has ever brought help and comfort from the new world to the old'. [90]

Yet in April 1945, amid Roosevelt's death and Hitler's defeat, the war's legacy seemed uncertain. Would the United States again pull back from global responsibilities? Would a fading Britain be left to confront its own fate? Much of Winston's labour for the rest of his life would be devoted to consecrating those two conjoined special relationships – with the United States and with its presidents – that he had commenced in tandem with Franklin D. Roosevelt. Both relationships were products of wartime reality but also of his creative imagination. The America he came to love was anglophile and anglophone: bound into the 'English-speaking peoples'. He took much less account of its ethnic and sectional diversity. Similarly, his view of FDR played down the President's rooted antipathy to the British Empire and his growing determination, as the war progressed, to forge new ties with the Soviet Union.

And it is ironic that the success that Winston did achieve after 1945 in advancing the 'fraternal association' of Britain and America in fact turned less on the White House than on the Kremlin.

THE FATES DECIDE.

From his eyrie at Berchtesgaden, Hitler contemplates his future as
the Big Three draw closer (Ernest Shepard, *Punch*, 19 May 1943).
But which of the triumvirate will be the real victor?

7

Josef Stalin

The Seductions of Summitry

Perhaps you think that just because we are the allies of the English that we have forgotten who they are and who Churchill is. They find nothing sweeter than to trick their allies ... Churchill is the kind who, if you don't watch him, will slip a kopeck out of your pocket ... Roosevelt is not like that. He dips in his hand only for bigger coins.

Josef Stalin, 5 June 1944[1]

Poor Neville Chamberlain believed he could trust Hitler. He was wrong. But I don't think I'm wrong about Stalin.

Winston S. Churchill, 23 February 1945[2]

Bonding with Franklin Roosevelt was, for Winston, a genuinely 'special relationship'. More surprisingly, the same was also true with Josef Stalin. Not on account of personal affection or a sense of common values. But in the more literal sense of 'special', because Stalin stood out among Winston's great contemporaries as a totally unfamiliar human being who intrigued him deeply – far more so than the 'country gentleman' from the Hudson Valley. Such fascination was not unique to Churchill. His wartime Foreign Secretary Anthony Eden wrote in 1965 that, 'after something like thirty years' experience of international conferences of one kind or another, if I had to pick a team for going into a conference room, Stalin would be my first choice.'[3]

Winston's rapport with Stalin on a personal level coexisted with his rooted antipathy to the Soviet regime. During the civil war of 1918–21 he had been the leading exponent in the Lloyd George Cabinet of smothering Lenin's revolution in its cradle, and in the 1930s he sometimes debated whether Nazism or Bolshevism was the greater threat to Britain and its empire. However, from the moment Hitler invaded the Soviet Union (Operation Barbarossa) on 22 June 1941, Winston adopted Stalin's beleaguered country as a vital partner – a key member of what he called 'the Grand Alliance' in concert with America and Britain. But his wartime documents are full of periodic musings about the possible post-war threat from the Soviet Union, empowered and emboldened by victory. Although his darkest utterances often came at moments of particular exhaustion, the 'frenemy' counterpoint is recurrent and striking.

Essential ally yet lurking threat. How did Winston try to square the circle? As with Roosevelt and America, the answer lay in the leader himself and in that Churchillian propensity to see others in his own image. Or at least to persuade himself that, through personal contact, he could shape relationships to his and Britain's advantage. In the Soviet case, what emerged was his doctrine of 'two Stalins': on the one hand, the difficult but approachable human being; on the other, a tool of dark forces in the Kremlin. This remarkable illusion was testimony to the seductions of summitry.

*   *   *

Winston's mounting alarm during the 1930s about the menace of Hitler ended his earlier equivocations about whether fascism or communism represented the greater threat to Britain and its empire. It was a similar pattern to the way his anxieties in the 1920s about the growth of American power, especially at sea, were overshadowed. By 1938, he spoke of both the USSR and the USA as potential partners with Britain and France in the diplomatic containment of Nazi expansion. But options narrowed sharply during 1939.

On 31 March Neville Chamberlain guaranteed the independence

of Poland. This was a panicked reaction to Hitler tearing up the Munich agreement and marching into Prague. The PM was desperate to draw a line somewhere to deter further expansion, even though Britain had nothing to offer militarily if Hitler called their bluff. The Polish guarantee ruled out any chance of a meaningful alliance with the USSR, which had never accepted the post-1918 resurrection of the Polish state and against which the Bolsheviks fought a brutal war in 1920–1. Conversely, no free Polish government could imagine letting the Red Army onto its territory to fight the Germans. Lloyd George grasped this clearly, calling the guarantee an 'irresponsible gambler's throw', but Winston welcomed Chamberlain's declaration as long overdue. He resisted the idea that Britain now faced a stark either/or – Poland or the Soviet Union – and would spend endless hours in 1941–5 trying to square the circle.[4]

A gambler's throw by Stalin in 1939 would prove equally important for his subsequent relations with Churchill. On 22 August, a Nazi-Soviet non-aggression pact was signed. This secured Stalin, for the moment, against German attack – allowing time for accelerated rearmament – and left Hitler free in September to turn west against the other capitalist powers: Britain and France. In accordance with the pact's secret protocol Hitler and Stalin carved up Poland between them. The Soviet leader then took advantage of France's collapse in June 1940 to annex the Baltic states of Estonia, Latvia and Lithuania.

On 1 October 1939, in his first radio broadcast of the war, Winston chose not to castigate Stalin for his cynical collaboration with Hitler. 'We could have wished that the Russian armies should be standing on their present lines as the friends of the allies in Poland, instead of as invaders. But that the Russian armies should stand on this line was clearly necessary for the safety of Russia against the Nazi menace.' He told his listeners: 'I cannot forecast to you the action of Russia. It is a riddle wrapped in a mystery inside an enigma; but perhaps there is a key. That key is Russian national interest.'[5] This would be Winston's refrain throughout the war, with that 'interest' being seen through Churchillian eyes.

And so, despite the Nazi-Soviet pact, Winston still held open the possibility of cooperation with Moscow. After the fall of France, he argued that Soviet annexation of the Baltic states 'may well have been justified in self-defence' because of 'the magnitude of the German danger now threatening Russia'. And he wrote to Stalin personally, asserting that, because Britain and Russia 'lie not in Europe but on her extremities', this left them 'better enabled than others less fortunately placed to resist German hegemony'.[6]

At any event Churchill – unlike Stalin – was well prepared for Operation Barbarossa. Immediately he heard the news, early on Sunday 22 June, he arranged to make a radio broadcast at 9 p.m. that evening. As he told Jock Colville, his private secretary, 'if Hitler invaded Hell, I would at least make a favourable reference to the Devil in the House of Commons.' Aware of the visceral anti-communism of the Tory party, he did not share his text with Cabinet colleagues, or even with Foreign Secretary Eden. 'No one has been a more consistent opponent of Communism over the last twenty-five years,' he told listeners. 'I will unsay no word that I have said about it. But all this fades away before the spectacle that is now unfolding.' He insisted that 'any man or state who fights on against Nazidom will have our aid'.[7]

Words were one thing, deeds quite another. Although by mid-July Winston was talking publicly of the USSR as 'our Ally', the British Army – in retreat all around the Mediterranean – had little aid to spare and doubted the Red Army's chances. Winston embellished his messages with glowing phrases – such as 'we are watching with admiration and emotion Russia's magnificent fight' – which the FO feared would have 'the worst effect on Stalin', because 'guff' was 'no substitute for guns'.[8]

As the German armies surged on towards Moscow and Leningrad, rounding up Russian soldiers in their tens of thousands, Stalin's pleas became truly fantastic. On 3 September he told Churchill to establish 'this year a second front somewhere in the Balkans or France', sufficient to 'divert from the Eastern Front some 30 to 40 German divisions'. Ten days later he claimed that 'Great Britain could without any risk land in Archangel 25–30 divisions or transport them across Iran to the Southern regions of the USSR'. Even if it were possible to deal with the logistical challenges of these random proposals, Churchill did not have twenty-five to thirty combat-ready divisions in the whole of the British Army.[9]

By mid-October, Moscow was gripped by panic and looting. Foreign embassies were moved to the Urals and a special train stood ready to evacuate Stalin and the Soviet leadership. Although order was restored in a few days and 'the Boss' stayed put, the crisis left its mark on Winston. On 24 October he rated 'as evens' the chances of Moscow 'being taken before the winter'. Next day he predicted that 'in a month or so' the USSR 'will have been reduced to a second-rate military Power' – allowing Hitler to redeploy two-thirds of his army against Britain.[10]

By November 1941, Churchill and Stalin seemed almost on two separate planets. Wary of providing further munitions, the PM offered to send two generals – neither of them Churchill intimates – 'to clear things up and to plan for the future'. Stalin rejected the idea with unconcealed sarcasm, saying that unless they came with authority to reach firm agreement on 'war aims' and 'mutual military assistance against Hitler in Europe' it 'would be very difficult to find the time' to meet them. This was virtually a slap in the face and Winston was furious. 'His face was white as chalk and he was breathing heavily', noted Russian ambassador Ivan Maisky in his diary. Eden begged Maisky to elicit some kind of olive branch. Grudgingly, Stalin said that his message had been 'exclusively of a business nature' and did 'not impugn any members of the British government, especially Premier Churchill' – adding that he was 'too burdened with events at the front to pay even a moment's attention to personal matters'.[11]

This message did something to clear the air. Winston responded by taking up a suggestion from Eden and Maisky and offered to send the Foreign Secretary himself, together with 'high military and other experts', in order to 'discuss every question related to the war'. He assured the Soviet leader that he wished to replicate his 'personal correspondence' with Roosevelt 'and 'work on equal terms of comradeship and confidence with you'. Stalin sent a cordial reply, welcoming Eden's visit. Then on 30 November, out of the blue, he sent another telegram: 'Warm wishes on your birthday. From the bottom of my heart wish you strength and health which are so necessary for the victory over the enemy of mankind – Hitlerism. Accept my best wishes'.[12]

Stalin was not in the habit of sending birthday greetings, least of all to bourgeois imperialists. The bright idea probably came from Maisky, who had known Churchill for years, but Stalin's readiness to take it up shows he was learning the ways of diplomacy and responding to the PM's desire to personalise the Soviet-British relationship. On 21 December the PM reciprocated with birthday greetings to Stalin, and these exchanges became the norm for the rest of the war. (Roosevelt did not initiate the practice until the end of 1944, just before the Yalta conference.) And so, 1941 ended on a positive note. But it would not have escaped Stalin's eagle eye that the Prime Minister had gone to Washington for Christmas, courting Roosevelt, while his deputy was sent to Moscow.

Eden's visit to the Soviet Union was the first by a British foreign secretary. Ostensibly his task was to discuss a formal treaty of alliance, but Stalin suddenly enlarged the agenda. He wanted Allied approval of the Soviet borders as they stood when Germany attacked on 22 June 1941. But those were essentially the borders conceded under the Nazi-Soviet pact of 1939, including eastern Poland and the Baltic states of Estonia, Latvia and Lithuania. Eden was sympathetic on the Baltics, judging that Stalin was 'a political descendant of Peter the Great not Lenin' – a man guided by realpolitik, not ideology, who regarded the border issues as 'the acid test' of Britain's readiness to cooperate.[13] But Roosevelt and the State Department strongly objected to such a breach of the Atlantic Charter and Churchill initially agreed.

The British felt caught between their two allies. 'Soviet policy is amoral,' Eden told the Cabinet. 'United States policy is exaggeratedly moral, at least where non-American interests are concerned.'[14] The War Cabinet was divided and Eden kept up the pressure on the PM – now harried by the fall of Singapore and by demands in Britain for an early second front to aid 'Our Gallant Russian Allies'. On 7 March a weary Churchill cabled FDR that the 'increasing gravity of the war has led me to feel that the principles of the Atlantic Charter ought not be construed so as to deny Russia the frontiers she occupied when Germany attacked her'.[15] He probably saw this as a way to propitiate Stalin and thereby head off pressure for a 'suicidal' attempt to cross the Channel that year.

But Roosevelt's priorities were the opposite. In a significant message to Stalin on 11 April – not copied to Winston – FDR proposed a 'meeting of minds in personal conversation' between the two of them in the summer, perhaps near their 'common border off Alaska'. In the meantime, he urged Stalin to send Foreign Minister Vyacheslav Molotov to Washington to discuss 'a very important proposal involving the utilization of our armed forces in a manner to relieve your Western front'. He was referring to Gen. George Marshall's plan for a cross-Channel attack, which had recently been given to Churchill.

Molotov therefore embarked on some intensive shuttle diplomacy in order to sort out these intricate diplomatic and military issues. First he travelled to Britain, arriving on 20 May, where the British were now ready to concede Soviet annexation of the Baltic states, part of the Tsarist empire before the Great War. But they stood firm on the pre-war border of Poland, guaranteed by Chamberlain in 1939. Instead, the FO drafted an alternative treaty, avoiding any territorial issues, which simply committed the two countries to a wartime alliance and a twenty-year pact of mutual assistance. On 24 May Molotov forwarded the British text to Moscow with a brusque comment: 'We consider this treaty unacceptable, as it is an empty declaration which the USSR does not need.'[16]

Stalin's reply that evening was another bombshell:

We have received the draft treaty Eden handed to you. We do not consider it an empty declaration but regard it as an important document. It lacks the question of security of frontiers, but this is not bad perhaps, for it gives us a free hand. The question of frontiers, or to

be more exact, of guarantees for the security of our frontiers at one
or other section of our country, will be decided by force.

Stalin instructed Molotov to sign Eden's draft treaty as soon as possible,
with a couple of small amendments, and then fly to America. The Soviet
Foreign Minister sent a grovelling apology and did what he was told.
Widely seen in the West as the tough guy – 'Stone Arse' or 'Mr Nyet' –
Molotov was ultimately Stalin's lackey.[17]

The British were astonished at the volte-face but also delighted.
Churchill assured Roosevelt that the treaty was now 'entirely compat-
ible with our Atlantic Charter', ironically praising Molotov as 'a
statesman' with real 'freedom of action'.[18] Stalin probably saw the futility
of further wrangling with Washington about the USSR's western
borders. The US ambassador in London, John G. Winant, had advised
Maisky that it would 'complicate Roosevelt's position' because the
President believed 'the second front was more important than the
treaties'. This reinforced Soviet hopes that FDR could pressure
Churchill to override the British military and mount a cross-Channel
attack in 1942.[19]

Stalin was probably also mindful of new disasters on the front,
where major Nazi operations had resumed after the spring thaw, shattering his earlier hopes of 1942 as the year of decisive victory. By late
May a massive German pincer offensive around Kharkov had eliminated three rifle armies and a tank army from the Soviet order of battle.
So Stalin re-focused on trying to secure an early second front and
eschewed further diplomatic haggling – persuading himself, as he told
Molotov, that he could eventually gain more on the battlefield than at
the negotiating table.

That belief seemed warranted when Molotov reached the White
House on 29 May. Keen to build a relationship with Stalin, yet aware
of the chronic lack of shipping, Roosevelt offered Molotov the possibility of a limited operation of six to ten divisions and made a comment
that enraged Churchill when it got back to London about having to
risk 'another Dunkirk'.[20] In the words of the American minutes, the

President 'authorized Mr Molotov to inform Mr Stalin that we expect the formation of a second front this year'.[21]

Molotov was no more impressed with the breezy US President than with the evasive British Prime Minister. But directives from 'the Boss' in Moscow again took a more positive line. Acting on those instructions, Molotov made sure that the communiqué included this statement: 'In the course of the conversations, full understanding was reached with regard to the urgent task of creating a second front in Europe in 1942.' This wording was, of course, ambiguous. It could signify that they agreed the task of creating a second front was urgent, or that they actually agreed to mount a second front in 1942. Marshall strenuously objected to including any date but FDR was adamant. He told Churchill, 'I am especially anxious that he carry back some real results of his Mission and that he will give a favorable account to Stalin' to bolster Soviet morale.[22]

But when Molotov returned to London, he found Churchill more averse than before to making any commitments about 1942. At the end of their meetings on 10 June, the PM gave Molotov an aide-mémoire seeking to clarify FDR's vague but upbeat comments about 1942:

We are making preparations for a landing on the Continent in August or September 1942 . . . It is impossible to say in advance whether the situation will be such as to make this operation feasible when the time comes. We can therefore make no promise in the matter, but, provided it seems sound and sensible, we shall not hesitate to put our plans into effect.

Having reserved Britain's position on 1942, the PM was, however, far more expansive about 1943:

Finally, and most important of all, we are concentrating our maximum effort on the organisation and preparation of a large scale invasion of the Continent of Europe by British and American forces in 1943. We are setting no limit to the scope and objectives of this campaign, which will be carried out in the first instance by over a million men, British and American, with air forces of appropriate strength.[23]

Both Western leaders had therefore stuck out their necks about the second front: Roosevelt for 1942, Churchill for 1943. Their assertions did not persuade Stalin, but they provided him with ammunition aplenty in the months to come.

During the summer, it became clear to FDR that Churchill could and would resist any cross-Channel attack in 1942, and so the President shifted his support to the North Africa option. This was, however, concealed from Stalin. Winston's messages to Moscow that summer were particularly concerned with the Arctic convoys, bringing essential supplies from Britain and America to the USSR's northern ports. After convoy PQ 17 lost twenty-three of its thirty-four merchant ships, the Cabinet decided that no further convoys must sail during the summer months of 'perpetual daylight'. On 17 July Winston sent a long cable to Stalin, justifying the suspension because, if the Royal Navy lost some of its battleships, 'the whole command of the Atlantic would be lost' and 'the building up of a really strong second front in 1943 rendered impossible'.[24]

Churchill's message caught Stalin on the raw, just as the Germans were thrusting towards the industrial and transport hub of Stalingrad. He reminded the PM that 'in war no important undertaking could be effected without risk or losses. You know, of course, that the Soviet Union is suffering far greater losses.' He also complained that 'in spite of the agreed communiqué concerning the urgent tasks of creating a Second Front in 1942, the British Government postpones this matter until 1943.' As with the similar flare-up in November 1941, it was Maisky and Eden, the diplomats, who moved things on. 'Two great men have clashed,' the Foreign Secretary observed to the ambassador with a faint, perhaps sardonic smile. 'They've had a tiff . . . You and I need to reconcile them . . . Too bad they've never met face to face!'[25]

Being a leader who relished adventure and believed in personal diplomacy, Winston embraced the idea with enthusiasm.[26] He composed a message for Stalin about hopefully resuming the convoys in September and proposed a meeting between the two of them to 'survey the war together and make decisions hand-in-hand. I could then tell you the plans we have made with President Roosevelt for offensive action in 1942.' He said he would also bring Sir Alan Brooke, Chief of the Imperial General Staff – Britain's top general. Maisky cabled the message to Stalin. Before the end of the day, he had received a warm acceptance.[27]

For more than a year, the Prime Minister of Great Britain and the General Secretary of the Communist Party of the USSR had been developing what one might call an 'epistolary relationship'. That's to say, one conducted through letters and telegrams, often composed in haste and under stress, which required much reading between the lines. Now the PM finally had a chance to forge a personal relationship, face-to-face. The five intense days he spent in Moscow (12–16 August 1942) would define his attitude to Stalin for the rest of his life. But, as in the case of relations with Roosevelt, Winston tended to see what he wanted to see.

* * *

The Moscow trip was sandwiched between Winston's two visits to Cairo. Anxious that Britain not shoulder the blame alone for the failure to mount a second front in France in 1942, he secured FDR's agreement to take with him the tycoon Averell Harriman, who had managed the US side of an Allied supply mission to Moscow the previous September. On 10 August Churchill and Harriman flew to Tehran where liaison was arranged with Soviet air command for the flight to Moscow. They travelled in a converted Liberator bomber, unheated and equipped with mattresses and some blankets on shelves instead of beds. Above 12,000 feet they had to suck on oxygen masks; en route there was always a risk from stray German fighters. US General Douglas MacArthur, no Anglophile, observed later that Churchill deserved a Victoria Cross, Britain's highest gallantry award, for the journey alone.[28] Churchill's plane landed at Moscow's main airport about 5 p.m. on 12 August. Pumped up with excitement, instead of taking a rest, he was driven to the Kremlin for his first encounter with Stalin at 7 p.m.

Stalin was attired in standard Communist Party dress – 'lilac-coloured tunic, buttoned up to the neck' with 'cotton trousers stuffed into long boots'. But to one of the PM's military secretaries, he seemed like a 'little peasant, who would not have looked out of place in a country lane with a pickaxe over his shoulder'.[29] The first half of the meeting was hard going. Churchill explained in detail why the Allies could not mount a cross-Channel attack in 1942. Stalin insisted that one could not win a war without taking risks, nor train troops without bloodying them in battle. But he warmed up a bit when the PM moved on to air operations, proclaiming his intention to 'shatter almost every dwelling in almost every German city'. Winston then revealed Operation Torch, sketching a crocodile to depict his idea of attacking what he called the 'soft belly' of the Axis in the Mediterranean before striking at its 'hard snout' in France. Stalin seemed to grasp its strategic value and the PM felt that they parted after four hours in an atmosphere of goodwill. He returned tired but elated to his lodgings in State Villa No. 7 (Stalin's dacha at Kuntsevo). 'My strategy was sound,' he told his entourage. 'For an hour and a half I told him what we could *not* do . . . Stalin said he was, of course, very, very disappointed . . . Then I told him we could do. He ended enthusiastic – in a glow.'[30]

Next day, 13 August, he met with Molotov and also briefed Brooke and others about his success the previous evening. 'Unfortunately,' according to Air Marshal Arthur Tedder, 'he rather let himself go, speaking of Stalin as just a peasant, whom he, Winston, knew exactly how to tackle.' Being sure the rooms were bugged, Tedder pushed a warning note across the table, whereupon the PM broke off and delivered what he called a few 'home truths' to 'any secret eventual listeners'. According to Cadogan's diary these included such choice lines as 'The Russians, I am told, are not human beings at all. They are lower in the scale of nature than the orang-outang. Now then, let them take them down and translate it into Russian.' The PM clearly enjoyed getting that off his chest, but one wonders how he imagined his 'peasant' sneer and racist gibe would help smooth relations with a man who presumably had not forgotten choice phrases from twenty years before, such as 'the foul baboonery of Bolshevism'.[31]

At 11 p.m. that evening, Winston went again to the Kremlin. The second meeting was very different from the first. The Soviet leader accused him of going back on what had been 'pre-decided' during Molotov's visit to London, which 'found expression in the agreed Anglo-Soviet Communiqué published on June 12th'. He even insinuated that British soldiers were cowards.[32] Stalin delivered all this in a low voice, puffing on his pipe and as usual rarely looking his interlocutor in the eye. Bristling at the criticisms and frustrated by poor translation, the PM exploded into a passionate defence of his own sincerity and exclamations about Britain having had to fight alone for a year in 1940–1. The tirade went on for about five minutes, during which neither interpreter could say anything. Stalin, smiling, declared: 'I do not understand the words, but by God I like your spirit.' The meeting eventually ended about 12.45 a.m. Churchill went to bed angry and confused.[33]

Next morning, he sent the following analysis to the War Cabinet in London:

> We asked ourselves what was the explanation of this performance and transformation from the good ground we had reached the night before. I think the most probable is that his Council of Commissars did not take the news I brought as well as he did. They perhaps have more power than we suppose and less knowledge. And that he was putting himself on the record for future purposes and for their benefit and also letting off steam for his own.[34]

His concept of 'two Stalins' – friendly in person but aggressive when pressed by his colleagues – dates from this time.

On 14 August the PM responded to the main points of Stalin's message in a blunt memo, building on his remarks at the Kremlin two days earlier, which sought to represent Torch as a 'Second Front' against the Germans. This was strictly true, but he was using the term very differently from Stalin, who meant a large-scale assault on France.[35] Tired and frustrated, still angry at the insults about the British Army, Winston talked of going home straight away and sulked through most of a bibulous Kremlin banquet that evening. Sensing the need to make some amends, Stalin said at one point, 'I am a rough man, not an experienced one like you,' and asked that his 'roughness' not be misunderstood. The PM put on a pleasant face for some photos together, but then abruptly said 'Goodbye' and marched out.[36]

Next morning Sir Archibald Clark Kerr, the British ambassador, tried to persuade Churchill that he must meet Stalin again before leaving Moscow. Taking his courage in both hands, the ambassador enticed the grumpy Churchill outside for a walk – less confrontational than talking face-to-face and safe from Russian bugging devices. Clark Kerr said that at the first meeting Churchill had used his 'charm' to 'admirable effect' but on day two he had let the Soviet leader get under his skin. You are 'an aristocrat and a man of the world', he told the PM, whereas the Russians were 'straight from the plough or the lathe . . . rough and inexperienced'. Yet instead of loftily recognising this, Churchill had taken offence. 'That man has insulted me,' Winston exclaimed. 'I represent a great country and I am not submissive by nature.' Clark Kerr pressed on. The PM must not 'leave Russia in the lurch', whatever had been said by Stalin.

Gradually Churchill mellowed. Cutting to the chase, Clark Kerr said he should ask Stalin for another talk, just the two of them. Given the Soviet leader's conciliatory mood the previous evening, such a meeting was likely to go well, especially if Churchill turned on the charm again. Suddenly Winston strode back to the dacha and summoned Cadogan to join them. He pointed at Clark Kerr – 'He says it's all my fault' – and then chuckled. The black mood had lifted. A meeting was fixed up for 7 p.m. that evening at the Kremlin.[37]

The talk was businesslike, but after about ninety minutes Churchill stood up to leave, explaining that his plane would take off at dawn next morning. Stalin then proposed they have a farewell drink or two. Churchill said he was 'in principle always in favour of such a policy' and so they adjourned to the Soviet leader's apartments on the other side of the Kremlin. In attendance was Churchill's new interpreter, Major Arthur Birse – son of a Scottish businessman and a Russian mother – who was not only truly bilingual but also chatted easily with Molotov and even Stalin. Winston quickly warmed to Birse as an 'excellent interpreter', using him at all subsequent meetings with the Soviet leader. Birse's role that evening was clearly vital.[38]

Churchill enjoyed meeting Stalin's daughter Svetlana – 'a handsome red-haired girl'. Over the next few hours, he sampled a rolling banquet of 'choice dishes' and 'excellent wines', topped off about 1.30 a.m. by a 'suckling pig', at which Stalin hacked with gusto. Apart from a few gibes about the Arctic convoys, 'the Boss' was in good humour, possibly heeding Maisky's advice that the key to getting on with Churchill was having 'a purely private chat on varied themes'. Talk ranged widely over operations in Norway, the Munich conference, Maisky ('he speaks too much'), the liquidation of the wealthier peasants (kulaks) during agricultural collectivisation in the 1930s, and a possible visit by Stalin to London (Churchill promised 'a magnificent reception'). When the PM waxed eloquent about the military genius of his ancestor John Churchill, first Duke of Marlborough, scourge of Louis XIV's armies, Stalin – with what Birse called 'a sly, mischievous look' – said he thought the Duke of Wellington was 'a greater general' because he had defeated Napoleon, 'the greatest menace of all time'. The PM eventually escaped at about 2.30, drove back to the dacha for a quick change, and reached the airport just in time to depart on schedule at 5.30. By then, to quote his memoirs, Churchill had 'a splitting head-ache, which for me was very unusual'. He slept off his hangover during the flight back to Tehran.[39]

That late-night booze-up with Stalin left an indelible impression on Churchill. 'For the first time we got on to easy and friendly terms,' he cabled the Cabinet. 'I feel I have established a personal relationship which will be helpful.' Later, back in London, he told Maisky: 'All these formal meetings, minutes, experts and other things – all this is nonsense. It is important to know the soul of the person with whom you work. On that evening, or rather night, I saw Stalin's soul.' Leaving aside the uncanny verbal parallel with President George W. Bush when asked in 2001 about how he got on with Vladimir Putin, there's no doubt that Churchill left Moscow convinced he could work man-to-man with Stalin – as long as those dark political forces in the Kremlin were kept at bay.[40]

Of course, the idea that Stalin was beholden to others seems bizarre today. None of Stalin's inner circle had any doubt who was 'Boss', as shown by Molotov's grovelling in May 1942 over the Anglo-Soviet treaty. Stalin exuded a quiet, often menacing authority. No ranter like Hitler or Mussolini, he was someone who spoke quietly and tersely. According to biographer Stephen Kotkin, Stalin 'was by inclination a despot who, when he wanted to be, was utterly charming' and 'an ideologue who was flexibly pragmatic'.[41]

During his short visit to Moscow in August 1942, Winston had glimpsed some of the paradoxes, especially the mix of charm and brutality. Listening to his host talking about the liquidation of the kulaks to create collective farms ('difficult – but necessary'), he had a 'strong impression' of 'millions of men and women being blotted out or displaced for ever'. But he held his peace: 'With the World War going on all around us it seemed vain to moralise aloud.'[42] Above all, he experienced the volatility of Stalin's moods, which he chose to explain in terms of the 'two Stalins'. That concept allowed him to retain his rooted belief in the malevolence of Bolshevism in tandem with a new hope that his own diplomatic skills had forged a personal relationship with the Soviet leader. In this way, Stalin became cast almost as the 'moderate' among Moscow hardliners.

The 'two Stalins' trope helped Winston get through the winter of 1942–3. In October, after failing to receive a response to a message about a new postponement of Arctic convoys, he mused to FDR 'whether anything has occurred inside the Soviet Animal to make it impossible for Stalin to give an effective reply ... It may be that the Russian army has acquired a new footing in the Soviet machine.' But Roosevelt was 'not unduly disturbed' about the silence from Moscow, remarking, 'I have decided that they do not use speech for the same purposes that we do.'[43]

This was an astute comment. Stalin did not share Churchill's logorrhoeic tendencies: if there was nothing to say, he did not say anything. And in October 1942 his attention was almost entirely absorbed in planning how to break the German grip on Stalingrad. Eventually Churchill also concluded that this was a time for silence. On 27 October he told Eden it would be 'a great mistake to run after the Russians in their present mood', adding, 'the only thing that will do any good is fighting hard and winning victories . . . Should success crown our efforts, you will find that we shall be in a very different position.'[44]

Up to a point Winston was right. After his cable on 5 November announcing victory at El Alamein and the Torch landings, Stalin reciprocated on the 20th with positive news about the Soviet pincer operation to relieve Stalingrad. Whereupon Winston fired back a long message of war news, prefaced with an assurance that 'I regard our trustful personal relations as most important to the discharge of our duties to the great masses whose lives are at stake.'[45]

At the end of the year, as in 1941, birthday greetings were exchanged. And with plans for 1943 now pressing, both Churchill and Roosevelt hoped for a Big Three meeting in January. But when they put the idea to Stalin, the reply was a polite negative. His excuse – the climax of the battle for Stalingrad – was plausible enough, but probably not the sole reason. Fear of air travel, reluctance to venture outside the NKVD security net, and a desire to strengthen his military-strategic position before entering into decisive discussions with his allies – these probably also played their part. So it was that at Casablanca in mid-January 1943, Churchill and Roosevelt met *à deux* for nearly two weeks. When FDR pondered Stalin's motives for absence, Churchill told him:

Stalin is a realist. You can't catch him with words. Had Stalin come to Casablanca, the first thing he would have asked you and me would have been: 'How many Germans did you kill in 1942? And how many do you intend to kill in 1943?' And what would the two of us have been able to say? We ourselves are not sure what we are going to do in 1943. This was clear to Stalin from the very beginning. So, what would have been the point of him coming to the conference?[46]

But Churchill and Roosevelt did themselves no favours with a joint report on Casablanca on 26 January that was vague and inept. Stalin's reply came straight to the point. 'As I understand that, by the decisions taken regarding Germany, you yourselves set the task of crushing it by opening a second front in Europe in 1943, I should be very obliged to you for information on the concrete operations planned in this respect and on the scheduled times of their realization.'[47]

Next morning, 31 January, Field Marshal Friedrich Paulus surrendered at Stalingrad, his gaunt, unshaven face captured in photographs that went around the world. Within days, millions of Germans knew their country had experienced a catastrophic defeat. Savouring the Soviet triumph, Maisky mused in his diary about whether a second front might be needed after all – balancing the extra cost in Russian lives against the Red Army 'entering Berlin first and thereby having a decisive influence on the peace terms and on the situation in the post-war period'. That, of course, was what Stalin had been getting at when he told Molotov in May 1942 that 'the question of frontiers' would be 'decided by force'.[48]

Winston persisted in explaining away ups and downs in the correspondence with Stalin within the 'two Stalins' framework.[49] In mid-April he told FDR, 'I continue to have very agreeable correspondence with Joe.'[50] And he did not allow that relationship to be disrupted by Berlin's discovery of over 4,400 bodies of Polish officers in Katyn Forest, near Smolensk – an atrocity which the Nazis attributed to the Red Army in 1940. Moscow in turn blamed it on the Germans during the invasion of 1941. On 16 April the Polish government-in-exile in London asked that Berlin's claims be investigated by the International Red Cross (IRC). Stalin sent Churchill a vituperative message, stating that Polish complicity in 'this vile fascist calumny' was a 'treacherous blow to the Soviet Union' at a time when the USSR was 'making the greatest possible efforts to defeat the common foe of all the freedom-loving countries'. Consequently, Moscow had decided to 'interrupt' relations with the Polish government in London.[51]

Stalin was lying about Katyn – we now know that he authorised the mass executions in March 1940 – and had clearly decided that attack was the best form of defence. But he needed to see how his allies would react. In the event, he need not have worried. 'Even if the German statements were to prove true, my attitude to you would not change,' Churchill told Maisky. 'You are a brave people. Stalin is a great warrior, and at the moment I approach everything primarily as a soldier who is interested in defeating the common enemy as quickly as possible.'[52] This would remain the PM's approach. 'I think it would be a pity', he cabled Clark Kerr on 2 May, 'that our Polish discussions with Stalin should interrupt the more or less weekly flow of friendly messages I have been sending him about operations. I am sure these give him pleasure and maintain our indispensable contact.'[53]

In any case, Churchill's mind was set on his next conference with Roosevelt. Codenamed 'Trident', this was intended to ensure British and American strategy were in concert now that victory in North Africa had finally been gained. Given the fiercely competing interests in play, the final strategic overview document was a mish-mash. And once again after these fraught Anglo-American discussions, the Stalin factor was neglected. Churchill and Roosevelt left the long-suffering General Marshall to convey a summary of Trident's outcome to the Kremlin. No wordsmith, the US Army Chief of Staff simply pulled together passages from the conference conclusions in ponderous language that made little attempt to sugar the unpalatable decisions that had been taken. His text was nodded through by Churchill and Roosevelt, by then on separate continents, with minimal tweaks.

The resulting message, sent on 2 June, was full of plans for the air offensive and for knocking Italy out of the war. Only at the end was it mentioned that the build-up in Britain 'should proceed at a rate to permit a full-scale invasion of the Continent to be launched at the peak of the great air offensive in the Spring of 1944'. So Stalin – still officially expecting an invasion of France in August or September 1943 – was informed *en passant* that there would be an eight-month delay. No attempt was made to explain the logistical constraints of global warfare, let alone offer some form of apology. The two leaders seem to have learned nothing from their tone-deaf message after Casablanca.[54]

Stalin's reply on 11 June was forensic, citing past cables to document how the second front had been postponed from 1942 to 1943, and then to 1944. This latest decision, he declared, would create 'exceptional difficulties for the Soviet Union which has already been fighting for two years ... not only for its own country but also for the Allies', and – he added – 'almost in single combat'.[55] He followed up on 24 June by concluding ominously that the whole business called into question Soviet 'confidence in the Allies'. This time Winston fired back an aggrieved reply which reminded Stalin that 'until 22nd June 1941 we British were left alone to face the worst that Nazi Germany could do to us' and spelled out his own case, asserting, 'I am satisfied that I have done everything in human power to help you.'[56]

The PM then waited for a reply. None came. Instead Maisky was summoned home to Moscow for 'consultations', together with his ambassadorial counterpart in Washington, Maxim Litvinov – the pair being replaced in due course by young Molotov protégés who were largely messenger boys. Brooding over the silence and Hitler's delay in launching his summer offensive, Winston suddenly became worried. He told Clark Kerr, 'this is probably the end of the Churchill-Stalin correspondence from which I fondly hoped some kind of personal contact might be created between our two countries.' His fertile, often fretful mind was now in full flight about a repeat of Stalin's 1939 deal with Hitler.[57]

This dark moment coincided with a delicate phase in Winston's relations with the President. It was also on 24 June that Harriman told Churchill that in May FDR had sent Joseph E. Davies, US ambassador to the USSR in 1936–8, to the Kremlin with a letter proposing a meeting between the President and the General Secretary – explicitly without Churchill. Stalin had not taken up the proposal, but Harriman's leak infuriated Winston. He sent an indignant message to FDR, only to receive a bare-faced lie that the meeting *à deux* had been Stalin's suggestion. The PM was deeply hurt at the deception, which he took as both a personal affront and an intimation that the balance of the alliance was shifting. But then he changed his mind in view of all the worrying signals from Moscow. On 29 June he told FDR he would 'no longer deprecate' a meeting between Roosevelt and Stalin, and indeed considered this to be 'important' if it could be arranged.[58]

Stalin maintained his silence all through July 1943. The Soviet embassies in London and Washington repeatedly stated that he was 'at the front', but Stalin was no Churchill and kept himself well away from danger. That standard Soviet form of words was accurate only in the sense that Stalin was totally absorbed with the German offensive, which finally opened on 5 July. Meanwhile, he was happy to let his allies stew in the juice of their own anxieties. Twice in three months, over Katyn and Trident, he had shown himself the master of psychological diplomacy – a far cry from the apprentice of autumn 1941. And by the time he was ready to reply to his allies, the Soviet military position had been utterly transformed.

* * *

For the third summer in succession, Hitler mounted a massive offensive in the USSR, this time to pinch out the Kursk salient from north and south. Unlike 1941 and 1942, however, the high command in Moscow had properly anticipated the German thrust. Equally important, they dissuaded 'the Boss' from any premature offensive. Instead, Soviet forces soaked up the initial German attack in massive tank battles and then drove deep into Ukraine. On 8–9 August Stalin finally resumed communication with his two partners, much to their relief. As Winston put it to King George VI, the 'Great Bear' was again 'speaking, or at least growling'.[59]

Now far stronger on the battlefield, Stalin asserted himself against his allies. He politely rebuffed Roosevelt's continued nudges about an early meeting between the two of them and renewed his proposal that, when they did meet, Churchill should be included. To give himself time before that summit, and with the aim of forcing his allies to show their hand, Stalin also proposed a preliminary meeting of 'responsible representatives'. This idea became the Conference of Foreign Ministers. Delighted, Churchill and Roosevelt agreed.

For Winston, still unsettled by the summer revelations about FDR's attempt to fix a meeting with Stalin behind his back, it now seemed vital to ensure that he and the President were on the same page. The four weeks he spent in North America in August and September, mostly with FDR, were intended to promote that consensus. On 19 August the two of them signed a top-secret agreement on 'Tube Alloys' (codeword for the atomic bomb). It included pledges that Britain and America would not use the weapon on 'third parties' without 'each other's consent', nor 'communicate any information about Tube Alloys to third parties except by mutual consent'. The most significant third party was, of course, the other member of the Big Three. Roosevelt, like Churchill, was clear that 'only two of them would have the bomb'. Despite the secrecy of his allies, Stalin did get the message. A report on the signing of the British-American nuclear agreement arrived in Moscow via Soviet military intelligence in early September.[60]

Although each of the Big Three tried to arrange the Foreign Ministers conference and the summit in a place that suited him, Stalin capitalised on the evident relief in London and Washington that he had broken his ominous six-week silence. He secured agreement that the conference would be held in Moscow in October, batting aside the suggestion of London from the other two. As for the Big Three conclave at the end of November, Stalin stuck to Tehran – the most desirable venue for him outside the USSR on account of security and communications. Winston was amenable but FDR fought hard to avoid a long and arduous trans-oceanic 6,000-mile journey to the Iranian capital, touting various other places around the Mediterranean. Stalin, as usual, cited the insuperable demands of 'The Front', but his root concern was status: he was now adamant that the victorious USSR should be treated as an equal by its two Western partners. That meant they must come to him.[61]

At Tehran, Winston was often isolated against the other two. That was most evident over the conference's firm decision to mount Overlord in May 1944. But he was also hurt by Roosevelt's deliberate cosying up to Stalin. The President stayed in the Soviet residence – indeed he secretly invited himself there – and ostentatiously sided with Stalin in a dinner joke that escalated into a full-blown row about the latter's proposal to shoot 50,000 German officers after the war. When (perhaps mindful of Katyn) the weary PM took offence, FDR – clearly enjoying Winston's discomfiture – grandly proposed a compromise of 49,000. At this point the PM got up and walked out, chased by Stalin and Molotov who insisted it was all just a bit of fun.

Yet too much can be made of the apparent Roosevelt-Stalin axis. FDR was mainly trying to show Stalin that he and Winston were not in each other's pocket. And, despite Stalin's persistent needling of the PM for being pro-German, there were cordial moments. After FDR had left the dinner for Winston's sixty-ninth birthday on 30 November, Stalin had a tipsy talk with the PM, recorded by Churchill's doctor, Lord Moran.

'I want to call Mr Churchill my friend.'

'Call me Winston. I call you Joe behind your back.'

'No, I want to call you my friend. I want to be allowed to call you my good friend.'

Once that had been agreed, Churchill declared: 'I drink to the Proletarian masses.'

'I drink to the Conservative Party,' Stalin replied, whereupon they tottered off to their beds around midnight. ('What piffle great men sometimes talk,' Clark Kerr observed *sotto voce* to Moran.)[62]

After Tehran, struck down by pneumonia, Winston entered the dark valley again, brooding about what was portended by the growth of Soviet power. But that made him cling even more to his budding relationship with Stalin. 'I only wish we could meet once a week,' he cabled the Kremlin at the end of December. If that happened, he told a journalist friend on 27 January 1944, 'there would be no trouble at all. We get on like a house on fire.' And in the Commons a month later he extolled the benefits of regular meetings between the 'chief representatives' of 'the three great Powers': 'By such meetings, both formal and informal, all difficulties could be brought out freely and frankly, and the most delicate matters could be approached without the risk of jars or misunderstandings, such as too often arise when written communications are the only channel.'[63]

The 'trouble' that most worried Winston was how to square the circle on Poland. From the New Year of 1944 he spent hours arguing with the London Poles and composing messages to Stalin in a search for agreement on the Polish-Soviet border as prelude to a post-war Polish government that would be free but also friendly to the USSR. The Poles were, however, intractable on territory, while Stalin kept insisting that they were incurably Russophobe. By April the PM had slumped into gloom, telling Eden, 'Although I have tried in every way to put myself in sympathy with these Communist leaders, I cannot feel the slightest trust or confidence in them. Force and facts are their only realities.' Yet it is noteworthy that he attached the blame not to Stalin but 'these Communist leaders'.[64]

The PM became increasingly preoccupied by the Overlord landings. On 6 June he sent an 'Everything has started well' telegram to Moscow. Stalin responded with surprisingly florid congratulations, declaring that Napoleon had 'failed ignominiously' when he tried to cross the Channel; likewise the 'hysterical' Hitler. 'Only our Allies have succeeded in realising with honour the grandiose plan of the forcing of the Channel. History will record this deed as an achievement of the highest order.'[65] Then, while his allies were stuck for weeks in the hedgerows of Normandy, Stalin delivered with interest on his side of the bargain struck at Tehran, when he had promised the Red Army would time its summer offensive to support Overlord. On the night of 22 June 1944 – the third anniversary of Barbarossa – Operation Bagration opened in Belorussia. Over the next five weeks, Soviet troops advanced over 400 miles, driving to the edge of Warsaw and destroying some twenty German divisions.

The Soviet advance triggered an uprising on 1 August by the Polish

Home Army, who were desperate to seize Warsaw from the Germans before the arrival of their other enemy, the Russians. But the Red Army stopped on the outskirts of the city and let the battle unfold. In part the halt reflected the exhaustion of troops and tanks after their headlong advance, but Stalin was also perfectly happy to let the Nazis destroy the Poles. Not only did he fail to help the Home Army, he also denied the Allies use of air bases on Soviet-controlled territory to refuel after their own supply drops. Churchill became almost frantic, but FDR did not wish to make a big issue out of Warsaw in view of 'the long-range general war perspective'. Stalin echoed his line over Katyn, calling the rising 'a reckless and terrible adventure' by 'a group of criminals', intended to 'seize power'. By the time the Red Army resumed its advance in mid-September, the Polish insurgents had lost the battle. Victorious Nazis systematically destroyed the city.[66]

The Red Army was now flooding into the Balkans, taking control in Romania and Bulgaria, while Tito's communist Partisans tightened their grip on Yugoslavia. So the PM proposed himself for a second solo visit to Moscow. Realising, perhaps, that his gamble on Stalin now lay in the balance, he had in mind a bizarre – even desperate – ploy.[67]

Churchill and Eden landed in the Soviet capital on 9 October and met Stalin at 10 p.m. that evening. Winston opened with his now customary refrain about how, by talking to each other, he and Stalin could 'clear away many questions' about which they had been writing 'for a long time'. And then, according to notes by the British interpreter – Arthur Birse again – the PM 'produced what he called a "naughty document" showing a list of Balkan countries and the proportions of interest in them of the Great Powers'. He pushed it across the table, adding 'that the Americans would be shocked if they could see how crudely he had put it'. But, he grinned, 'Marshal Stalin was a realist' and 'he himself was not sentimental' – noting that he had consulted neither Cabinet nor Parliament.[68]

The PM's 'naughty' list enlarged an understanding of May 1944 between the two governments. In Romania, Churchill allotted Russia 90 per cent and 'the others' 10 per cent; in Greece, Britain would have

90 per cent and 'the others' 10 per cent. In Bulgaria, Russia should get 75 per cent and the others 25 per cent, while in both Yugoslavia and Hungary he proposed 50:50 splits. According to Churchill, Stalin marked the document with a tick and pushed it back across the table. Later, the Soviet leader quibbled about the figure for Bulgaria, and the two leaders agreed that Eden and Molotov should firm up the details next day.[69]

Percentages had come out of the blue. Churchill had not broached the idea even to Eden, who was left to work out with Molotov what the numbers might signify.[70] Nor, it seems, did Churchill himself have much idea. Asked later by a sceptical Cabinet, he said the 'system of percentages' was intended 'to express the interest and sentiment' with which the two governments 'approach the problems of these countries', so that 50:50 would imply 'joint action and an agreed policy', whereas 90:10 would indicate that one power would 'play a leading part'. But the PM had never used percentages before, nor would he do so again. He clearly wanted to win Stalin's trust, building on their man-to-man evening the last time he had been in the Kremlin, on the night of 15 August 1942. Perhaps he thought numbers would lend precision to his proposals, unlike vague terms such as 'predominance' or 'influence'. Or maybe, as a passionate theatre lover, he saw the sheet of paper pushed across the table as almost an act of melodrama – a ploy to grab Stalin's attention in a darkened Kremlin room.[71]

At any event, 'as theatre, it was brilliant' but 'as diplomacy, it was amateurish.'[72] Stalin did respect the 90 per cent British stake in Greece, not protesting later when British troops, presided over by the PM, took on the Greek communists. But the 50:50 deal for Yugoslavia failed to stick because of Tito's non-cooperation. And within months the PM, increasingly unhappy about the brutal imposition of Soviet rule in Romania, was lamenting how his hands had been tied by the 90 per cent deal he made with Stalin. Nevertheless, in October 1944 the PM left Moscow in high spirits. Not only had Stalin attended a reception at the British Embassy (for the first time ever), he also came to see Winston off at the airport, waving his handkerchief as the plane taxied along the runway. And there were more flashes of that dry Stalin humour. During the conference, when someone spoke of the Big Three as the Holy Trinity, Stalin quipped, 'If that is so, Churchill must be the Holy Ghost. He flies around so much.'[73]

'This memorable meeting in Moscow has shown that there are no matters that cannot be adjusted between us when we meet together in frank and intimate discussion,' Winston wrote in a thank-you message.[74] But he also sensed 'strong pressures in the background, both party and military' and clung onto that earlier notion of the 'two Stalins'. 'There is no doubt', he cabled the War Cabinet, 'that within our narrow circle we have talked with an ease, freedom and beau gest [sic] never before attained between our two countries. Stalin has made several expressions of personal regard which I feel sure were sincere. But I repeat my conviction that he is by no means alone.'[75]

Unsettled by Churchill's Moscow visit, Roosevelt now pushed ahead with plans for a second meeting of the Big Three. He toyed with at least ten possible Mediterranean venues, but was unable to deflect Stalin from Yalta in the Crimea. Once again, Roosevelt and Churchill had to go to him – and to get there via long and difficult journeys that served only to damage their health. The conference (4–11 February 1945) has become notorious, largely because US Republicans and French Gaullists alike damned it as the moment when the Western Allies divided Europe, handing over the eastern half to the Soviets. But that is not true, because the Red Army already controlled much of Eastern Europe – its position the combined legacy of the delayed second front and the surging Soviet victories in 1943–4. Before leaving Washington FDR told senators privately that 'the Russians had the power in Eastern Europe, that it was obviously impossible to have a break with them and that, therefore, the only practicable course was to use what influence we had to ameliorate the situation.' The PM was equally conscious of the limits of Western influence, at times bleakly so. 'Make no mistake,' he told Jock Colville on 23 January, 'all the Balkans, except Greece, are going to be Bolshevised; and there is nothing I can do to prevent it. There is nothing I can do for poor Poland either.' But that was not his considered policy:

like FDR, but with far more energy, at Yalta he did try to 'ameliorate' the situation, conscious of the debt of 'honour' bequeathed him by Chamberlain's 1939 guarantee of Poland's independence.[76]

The border issue was settled by 'moving' Poland westwards: allowing the USSR to regain Ukrainian areas in the east, while compensating the Poles with German territory in Silesia and Pomerania. The hardest nut remained the Polish government, given that the Red Army had already installed Stalin's placemen in the city of Lublin. After much haggling it was agreed that the Lublin regime would be 'reorganized' by including some new faces from Poland and abroad and that 'free and unfettered elections' would be held 'as soon as possible'. Both Roosevelt and Churchill said later that this formula was 'the best' they could get. And each had other issues on his mind as well. Winston was particularly anxious to avoid imposing another punitive peace on Germany, and – to Stalin's evident irritation – he firmly resisted Soviet demands for reparations and dismemberment. FDR's priorities were Soviet membership of the United Nations, the keystone of his post-war architecture, and also firming up Stalin's commitments to join in the war against Japan, a matter on which the PM strongly agreed.[77]

So Yalta has to be seen in the round. Diplomacy in 1945 could not salvage what had been decided on the battlefield in 1942–3. But Yalta did need to be sold to the public in Britain and America, and here both Western leaders offered immense hostages to fortune. The President hyped up the agreement on the UN as 'a turning point' both in American history and in 'the history of the world', because it should 'spell the end' of 'spheres of influence'.[78] And on Poland, Winston stuck out his neck repeatedly, while also agonising in private about what he was saying. Meeting Government ministers on 23 February, he made the remarkable statement: 'Poor Neville Chamberlain believed he could trust Hitler. He was wrong. But I don't think I'm wrong about Stalin.' Yet that evening, Jock Colville found Winston in his cups and 'rather depressed, thinking of the possibilities of Russia one day turning against us, saying that Chamberlain had trusted Hitler as he was now trusting Stalin (though he thought in different circumstances)'. Despite these dark thoughts, on the 27th Winston told MPs: 'The impression I brought back from the Crimea, and from all my other contacts, is that Marshal Stalin and the Soviet leaders wish to live in honourable friendship and equality with the Western democracies. I feel also that their word is their bond.'[79]

By March 1945, however, the Yalta agreements seemed to be breaking down. The Soviets dragged their feet on repatriating Allied servicemen from German prisoner-of-war camps. They did not send representatives to London to start up the new Control Commission for Germany. In Romania they forced the King to appoint a new government dominated by communists. And in Poland they allowed the Stalinist provisional government to veto candidates for its own 'reconstruction' and to exclude Western observers, while potential rivals in Poland were butchered or sent to the camps.

Did all this signal a sinister shift in Kremlin policy? In London the 'two Stalins' hypothesis kicked in again. Among those blamed for what was happening in Eastern Europe were Molotov, 'Party bosses behind the scenes' and 'Army marshals at the front'.[80] In one message to FDR, Winston wrote darkly about 'the Soviet leaders, whoever they may be'. He subjected the President to a steady barrage of telegrams, mainly on Poland, where he bemoaned the sinister 'veil' or 'curtain' that was coming down on events and urged an early joint appeal to Stalin as 'the only way to stop Molotov's tactics'. Winston claimed that Poland was 'the test case between us and the Russians of the meaning which is to be attached to such terms as Democracy, Sovereignty, Independence, Representative Government and free and unfettered elections'.[81]

Roosevelt, by contrast, wanted to 'minimize the general Soviet problem as much as possible' – in other words, he was not keen to get worked up about the latest telegram or constantly badger Stalin. 'We must be firm, however, and our course thus far is correct.' That was his line to Churchill in a message that arrived on 12 April.[82] But a few hours later the President dropped dead. His demise not only caused Winston deep distress but also removed an essential balancing mechanism in the PM's relations with Stalin. Sometimes he had prodded

FDR on; on other occasions the President had restrained his volatility. Now he was in a whirl.[83]

Harry Truman, the new president, seemed no great help. On 23 April he gave Molotov a stiff talk about Poland, telling the Soviets to stick to the Yalta agreements, but over the next few weeks he found time to read those agreements and realised how 'elastic' they were.[84] Victory in Europe was celebrated on 8 May but Churchill's wartime coalition broke up, and so he formed a Tory government ahead of a general election in July. On 12 May he used the term 'iron curtain' for the first time, in a message to Truman. And then, in deep secrecy, he instructed his military planners to examine how to 'impose upon Russia the will of the United States and British Empire' in order to get 'a square deal for Poland'. The date for the opening of hostilities would be 1 July 1945. The plan was labelled 'Operation Unthinkable'.

The military was instructed to assume, first, that US armed forces would be fully involved and that the war had 'the full support' of American and British public opinion. Secondly, they could 'count on the use of German manpower and what remains of German industrial capacity'. Attacking a still popular ally just three months after the war's end, with the aid of the former enemy, was, of course, inconceivable. What's more, the planners warned that 'the only way we can achieve our object with certainty and lasting results is by victory in a total war' which, on the most hopeful scenarios, 'would take us a very long time'.[85] (Brooke called the whole idea 'fantastic and the chances of success quite impossible. There is no doubt that from now onwards Russia is all powerful in Europe.') Faced with this grim prognosis, Churchill backed off, telling the military that 'this remains a precautionary study of what, I hope, is still a purely hypothetical contingency.'[86]

We shall probably never know what was going on amid Winston's mental turmoil at this time. But this proved a blip. Having stared into the abyss of a third world war, he reverted to his familiar claim that the best chance of resolving differences was by talking with Stalin. Truman, however, continued to chart his own course. At the end of May Harry Hopkins was sent to Moscow to sort out the balance of

the Polish government – largely on Stalin's terms and without reference to London. And when the three leaders met at Potsdam at the
end of July, the interlinked compromises on Germany and Poland
were decided largely by the USA and the USSR. Cadogan reflected
sadly that Potsdam was a meeting of the 'Big 2½'.[87]

To complete Winston's misery, in the middle of the conference he
returned to London for the result of the general election only to learn
that Labour had won a landslide victory. It was the worst Tory defeat
since that of 1906, which had catapulted Winston into office. But then
he had been a young Liberal; now he was the leader of the Tory party.
As the family lunched in sepulchral gloom on 26 July, Clementine –
aware of her husband's utter exhaustion – declared brightly that 'it
may well be a blessing in disguise.' Looking at her, he grunted, 'At the
moment it seems quite effectively disguised.' A few days later Truman
sent him warm wishes for 'the happiest possible existence from now
to the last call'.[88]

* * *

The wheel had come full circle in the course of five momentous years.
On 10 May 1940 Winston Churchill finally attained the greatness he
had coveted for so long – only to realise a few days later, hearing
Gamelin's hopeless '*Aucune*' in Paris, that his was a poisoned chalice.
After France surrendered, he had to contrive completely new alliances
with the United States and the Soviet Union within which Great Britain
was fated to be the junior partner. The problems that this entailed
were contained to some extent during the war, but they had to be
faced from the summer of 1945.

Yet the election result on 26 July meant that Churchill would not
have to deal with them. The cup was now passed to Clement Attlee.
Instead, Winston spent another period in the political wilderness, as
in the years 1929–39 – again spared the invidious choices of office
and free to speak out on international affairs. In other words, he could
once more have his cake and eat it. The big difference with the 1930s
was that by 1945 he was a world-renowned statesman. During these

second wilderness years, therefore, his prophetic voice had far greater resonance than in the 1930s.

The speech that echoed loudest was delivered at Fulton, Missouri, on 5 March 1946. The invitation from the President of Westminster College would probably have received a polite rejection, like hundreds of others, but for the postscript from the President of the United States, which offered to introduce him at this 'wonderful school in my home state'. In that case, Winston replied, 'I should feel it my duty – and it would also be a great pleasure' to deliver an address 'on the world situation'. With Truman on the podium beside him, he knew the world would listen.[89]

His own title for the speech – added at the last minute – was 'The Sinews of Peace'. Dismissing talk that war with the USSR was inevitable, he called again for 'a good understanding with Russia' backed by 'the whole strength of the English-speaking world'. What caught global attention, however, was this sentence: 'From Stettin in the Baltic to Trieste in the Adriatic, an iron curtain has descended across the Continent.' East of that line, said Churchill, people were subject to 'a very high and, in many cases, increasing measure of Soviet control'. Stalin blasted the speech as 'a call to war with the Soviet Union'. He said Churchill was arguing that the English-speaking peoples, 'being the only valuable nations, should rule over the remaining nations of the world'. This, he asserted, was a 'racial theory' based on language – 'one is reminded remarkably of Hitler and his friends.'[90] Stalin probably wanted to show he would not be intimidated by the West – even though the US now possessed the atomic bomb – while also seeking to mobilise the Soviet population against a new enemy in order to restore tight social control after the war years. Whatever Stalin's motivation, it was his high-profile rebuttal as much as Churchill's own words which ensured that the Fulton speech went down as one of the opening salvoes in the Cold War.[91]

Yet, for Winston, Fulton had served its purpose. The President of the United States had sat alongside him as he spoke; the leader of the Soviet Union had denounced him as a budding Hitler. His words had echoed around the world, including soundbites such as 'iron curtain' and 'special relationship' – previously used in private correspondence. Buoyed up at being the centre of attention once more, Winston dismissed rumours about his imminent retirement as Tory leader. He was also fired up by a belief that the Labour Party was selling off the empire and selling out the country, declaring on 27 June: 'A short time ago I was ready to retire and die gracefully. Now I'm going to stay and have them out.' His crony and fixer, the newspaper editor Brendan Bracken, summed up the new mood: Churchill was 'determined to continue to lead the Tory party till he becomes Prime Minister on earth or Minister of Defence in Heaven'.[92]

Although, thanks to Stalin's vehemence, Fulton became known as the 'iron curtain' speech, Winston's main aim had been to rebuild the Anglo-American relationship, playing up the Soviet threat as justification. The deepening Cold War did indeed draw the US into unprecedented acts of cooperation: Marshall Aid, the Berlin Airlift and the North Atlantic Treaty. Speaking in Boston on 31 March 1949 just before the treaty was signed, Winston was quietly jubilant: 'Three years ago I spoke at Fulton under the auspices of President Truman. Many people here and in my own country were startled and even shocked by what I said. But events have vindicated and fulfilled in much detail the warnings which I deemed it my duty to give at that time.' For that achievement he credited 'fourteen men in the Kremlin' who 'cannot afford to allow free and friendly inter-course to grow up between the vast area they control and the civilization of the West'.[93]

But Winston was still thinking about the 'sinews of peace'. He continued his wartime practice of sending birthday greetings to Stalin in December 1945, and again the following year, despite the abuse about Fulton. In January 1947, Field Marshal Montgomery returned from a visit to Moscow with a message from Stalin noting that they disagreed now 'on many political matters' but expressing 'the greatest respect and admiration for what you had done during the war years'. Winston responded in kind, writing to Stalin:

I always look back on our comradeship together, when so much was
at stake, and you can always count on me where the safety of Russia
and the fame of its armies are concerned. I was also delighted to hear
from Montgomery of your good health. Your life is not only precious
to your country, which you saved, but to the friendship between
Soviet Russia and the English-speaking world.[94]

One shouldn't make too much of such diplomatic pleasantries, but
they suggest that Winston had not entirely lost his faith in the Soviet
leader.

Certainly, as 10 Downing Street beckoned again, that facet of Fulton
became prominent. In February 1950, Winston called for 'another talk
with the Soviet Union at the highest level', adding that it was 'not easy
to see how matters could be worsened by a parley at the summit'. Thus
he coined another resonant slogan for the lexicon of diplomacy, to
complement 'iron curtain' and 'special relationship'. At the end of the
election campaign in October 1951, he told a crowd in Plymouth that
'a lasting peace settlement' was 'the last prize I seek to win', adding that
'all the day-dreams and ambitions of my youth have not only been
satisfied, but have been surpassed. I pray indeed that I may have this
final opportunity.' And on 6 November 1951, soon after starting his
second term as PM, he promised the Commons 'a supreme effort to
bridge the gulf between the two worlds, so that each can live its life,
if not in friendship at least without the fear, the hatreds and the frightful
waste of the "cold war".'[95]

Summitry became both the passion and the pretext for Winston's
second term. Reminiscing with Soviet ambassador Andrei Gromyko
in February 1953 about wartime summits, he said his 'percentages'
meeting with Stalin in Moscow in 1944 had been 'the highest level
we ever reached'.[96] Nevertheless, he responded with alacrity to the
news of Stalin's death on 5 March 1953, sensing a relaxation of tension
under the new reformist leadership and calling anew for 'a conference
at the highest level' involving 'the smallest number of Powers and
persons possible'.[97] In November 1954, he made his most direct attack

on Stalin. Speaking about the transformation of Germany from enemy to ally in a single decade, he said that this had been brought about 'by the policy of Soviet Russia itself and above all by Stalin, the Dictator, who was carried away by the triumphs of victory and acted as if he thought he could secure for Russia and Communism the domination of the world'.[98]

That was not, however, his final verdict. In April 1956, he told US President Dwight Eisenhower that 'Stalin always kept his word with me', citing the percentages deal of 1944 when he told the Soviet leader, 'You keep Rumania and Bulgaria in your sphere of influence, but let me have Greece.' To this bargain, Churchill declared, Stalin 'scrupulously adhered'. And it was his abiding refrain in later life that Stalin 'never broke his personal word to me'. Years later his private secretary still puzzled over what he termed this 'remarkable blind spot in judging Stalin'.[99]

Yet is 'blind' really the right word? As when dealing with Roosevelt, Winston saw what he wanted to see. Not, of course, a 'special relationship' between their two countries: exactly the opposite. But grounds for hope that, by talking man-to-man, they might prevent the Cold War escalating into a third world war and global nuclear destruction. Of course, the obsession with summitry in his second term was partly to justify what he called 'staying in the pub till closing time'. But it was also infused with yearning for a better future than a crude balance of terror – or, worse, its breakdown. One of the last novels Winston read (twice) was Nevile Shute's *On the Beach*, an apocalyptic evocation of the aftermath of nuclear war. He also watched the movie.[100] As a Victorian optimist, he wished to look into the future with hope. Churchill needed 'his' Stalin.

'Je suis prisonnier': De Gaulle with his English minder in Marrakech
(13 January 1944). Yet 'Le Grand Charles' would have the last laugh.

8

Charles de Gaulle

'A Certain Idea'

Churchill was magnificent until 1942. Then, as if exhausted by such a great effort, he passed the torch on to the Americans and abased himself before them.

Charles de Gaulle, January 1963[1]

I should be sorry to live in a country governed by de Gaulle, but I should be sorry to live in a world, or with a France, in which there was not a de Gaulle.

Winston S. Churchill, note 1947[2]

'*Toute ma vie, je me suis fait une certaine idée de la France.*' Thus the Proustian opening of Charles de Gaulle's memoirs of the Second World War. And for most of his life he also entertained a certain idea of himself as the incarnation of what he considered France's quintessential greatness: '*la France ne peut être la France sans la grandeur.*' The adjective 'certain' conveys something rock solid yet also sublimely mystical.[3] In similar vein, Winston Churchill saw himself as embodying Great Britain and its empire. Both men were fervent patriots, with a profound sense of national history. As such, they were bound to clash, and did so repeatedly in 1940–4 when this tall, proud Frenchman bristled with resentment at his humiliating dependence on Churchillian hospitality. After the war, each spent time in the political wilderness, using his enforced leisure to shape the verdict of history through weighty tomes of war memoirs. Winston's political swansong occurred in 1951–5; de Gaulle's came later but far more emphatically as founding President of France's Fifth Republic between 1958 and 1969.

During those post-war years, each set the pattern for his country's role in the new Europe. Winston wanted Britain to have its cake and eat it: trying to retain a global role, in a special relationship with the US, while influencing European affairs from the edge. De Gaulle, still smarting from the hurts inflicted on his sensitive Gallic skin by Churchill and FDR, blocked Britain's bid to 'join Europe' all through the 1960s. Now it was Winston's turn to resent de Gaulle's treatment of Britain. By the time Britain did join, in 1973, the European Economic Community had set firm under French hegemony. Nevertheless, they saw in one another the marks of greatness. Even if neither could have endured life in a country ruled by the other, they would probably have agreed that the world was the richer for having Churchill and de Gaulle in the ring together.[4]

* * *

Winston, despite his ardent patriotism, was a noted Francophile. This started young. Visiting the Place de la Concorde in Paris with his father in 1883, aged nine, he noticed that one of the eight statues representing great French cities was covered by black crêpe and wreaths of flowers. 'Why?' he asked, and was told it was a sign of mourning for Alsace and Lorraine, the two provinces seized by Germany in the Franco-Prussian war. His father explained that the French were 'very unhappy about it and hope some day to get them back'. Winston said to himself, 'I hope they will get them back.'[5]

'Ever since 1907,' he wrote during the Second World War, 'I have in good times and bad been a true friend of France.' That was the year he attended the French military manoeuvres. Whereas similar visits to Germany in 1906 and 1909 left him with an abiding sense of its army as 'a terrible engine', his reaction to L'Armée de Terre was very different. Winston was captivated by their blue tunics and red trousers.

Recalling the sight in 1946, he wrote: 'When I saw, at the climax of these manoeuvres, the great masses of the French infantry storming the position, while the bands played the "Marseillaise," I felt that by those valiant bayonets the rights of man had been gained and that by them these rights and also the liberties of Europe would be faithfully guarded.' The blue and red uniforms were abandoned after the carnage of August 1914, but Winston retained his romanticised faith in the French army right up to the debacle of 1940.[6]

That was when the two men first met. De Gaulle was already aware of Churchill, a Cabinet minister during the Great War and in the Thirties a trenchant critic of appeasement. But it's unlikely that the towering Frenchman (he was 6ft 5in tall) had registered in Winston's consciousness. Born in 1890, and therefore sixteen years Winston's junior, he was a professional soldier, wounded several times during the Great War and eventually captured at Verdun in 1916. He then spent two and a half years in German prisoner-of-war camps, despite repeated efforts to escape. During the interwar years he served as a staff officer and lecturer on military history, but his main claim to fame was the short book he published in 1934 entitled *Vers l'Armée de Métier*, which advocated an elite force of motorised, armoured divisions to bring mobility back to the battlefield. Such ideas were not novel – de Gaulle drew heavily on French and British military thinkers such as Joseph Aimé Doumenc, J.F.C. Fuller and Basil Liddell Hart – but it took real courage for a young colonel to champion them against the defensive orthodoxy of the high command, not least his former patron Marshal Philippe Pétain.

The book was translated into English under the title *The Army of the Future*, but this was not until 1940 and, although Churchill became vaguely aware of de Gaulle's ideas during a visit to Paris in March 1938, he did not take them seriously. In fact, they were diametrically opposed to his own strategic thinking at the time which, as we saw in Chapter 4, argued that tanks had had their day and assumed the supremacy of the defence.

On 6 June 1940, in the dying weeks of Paul Reynaud's premiership, Brigadier General de Gaulle was abruptly promoted to Under Secretary for National Defence. Three days later he was sent to London to show the British a French general with real aggressive spirit. During the period 9–16 June he had four meetings with Churchill, on either side of the Channel. In a last effort to keep France in the fight, they concocted a declaration of union between the two countries, which was approved by a sceptical British Cabinet. But by the time they met for a fifth time, on 17 June, Reynaud had resigned, Marshal Pétain was seeking an armistice and de Gaulle had taken a plane to London. His defiance was almost ludicrous. Before leaving Paris, he had announced calmly, as if stating a fact: 'The Germans have lost the war. They are lost and France must keep on fighting.'[7]

De Gaulle's defiance was instinctive. 'The defeated,' he declared, 'are those who accept defeat.'[8] But, in common with Winston's own pugnacity in 1940, he needed rationalisations as well. 'This war is not finished by the battle of France. This war is a world war,' he announced to his compatriots via BBC radio on 18 June. 'For France is not alone! ... She has a vast Empire behind her. She can ally with the British Empire that commands the sea and continues the fight. She can, like England, draw unreservedly on the immense industrial resources of the United States.' Fine words, but broadcast from a country under threat of imminent invasion, by a junior general challenging the authority of a marshal of France. To de Gaulle's fury, his words were not deemed important enough to be recorded for posterity by the BBC.

He could have done nothing in exile without Churchill's support. It was the PM – overruling the Foreign Office and War Cabinet, who both still hoped to keep Pétain in play – who allowed him to use the BBC. Otherwise, de Gaulle's now immortal 'Appel' of 18 June – one of twenty broadcasts he made during June and July 1940 – would have been impossible. This was a debt the General never forgot in all their subsequent altercations. And on 28 June Churchill announced that the British Government recognised de Gaulle as 'leader of all Free Frenchmen, wherever they may be, who rally to him in support of the Allied cause.' Winston, for his part, desperately needed to create the impression that Britain was not entirely alone. He made his own dramatic appeal to the

people of France, in French over the BBC, on 21 October. '*Français.
C'est moi. Churchill*'. With appropriate reference to luminaries such as
Napoleon Bonaparte and Léon Gambetta, champion of the third French
republic in 1870, he assured his audience, 'Never will I believe that
the soul of France is dead. Never will I believe that her place among the
greatest nations of the world has been lost for ever.'[9]

A crucial moment for both men was Britain's destruction of the
French fleet at Mers-el-Kebir on 3 July.[10] De Gaulle's first reaction was
explosive. He told a British liaison officer that he would now have to
decide whether to continue cooperating with Churchill's government
or else 'withdraw to private life in Canada'. But by the time he spoke to
the people of France on 8 July, his tone had softened. He did not deny
the 'grief and anger' felt by himself and his countrymen – feelings that
came from 'the innermost depths of our being'. But, he added, 'from
the point of view of ultimate victory and the deliverance of our country',
since the Vichy government had placed 'our ships at the mercy of the
enemy', he had 'no hesitation in saying that they are better destroyed'.[11]

Despite growing respect, relations between the two men were always
calculating. The problem was that in June 1940 Winston thought he
was backing a military leader who could serve as a temporary rallying
point for French resistance. His support was also 'a slightly impulsive
gamble', observes de Gaulle biographer Julian Jackson, because 'the
romantic and sentimental side of his nature was seduced by the quixotic nobility of the General's solitary struggle'.[12] But since no French
politician of note fled to Britain, de Gaulle became, *faute de mieux*, a
political figure as well; which, of course, was what he intended. For
three years, Churchill tried to avoid a total embrace: he took the line
that 'de Gaulle was not France, but Fighting France'. The General would
have none of this. Told during one meeting that the British Government
was working for '*La France entière*', he exploded: '*La France entière!
C'est la France libre, c'est moi*'.[13]

In 1940–1 the British kept open contacts with Vichy via the Madrid
embassy and other intermediaries. They also tried to rally alternative
leaders in French North Africa. And, after the failure of an attempt

to seize Dakar in September 1940, which the British blamed partly on leaks from de Gaulle's forces, they tried to keep tight control of subsequent operations. 'You think I am interested in England winning the war?' de Gaulle asked one of his British liaison officers. 'I am not. I am only interested in France's victory.' Told that these victories were one and the same, he snapped back, 'Not at all.' Further signs that the British were trespassing on French territory produced new explosions of Gaullian rage, fuelled by his innate suspicion of perfidious Albion – as in May 1942 when the British took control of the French island of Madagascar without even informing de Gaulle in advance. 'There is nothing hostile to England that this man may not do once he gets off the chain,' Churchill warned Eden.[14]

Yet, somehow, their personal relationship survived. One colourful anecdote comes from Jock Colville, Winston's private secretary. In September 1941 de Gaulle was summoned to 10 Downing Street for a formal rebuke over his latest maverick act. Beforehand, the PM announced that he would speak only in English, with Colville as inter-preter. Given Winston's franglais, this might seem an act of kindness, but the PM clearly intended to signify profound disapproval. When de Gaulle arrived in the Cabinet Room, Churchill declared sternly, 'General de Gaulle, I have asked you to come here this afternoon.' He then paused for translation. '*Mon Général*,' Colville began, '*je vous ai invité de venir cet après-midi.*' Winston stopped him: 'I didn't say *Mon Général* and I did not say that I had *invited* him.' Colville stumbled through a few more sentences, with frequent corrections, and then de Gaulle replied. After Colville had translated the first sentence, the general interjected, '*Non, non, ce n'est pas du tout le sens de ce que je disais.*' Colville had no doubt that he had rendered an accurate translation but Churchill said that, since he clearly couldn't do the job, he had better find someone who could. Suppressing his indignation, Colville called in Nicholas Lawford of the Foreign Office, a fluent French-speaker. But within minutes Lawford stomped out of the Cabinet Room, furious to have been told that, since he could not speak French properly, the two leaders would manage alone. After an hour, an anxious Colville was about to enter the room with a bogus message when suddenly the bell rang. He found Churchill and de Gaulle sitting side by side, chatting amiably in French, with the general smoking one of Winston's cigars.[15]

After the attack on Pearl Harbor in December 1941, the troubled Anglo-French marriage was further complicated by the appearance of a third party. De Gaulle had two reactions. First, confirming his his 'Appel', that 'this war is over ... In this industrial war, nothing can resist the power of American industry.' But then he added: 'From now on, the British will do nothing without Roosevelt's agreement.' It was a shrewd prophecy. Winston informed Eden in November 1942: 'My whole system is based on friendship w[ith] Roosevelt.'[16]

The US President, for his part, was confident he could still exert influence over Pétain and Vichy, and had no time for de Gaulle. But the General was no more willing than Winston to preside over the liquidation of his country's once great empire. Over Christmas and New Year 1941–2, there was a flaming row when three Free French corvettes and some 200 troops unilaterally occupied the Vichy-controlled islands of St Pierre and Miquelon, in the Gulf of St Lawrence. 'The trouble with de Gaulle is that he sees himself in the role of Joan of Arc, liberating his country from Vichy,' Eden noted, 'and cooperation with the Allies is secondary in his mind.'[17]

FDR persisted in cultivating Vichy. In November 1942 he insisted that the initial Torch landings in Algeria and Morocco should be a purely American affair, arguing that if no British or Free French forces were involved the Vichy authorities would cooperate with their liberators because the US was renowned as an anti-imperialist power. De Gaulle was informed of the operation only as the troops were going ashore. 'Well, I hope the people of Vichy throw them into the sea' was his vituperative reaction when awakened with the news, standing there in his pyjamas.[18] To compound matters, after FDR's hopes of no resistance proved delusory, the US military concluded a deal on 10 November with Admiral François Darlan, Pétain's deputy, who had been captured in Algiers. Darlan was allowed to assume power in French North Africa in return for declaring a ceasefire. De Gaulle's anger was matched by British incredulity and waves of criticism in the US.

Although unhappy, Winston kept faith with FDR. On 26 November he told Eden that Darlan had 'done more for us than de G[aulle].' He was gratified that the Admiral kept his promise and scuttled the French fleet rather letting it fall into German hands.[19] On 10 December, in a secret speech to the Commons, the PM combined pragmatic defence of the Darlan deal with warnings that de Gaulle was by no means 'an unfaltering friend of Britain' but was, rather, 'one of those good Frenchmen who have a traditional antagonism' ingrained in their hearts 'by centuries of war against the English'. He told MPs that he continued to maintain 'friendly personal relations' with de Gaulle and intended to help him as far as possible because he had 'stood up against the men of Bordeaux and their base surrender' in June 1940. Nevertheless, 'I could not recommend you to base all your hopes and confidence upon him.' Winston then shared with the Commons his own 'certain idea': 'I have lived myself for the last 35 years or more in a mental relationship and to a large extent in sympathy with an abstraction called France. I still do not think it is an illusion. I cannot think that de Gaulle is France, still less that Darlan and Vichy are France. France is something greater, something more complex, more formidable than any of the sectional manifestations.'[20]

This whole uneasy balancing act was brought to an end by Darlan's murder in Algiers on Christmas Eve at the hands of a young royalist. Who was really behind the shooting remains a matter of debate, but, as historian François Kersaudy nicely put it, rarely has a political assassination been 'so unanimously condemned and so universally welcomed'.[21]

With Darlan eliminated and all of France now occupied by Hitler, the Vichy option was clearly dead. But the Allies still tried to dream up alternative Frenchmen. At Casablanca in January 1943 Roosevelt and Churchill pressed de Gaulle to work with their preferred figure, General Henri Giraud, in a unified administration of French North Africa. Giraud, lionised for his daring escape from Nazi captivity, was intended by FDR to galvanise and lead the French army in North Africa. But de Gaulle – so far totally ignored by the Allies during the North African campaign – intended to absorb Giraud in a political structure headed by himself as the true representative of the Republic. He told an aide:

'I cannot compromise with the fundamental interests of France.'

'Could there not be a transitional stage, which would be a kind of duumvirate?'

'A lame solution.'

'On occasion it is necessary to limp along a little before being able to walk straight. There were sometimes two consuls in Rome.'

'But in France there was a First Consul.'[22]

That triumphant invocation of Napoleon ended the conversation. But the Americans did not 'come round' as de Gaulle predicted. And at Casablanca Winston warned him in a 'pretty rough' exchange that if he failed to reach an accord with Giraud and ended up as 'an obstacle to French unity', then 'I should not hesitate to speak in public about these matters.' As the general stalked off, head in the air, the PM remarked: 'His country has given up fighting, he himself is a refugee, and if we turn him down he's finished. Well, just look at him! Look at him! He might be Stalin, with 200 divisions behind his words.'[23] But eventually de Gaulle did a deal with Giraud – sealed by a frigid handshake captured on film as President and Prime Minister watched in genial satisfaction at the 'shotgun wedding'. FDR left Casablanca convinced that de Gaulle saw himself as a combination of Joan of Arc and Clemenceau but also hopeful, in his usual breezy way, that he had now fixed the French problem. Yet, despite starting with a much weaker hand, during 1943 de Gaulle outplayed Giraud and remorselessly enlarged his authority within their combined French Committee of National Liberation (CFLN). Soon he did, indeed, end up as 'First Consul'.

Watching the drift of events, FDR pressed hard for Britain to break with de Gaulle. When Winston stayed in Washington in May 1943, he was fed daily stories about the general's machinations and eventually cabled the Cabinet on 21 May with a diatribe about 'this vain and even malignant man' who 'hates England and has left a trail of Anglophobia behind him everywhere', asking 'whether we should not now eliminate de Gaulle as a political force'.[24] But Eden – consistently more sceptical about America than Churchill and more supportive of France – stiffened the Cabinet. As he privately acknowledged, it was much easier to stand up to Winston *in absentia* – in person the PM's belligerent loquacity usually wore the opposition into silence if not assent. In July 1943, however, Prime Minister and Foreign Secretary did clash head on. Eden argued so strongly for political recognition of de Gaulle that Churchill warned him 'we might be coming to a break.' This remark was in response to a paper from Eden arguing that 'in dealing with European problems of the future, we are likely to have to work more closely with France even than with the United States.' An angry Winston asserted that de Gaulle was 'thoroughly anti-British' and showed 'many of the symptoms of a budding Führer'. He told Eden, 'I am resolved never to allow de Gaulle or his followers to cloud or mar those personal relations of partnership and friendship which I have laboured for nearly four years to develop between me and President Roosevelt by which, I venture to think, the course of our affairs has been notably assisted.'[25] This exchange revealed very clearly the two men's differing priorities. For all his Francophilia, Churchill would side with the US when the chips were down. In the last analysis, Eden would go the opposite way – as Suez in 1956 was to show dramatically.

Caught between Roosevelt and Eden, it's not surprising that Winston frequently lost his cool. Nevertheless, however, his personal relationship with de Gaulle survived. In March 1943, for instance, he refused permission for the general to visit Africa and the Middle East, fearing more anti-British agitation. *'Je suis prisonnier,'* de Gaulle exclaimed when they met. *'Bientôt vous m'enverrez à l'Iloman.'* A puzzled Churchill asked him to repeat the last word. After three attempts, he gathered that de Gaulle meant the Isle of Man – a remote island off the northwest coast of England where enemy aliens were being detained.

Whereupon, in his best French, the PM declared: '*Non, mon Général, pour vous, très distingué, toujours la Tower of London.*' Once again, a sulphurous start was alchemised into an amicable conclusion. Each man entertained a regard for the other that somehow survived their political differences and volcanic rows.[26]

At the end of 1942 Winston had sent Harold Macmillan, a Tory MP, to Algiers as British Minister Resident in North Africa. There Macmillan became much involved in negotiations over the CFLN. On 1 June 1943, he noted in his diary: 'One comes away, as always after conversation with de Gaulle, wondering whether he is a demagogue or madman, but convinced that he is a more powerful character than any other Frenchman with whom one has yet been in contact.' Able to converse tolerably in French, Macmillan spent a fair amount of social time with de Gaulle, chatting about politics, religion, history and the classics. 'But I'm afraid he will always be impossible to work with. He is by nature an autocrat. Just like Louis XIV or Napoleon. He thinks in his heart that he should command and all others should obey him.' Macmillan's relationship with de Gaulle, initiated in wartime North Africa, would cast a long shadow over the post-war history of their two countries.[27]

By the end of the year de Gaulle had full control of the CFLN, entirely forcing out Giraud. Yet nothing was decided by Churchill and Roosevelt about the future government of France itself. And major decisions that autumn showed that de Gaulle still stood on the margins of the Allied war effort – not consulted about the Italian surrender, left off the new European Advisory Committee and excluded from the Big Three meeting at Tehran.

At every step of the way, de Gaulle insisted on his dignity as the personification of France. After a difficult dinner in Marrakech in January 1944, Winston exclaimed, '*C'est un grand animal!*' A couple of weeks later he told friends in London about it, contrasting how he and de Gaulle treated their respective positions of diplomatic dependence: 'Look here! I am the leader of a strong, unbeaten nation. Yet every morning when I wake up my first thought is how I can please

President Roosevelt, and my second is how I can conciliate Marshal Stalin. Your situation is very different. Why then should your first waking thought be how you can snap your fingers at the British and Americans?'

As far as de Gaulle was concerned, however, the essential negotiating ploy, for a leader in his position, could only be the eternal '*Non*'. As he explained later to a wartime colleague: 'Begin by saying "no"! Two things will follow. Either your "no" is destined to remain a "no" and you have shown yourself to be someone of character. Or finally you send up saying "yes". But then (a) you have given yourself time to reflect; (b) people will be all the more grateful for the final "yes".'[28]

Gaullian tactics were dramatically in evidence in the run-up to D-Day. As with Operation Torch, Roosevelt refused to bring de Gaulle into the planning. It was only after repeated pleas from Eden that Churchill summoned the general from Algiers on 4 June in order to tell him that his country was about to be liberated. 'Otherwise,' the PM cabled Roosevelt, 'it may become a very grave insult to France.'[29] But FDR still refused to accept the CFLN as France's provisional government, and de Gaulle was furious that the Allied Supreme Commander, General Dwight D. Eisenhower, planned to impose a government of occupation, complete with its own 'French' currency. According to the British record, the PM then stated 'bluntly' as tempers rose that 'if after every effort had been exhausted, the President was on one side and the French National Committee of Liberation on the other', he 'would almost certainly side with the President' and that 'anyhow no quarrel would ever arise between Britain and the United States on account of France.' The version in de Gaulle's memoirs is more colourful, with Churchill declaring, 'You must know that when we have to choose between Europe and the open sea [*le grand large*], we shall always choose the open sea. Each time I have to choose between you and Roosevelt, I will choose Roosevelt.'

Whatever the PM actually said, that was how de Gaulle remembered his words. As Julian Jackson observes, 'they rankled for the rest of his life.'[30]

During the night before D-Day, 5–6 June, there were acrimonious exchanges about protocol and policy between de Gaulle and Churchill – both weary and worried about what the dawn would bring. At one point Churchill ordered de Gaulle to be sent back to Algiers, 'in chains if necessary', insisting that 'he must not be allowed to enter France.' It took all Eden's finesse to have the order rescinded.[31] Eventually the General was allowed to set foot on French soil on 14 June, almost exactly four years since he had departed. Roosevelt assumed that he would soon be eclipsed by other figures, but de Gaulle was determined to prove him wrong, starting with a walkabout in Bayeux on 14 June, played up by Free French publicists. In 1940, for most French foes of Pétain and Hitler, de Gaulle had simply been a voice. Gradually his face, with that long nose, became well known. But June 1944 began the incarnation, as de Gaulle was seen and touched by the French in their millions.

Above all, on 25 July in his brilliantly staged entry into Paris. Eisenhower had been persuaded to let a French armoured division liberate the city after the Germans left without a fight. At the Hôtel de Ville, de Gaulle delivered a rhetorical *tour de force*: 'Paris! Paris outraged! Paris broken! Paris martyred!' A long pause. 'But Paris liberated! Liberated by itself, liberated by its people with the help of the armies of France, with the help and assistance of the whole of France, of that France which fights, of the only France, of the true France, of eternal France.' No reference to Churchill's Britain, where he had been given sanctuary. No thanks to the Allied armies who had made the liberation possible. No allusion to the Resistance who had harried the Nazis at great personal cost for four years. Next day he walked slowly down the Champs-Elysées to show himself to his people. The crowd was immense. 'It looked more like the sea,' de Gaulle rhapsodised in his memoirs. 'Perhaps two million souls.' No one knows, but Jackson suggests it was 'probably the largest gathering of its kind in the history of France ... The voice from London was made flesh at last.'[32]

Even Winston, a superb showman, could not have matched this Gaullian extravaganza – hence his grudging admiration for *le grand animal*. FDR, too, relented. After the tidal wave of support accorded the General on French soil, Roosevelt finally received him at the White House. Full diplomatic recognition followed at the end of October. The gesture resolved Winston's problem in juggling Roosevelt and de Gaulle and paved the way for his own visit to Paris. On Armistice Day, 11 November, the two leaders made their own promenade down the Champs-Elysées to cheers from hundreds of thousands of Parisians. They paid their respects at Clemenceau's statue, Foch's grave and Napoleon's tomb, where the PM spent a long moment, murmuring to his host, 'In all the world there is nothing greater.' During lunch, both men were gracious and expansive in their speeches: de Gaulle toasted the fidelity of 'our old and gallant ally, England', while Churchill, close to tears, welcomed France back to the ranks of 'the great nations' and praised 'the capital part' played by de Gaulle in the transformation of his country's fortunes.[33] But their business discussions over the next two days showed that for Winston sentiment did not outweigh realpolitik. According to de Gaulle's memoirs – though again not found in the British record – when he suggested an exclusive bilateral alliance of the sort mooted during the crisis of June 1940, the PM reiterated that he wished to work first with the US, using his close personal tie with FDR to persuade and guide the Americans to use their 'immense resources' to best advantage.[34] Winston's message remained clear. '*Entente cordiale – mais oui!*' But there was only one 'special relationship'.

Given Churchill's priorities and Roosevelt's prejudices, France, even after liberation, would therefore remain on the margins. FDR, in fact, was not merely Gaullophobe but Gallophobe, entertaining profound doubts about the future of France itself. In December 1944, as Greece descended into civil war, he told another British minister that 'no doubt we should see the Greek situation repeated elsewhere, probably in France' and that he was 'determined that American troops should not be mixed up with the French civil war'.[35] Clearly the President had no faith in France as a cohesive state, let alone a great power. His confidant Harry Hopkins told de Gaulle in January 1945 that the root problem was the shock felt in Washington at the French collapse in

1940. America's traditional assumptions about the power and status of France had been destroyed in an instant.[36]

Winston had a much higher estimation of France, especially after his visit in November 1944. But when Eden started to press the idea of a 'Western European bloc' centred on France, as a contribution to continental security, the PM was scathing:

> Until a really strong French Army is again in being, which may be more than five years away or even ten, there is nothing in these countries but hopeless weakness. The Belgians are extremely weak, and their behaviour before the war was shocking. The Dutch were entirely selfish and fought only when they were attacked, and then for a few hours. Denmark is defenceless, and Norway practically so. That England should undertake to defend these countries, together with any help they may afford, before the French have the second Army in Europe, seems to me contrary to all wisdom and even common prudence. It may well be that the Continent will be able to fire at us, and we at the Continent; and that our island position is damaged to that extent. But with a strong Air Force and adequate naval power, the Channel is a tremendous obstacle to invasion by armies and tanks.[37]

In short: 1940 reigns supreme.

Just before Churchill's visit, de Gaulle requested an invitation to the Kremlin, judging the trip and the attendant publicity as essential to help re-establish France as a great power. Ever since June 1941 he had seen Soviet Russia not only as a military asset but also as a potential 'balancing element against the Anglo-Saxons'.[38] The December 1944 visit sent shockwaves through London and Washington but the treaty of friendship signed with Stalin offered nothing on the future of Germany and generally made clear that France did not count for much in Soviet policy.

This was underlined at the Yalta conference in February 1945, from which de Gaulle was entirely excluded. It was only after repeated pressure from Churchill and Eden that France was given an occupation zone in Germany and a seat on the Allied Control Commission. Stalin and FDR indicated that this was an act of 'kindness' on their part rather than a recognition of international realities. In developing his case, the PM even said he did not want the French in Big Three meetings, at least for a considerable time, and that this concession over Germany would help 'satisfy their amour propre'. Stalin doubted it would, whereupon Churchill declared 'that theirs was a very exclusive club and that the entrance subscription was the possession of at least five million soldiers or their equivalent'.[39] This statement pointed to Winston's real concern: FDR's reiteration at the conference that he did not expect Congress to keep an army in Europe for more than two years after the war.[40] That fact strengthened Winston's desire to find another European partner to help keep Germany down and, perhaps, as some British military planners argued, also to offset the growing power of Russia.

So victory in 1945 had a bitter taste for de Gaulle, who was still struggling to regain France's place at the top table. And it turned sour for Winston, too, as he tried ineffectually to persuade the US to take a firmer line against Soviet expansion. Moreover, for both men, personal tragedy soon intervened. In July Churchill found himself voted out of Downing Street by the British electorate. Although in November the French Assembly elected de Gaulle President of the new Fourth Republic, he had no control over the government amid a melee of parties that replayed the squabbles of the 1930s and undermined his sense of rightful leadership. On 20 January 1946 he resigned, probably intending it as a tactical retreat: 'I thought the French would recall me very quickly,' he admitted a few years later.[41] But they didn't. Churchill returned to power in 1951; de Gaulle had to wait until 1958.

* * *

After 1945, Churchill and de Gaulle kept in touch. When Winston was at Antibes in September 1948, he learnt that de Gaulle was in the vicinity and sent a note of greeting. This elicited a very cordial handwritten reply in French in which the General expressed 'all the admiration and friendship which I have for you. If your journey happens to take you near Colombey-les-Deux-Eglises before leaving France, my wife and I will be very happy and indeed honoured to receive you there in complete privacy.' Winston did not avail himself of this opportunity to visit the de Gaulles at their country house in Champagne.[42] Which is a pity. When Konrad Adenauer accepted a similar invitation to Colombey in 1958, this personal hospitality *chez de Gaulle* proved a breakthrough moment in relations between the two men and their two countries. But by then Adenauer was West Germany's Chancellor and de Gaulle once more President of France. A decade earlier, Churchill and the General were merely private citizens.

Winston's view of post-war France and Germany was shaped by his vision of a 'United Europe'. In late 1946 he drew the General's attention to his speech on that theme at Zurich on 19 September, when Winston had lamented 'the tragedy of Europe', ravaged in a 'series of frightful nationalistic quarrels, originated by the Teutonic nations in their rise to power'. Of course, he said, 'the guilty must be punished' and Germany 'deprived of the power to rearm and make another aggressive war'. But then 'there must be an end to retribution.' And he added that famous remark calculated to 'astonish you', declaring: 'The first step in the re-creation of the European family must be a partnership between France and Germany' to build 'a kind of United States of Europe'.[43]

Winston then sent his son-in-law Duncan Sandys to investigate the General's attitude, but Sandys' summary of their talk was discouraging. 'All Frenchmen were violently opposed to recreating any kind of unified, centralised Reich, and were gravely suspicious of the policy of the American and British Governments. Unless steps were taken to prevent a resuscitation of German power, there was a danger that a United Europe would become nothing else than an enlarged Germany.' The only way to win over the French, stated de Gaulle, was for France to 'come in as a founder partner with Britain', with both having previously reached 'a precise understanding' about their attitude towards Germany.[44]

De Gaulle's suspicions of Churchill as a European could only have been strengthened by Winston's speech to the Tory party conference on 9 October 1948 about 'three great circles among the free nations and democracies': 'the British Commonwealth and Empire'; 'the English-speaking world', including the United States; and, thirdly, 'United Europe'. He then drew attention to the special position of Britain within this 'majestic' global geometry: 'If you think of the three interlinked circles you will see that we are the only country which has a great part in every one of them. We stand, in fact, at the very point of junction, and here in this Island at the centre of the seaways and perhaps of the airways also, we have the opportunity of joining them all together.'[45]

Returning to this theme in a Cabinet paper in late 1951, at the start of his second premiership, Winston welcomed the European Coal and Steel Community (ECSC) as 'a step in the reconciliation of France and Germany' which was 'probably rendering another Franco-German war physically impossible'. He felt Britain should 'favour the movement to closer European unity and try to get the United States' support in this work'. But he also reiterated the lessons of 1940 and his concept of the three circles:

> I should resist any American pressure to treat Britain as on the same footing as the European States, none of whom have the advantages of the Channel and who were consequently conquered. Our first object is the unity and the consolidation of the British Commonwealths and what is left of the former British Empire. Our second, the 'fraternal association' of the English-speaking world; and third, United Europe, to which we are a separate closely- and specially-related ally and friend.[46]

Most leading Tories in the 1950s agreed with Winston that Britain could have its cake *and* eat it, if the country kept moving nimbly between the three circles. Indeed, this Churchillian conceit about British power was shared by both main parties and it endured long

after Winston's political life was over. In 1955 the six members of the
ECSC invited Britain to join in talks about further integration. After
some debate, the government of his successor, Anthony Eden, sent
only a senior official from the Board of Trade, simply to observe
proceedings. Most of Whitehall believed that the negotiations would
collapse given the febrile volatility of French politics, and the issue
was hardly discussed in Cabinet. Such complacency, even arrogance,
about countries that had recently been either vanquished enemies or
feeble allies has been dubbed 'the price of victory'.[47]

Eden's Government failed to anticipate the unlikely alliance forged
by Guy Mollet, France's Prime Minister in 1956, and Chancellor
Adenauer in Bonn. Although Mollet was a socialist and Adenauer a
Christian Democrat, both were committed to Franco-German
rapprochement, and Mollet's determination was reinforced when Eden
lost his nerve during the Anglo-French military operation to regain
control of the Suez Canal in November 1956 and accepted a ceasefire.
The French were furious at British perfidy: Adenauer reputedly told
Mollet that 'Europe will be your revenge.'[48] And so the Treaty of Rome
was signed in March 1957, without Britain. Although London's sticking
point is often described as the principle of national sovereignty, it was
really British unwillingness to abridge that sovereignty through
European as well as *transatlantic* interdependence. When the chips
were down, 'Europe' had indeed taken second place to the 'open sea'.

De Gaulle, out of office for most of the 1950s, remained a fierce
critic of the European project. But by the time he became President
of the newly constituted Fifth Republic on New Year's Day 1959, the
European Economic Community (EEC) was up and running. Equally
important, West Germany was a member of NATO and one of the
founding Six of the EEC. President de Gaulle therefore accepted the
Treaty of Rome as a fait accompli while trying to shape both the EEC
and the Franco-German partnership to his liking. Welcoming Adenauer
to Colombey was a first step in that strategy.

By the end of the decade, attitudes in London were shifting.
Although the economic case for Britain's entry to the EEC still seemed

evenly balanced, the geopolitical implications of staying out looked alarming. 'If the Community succeeds in becoming a really effective political and economic force,' a Whitehall committee advised, 'it will become the dominant influence in Europe and the only Western bloc approaching the importance of the big Two – the USSR and the United States. The influence of the United Kingdom in Europe, if left outside, will correspondingly decline.' Crucially, this might erode the 'special relationship' if Washington began treating the EEC as its main transatlantic partner.[49]

But when Macmillan, who had taken over from Eden as Prime Minister after the Suez debacle, knocked on the EEC's door in 1961, he found it firmly locked – with de Gaulle holding the keys. No less than Britain, the French retained global as well as European interests but they had managed to fit the former adroitly within the latter, and the President had no intention of relinquishing that advantage. Asked why France was so hostile to British entry, de Gaulle's agriculture minister informed his British counterpart with chauvinistic elegance: 'My dear chap. It's very simple. At the moment, with the Six, there are five hens and one cock. If you join (with the other countries), there will be perhaps seven or eight hens. But there will be *two* cocks. Well, that's not so pleasant.'[50]

Macmillan hoped that his efforts to help de Gaulle in North Africa in 1943 would now pay political dividends. During several meetings in 1960–2, he argued that the pair had much in common, including opposition to a federalist Europe and a German revival. But to no avail. 'He talks of Europe but he means France,' the PM fumed. 'His pride, his inherited hatred of Britain', including 'bitter memories of the last war', and 'above all, his immense vanity for France' proved stronger. Again and again 'he goes back to his disgust and his dislike, like a dog to his vomit.' De Gaulle did not believe that Britain's application to join the EEC reflected a fundamental change of heart from that expressed by the Churchillian phrase he still chose to recall from D-Day. He told Macmillan in June 1962: 'The sense of being an island remains very strong with you. England looks to the sea, to wider horizons. She remains very linked to the United States by language, by habits and by certain agreements.'[51]

And so, in a regal press conference on 14 January 1963, de Gaulle blocked Britain's application. He did so again in 1967 and it was only after his resignation in 1969 that negotiations resumed. By the time the UK did join, in 1973, the EEC's institutions had set firm in ways that did not suit British interests, and there was little prospect now of radical reform because the post-war economic boom had faded into a new era of oil shocks and stagflation. Britain became Europe's 'awkward partner'[52] – chafing against further integration as the EEC slowly evolved into the European Union, until the referendum for Brexit in 2016. Thereafter, instead of facing the problems of living with the Europeans inside the EU, the UK had to deal with the same problems from outside.

So it was Charles de Gaulle, not Guy Mollet, who had truly exploited Adenauer's invitation: 'Europe will be your revenge.' And he had done so in one of the most striking acts of post-war *realpolitik*, marking him out as a ruthless statesman. Britain's ambivalence towards the integration project in the decisive mid-1950s – when 'Europe' could still be shaped – had given him the chance. And although much of the responsibility for that lies with the Eden Government, Churchill's belief about Britain having its European cake and eating it surely played a part. His three 'majestic circles' could not be squared: that concept was not a realistic vision but a *trompe l'oeil* that flattered a country unwilling to face up to the true legacies of the Second World War.[53]

In any case, it was probably inevitable that a man with de Gaulle's personality would want to bite the hand that fed him. At Casablanca in January 1943 a tearful Winston had remarked to his entourage: 'England's grievous offence in de Gaulle's eyes is that she has helped France. He cannot bear to think that she needed help.' In similar vein, the ageing Macmillan opined to his biographer, 'Things would have been easier if Southern England had been occupied by the Nazis – if we'd had Lloyd George for Pétain . . . I may be cynical, but I fear it's true – if Hitler had danced in London we'd have had no trouble with de Gaulle.'[54] (Though, of course, much more trouble with Hitler.)

How Winston reacted in 1963 to de Gaulle's revenge is not known. By then, deaf and enfeebled, he took in little and said even less. There were unconfirmed rumours that he wanted de Gaulle's name to be removed from the guest list for his state funeral. And although he apparently joked that the funeral train must not leave London for the Oxfordshire village of Bladon from Paddington Station, because he wanted de Gaulle to endure Waterloo, in fact that station, next to the Thames, was the best place to transfer the coffin from boat to train. (In any case, the interment near Blenheim was strictly for the family and close friends.) When de Gaulle heard the news of Churchill's death he murmured, without obvious regret, 'Now Britain is no longer a great power.' And he did attend the funeral in St Paul's.[55]

Speculation aside, what we have is the image each wished to leave for the posterity of the other, because during their post-war wilderness years both worked assiduously on their war memoirs. Indeed, de Gaulle was the only one of Winston's great contemporaries to publish his own account, thereby allowing us – as it were – a two-way mirror. Churchill introduces de Gaulle early in Volume 2, *Their Finest Hour*. After a vivid depiction of the feebleness of Gamelin and the French high command at the Quai d'Orsay on 16 May 1940, de Gaulle is then brought on stage as the embodiment of 'Fighting France', in contrast with his now defeatist superiors. At Tours on 13 June Churchill glimpses him 'stolid and expressionless' at the end of a crowded passage. 'Greeting him, I said in a low tone, in French: "L'homme du destin."' When de Gaulle was asked in the 1960s by his biographer whether he had heard these words at the time, the General said 'no'. But he added: 'What is true is that we took to one other right away.'[56]

The 'man of destiny' tag also serves as an interpretative key to Churchill's treatment of de Gaulle throughout the memoirs. The reader is left in no doubt that this was a difficult, often turbulent relationship, but Winston's published verdict was moderated and modulated by hindsight in two main ways. The first simplification was political. From the competing wartime claimants, de Gaulle had triumphantly emerged as the representative of France. Churchill's memoirs (1948–54) therefore played down Britain's attempts to keep all options open, especially his dalliance with Vichy in 1940–2 and his brief but real enthusiasm for Admiral Darlan in the early days of Operation Torch.[57]

The other simplification was personal. By the time Churchill started writing, de Gaulle's first presidency was over but he had founded his own party and was clearly a major force in the polarised politics of the Fourth Republic. An eventual return to power seemed likely, and it was therefore deemed prudent to omit from documents quoted in the memoirs the more pungent Churchillisms. So, 'symptoms of a budding Führer' (July 1943) did not make it into print; nor did a remark to the War Cabinet in 1945 that de Gaulle's presence at Yalta 'would have wrecked all possible progress'.[58] Readers were also deprived of what was probably Winston's most honest verdict on the General, quoted as one of the epigraphs to this chapter, that he would 'be sorry to live in a country governed by de Gaulle' but would also 'be sorry to live in a world, or with a France, in which there was not a de Gaulle'. Yet there survived into print this very accurate rendition of his feelings in a passage on the Casablanca conference of 1943: 'Always, even when he was behaving worst, he seemed to express the personality of France – a great nation, with all its pride, authority, and ambition.'[59]

De Gaulle was slower to publish. It was not until his party's failure in the elections of June 1951 that the General retreated to Colombey and began to write. Unlike Churchill with his self-styled 'factory' of researchers and secretaries at Chartwell, de Gaulle operated a craft industry, scrawling out the draft by hand before it was typed up by his daughter.[60] He also produced a much cleaner narrative than Winston, who saved time and energy by reproducing masses of contemporary documents. 'I want to write a *work* [*une oeuvre*],' the General declared, adding caustically, 'unlike Churchill who has never written a properly composed book, just interesting observations and lots of documents' which amounted, he said, to 'one thing after another'.[61] Volume 1 (on 1940–2) appeared in 1954 and Volume 2 (1942–4) followed in 1956, but the last volume was not published until 1959, after de Gaulle had become President. Like Churchill, he made clear the extent and frequency of their differences. Less tied to the documents, he was also probably freer with his 'quotations' – notably that purple passage about choosing between 'Europe and the open sea' attributed to Churchill just before D-Day. Yet a long passage about their first meeting on 9 June 1940 includes this tribute:

> The harsh and painful incidents that often arose between us, because of the friction of our two characters, of the opposition of some of the interests of our two countries, and of the unfair advantage taken by England of wounded France, have influenced my attitude towards the Prime Minister, but not my judgment. Winston Churchill appeared to me, from one end of the drama to the other, as the great champion of a great enterprise and the great artist of a great history.[62]

Those last words can be read in several ways. '*Quel grand artiste!*', de Gaulle often exclaimed about his English protagonist, seeking to capture thereby Winston the performer's sense of the theatrical, being someone whom de Gaulle called 'a romantic type'.[63] But 'the great artist of a great history' also captures the way that a romanticised narrative of 'our island story' was integral to Winston's very being. And the *grand artiste* line could be applied to both of them. These were men with the confidence to seize the moment, however unpropitious it might seem. Leaders whose heroic sense of their country's past in turn shaped their vision for the future. Artists able to depict a vast historic canvas in bold, vivid colours. Above all, two men intoxicated by greatness. Given such larger-than-life personalities, it was almost inevitable they would clash – and the divergent legacies of 1940 made that clash more acrimonious. But it's likely that if the boot had been on the other foot, Winston would have been just as much of a pain to de Gaulle as the General proved for him.

'The great champion of a great enterprise and the great artist of a great history' has a strange echo of what Winston wrote in *Great Contemporaries* about Georges Clemenceau and Marshal Ferdinand Foch. Clemenceau, France's Prime Minister in 1917–20, was known as

'Le Tigre' and 'Père la Victoire' – nicknames that capture his character and his achievement. 'As much as any single human being, miraculously magnified, can ever be a nation, he was France,' Winston wrote in 1937. 'He represented the French people risen against tyrants – tyrants of the mind, tyrants of the soul, tyrants of the body, foreign tyrants, domestic tyrants . . . traitors, invaders, defeatists . . .' Clemenceau – an anti-clerical 'Radical' – was very different from the soldierly Foch. Appointed Supreme Allied Commander in March 1918 when the Germans nearly broke through, he pulled together the feuding French, British and American armies and gave them the cohesion needed to turn the tide and bring the war to its victorious conclusion. For Winston, the courtly courage of Foch expressed 'another France . . . ancient, aristocratic; the France whose grace and culture, whose etiquette and ceremonial has bestowed its gifts around the world'.[64]

Having depicted Clemenceau and Foch vividly but separately, Churchill concludes: 'In the combination of these two men during the last year of the War, the French people found in their services all the glories and vital essences of Gaul. These two men embodied respectively their ancient and their modern history'.[65] One wishes that he had returned to this theme in his final years. Might he have imagined the restless spirits of Foch and Clemenceau finding some kind of unity in the bosom of Charles de Gaulle?

Virtually the last encounter between Churchill and de Gaulle occurred in April 1960, when the latter – now President of the Fifth Republic, with a constitution much more to his regal liking – paid a state visit to London. This was his first time across the Channel since those fateful days in 1944. Intent on rehabilitating France as a great power, he obstinately spoke French as much as possible throughout the visit. One of the side-events was a meeting with Churchill, now 85 and fading fast. But when the President arrived – late – the old man dragged himself to his feet with sudden animation. '*Ah, mon général, c'est un grand plaisir de vous rencontre aujourd'hui.*' De Gaulle smiled warmly: 'Sir Winston, how good of you to be here!'[66]

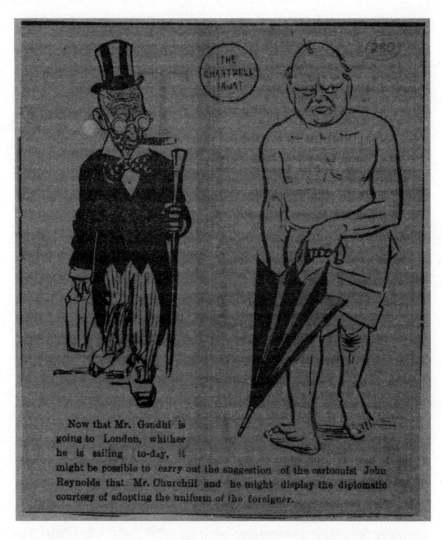

Now that Mr. Gandhi is
going to London, whither
he is sailing to-day, it
might be possible to carry out the suggestion of the cartoonist John
Reynolds that Mr. Churchill and he might display the diplomatic
courtesy of adopting the uniform of the foreigner.

On 29 August 1931, as Gandhi sets out for the Round Table conference
in London, cartoonist John Reynolds imagines the inconceivable.

9

Mohandas K. Gandhi

'Half-Naked' Power

With this, I am shaking the foundations of the British Empire.
                                        M.K. Gandhi, 6 April 1930[1]

It is alarming and also nauseating to see Mr. Gandhi, a seditious Middle Temple lawyer, now posing as a fakir of a type well known in the East, striding half-naked up the steps of the Viceregal palace, while he is still organising and conducting a defiant campaign of civil disobedience, to parley on equal terms with the representative of the King-Emperor.
                                        Winston S. Churchill, 23 February 1931[2]

'Posing as a fakir . . . striding half-naked'. One can almost hear the relish with which Churchill mouthed those choice phrases when addressing his constituents in 1931. This was the artistic showman in full flight. But there was a pungency, almost nastiness, as well – 'alarming', 'nauseating', 'seditious' – which recalls his denunciation of Russian Bolsheviks, a decade before, as baboons and vermin. The 'fakir' quote has been dismissed as an 'ignorant jibe',[3] but Winston did not waste his rhetorical blockbusters on minor targets. By the 1930s he bracketed Gandhi with Hitler as the two most dangerous threats to Britain's global position.

Yet there was a fundamental difference. The threat from the Führer could be understood in conventional power-political terms: Germany was rearming and that must be met by British rearmament. What really got under Winston's skin was that Gandhi was not playing the familiar game. This colonial subject trained at the Inns of Court, yet now dressed up as a 'half-naked fakir', seemed a conman: truly a faker. Worse still, his political creed of non-violence could not be overcome by force, and that challenged everything Winston had understood about power since his Sandhurst days. He would never have conceded to Gandhi the accolade of 'greatness', but the little Indian in his loincloth (dhoti) was able to mobilise power of a sort that Winston never dreamed of – as when he picked up a lump of salty mud from a beach in Gujarat in April 1930 to trigger mass protest. With such unlikely weapons, he helped liquidate the British Empire at its colonial heart in South Asia.

Winston's jousts with the Mahatma also exposed the complexity of his attitude to race and empire. Individual human cases could arouse his keen sense of injustice – the Amritsar massacre in 1919 being a striking example – and he frequently described paternalistic British rule as a defence against local oppression. At root, however, he saw the Empire as fundamental to Britain's position as a world power: global Britain, in his view, was essentially imperial Britain. And although he regarded some non-white groups more highly than others, he had no doubt about the superiority of the 'white race' and also of its civilisation. That's why the battle for the Indian Raj in the 1930s and 1940s became so crucial for his principles and his politics.

* * *

Churchill's axiomatic faith in the rightness of the British Empire and the superiority of the 'white race' was expounded in his very first major political speech, on leave from India, at Bath in July 1897, as the country was celebrating Queen Victoria's sixty years on the throne. He told cheering Tories:

> There are those who say that in this Jubilee year our Empire has reached the height of its glory and power, and that now we shall begin to decline, as Babylon, Carthage, Rome declined. Do not believe

these croakers, but give the lie to their dismal croaking by showing by our actions that the vigour and vitality of our race is unimpaired and that our determination is to uphold the Empire we have inherited from our fathers as Englishmen, that our flag shall fly high upon the sea, our voice shall be heard in the councils of Europe, our Sovereign shall be supported by the love of her subjects. Then shall we continue to pursue that course marked out for us by an all-wise hand and carry out our mission of bearing peace, civilization and good government to the uttermost ends of the earth.

Although Winston's language and tone would change over the years, that ebullient expression of late Victorian imperialism encapsulates his lifelong creed.[4]

At the turn of the century, making his name as a soldier-journalist in war zones from the Northwest Frontier of India to South Africa, Winston became known as one of the country's leading observers of empire. Yet his direct experience of the British world was distinctly limited in both time and space. After a year of military service in the Raj in 1896–7 – much of it, apart from the Malakand expedition, in barracks or on the polo ground – he never spent time in twentieth-century India. He did make several trips to North Africa and the Middle East, especially in 1942–3, but never visited Australia and New Zealand or Malaya, Singapore and Hong Kong – all of them significant regions of the Empire. And his last sight of a British colony in sub-Saharan Africa was in 1907–8, when visiting Kenya and Uganda as Under-Secretary for the Colonies. In short, this was an imperialist running increasingly on intellectual capital and roseate memories from the Victorian sunset.

By this time Gandhi, five years older than Winston, had become a well-known campaigner for Indian rights in South Africa. Having been called to the London Bar in 1891, he returned to India, but then moved to Natal in 1893 to act as a lawyer for an Indian trader in Durban. What was initially a one-year commitment turned into a career of political activism lasting more than two decades, during which Gandhi developed much of his basic philosophy. Natal was one of the two British colonies in South Africa, and it had brought in Indians as indentured labour to cultivate the sugar, coffee and tea plantations. The Indian community put down roots and prospered as farmers and traders. Yet Indians were denied the vote and suffered discrimination in civic life, being obliged, for example, to walk in the street rather than on public footpaths and denied first-class travel on trains. In 1894 Gandhi – himself the victim of such mistreatment – helped found the Natal Indian Congress. At this stage he was claiming the equal rights that Queen Victoria had promised the Raj in 1858, after the brutal suppression of what the British called the 'Indian Mutiny', and he still placed his faith in what has been called Britain's 'moral empire' whose values, he believed, would trump the aggressive imperialism of trade and territory.[5] Keen to show his loyalty to that (idealised) empire, Gandhi raised a group of more than a thousand Indian stretcher bearers. They supported British troops in the front line in the Boer War, notably in the brutal battle of Spion Kop in 1900 where, by happenstance, Winston served nearby as a runner between the embattled soldiers and British commanders.

It was only at the Colonial Office in 1905–8 that Churchill started to take seriously the place of Indians, and indeed Asiatics, in the British Empire. In East Africa he urged the case for Indian participation on the new legislative council: 'There can be no reason for excluding this large and meritorious class.'[6] But in South Africa, after the war ended in 1902, his priority was to conciliate the Boers. Worthy principles such as 'the safeguarding of all immigrants against servile conditions of labour', he told the Commons in February 1906, had to be adapted to 'existing circumstances' in particular colonies – distinguishing between 'harsh customs which we dislike' and 'positive cruelty' against which the British Government must act. He stressed the overriding need in South Africa for peace and reconciliation between 'the two European races' and asked the House to remember the colonists' anxieties about 'the ever-swelling sea of dark humanity' on which 'they float somewhat uneasily . . . one white man to five natives'. But Winston assured the House that 'we will endeavour as far as we can to advance the principle of equal rights of civilised men irrespective of colour.' This principle – borrowed from Cecil Rhodes – encapsulates Winston's racial philosophy: equal rights, but modified by the crucial criteria of 'civilised', and, of course, 'men'.[7]

To Gandhi in South Africa, the Liberal understanding of self-government simply meant leaving the white settlers to their own devices. In November 1906 he and a Muslim businessman, Haji Ally, arrived in London to lobby the Government. The only record of their meeting with Winston comes from Gandhi, who said he 'spoke nicely'. Ally protested his loyalty to the Crown, adding that he had been among the crowd welcoming Churchill to Durban after his escape from the Boers, whereupon Winston smiled, patted Ally on the back and 'said he would do all he could'.[8] But Winston never referred to the encounter. Certainly it did not change his thinking. After Louis Botha's Afrikaan Het Volk party won the February 1907 election, it immediately passed a law restricting immigration from India and requiring 'Asiatics' already in South Africa to register or leave. This pushed Gandhi into his policy of non-violent resistance (satyagraha) and his first period in jail. 'Please tell Botha', Winston cabled the British High Commissioner in South Africa, 'I am going to support his Government most strongly on the Indian question and that I thoroughly understand the views of white South Africa.'[9]

Over the next few years, Gandhi went to jail several times during campaigns of satyagraha. But he had not entirely lost his faith in the 'moral empire'. In 1914, as in 1899, he organised an Indian ambulance corps to offer non-violent support for the British Empire in the Great War and then sailed on from London to India, arriving in Bombay (Mumbai) on 9 January 1915. Having not set foot in his homeland for twenty-two years, he returned with a profound conviction that satyagraha was 'an infallible panacea' for 'the many ills we suffer from in India'. His sense of Indian identity had also been reconfigured by the long exile in London and Johannesburg. A Hindu, he had worked closely with Muslims. A native Gujarati speaker, he had dealt with

Indians speaking Tamil, Telegu, Hindi, Urdu and Bengali. These experiences nurtured a deep sense that national unity must somehow embrace religious and linguistic pluralism. And his disenchantment with the fruits of industrialism in Britain and South Africa left him determined to base India's future on a return to its peasant and craft traditions. 'For Gandhi, swaraj and swadeshi, freedom and self-reliance, went hand in hand.' He told a journalist in 1919, 'I want every man, woman and child to learn hand-spinning and weaving' – both to break the country's dependence on British textiles and also to bring people back to the traditions of village life.[10] Here was a vision of India fundamentally at odds with that of Churchill, who advocated economic development, firmly sponsored by the Raj, and a large Indian army to maintain British rule across South Asia and the Middle East.

At this stage Gandhi's aim was 'Home Rule' within the British Empire. Like the Irish leader John Redmond or David Ben Gurion in Palestine, he believed it necessary to support the war effort in order to buy British goodwill, offering 'ungrudging and unequivocal support to the Empire, of which we aspire, in the near future, to be partners in the same sense as the Dominions overseas'.[11]

Some politicians in London were sympathetic to this strategy, notably Edwin Montagu, the Secretary of State for India. His Government of India Act (1919) established the principle of 'dyarchy' by which some areas of provincial government – such as agriculture, health and education – were transferred to Indian ministers answerable to provincial councils, while security, defence and communications remained reserved for British officials. But Montagu's reforms, together with the Bolshevik Revolution and the Paris peace conference, aroused the expectations of Indians and provoked tougher government laws against subversion. Gandhi mobilised a satyagraha in protest, and his growing prominence gave him the chance to take leadership of the Hindu-dominated Congress party. But, as would happen on other occasions, he could not control the forces he aroused, or ensure that protests remained peaceful.

As violence escalated in the Punjab, a harsh regime of martial law was declared and on 13 April 1919 British troops fired on a motley crowd of protestors and pilgrims in the city of Amritsar who were defying the ban by congregating in Jallianwala Bagh, an enclosed park near the Sikh Golden Temple. Estimates of the death toll range from 400 to 1,000. The carnage severely damaged Britain's moral image in India and around the world.

The local British commander, Colonel Reginald Dyer, was censured by a committee of inquiry and Churchill, as Secretary of State for War, eventually had to speak about the case in a debate in the House of Commons on 8 July 1920. Passions were running high on both sides, many MPs condemning Dyer's brutality while others defended a 'gallant' soldier who had only done his duty. With the debate getting out of hand, Winston delivered a methodical and measured narrative of events, leading into a defence of Dyer's censure. He also underlined 'one general prohibition' of overriding importance, namely that against 'frightfulness' – meaning 'the inflicting of great slaughter or massacre upon a particular crowd of people, with the intention of terrorising not merely the rest of the crowd, but the whole district or the whole country'. Winston depicted Jallianwala Bagh as 'a monstrous event ... without precedent or parallel in the modern history of the British Empire'. Rule by terror was the practice of Bolsheviks but 'not the British way of doing things'. Roundly dismissing the claim that Dyer had 'saved India' by making an example of Amritsar, he insisted that 'our reign in India or anywhere else has never stood on the basis of physical force alone' – indeed, such a policy 'would be fatal to the British Empire'.[12]

It was a masterly speech, regarded by contemporaries as one of Winston's best, and it helped turn the mood of the House. That day, a motion endorsing Dyer was rejected by 230 votes to 129. The Amritsar denunciation of 'frightfulness' stands with his address to the Commons in February 1906 on 'equal rights for civilised men' as benchmark statements of his racial philosophy.

By this stage, however, Churchill had marked Gandhi down as a troublemaker and not a 'civilised' man. In October 1921 he suggested that Montagu have him 'arrested and deported from India'. He said at a dinner party that Gandhi 'ought to be lain bound hand and foot at the gates of Delhi and then trampled on by an elephant with the new Viceroy seated on its back'.[13]

By February 1922, now Colonial Secretary, Winston's attitude had hardened further against Montagu's reforms and their legacies. Speaking to fellow ministers, he dismissed the apparently prevalent idea that 'we were fighting a rearguard action in India, that the British raj was doomed, and that India would gradually be handed over to Indians'. On the contrary, he declared, 'we must strengthen our position in India.' He suggested that 'opinion would change soon as to the expediency of granting democratic institutions to backward races which had no capacity for self-government', and claimed that 'a way out of our difficulties might be found by extending the system of Native States, with their influential aristocracies and landed proprietors.'[14]

But Indian politicians had not forgotten Amritsar. For Gandhi it was a key issue pushing him into a 'non-cooperation' movement in 1921–2 under which Indians would undermine the Raj by boycotting British goods and progressively withholding taxes. This was when Gandhi adopted the loincloth, to show solidarity with the nakedness of the rural poor. Inverting the martial nationalism of Hindu extremists, he promoted what has been called 'a feminized patriotism' that made 'his life and body, his habits and posture' a demonstration that 'strength was with the victims of history.'[15] For Churchill, by contrast, the dhoti was a sign that Gandhi had deserted the realm of 'civilised men'. As non-cooperation degenerated into acts of violence, Winston became yet more sure that this man posed a mortal danger.

By now Winston had accomplished the remarkable political feat of 're-ratting', having returned to the Tory fold and then receiving the plum post of Chancellor from Baldwin in 1924. The PM even mused about him in February 1929 as a possible Secretary of State for India: 'He was very good all through the Irish troubles: he has imagination, courage: he is an imperialist; he is a Liberal.' Baldwin went on: 'BUT – we do know the risk. Should it be taken? . . . The Indian Question will be the biggest threat for the new parliament.' As for Winston, in a passage drafted for his memoirs, though not eventually published, he wrote: 'I was not attracted by this plan. My friendship with Lord Birkenhead, then at the India Office, had kept me in close touch with the movement of Indian affairs, and I shared his deep misgivings about that vast sub-continent.' Birkenhead considered it 'frankly inconceivable that India will ever be fit for self-government'.[16] In the event, any idea of Winston as Secretary of State for India vanished when the Tories lost their majority in the May 1929 election. Ramsay MacDonald's Labour Party formed the new government and it was ready to move vigorously down the road towards Dominion status.

Winston was now in his mid-fifties, and conscious that the clock was ticking. Admired for his ability and energy, he was damned for lack of balance and erratic judgment. Whenever Winston felt marginalised, his instinct had always been to force himself on others, and in 1930–1 that was what he did. Baldwin was struggling to hold his party together over the two great issues of tariff reform and Dominion status for India. On the former, Winston sided with the beleaguered Baldwin, remaining attached to Victorian doctrines of free trade. But the crisis that blew up over India in 1930–1 offered an apparently perfect moment – blending principle and opportunism – to take on his party leader.

* * *

It was Baldwin's government which had raised the political temperature back in 1927 by appointing a commission of inquiry to assess the implementation of the 1919 Government of India Act. The commission, chaired by the Liberal politician Sir John Simon, consisted entirely of British parliamentarians, and its arrival in India in February 1928 was greeted by mass demonstrations about the absence of Indian representation. Seeking to defuse the tension, in October 1929 Lord Irwin, the Viceroy, issued a brief statement on behalf of the British Government affirming that it was 'implicit' in the Montagu Declaration of 1917 that 'the natural issue of India's constitutional progress, as there contemplated, is the attainment of Dominion status'.[17] He proposed that once the commission had reported, a round table conference should be held to review the situation. While well intentioned, what became known as the Irwin Declaration raised nationalist expectations, which the Viceroy then dashed by rejecting all demands to discuss a timetable for India to become a Dominion.

On 16 November Winston published a long rebuttal of the Declaration in the *Daily Mail*, setting out principles to which he would adhere for the rest of his life. 'The rescue of India from ages of barbarism, tyranny and internecine war, and its slow but ceaseless march to civilisation constitute upon the whole the finest achievements of our history. This work has been done in four or five generations by the willing sacrifices of the best of our race.' He argued that the main obstacles to this work had been the baleful influence of Hinduism and, latterly, 'the growing lack of confidence at home in the reality of our mission' – which the Declaration would now reinforce with 'criminally mischievous' effects. He listed three horrific features of Indian life that would have to change before Dominion status could be conceded. First, this was a country that 'brands and treats sixty million of its members, fellow human beings, toiling at their side, as "Untouchables", whose approach is an affront and whose very presence is pollution'. Second, 'India is a prey to fierce racial and religious dissensions' and 'the withdrawal of British protection would mean the immediate resumption of medieval wars'. Nor, thirdly, was Dominion status attainable 'while the political classes in India represent an insignificant fraction of the 350 millions for whose welfare we are responsible'.[18]

It was in this fraught atmosphere that Gandhi launched his Salt March. Salt was a basic necessity, heavily taxed by the Raj but other-wise readily available in vast salt pans along the Indian coast. Free access to it was a non-sectarian issue of stark moral symbolism, and Gandhi exploited this superbly. He set out on 12 March 1930 with seventy-eight followers across Gujarat to Dandi on the coast, drawing massive crowds in what became a triumphal procession by this little 60-year-old man in his loincloth – captured for Indians and the world on film and newsreels. At Dandi, on 6 April, he stooped to pick up salt from the seashore and declared, 'With this, I am shaking the foundations of the British Empire.' His act electrified the country. Salt protests proliferated, as did boycotts of British cloth, goods and businesses. Civil disobedience, orchestrated by Congress party radicals, again often turned violent. On 5 May the Mahatma was arrested without trial. This only prompted further civil disobedience. By the end of 1930, some 60,000 Indians had been imprisoned.[19]

British policy was now at sixes and sevens. 'Irwinism' was denounced by much of the Tory party, with Winston in the vanguard. He warned Baldwin on 24 September, 'I must confess myself to care more about this business than anything else in public life.'[20] On the other hand, the Viceroy enjoyed the support of MacDonald's Labour Government and of Baldwin, his party leader and close friend. When his Round Table Conference met in London from November 1930 to mid-January 1931, it was boycotted by the Congress party, which now saw civil disobedience as a far more effective way to force the pace. Tory hardliners rallied against Baldwin. On 12 December 1930 Winston was the main speaker at the inaugural public meeting of the new 'Indian Empire Society'. He denounced the growing talk among Indian opinion of a post-Raj era, blaming its spread on British vacillation and weakness, and warned: 'The truth is that Gandhi-ism and all that it stands for will, sooner or later, have to be grappled with and finally crushed. It is no use trying to satisfy a tiger by feeding him with cat's-meat.'[21]

Once again Irwin opted for a bold stroke. Against all but the inner circle of his advisers, and to the disgust of critics in London, he decided to release Gandhi unconditionally on 25 January 1931, arguing that no progress could be made while the Mahatma was in prison. On the 27th, Winston resigned from the Tory front bench over its India policy. Meanwhile, Gandhi was even bolder. In a 'Dear Friend' letter, he asked for a 'heart-to-heart talk' with Irwin as soon as possible, adding, 'I would like to meet not so much the Viceroy as the man in you.' This audacious letter was signed 'Your faithful friend, M.K. Gandhi'. Irwin decided he had no choice but to accept – otherwise, he believed, the backlash across India would have undermined his strategy for ending civil disobedience, which was to turn public opinion against it. He told a close colleague, 'I have always thought that discussions about peace terms would in some form and at some time become inevitable.'[22]

And so, on 17 February 1931, the tiny brown figure, with his bald head and toothless smile, arrived at the viceregal palace in Delhi: an historic moment captured six days later in Winston's words to his constituents, which stand as an epigraph to this chapter.[23] That speech was a classic of Churchillian hyperbole. Gandhi actually shuffled in by a side door, but the idea of him 'striding' up the grand imperial staircase conveyed a shocking image of anti-imperial effrontery. 'Fakir' was strictly a Muslim holy man, yet the word slid neatly into 'faker' – which was Winston's polemical point: Gandhi was a London-trained lawyer turned political conman. And 'half-naked' was not merely a pejorative dismissal of Indian traditional dress, it also played on deeper 'civilised' beliefs about how political men should be attired, in antithesis to the stereotypically weak and feminised Hindu.[24]

Just before the Epping speech, Churchill had told an audience in Liverpool on 2 February that apparent British decline was actually 'a disease of the will power' which he blamed on the fact that 'we have carried the franchise to limits far beyond those who are interested in politics' – a dig at the expansion of female suffrage in 1918 and 1928. Asked directly in Glasgow on 5 February whether he had opposed votes for women, he replied that he had. But now 'I have got to put up with it.' He then warned his audience of 'the shame that would be theirs' if, in two decades or so, people were to look back and say: 'No sooner was the franchise extended than they muddled away the great Empire, the inheritance which rugged centuries had gathered together for them.' As historian Paul Addison observes: 'Evidently Churchill feared that women would be too preoccupied with hearth and home to sustain the politics of Empire.'[25]

There was, therefore, a lot going on behind that sneer about Gandhi. But Winston's essential argument was incontrovertible: Irwin had conceded a position of symbolic equality to the most potent Indian opponent of British rule, a man whom Winston damned later in the

Epping speech as a 'malignant subversive fanatic'.[26] Irwin – not sharing Winston's conviction that the Raj could and must be sustained – considered the risk to be worth taking in order to keep India in Britain's orbit by other means. He and Baldwin agreed that Churchill had lost his head over the Raj, failing to move with the times after the Great War and instead reverting to the mentality of a 'subaltern of hussars of '96'. Years later Irwin, by then further ennobled as the Viscount Halifax, still enjoyed telling a story about his offer to introduce Winston to some of the modern Indians who would be attending the Round Table Conference, so as 'to bring your ideas up to date'. He got a dusty reception. 'I am quite satisfied with my views on India', Winston replied, 'and I certainly don't want them disturbed by any bloody Indian.'[27]

So, was this a clash of two different views of past and future? Was Winston driven entirely by his stated conviction that India was 'the greatest question Englishmen have had to settle' since the Great War, on which the credibility of Britain's global power would depend?[28] Andrew Roberts, in his magisterial biography of Churchill, says that the stance he took on India, 'for which he quite consciously threw away what appeared to be his last chance of winning the premiership, cannot be understood except in the light of the secular religion that he had made of the British Empire, and his Whiggish conviction that it was central to Britain's historical mission of progress'. But was this simply an act of self-sacrificial principle? A quarter of a century earlier, when writing the life of Halifax, Roberts had suggested that Winston's 'vituperation' over the betrayal of India had 'more than a hint of political opportunism to it'.[29] And would this be so surprising? After all, his whole career had managed to interweave principle and politics, passionate conviction and personal advantage. His belief in the Raj was fortified by a sense that the mess Baldwin had got into over India and Imperial Preference finally signalled the Churchillian moment. On 26 February, after his 'naked fakir' speech, Winston wrote exultantly to Clemmie, 'There is no doubt that the whole spirit of the Conservative party is with me . . . It is astonishing looking back over the last six weeks what a change has been brought in my position . . . Anything may happen now if opinion has time to develop.'[30]

Nor did this optimism seem unwarranted. By 1 March, Baldwin felt so beleaguered that he was on the verge of resignation.[31] His inner circle dissuaded him from precipitate action, but the end seemed near. Suddenly, on 5 March it was announced that the talks Irwin had initiated with Gandhi had borne unexpected fruit: after much haggling, the Mahatma agreed to call off civil disobedience and committed the Congress party to participate in a new session of round-table talks. On the 5th, one of the Viceroy's London confidants wrote to him: 'Yesterday the [press] lobby opinion was that SB's resignation of the Leadership could not be postponed for more than a few days, but today his position is far stronger.'[32] On the other hand, Irwin agreed to release all those detained during the disturbances, and this Irwin-Gandhi 'Pact' was used by critics like Winston to denounce again the position of equality being conceded to a seditious agitator. Ironically, the same accusation of 'surrender' was directed against the Mahatma by Congress radicals. What drew Irwin and Gandhi together was not shared saintliness but a pragmatic belief in the morality of compromise.[33]

Bouncing back strongly, Baldwin addressed the Commons on 12 March 1931. He warned against 'extremists in India and at home' and, with relish, cited approvingly a speech delivered by an unnamed MP to the House in 1920 which, he said, stated with 'more lucidity of thought and felicity of style than I can ever hope to attain, being a man of plain speech'. Baldwin then quoted from that speech, with (doubtless) a broad smile on his face, passages such as 'Our reign in India or anywhere else has never stood on the basis of physical force alone', and the statement that 'the British way of doing things' had 'always meant and implied close and effectual co-operation with the people of the country'. The Commons was delighted. Ignoring cries of 'Name! Name!', Baldwin declared, 'I do not think there could be a better summing up of the situation', and ended by directly challenging his critics. If those who approached Indian constitutional development in 'a niggling, grudging spirit' proved a majority, 'in God's name let them choose a man to lead them.'[34]

The drama of the moment was recorded by one eyewitness. 'The late Premier and his Chancellor, both evidently moved by strong emotion, were within a few yards of one another. Churchill seated, with flushed features and twitching hands, looked as though about to spring.'[35] But by the time Baldwin sat down, to tremendous cheers, he had won over the House. Winston had been wrongfooted by Baldwin's deft and witty use of his own words from the Amritsar debate. When he spoke, he became increasingly petulant. There were still some choice Churchillian digs about the Mahatma. About his objectives: when he walked to Dandi a year ago 'he was not looking for salt, he was looking for trouble'. And about his integrity: 'Already Mr. Gandhi moves about – so I read in the "Times" newspaper – surrounded by a circle of wealthy men, who see at their fingertips the acquisition of the resources of an Empire on cheaper terms than were ever yet offered in the world.' But amid mounting interruptions, Winston sat down without delivering a strong peroration and was then lampooned by Colonel Josiah Wedgwood, a veteran radical: 'The Right Honourable Gentleman never gets older . . . he will remain for ever the brilliant witty irresponsible *enfant terrible* of this House.'[36]

Winston was now firmly stuck in the political wilderness. He had broken with Baldwin in the New Year when it seemed that India was sliding into anarchy and Baldwin's days were numbered. But then he had been left high and dry by the renaissance of Baldwin and Irwin during March. Although India soon descended into new violence, it came too late to retrieve Winston's political fortunes. His moment had passed (if it ever existed). Having nailed his colours to the mast on India, he had no choice but to follow the course he had chosen right through to its conclusion – thereby becoming ever more isolated from the Tory high command just as Baldwin became kingmaker of the new National Government formed under MacDonald's titular leadership in the wake of the financial crisis of August 1931. Inevitably, there was no place for Churchill. And the landslide for the new coalition in the October election decimated the ranks of the Indian Empire Society, leaving it with only 20 of the 615 MPs.[37] The National Government continued the old bipartisan policy, aiming at further round-table talks to achieve full Dominion status for India.

There is no place here to detail Winston's dogged war of attrition against the Government's India bill. Suffice to say it was the most monumental piece of parliamentary business of the interwar years: occasioning over 1,950 speeches in Parliament, containing 15.5 million words, and filling 4,000 pages of *Hansard*.[38] Along the way he underlined to the Commons his paternalistic view of the people of India: 'You cannot desert them; you cannot abandon them. They are as much our children as any children can be. They are actually in this world as the result of what this nation and this Parliament have done.' And in February 1935 he rejected any idea that the British were pulling out of India, asserting that 'we are there for ever.'[39] With typical Churchillian obduracy, he fought Mac-Donald and Baldwin all the way until the bill became law in August 1935. His barbs became increasingly sharp, even though Baldwin tried to maintain some semblance of bonhomie. On one occasion, Winston entered a small lavatory in the Commons, only to find Baldwin already relieving himself. There being no other place, Winston stood beside him at the urinals. After a moment's silence, Baldwin murmured, 'I am glad there's still one platform where we can meet together.'[40]

But after Parliament passed the Government of India Act, Winston changed, or modified, his tune. Concerned about the darkening situation in Europe, he tried to repair relations with Baldwin and the Tory leadership, and even reached out to Gandhi. In August 1935 the Indian industrialist Ghanshyam Das Birla was invited to lunch at Chartwell. G.D. Birla was one of the Mahatma's leading financial backers (as someone once said, 'it costs a great deal of money to keep Gandhiji in poverty'), and Winston put on an accomplished performance. Dressed in a workman's apron, which he wore right through lunch, he showed Birla the bricks he had been laying (his manly equivalent of spinning?). He spoke of India with 'great emotion', taking pride in calling himself a 'diehard', but said that 'Gandhi has gone very high in my estimation since he stood up for the untouchables' – a comment he also made to others.[41]

Winston did not repent his opposition to the India bill but it was now on the statute book – 'so make it a success', he told Birla. Asked what would constitute success, Winston answered: 'My test is improvement in the lot of the masses.' Circling back to the Mahatma, he remarked, 'I did not meet Mr Gandhi when he was in London [in 1931]. It was then rather awkward', before adding, 'I should like to meet him now. I would love to go to India before I die. If I went there, I would stay six months.' He told Birla he was 'genuinely sympathetic' to India but had 'real fears about the future' and called the country 'a real burden on us', explaining that 'we have to maintain an army and for the sake of India we have to maintain Singapore and Near East strength. If India would look after herself, we would be delighted.'[42]

In a cordial letter a month later, Birla informed Churchill that Gandhi was 'very much interested' to hear of the meeting at Chartwell. Harking back to 1908, he had said, 'I have got a good recollection of Mr Churchill when he was in the Colonial Office and somehow or other since then I have held the opinion that I can always rely on his sympathy and goodwill.'[43]

Quite what one should make of these flutterings of *politesse* by Churchill and Gandhi is unclear. But they do hint at some kind of rapprochement in 1935. And there is no doubt that the late 1930s did provide a brief respite in Anglo-Indian tensions. The Government of India Act had backed away from any declaration of Dominion status: that was one achievement of Churchill and the diehards. And its plan for an All-India Federation was aborted when, late on, most of the 600 princely states decided to opt out. However, plans for greater provincial autonomy came into effect in 1937 and Congress chose to contest the elections, winning victories that enabled them to form majority governments in seven of the eleven provinces of British India – those areas under Britain's direct rule. Although the Act left the provincial governors and the Viceroy with 'special responsibilities' that amply buttressed imperial power, it had greatly boosted the authority of Congress. Gandhi encouraged sceptics like Jawaharlal Nehru to accept the burdens of office, arguing that, although the Act was 'universally regarded as unsatisfactory for achieving India's freedom', it could be considered as 'an attempt, however limited and feeble, to replace the rule of the sword by the rule of the majority'. One small but symbolic victory was the instruction issued to all the (mostly British) officials in the Central Provinces by order of their new Congress government: 'In future Mr Gandhi should be referred to in all correspondence as "Mahatma Gandhi".'[44]

As the decade progressed, some commentators discerned a growing extremism on Gandhi's part. The Mahatma had fasted before, but in September 1932 he talked for the first time of a 'fast unto death'. Was this not a coercive strategy at odds with the original principles of satyagraha? One who thought so was the South African premier Jan Christian Smuts, an old foe of Gandhi in the Boer War, who described this as 'persuasion by semi-starvation'. He noted parallels with the 'Suffering Servant' in the Judaeo-Christian scriptures but also discerned worrying similarities with the way contemporary dictators tried to 'overwhelm the public mind, not by reason but by play on the emotions, many of them of an irrational character'. Smuts called this 'Gandhi's distinctive contribution to political method', observing that it had 'worked wonders in India', carrying him to 'heights of achievement' probably 'unattainable otherwise'.[45]

Smuts' commentary was one of a volume of essays intended for Gandhi's seventieth birthday in October 1939. By the time it was published, however, a new war had broken out in Europe, which brought down the Chamberlain government in May 1940 and went global in 1941–2. Amid this radically transformed landscape, Winston had to grapple anew with Gandhi's unorthodox 'political method' – this time not as a truculent backbencher but as the King-Emperor's First Minister.

* * *

From day one, the war upset the limited progress made in the late 1930s. On 3 September Lord Linlithgow (Viceroy, 1936–43) declared that India was at war with Germany – speaking for 320 million people without consulting any of their politicians. He did, however, ask Gandhi to meet him. Afterwards, the Mahatma issued a statement stating that his own sympathies 'were with England and France from the purely humanitarian standpoint' and saying that he 'broke down' when imagining the possible destruction of the Houses of Parliament and Westminster by aerial bombing. Here was a reminder that, on a personal level, Gandhi was indeed 'at home' in London, a city in which he had lived for long periods: in 1888–91, 1906, 1909, 1914 and 1931. But Gandhi also made clear to the Viceroy that it was Congress who decided policy. And its position, said Gandhi on 23 October, was that it simply wanted a British commitment to India's independence after the war, according to a charter 'framed by her elected representatives'.[46]

Linlithgow indicated that there would be no movement beyond the 1935 Act, and so the Congress party resigned from the provincial ministries. Further complicating the situation, in March 1940 the Muslim League, meeting in Lahore, declared its commitment to a separate Islamic state – Pakistan – asserting that Islam and Hinduism were not merely unique religions but 'different and distinct social orders' and it was 'a dream' to imagine that they could 'ever evolve a common nationality'. Gandhi refused to take seriously the 'two-nations' philosophy of the League's leader, Mohammad Ali Jinnah – calling it an 'untruth' and doubting that Muslims would ever opt for what he called 'vivisection'.[47]

Sharing the general Congress belief that British policy was one of divide-and-rule, Gandhi would have been interested to know that Churchill, by then First Lord of the Admiralty, had told the Cabinet in February 1940 that he 'regarded the Hindu-Muslim feud as a bulwark of British rule in India'. Endorsing 'a firm stand' against the 'immoderate demands' of Congress, Churchill felt confident that 'a method of government which kept India quiet for the duration of the war would be certain of the approval of the country as a whole.' By 'the country', he meant of course Britain, not India.[48]

Such complacency was shattered by the events of May 1940. On the 26th, as the remnants of the British Expeditionary Force retreated to the beaches of Dunkirk, the Mahatma asked the Viceroy: 'Assuming that things are as black as they appear to be for the Allied cause, is it not time to sue for peace for the sake of humanity'. He added, 'I do not believe Herr Hitler to be as bad as he is portrayed'. Linlithgow, who had two sons and a son-in-law on active duty, sent a polite letter of rejection, whereupon Gandhi went public. On 18 June – the day Winston predicted to the Commons that, if the British Empire lasted a thousand years, men would still say that 1940 was its 'finest hour' – Gandhi wrote a newspaper article advising the nations of Europe on 'How to Combat Hitlerism'. Although admitting that Nazism meant 'naked, ruthless force' and predicting that Germany would 'not be able to hold all the conquered nations in perpetual subjection', he insisted that Hitlerite violence could not be combated by counter-violence and commended the 'rare courage' of 'French statesmen' in signing an armistice to avoid 'senseless mutual slaughter'. As ever, he cited his philosophy of 'non-violent resistance' as the panacea, and expressed the wish that England and the other nations of Europe had adopted such a course from the start of the conflict. Of course, he admitted, 'Hitler would have got without fighting what he has gained after a bloody fight', but 'Europe would have added several inches to its moral stature'. In order to ram home his message, he also wrote an open letter 'To Every Briton' on 2 July 1940 – just as Churchill was about to launch his ruthless attack on the French fleet, to ensure it did not fall into German hands. His letter invited the British to 'fight Nazism without arms'. This meant that 'you will invite Herr Hitler and Signor Mussolini to take what they want of the countries you call your possessions' and indeed to 'take possession of your beautiful island, with your many beautiful buildings'. Yes, Gandhi admitted, 'you will give all these, but neither your souls, nor your minds.'[49]

There is no evidence that Winston read these articles, but they reveal that he and the Mahatma now inhabited totally different universes. Winston's main interest in south Asia that summer was rapid mobilisation of reliable Indian troops, both to free up British regulars from garrison duty in India and also to reinforce battlefronts in the Middle

East. He complained to Leo Amery, the Secretary of State for India, that 'the assistance of India this time is incomparably below that of 1914–18.' But Amery – who had sparred with Churchill ever since Winston had pushed him into the school swimming pool at Harrow – took a different view. He considered that the need to galvanise Indian support, and also the growing rift between Hindu and Muslim 'factions', with its 'real danger of drift towards civil war', were both compelling reasons for issuing a clearer timetable for constitutional advance, going beyond 'Dominion status, to 'enable India's new self-devised constitution entering into force within a year of the conclusion of the war'. Winston, by contrast, continued to see the Hindu–Muslim split as beneficial to British rule and deplored any new parliamentary debate on India at a time when Britain faced possible invasion. Despite this crisis at home, he devoted two lengthy Cabinet meetings in July to crushing what he called Amery's blueprint for 'virtually an independent India'.[50]

Gandhi wished to maintain some kind of peaceful struggle for Indian freedom during the world war. In the autumn of 1940, he launched a restricted campaign of civil disobedience. By December 1940 several thousand protesters were in prison, but the authorities decided not to arrest Gandhi for fear of inflaming the situation. On the 24th the Mahatma wrote a 'Dear Friend' letter to Hitler, urging him to 'make an effort for peace' during the Christmas season. Like an earlier letter in July 1939, this was suppressed by British censors, but it reveals again the Mahatma's distinctive take on the war. While not believing 'that you are the monster described by your opponents', he told the Führer, he also had 'no doubt that many of your acts are monstrous and unbecoming of human dignity . . . Hence we cannot possibly wish success to your arms.' But, Gandhi continued, 'ours is a unique position. We resist British imperialism no less than Nazism. If there is a difference it is in degree.' Asserting his continued fidelity to non-violence, he said it remained to be seen whether Germany's 'organized violence' would prove more powerful than Britain's. 'We know what the British heel means for us and the non-European races of the world. But we would never wish to end British rule with

German aid.'[51] Again, his complete divergence from Churchill's worldview is clear.

The crisis in India following the fall of Singapore and Japan's conquest of Burma prompted the Mahatma to mount a new campaign. On 8 August 1942 the All-India Congress Committee passed a resolution sanctioning 'a mass struggle on non-violent lines on the widest possible scale', which would 'inevitably be under the leadership of Gandhiji'. The British were ready. In 1920 they had waited more than a year to lock him up, and in 1930 they had let him make his Salt March in the eye of the world's media before taking action. In 1942, however, they moved within twenty-four hours. At 5 a.m. next morning, 9 August, Gandhi was arrested at G.D. Birla's residence in Bombay and taken with other Congress leaders to Poona. This time he was housed not in the Yerwada prison but in a large two-storey house leased from the Aga Khan. (It was hoped that American opinion might be appeased to know that the Mahatma was being held in the so-called 'Aga Khan Palace'.) Nehru and other Congress leaders were also rounded up and detained in an old Mughal fort in the centre of India. The Viceroy justified the operation as a response to Congress's 'totalitarian policy' of imposing its view on all Indians – a deliberate coupling of the party with the values of the Axis powers. Churchill, then in Egypt, was pleased at the news. But Smuts, dining with him, was not. Gandhi, he told Winston, was 'a man of God', whereas 'you and I are mundane people. Gandhi has appealed to religious motives. You never have. That is where you have failed.' Winston, grinning, had the last word: 'I have made more bishops than St. Augustine.' Smuts did not consider this a joking matter. According to Churchill's doctor, 'his face was very grave.'[52]

The Congress party's 'Quit India' campaign went ahead despite the loss of its leaders. Winston, already on edge as Rommel's army menaced Cairo, did not restrain his anger. 'I hate Indians,' he exploded to Amery on 9 September 1942. 'They are a beastly people with a beastly religion.' Next day he let rip to the House of Commons: 'The Indian Congress Party does not represent all India. It does not represent the majority of the people of India. It does not even represent the Hindu masses. It is a political organisation built around a party machine and sustained by certain manufacturing and financial interests.' The PM declared that Congress had 'now abandoned in many respects the policy of nonviolence which Mr. Gandhi has so long inculcated in theory, and has come into the open as a revolutionary movement designed to paralyse the communications by rail and telegraph and generally to promote disorder'. The campaign, he said, had the 'intention or at any rate the effect of hampering the defence of India against the Japanese invader'; he suggested it had been 'aided by Japanese fifth-column work on a widely extended scale'.[53] He told Roosevelt that 'Gandhi was prepared to negotiate with the Japanese on the basis of a free passage for Japanese troops through India in the hopes of their joining hands with Hitler.' And he added: 'I have no doubt that the Congress would have the use of sufficient Japanese troops to keep down the composite majority of 90 million Moslems, 40 million untouchables and 90 million in the Princes' states.' When the Chinese leader Chiang Kai-shek expressed his concern about how Gandhi was being treated, Winston told him brusquely, 'I think the best rule for Allies to follow is not to interfere in each-other's internal affairs.'[54]

The Mahatma was not released until May 1944; Nehru and the Congress leadership only in June 1945. Their long absence from the political stage after August 1942 had two important consequences. First, it meant that the 'Quit India' movement they had started fell into the hands of younger radicals – students in the cities, peasant activists in the countryside – targeting police stations, post offices, railways and factories in what became overtly 'anti-state' campaigns, often anti-Muslim as well. Even more than in previous protests, Gandhi was invoked as 'the millenarian inspiration for acts that could be carried out in his name', even if they breached his philosophy of peaceful protest. It was the 'biggest civilian uprising in India since the great rebellion of 1857'. The British crackdown was brutal, with hundreds of deaths and 100,000 arrests, and within a few months India was brought largely under control. The damage to Britain's image was immense, yet the turmoil was also a setback for Gandhi. It cast doubt on 'the viability of non-violence as a political mode except in very restricted, small-scale situations, where its exponents could be carefully disciplined and deployed'.[55]

Secondly, while Congress leaders were politically marginalised, Jinnah – supportive of Britain's war effort – had free rein to build up the Muslim League's political base. Moving to and fro across northern India, he brokered deals with political bosses in key Muslim-majority provinces such as the Punjab, Bengal, Sind and the Northwest Frontier. In the process, as he travelled the country, a party originally representing mainly aristocrats and landlords gradually developed a following among peasants and the urban poor, playing on fears of Hindu domination. And Jinnah – once aloof and snobbish, speaking mostly in English rather than Urdu – transformed himself into a leader with a mass following, as the 1946 elections would later show. Congress was never able to regain the grip it had exerted over the nationalist movement in the 1930s.[56]

Chafing at exclusion from active politics and aggrieved at British portrayal of him as Tokyo's tool, Gandhi announced in February 1943 that he would embark on a new fast, to last for twenty-one days. Once again, the War Cabinet was at odds with Linlithgow, the Viceroy, whose (largely Indian) Council wanted to release him for the duration of the fast. The Council wanted to avoid any risk that the Mahatma might die while in British detention, but the War Cabinet believed that yielding to Gandhi's threatened hunger strike would 'create an impression of great weakness'. Winston was 'more genially aggressive than ever', Amery noted in his diary. The PM did not care if the issue split the Viceroy's Council: 'What did it matter if a few blackamoors resigned! We could show the world we were governing.' Amery felt that Churchill's head had been 'completely turned by the turn of the tide in the war' after Alamein and he had 'not the slightest idea how little that has affected India or the public here or in America about India'.[57]

In the event, Gandhi rejected anything except unconditional release and began his water and fruit-juice fast in the Aga Khan's Palace on

10 February. After ten days, there were reports that he was close to death, but the PM never took them seriously. Ironically, at almost the same time, he was himself stricken with a severe bout of pneumonia that seemed for a time to be life-threatening. The hunger strike revived Winston's 1931 obsession about the fakir-faker. 'I have heard that Gandhi usually has glucose in his water when doing his fasting antics,' he wrote to Linlithgow on 13 February. 'Would it be possible to verify this?' No evidence was obtained, but the PM did not abandon his suspicion, which was widely shared in London and Delhi.[58] Throughout, though, Winston talked about Gandhi in a more jocular tone than in 1931 – referring, in a letter to the King, to 'the old humbug' and wondering 'whether his fast is *bona fide*'. He took the same line with Smuts: 'I do not think Gandhi has the slightest intention of dying, and I imagine he has been eating better meals than I have for the last week. It looks highly probable he will see his fast out. What fools we should have been to flinch before all this bluff and sob-stuff.'[59]

Winston's illness in February 1943 gave him a rare opportunity for reflection. (For one whole week the only message he dictated was a thank-you to the King for a get-well greeting.) The fruits of his thinking with regard to India are evident in the text of two speeches he drafted in March but did not deliver. One of these was intended for the Commons debate on India on 30 March. In this Winston waxed lyrical about the eighty-year peace Britain had brought to India, at a time when Europe was wracked by conflicts and America wrestling with the legacies of a 'most bloody', if 'glorious', civil war. He wished to tell the Commons, as he did *Daily Mail* readers in November 1929, 'We should be proud of our work in India. We should look at it as one of the noblest works that any European nation or white race has ever accomplished.' He also prepared a long tribute to the Indian Army, nearly two million strong, and unlike 'all other armies now fighting in the world war' because 'they are all volunteers.' By contrast Gandhi, in his 'baffled malice', had dubbed them 'mercenaries' and had tried to undermine India's war effort. In short it was little wonder that 'for the ten years before the war, I warned our British people against Hitler and Gandhi.'[60]

'Hitler and Gandhi' – depicted as a devilish duo. Utterly different in personality and values but, for Winston, conjoined as the greatest threats to Britain and its righteous empire.[61] Such convictions probably affected his response to the appalling famine that engulfed Bengal in 1943–4. Debates about its causes still rage today; the balance between natural disasters (such as the cyclone of 1942) and man-made factors remains in dispute, though generally tilting to the latter. Japan's conquest of Burma, source of much of Bengal's grain, was a catalyst, prompting a flood of refugees and rampant inflation. But at the heart of the story are Britain's priorities for winning the war, coupled with the remoteness of the Indian peasant from the mentality of Whitehall. Policies for 'belt-tightening' and 'making do', which might have worked in Britain in 1940–2, meant the difference between life and death for hundreds of thousands already on the edge of starvation. And London's number one shipping priority in 1943–4 was the build-up of resources in Britain for D-Day. Winston got involved occasionally, for instance trying to drum up Australian wheat, but his preoccupation was to defeat Hitler, not to aid what he considered a country whose corrupt and duplicitous leaders, headed by their spurious saint, showed no appreciation of what Britain was doing for them. The death of two or three million Indians was certainly not a Churchillian 'genocide', as has sometimes been implied, but it is hard to dispute this statement of Lord Wavell – Linlithgow's successor as Viceroy – that it was 'one of the greatest disasters that has befallen any people under British rule, and damage to our reputation both among Indians and foreigners in India is incalculable'.[62]

Wavell had not been Winston's first choice to replace Linlithgow, a fellow enthusiast for the Raj whose tenure had been prolonged to a total of seven years. The taciturn Wavell was one of the generals the PM had sacked during his quest for desert victory, but his two years of on-the-spot experience as Commander-in-Chief in India outweighed the doubts in this case. As Viceroy-designate, Wavell wanted licence to make cautious moves on the political front, especially bringing 'the leaders of the Indian political parties into the Executive Council' if Gandhi, Nehru and their colleagues promised 'whole hearted support of the war effort' and no resumption of civil disobedience. But Churchill stamped firmly on the whole idea. His conclusion was both blunt and familiar: 'Victory is the best foundation for constitutional departures.' At a long Cabinet meeting on 7 October 1943, the PM said that he 'did not by any means rule out the idea that further progress might be made during the war', but he was 'disappointed that the suggestions put forward took the form of resuscitation of the same old political arguments with the same old political leaders'.[63]

Wavell, who attended the meeting, found it 'worse even than I had expected', dominated by the PM 'who waved the bogey of Gandhi at everyone'. According to Amery, Churchill privately indicated that 'only over his dead body would any approach to Gandhi take place.'[64] When he was out in India, the new Viceroy found the PM equally cantankerous. On 4 May 1944 Wavell cabled London saying that, in view of a grave deterioration in Gandhi's health (including severe malaria and kidney problems), he asked for approval to release him unconditionally from prison. This was granted by the War Cabinet. But at the end of May Winston told Wavell: 'I assented to your letting Gandhi out on the grounds of his grievous state of health. He seems to have recovered a good deal of political vitality since then. He is a thoroughly evil force, hostile to us in every fibre, largely in the hands of the native vested interests and frozen to his idea of the hand-spinning wheel and inefficient cultivation methods for the over-crowded population of India.'[65] A 'thoroughly evil force' who was 'out of touch' with the 'real' India – a kind of Asian Luddite: here was Winston's considered view of Gandhi.

The stalemate in India continued for the rest of Winston's tenure as Britain's war leader. En route to Yalta and ill with a high temperature, he wrote dolefully to his wife: 'I have had for some time a feeling of despair about the British connection with India, and still more about what will happen if it is suddenly broken.' He confessed to her his support for partition and Jinnah's idea of Pakistan. At the end of February – back from Yalta and after a well-lubricated dinner – he indulged in another of his rants about India. According to his private secretary, 'the PM said the Hindus were a foul race "protected by their mere pullulation from the doom that is their due"' and expressed the wish that Air Marshal Harris 'could send some of his surplus bombers to destroy them'. These remarks echoed a similar outburst against the 'baboos' and in favour of Pakistan over dinner in March 1943, when he got into an argument with Tory politician R.A. Butler about the merits of holding India together: 'If our poor troops have to be kept in a sweltering, syphilitic climate and lice-infested barracks for the sake of your precious unity, I'd rather see them have a good civil war.' Clemmie remonstrated with him: 'Winston, you don't mean what you're saying.' 'No,' he replied, 'but when I see my opponents glaring at me, I always have to draw them out by exaggerated statements.'[66]

Some of these outbursts were probably tactical, but one has to say that it was only about the Indian 'baboos' and the Bolshevik 'baboons' that Winston really lost his rag. For him, these were both issues of the heart – indeed of the gut. He managed to hold his line on India for the rest of the wartime coalition but, after Labour resigned from the coalition in May 1945 and Winston formed a caretaker Tory government prior to a general election, he was persuaded to release the Congress leaders and make some kind of constitutional move in order to avoid India becoming an election issue. At the end of May the new Cabinet allowed Wavell to go ahead with his 1943 plan to call a conference of Indian political leaders and, from among them, to form an Indianised Viceroy's Council. The conference duly convened in Simla in July, only to be torpedoed by Congress's demand that one of their members of the Council should be a Muslim and by Jinnah's insistence that all Muslims on the Council had to be members of his League. Gandhi blamed Jinnah for the breakdown of the conference, while Wavell thought the collapse revealed 'more openly than ever before the great rift between Hindus and Muslims, which the events of the last few years have accentuated'. But Amery reflected in December 1947 that 'the real wrecker' was 'perhaps the long delay' before Wavell had been 'allowed to try' his plan. In other words, he blamed Winston.[67]

* * *

Whoever or whatever was to blame, the still-born Simla Conference was the finale of Winston's long fight to hold onto the Raj. After the Labour landslide of 26 July 1945, he became only a bystander, albeit a vociferous one, as the new government moved rapidly, amid mounting chaos, to Indian independence and partition on 15 August 1947. Winston's commentary on those tragic years is more relevant to the Churchill-Attlee saga described in the next chapter. Of note here is his telling silence after 1945 about the fate of the 'half-naked fakir' and what, in conclusion, this tells us about his conceptions of political power and historical greatness.

After Gandhi's release from detention in May 1944, when he was trying to draw the British into talks, he wrote a letter to Churchill. It began 'Dear Prime Minister', not 'Dear Friend' (as to Irwin and Hitler), but was certainly proffered as a (rather bizarre) olive branch:

> You are reported to have the desire to crush the simple 'naked fakir' as you are said to have described me. I have been long trying to be a fakir and that naked – a more difficult task. I, therefore, regard the expression as a compliment though unintended. I approach you then as such, and ask you to trust and use me for the benefit of your people and mine and through them those of the world.

Winston had no intention of opening a correspondence. He asked Wavell to send a single sentence in reply: 'The Prime Minister desires me to acknowledge with thanks the receipt of your letter of July 17 to him.'[68]

In 1946–7 Winston's public comments on India were mostly directed against the Labour Government. Representing himself now as a committed supporter of Dominion status, he castigated Attlee and his colleagues for rushing headlong into a Congress-controlled government and finally partition. Predicting immeasurable 'misery and bloodshed' as Britain's 'mighty and wonderful empire' descended into 'civil war', he contrasted London's 'unparalleled act of voluntary abdication' with Soviet Russia 'expanding or seeking to expand in every direction.'[69] But, already inclined to the Pakistan option, he and the Tories did not vote against Labour's policy, or try to delay it. And in 1949 Winston welcomed the decision of the new Indian republic, led by Nehru, to remain in the Commonwealth with the British monarch at its head. Over time, in fact, he developed a good relationship with the new Indian leader – who did not dress in a loincloth and, as a fellow Old Harrovian, happily sported the old school tie. 'I get on very well with him,' Winston remarked in 1955, lauding Nehru and his Non-Aligned movement as a bastion against communism in Asia.[70]

After the war the Mahatma felt marginalised. 'No one listens to me any more,' he lamented on 1 April 1947. 'I am a small man. True, there was a time when mine was a big voice . . . I am crying in the wilderness.' For him, partition was a 'spiritual tragedy', which meant that 'thirty-two years of work have come to an inglorious end.'[71] Gandhi's sense of failure was understandable. The India that became independent in 1947 seemed the antithesis of his dreams – defined by democratic politics, run by a strong state, committed to industrial development rather than village values, with its unity irretrievably shattered by communal hatreds.[72] Yet, nowadays, the post-1945 years are usually seen as Gandhi's apotheosis. One biographer, in Churchillian mode, has even called them Gandhi's 'finest hour' – more so than the Salt March of 1930 – arguing that his 'unique personal qualities and true greatness' were 'never more evident than in the last months of his life.'[73]

Unable now to summon up another satyagraha, Gandhi walked hundreds of miles in personal missions to calm communal strife. On 1 October 1947, just before his seventy-eighth birthday, he began another 'fast unto death' to end violence between Muslims and Hindus in Calcutta, desisting four days later when peace had been restored. He fasted again in mid-January to protest at anti-Muslim violence in Delhi. And then, on 30 January 1948, he was shot dead by a militant Hindu nationalist.

The assassination had a cathartic effect on the whole country, cleverly managed by Nehru and Congress through the state funeral in New Delhi and then the distribution of the ashes across the country.

'Gandhi martyred proved even more powerful a bond for Indians than he had been alive,' writes biographer Judith Brown. 'He became a national symbol, and in time, almost a myth; his name invoked in times of national crisis and disunity.'[74] And also an international inspiration, whose philosophy of 'non-violence' was embraced by African nationalist leaders such as Kwame Nkrumah and Kenneth Kaunda, by Martin Luther King and the American Civil Rights Movement, and even by the German 'Green' activist Petra Kelly. 'As an iconic figure', writes David Hardiman, Gandhi has proved 'very durable'.[75]

Yet Gandhi's resurrection passed Churchill by. His post-war speeches hardly mentioned the man and, unlike Labour politicians, he made no statement about the assassination.[76] In fact, it is in Churchill's war memoirs that we find his last words on Gandhi. The 'half-naked fakir' phrase does not appear in Volume 1, published in October 1948, but the conman image is still there in the form of a sardonic reference to Gandhi's release from 'commodious internment' by Lord Irwin in 1931. That image reappears in Volume 4 (1950), when discussing his February 1943 fast while 'in detention under the most favourable conditions in a small palace in Poona'. After telling his readers that in 1943 'most active world-wide propaganda was set on foot that his death was approaching', Winston added: 'it was certain, however, at an early stage that he was being fed with glucose whenever he drank water' and that, once 'convinced of our obduracy, he abandoned his fast'. When Volume 4 was published, these remarks caused 'a furore' in India, and the doctors who had attended Gandhi in 1943 issued a statement denying the glucose accusation. The passage was cut from future reprints.[77] In the same volume Winston also contrasts Nehru's determination in 1942 to resist a Japanese attack with 'the total pacifism of Gandhi'. A claim that the old man 'may well' have been willing to 'give the Japanese free passage across India to join hands with the Germans in return for Japanese military aid to hold down the Moslems and secure the All-India Dominion of the Hindu' was cut on the advice of the Cabinet Secretary in view of 'all the commotion which it seems likely to cause'.[78]

Why would Winston never extend the accolade of greatness to this remarkable little man? Most of all, of course, because of Gandhi's remorseless campaign against the Raj. The British Empire was what Andrew Roberts has called Winston's 'secular religion',[79] one he had defended passionately against foreign foes and 'dismal croaking' at home throughout his life since those subaltern days in 1897. Yet, to quote Judith Brown again, the Raj 'was in the long term a vulnerable super-structure raised over an ancient and complex society over which it had little control'. Stability depended on retaining the 'formal or informal collaboration of certain key groups of Indians, and the acquiescence of the vast majority'. In this battle for hearts and minds, Gandhi's satyagraha was hugely important. It 'encouraged Indians to shed their ingrained fear and acceptance of the raj, and to realize their own strength', not least through mundane acts such as singing patriotic songs, boycotting British goods and spinning their own cloth. This was a battle which Britain could never win by force of arms – as Baldwin, Irwin and Wavell acknowledged, but Churchill did not.[80]

'Secular religion' has a further implication. Winston – as Smuts noted in 1942 – had limited feel for the spiritual dimension of life and living. Other British politicians shared his wariness of Gandhi, but Attlee and Irwin were men of faith who could respect Gandhi's saintliness while also being alert to his cunning. Where they were at least ambivalent, Winston was utterly condemnatory; as historian Faisal Devji has observed, it was 'not so much the ill effects of the Mahatma's policies' but rather 'his potential for hypocrisy' that proved 'the dividing line between those who supported and opposed him'.[81] In 1943, most British leaders were fed up with Gandhi, but that did not prevent them from offering more generous appraisals after his death.

For Winston, Gandhi's perceived 'hypocrisy' was evident in two additional ways: dress and fasting. As he declared repeatedly, the British Empire had a moral purpose – to elevate people from 'barbarism' to 'civilisation'. In his mind Gandhi had deliberately reverted to barbarism for political reasons by abandoning Western suits of the sort worn by Jinnah to adopt the garb of the rural poor. Indeed, his loincloth and shawl seemed almost feminine, as did Gandhi's insistence on spinning, which was conventionally women's work. On these issues of attire, Gandhi therefore challenged Winston's creed of manliness, which valorised physical and moral courage, as shown by soldiers who won the Victoria Cross, or by FDR's battle against polio. One might, of course, argue that fasting to the verge of death requires immense courage, but that kind of strength through weakness was foreign to Churchillian values. Yet the moral power of self-sacrifice was clearly immense – moving millions in India and across the world. Hence Winston's persistent efforts to present 'fast' as 'farce': another charade in the conman's bag of tricks.

In short, Gandhi not only tried to subvert the British Empire to which Winston devoted his life but also challenged the values of European civilisation and martial manliness on which it – and Winston's faith – were founded. Worse still, the Mahatma succeeded. Little wonder that Churchill could not abide Gandhi.

'All Behind You, Winston', 14 May 1940: an autographed
copy of David Low's celebrated cartoon of the wartime coalition
was on Attlee's bedroom wall when he died. Clem watched
Winston's back, but also advanced his own agenda on the quiet.

10

Clement Attlee

'A Very Modest Fellow'

He is an admirable character, but not one with whom it is agreeable to dine.

Winston S. Churchill, July 1948[1]

I used to compare him to one of those layer cakes. There was a layer of the seventeenth century, a layer of the eighteenth century, a layer of the nineteenth century, and possibly even a layer of the twentieth century. One never knew which layer would be uppermost.

Attlee on Churchill, 21 April 1963[2]

On the train from Washington DC to Fulton, Missouri, in March 1946, Winston Churchill and Harry S. Truman had plenty of time to chat. According to Clark Clifford, Truman's aide, at one point the President asked about Clement Attlee, who had taken over as Prime Minister a few months before. After a chilly silence, Winston grunted, 'There is less there than meets the eye.' Persisting, Truman observed, 'he seems to be a very modest fellow.' Churchill agreed: 'He has much to be modest about.'[3]

Clark Clifford was known as an inveterate gossip, but Winston could be very waspish behind people's backs. Whatever the truth of the anecdote, there was a great deal more to the relationship between Churchill and Attlee than those oft-quoted one-liners suggest. 'Clem' made a career out of being underestimated. Like Winston, he had steel in his nature, yet it had been forged in the slums of London as well as on the frontiers of Britain's empire. And as deputy PM, in fact or name, for the whole of the Churchill's war premiership, he 'quietly stamped his own seal on Whitehall, extending his influence across the entire field of government'.[4] This laid the foundations for his own transformational administration in 1945–51.

Here were two sharply different conceptions of political leadership and of what did or could make Britain 'Great'. Like Gandhi, Attlee showed up Churchill in a less heroic light. By 1945 Winston's rooted anti-Bolshevism had hardened into ideological rigidity. A Liberal reformer before 1914, he was now unwilling to rethink the role of the state in the renovation of post-war capitalism. Attlee was more attuned to the voices of a people who had sacrificed lives, wealth and happiness in a thirty years' war against foes abroad and poverty at home. An ardent imperialist when young, he also became more aware than Winston of the winds of change blowing through the British Empire. During his premiership, Attlee not only presided over independence for India but also questioned why, in the nuclear age, Britain needed to maintain a large military presence in the Middle East. Churchill and Attlee were both patriots, but for Clem, unlike Winston, socialism defined his sense of Britain and its greatness, past and future.

* * *

On 15 November 1922 Clement Richard Attlee was elected as MP for Limehouse, in the East End of London. That was the same day on which Winston, famously, found himself without a seat and without an appendix. As Attlee began his parliamentary career, Churchill was out of the Commons for the first time in twenty-two years – seventeen of them as a government minister.[5] But his was experience derived from high office, through seeing a wide range of Britain's problems from the top down; whereas Attlee had come to socialism from the bottom up, living in London's docklands.

That wasn't how he started out. Attlee grew up in Putney, a prosperous southwest London suburb. His father, Henry, was a solicitor in a well-established firm in the City of London and the family lived in a comfortable house with its own tennis court, gardener and three domestic servants. What he took from his home was the deep ethical commitment of both his parents and also, thanks to several years of home schooling by his mother, a love of history, poetry and languages, with a facility in French and Italian that lasted all his life. He arrived at Oxford in 1901 as a convinced Tory imperialist – much like Winston (eight years older), who entered the Commons that same year. Attlee read history, with a particular interest in the Italian Renaissance, and developed a sneaking regard for what he called 'strong, ruthless rulers'. Yet he left no real mark. One tutor described him as 'a level-headed, industrious, dependable man with no brilliance of style or literary gifts but with excellent sound judgement'.[6] In short, almost the exact opposite of Churchill. After Oxford, Attlee returned home to Putney and trained as a barrister. But then, in October 1905, 'an event occurred which was destined to alter the whole course of my life'.[7]

His family had a strong tradition of social service. His old school, Haileybury, ran its own boys' club in Stepney, in the East End, and young Attlee paid it a visit one evening after work. Most of the teenagers were scruffy van boys by day, engaged in sweated labour to help keep their families going. But on club evenings they dressed in the uniform of Territorial Army cadets, taking pride in their smart appearance, and were put through drill and physical training that improved their fitness and fostered discipline and teamwork. Attlee was hugely impressed. In 1907 he took over as club manager and lived in the East End until the Great War broke out. In the process, his eyes were opened to poverty and deprivation. Churchill had similar glimpses as an MP in Manchester and Dundee, pushing him towards the doctrines of New Liberalism about rebalancing individualism and collectivism. According to historian Paul Addison, Winston 'alternated between radical attacks on privilege and a conservative vision of social reform', often intended as an antidote to socialism. The radicalism 'was to prove transitory' but the paternalism 'was to endure'.[8] For Attlee, however, living day by day in East London severed him entirely from the do-gooder Liberalism of his parents. And in January 1908, listening to 'a fiery little Welshman' called Tommy Williams proclaiming his socialist faith, Attlee found himself saying 'I am a socialist too.'[9]

Henry Attlee was not happy with his son's dramatic conversion, but he died in 1908. Consequently, Clem's yearly income rose to £400 a year, allowing him to become a professional politician. Yet he was never an orator or an ideologue: 'The people I admired were those who did the tedious jobs, collecting our exiguous subscriptions, trying to sell literature, and carrying the improvised platform from one street corner to another. They got no glamour . . . but, uncomplainingly, they worked to try to help on the cause.'[10] These were the political virtues he would cherish all his life, gaining him a superficial reputation for colourless efficiency. But his politics were rooted in the human sympathies kindled at Haileybury House and in the socialist romanticism of William Morris, which appealed to his heart as well as his head. Attlee was a political foot-soldier who climbed through the ranks to become an officer. Churchill had been a field marshal since childhood.

Although Attlee's socialism was local and communitarian, it was in no way incompatible with service to the nation. In 1914 many Labour men refused to fight in what they saw as an imperialist war. Among them were Ramsay MacDonald, who resigned as party leader, and Attlee's brother Tom, a conscientious objector who would suffer cruelly for his Christian pacifism. Clem, however, had no doubt about his duty to fight, although at 31 he was officially a year over the enlistment age. He commanded a company of the South Lancashire Regiment, some 800 lads from around Wigan, Warrington and Liverpool, in the Gallipoli campaign, helping to hold the perimeter line during the evacuation from Suvla Bay. When the South Lancs were redeployed to Mesopotamia, Captain Attlee was wounded in the attack on Kut. After a long recuperation learning to walk again, he went out to the Western Front, now as a major, and celebrated the Armistice with another spell in hospital. Those months of service abroad confirmed his deep patriotism. As he wrote in 1918: 'It was not until the Great War that I fully understood the strength of the ties that bind men to the land of their birth.'[11]

For Major Attlee, social service and national service had become two sides of the same coin. True patriotism meant fighting for Britain's freedom and also striving to make the country a better place. Demobilised in January 1919, he went straight back to the East End and was co-opted by the new Labour majority on the borough council to serve as Mayor of Stepney – at 36 the youngest in its history. To a party still haunted by conscientious objection, a former officer with a distinguished war record was a huge political asset. During these years Attlee set out a conception of socialism that would last a lifetime. It makes an interesting comparison with the Churchillian worldview. Attlee argued that 'the fact that we live in societies implies that we have certain rights and duties as members.' What concerned him was that, in recent times, rights had taken precedence over duties. This he blamed largely on 'the dominant idea of the nineteenth century, the exaltation of the individual at the expense of society, and the theory that the less the organised community interfered with the individual the better.' Here he was attacking head-on the laissez-faire verities of Victorian liberalism. Instead, in the new era of socialist democracy, 'we now have the conception that it is the duty of the State to act as the coordinating factor in making all individual effort work for the good of the citizens.'[12]

Contrast this optimistic view of the future with Winston's jeremiad during his abortive election campaign in November 1922, delivered on Armistice Day. His speech notes express graphically his sense of decline:

> What a disappointment the Twentieth Century has been
> How terrible & how melancholy
>   is long series of disastrous events
>   wh[ich] have darkened its first 20 years
> We have seen in ev[ery] country a dissolution,

a weakening of those bonds,
  a challenge to those principles
   a decay of faith
    an abridgement of hope
     on wh[ich] structure & ultimate existence
      of civilised society depends.[13]

Attlee was probably unaware of that speech. But he would hear similar philippics from Winston over subsequent decades. That may be why in 1963, when speaking of the Churchillian mind as a 'cake' with rich layers from the seventeenth, eighteenth and nineteenth centuries, he only said 'possibly even' about any layer from the present day. At heart Winston was a nineteenth-century Whig who struggled against the twentieth century, whereas Attlee wrote off the Victorian era and looked forward to bright possibilities dawning in his own time.

In January 1924 Ramsay MacDonald formed a minority Labour government after the Tory election defeat, and Attlee had his first taste of office as one of the under-secretaries at the War Office. But Labour could govern only with Liberal support. When that was withdrawn and another election ensued, Baldwin and the Tories returned to power in November – Winston among them. By then he had not only found a party and a seat again but also high office, being Baldwin's surprise choice as Chancellor of the Exchequer. And, as MP for the Epping Division of Essex, he also acquired Mr and Mrs C.R. Attlee as two of his constituents.[14] With Clem now on the Opposition front bench, the two men became Commons adversaries. That would be their political posture for the next three decades, except during Churchill's wartime coalition of 1940–5.

In the mid-1920s, Attlee spoke frequently in the Commons, particularly on the rates and electricity – topics that he knew well from his Stepney days. Occasionally he crossed swords with Churchill, as on 15 June 1925 during a debate on Winston's Budget, when they traded blows about the pros and cons of capitalism.[15] That exchange was typical of the two men's rhetorical positions at the time: Clem's utopian socialism, Winston seeing Reds under every bed. But in the late 1920s such parliamentary duels became less frequent because, in November 1927, Attlee reluctantly accepted MacDonald's request to serve on the new Statutory Commission for India. He could see that this might prove a poisoned chalice but, as biographer Kenneth Harris observed, his selection 'launched him, against his will, on a preoccupation with India that lasted the rest of his political life' – and also generated his fiercest conflicts with Winston.[16]

The commission paid two visits to India: a reconnaissance in February–March 1928, and then a detailed exploration from October 1928 until April 1929, during which his wife Violet, to her lasting delight, was able to come out for three months. The work in and on India stood Attlee in good stead. He saw the country first-hand in a way Winston never did in the twentieth century, visiting all but one of the provinces of British India. What's more, he did not come home with a Churchillian disdain for the Hindus and their culture. And in December 1931 he addressed the Commons at length about what he had learned, prodding frequently at Winston in a speech that outlined the principles which would guide him thereafter.

'There are various stages of knowledge of India,' he warned MPs. 'I have only reached the second stage, when one knows how little one knows. I cannot possibly compete with the easy dogmatism of knowledge that belongs only to inspired people like Lord Rothermere and the right hon. Gentleman the Member for Epping.' In another jab at Winston, he observed that 'the Indian problem is not a static problem. You cannot say that because you knew the Indian problem 20 years ago you know it now.' Declaring that Labour recognised 'very fully the right of India to self-government', Attlee lamented what he considered Winston's 'total failure to grasp the essentials of the Indian problem' – namely the desire for 'status and self-respect'. He surmised that Churchill had 'at the back of his mind something that flatters his national self-respect in some kind of feeling of Imperial domination. That is not understandable to me.' He was sure that India was 'suffering from a variety of economic and social ills that will require a giant's hand to remove them', but, equally, that this 'giant's hand cannot be an alien hand. It can only be done by the people of India themselves.'[17]

In the 1930s Attlee's constitutional road map extended only as far as Dominion status, which would put India on a par with countries like Australia. This seemed the limit of practical politics until communal tensions had been addressed, the princes brought into discussions and the officer corps of the Indian army Indianised. But his new familiarity with South Asia and his mantra that 'the Indian problem is not a static problem' prepared him to take radical action when he became PM.

By the time Attlee delivered this speech his own political position had changed dramatically. For five months in 1931 he enjoyed his first taste of junior ministerial office, as Postmaster-General. But when the Labour Government fell apart over the financial crisis of August 1931 and MacDonald then formed a National Government, Attlee was out of a job. In the election that followed the National Government won a landslide victory but MacDonald was now dependent on the Tories, while the Labour Party was reduced from 287 MPs to 52. Attlee narrowly kept his seat in Limehouse. Already disenchanted with MacDonald, he became a bitter critic, accusing him of perpetrating 'the greatest betrayal in the political history of this country'.[18] Yet that 'betrayal' was Clem's chance. With most of the Labour titans toppled in the election or deserting to 'the enemy', the Parliamentary Labour Party elected him deputy leader, to serve under George Lansbury.

Attlee, who loved watching cricket, was still described as a 'second eleven' man – a solid all-rounder rather than a star player. He didn't have the style and charisma of Stafford Cripps, a wealthy barrister and ardent left-winger. But at the end of 1933 he became acting leader for nine months while Lansbury was ill. One of his main concerns was the National Government's White Paper on India, which was being frustrated at every turn by Winston. Clem told his brother that Churchill had 'really persuaded himself that he is right about the imminent dissolution of India and the Empire' and was now pursuing his fight against Dominion status despite the damage this was doing to his position within the Tory party. 'Trouble with Winston,' Clem once observed: 'he nails his trousers to the mast and can't climb down.'[19]

Yet Attlee had a similar sartorial problem when he debated rearmament in the 1930s. Labour had taken its cue from Lansbury's ardent Christian pacifism and Attlee was initially a willing spokesman. On 7 November 1933, having told the Commons, 'I loathe and detest the present German regime and the whole spirit of the Nazi movement,' he argued that 'nowadays we have to realise that the whole conception of nationalism is out of date, that we need internationalism.' This meant that 'if you want full security you have to surrender sovereignty ... You have to make the League of Nations a real League and you have to put loyalty to the League of Nations above loyalty to your country.' He and Winston took revealingly opposite views of the notorious vote in February 1933 by the Oxford Union debating society: 'That this House will in no circumstances fight for its King and Country.' To Churchill this was an 'abject, squalid, shameless avowal' of socialist pacifism, whereas Attlee saw it as 'a vote for internationalism against nationalism, a vote *for* the League.'[20] Every year in the early 1930s, despite Nazi rearmament, Labour opposed the annual defence estimates. In October 1934 Attlee declared: 'We want to see put on the Statute Book something which will make our people citizens of the world before they are citizens of this country.' Winston was so struck by that line that he kept a note of the speech in his papers and sometimes taunted Attlee about it, even after 1945.[21]

The turning point came in October 1935 over Mussolini's invasion of Abyssinia, which took place while the party conference was in session. Faced with a motion from Ernest Bevin and other union leaders for sanctions against Italy, Lansbury and Cripps opposed it, whereas Attlee placed his commitment to the League above his opposition to armaments. 'We are against the use of force for imperialist and capitalist ends,' he declared, 'but we are in favour of the proper use of force for ensuring the rule of law.' After the motion passed, Lansbury resigned as leader of the Parliamentary Labour Party. Exploiting the confusion, Baldwin – now PM – called a snap election. Although his National Government triumphed, Labour raised its tally of seats to 154. Several party heavyweights returned to the Commons but Attlee was confirmed as leader, supported by the union MPs who had worked with him since 1931. His critics were scathing. 'A wretched, disheartening result,' groaned Hugh Dalton, a Labour intellectual. 'And a little mouse will lead them.'[22]

Few thought that Attlee would last long. Yet, through his customary hard work and an ability to defuse crises, he gradually established himself. In the summer of 1937 Labour finally agreed to stop voting against the defence estimates – a change of policy that Attlee, too, was now ready to embrace. The party conference promised to 'unhesitatingly maintain such armed forces as are necessary to defend our country and to fulfil our obligations as a member of the British Commonwealth and the League of Nations.'[23] And in December 1937 he spent a week in war-torn Spain, talking with the embattled Republican government and meeting victims of air raids. He also visited the XI International Brigade on the front line, especially its 'British Battalion', whose No. 1 company thereafter took the name 'The Major Attlee Company'. A photo of him giving the Republic's clenched-fist salute outraged Tories but delighted the left. Not only did it mark Attlee out from the Government's fence-sitting policy of non-intervention, it displayed a growing awareness of gesture politics that belied his grey reputation.[24]

On the other hand, his essentially bourgeois image, with pipe and hat, helped reassure many voters that the Labour Party was not run by left-wing revolutionaries. In 1931 Clem, Vi and their four children had moved from Winston's constituency into a larger house in the northwest London suburb of Stanmore. Although now able to afford a maid and a cook, the family remained careful about money. 'I have my little car,' Vi told a newspaper interviewer in 1937, 'but my husband uses the tube. Quicker and cheaper.' (Not a Churchillian mode of transport – his wife observed in April 1945 that Winston had only used the London Underground once in his life: during the General Strike of 1926. She said she deposited him at South Kensington but 'he went round and round' – presumably on the Circle Line – 'not knowing where to get out, and had to be rescued eventually'.)[25] In mid-1939 the Attlee family took in Paul Willer, a Jewish refugee from Nazi Germany, who stayed with them for four months until war began. Arranged through their local church, their hospitality remained a secret until 2018, and Attlee made no political capital out of it. He was 'a modest man', Willer recalled. He did not try to glorify himself in any way – 'a gentle man and a gentleman'.[26]

After Chamberlain returned from Munich proclaiming 'peace for our time', Churchill and Attlee both vehemently attacked the agreement. Winston's denunciation of it on 5 October is famous: 'a total and unmitigated defeat . . . a disaster of the first magnitude'. Yet Attlee's assault two days earlier had been no less striking and also more barbed. His dislike of Chamberlain went deep. 'He always treated us like dirt,' he said in 1965. 'I thought he was absolutely useless for foreign affairs – ignorant and at the same time opinionated.'[27] On 3 October, he attacked the PM in very personal terms, to cries of 'No' and 'Oh!' from some MPs. 'It was his determination to try to get something which he thought Herr Hitler would accept, and then he brought it and forced it on President Benes. That is not negotiation. That is merely delivering an ultimatum on behalf of one side.'[28]

Despite this trenchant speech, many still saw Attlee as a caretaker. That spring he did himself no favours nationally when Labour decided to oppose the Government's introduction of conscription – a mistake he later described as part of 'the hangover from the last war' when conscription was hugely controversial.[29] By now Winston's stock was rising. In June he published *Step by Step*, a collection of his newspaper articles on foreign affairs over the previous three years. Attlee was sent a copy. 'My dear Winston,' he replied. 'Thank you so much for sending me your book. It must be a melancholy satisfaction to you to see how right you were.'[30]

While Winston returned to the Admiralty on the outbreak of war, questions were still being raised about Attlee. According to a profile in the *Daily Mail* in December, 'Nobody looks less like a typical major than the Leader of the Opposition. Instead of being stocky and fierce, he is slim and gentle. As he talks, he clasps his hands, intertwines his fingers so hard that the knuckles show white, even when he is saying something that doesn't touch the emotions.'[31]

But then on 8 April 1940, Nazi Germany's onslaught on Norway transformed the positions of both Churchill and Attlee. Chamberlain's crowing on the 4th that Hitler had 'missed the bus' came back to haunt him as the hasty British attempts to intervene in Norway became embarrassing failures. Attlee called for a full debate and on 7 May, after Chamberlain's testy self-defence, he led off for the Opposition. Avoiding direct criticism of Churchill, he directed his fire at Chamberlain. 'The Prime Minister talked about missing buses. What about all the buses which he and his associates have missed since 1931? They missed all the peace buses but caught the war bus.' The British people, Attlee declared, 'see everywhere a failure of grip, a failure of drive'. In short, 'there is a widespread feeling in this country' that 'to win the war, we want different people at the helm from those who have led us into it.'[32]

His speech cued others on all sides of the House to speak out. 'Missed the Bus!' became a frequent jeer at the PM. The vote of 281 to 200 left no doubt that Chamberlain, at the very least, would have to form a coalition. Attlee and his deputy, Arthur Greenwood, made clear that Labour would not serve under Chamberlain, but probably would do so under someone else. This position was then confirmed at the Labour Party Conference, meeting in Bournemouth. By the time the two of them returned to London on the evening of 10 May, Hitler had invaded the Low Countries, Halifax had ruled himself out as PM, and Winston had been asked by the King to form a new government. Attlee and Greenwood were driven straight from Waterloo Station to the Admiralty, where Winston appointed them to his new five-man War Cabinet. The other two members were Chamberlain and Halifax, retained to keep the Tories loyal. Thus began the wartime coalition. By the time it ended in May 1945, only Churchill and Attlee were left in the War Cabinet. For the next five years the adversaries were allies – of a kind.

* * *

Attlee became a member of the three key wartime committees. Alongside the War Cabinet, he was appointed to the Defence Committee, which shaped strategy, and the Lord President's Committee, in control of domestic policy. He was the PM's deputy on the first two bodies as well as the initiator of the third, which he took over as Lord President in September 1943. He also deputised in the Commons when Winston was away at wartime conferences, and was formally appointed as Britain's first Deputy Prime Minister in February 1942. To many Labour left-wingers, his support of the Tory premier seemed supine. But Attlee had no doubt about Winston's capacity as a war leader. Asked in the 1960s which Churchillian traits he most admired, Clem replied, 'Courage, imagination, a great knowledge of things.' Yet, he added, Churchill 'wanted someone by him at a certain point to say, "Now don't be a bloody fool." '[33]

Public loyalty, private candour: that, in effect, was Attlee's mantra. It was evident from the first critical weeks of the war coalition. He did not quibble about the distribution of offices, as had happened with Asquith and Lloyd George during the Great War. He and Greenwood robustly rebutted Halifax's idea of exploring the chances of a negotiated peace when the British troops were trapped on the beaches of Dunkirk. (His direct experience at Gallipoli in 1915 made him optimistic about the chances of successful evacuation.) And the man who in the 1920s had inveighed against the immorality of war had no doubt in May 1940 that bombing German cities was both strategically sound and morally justified, because this war was a straight battle between good and evil.

One of the most celebrated British cartoons of the war was 'All Behind You, Winston' by the New Zealand artist David Low, published

in the *Evening Standard* on 14 May. It showed the new PM, jacketless
and rolling up his sleeves, marching forward pugnaciously – followed
by a phalanx of ministers, similarly dressed, headed by Attlee, Bevin
and Herbert Morrison. Clem loved the cartoon and secured a signed
copy from Low. When Attlee died – in a tiny flat in King's Bench
Walk – there were two pieces of art in his bedroom: a portrait of him
as Prime Minister, and 'All Behind You, Winston'.[34] Major Attlee was
immensely proud of his war record in this war as well as the last. And
Winston – not even leader of the Tory party till Chamberlain's death
in November 1940 – needed such loyalty. Indeed, he seems to have
often found Attlee easier to talk with than many members of his own
party. Attlee gave that loyalty readily. But it was not unconditional.
He had firm ideas about the peace that must follow, and was determined that Labour should use its time in office to quietly prepare the
way towards a better world for working people than had come about
after the Great War. Clem watched Winston's back, but also worked
behind his back to advance Labour's agenda.

The PM was firmly opposed to talking about peace aims. In May
1941 he told Eden, 'I am very doubtful about the utility of attempts
to plan the peace before we have won the war.'[35] But his hand was
forced by the Atlantic meeting in August, when Roosevelt insisted
on a formal declaration, which had to be improvised on the spot by
Churchill and Cadogan of the Foreign Office. When the PM asked
London for comments, Attlee moved with alacrity, summoning two
meetings of the War Cabinet at 1.45 a.m. and 10 a.m. on 12 August
to discuss texts and redrafts. One proposal from Attlee and the Labour
members became, virtually unchanged, point five, asserting that their
countries 'desire to bring about the fullest collaboration between all
nations in the economic field with the object of securing, for all,
improved labour standards, economic advancement, and social
security'. Attlee's telegram to Winston warned: 'The omission of a
paragraph on these lines would be most marked and would have an
unfortunate effect on public opinion in this country and the
Dominions and on the Allied Governments.' It was also Attlee who

announced the declaration to the world on 14 August. The radio broadcast had been hyped in advance, but his dry, terse style added to the general sense of anti-climax in Britain when the hoped-for US declaration of war turned out to be merely a declaration of war aims. The story of the Atlantic Charter is a good illustration of Clem's skills behind the scenes and his limitations front-of-house.[36]

Attlee told a meeting of West African students in London that the charter would apply to 'all the peoples of the world'. Winston, however, clamped down hard on that idea, telling the Commons on 9 September that 'at the Atlantic meeting, we had in mind, primarily, the restoration of the sovereignty, self-government and national life of the States and nations of Europe now under the Nazi yoke, and the principles governing any alterations in the territorial boundaries which may have to be made. So that is quite a separate problem from the progressive evolution of self-governing institutions in the regions and peoples which owe allegiance to the British Crown.'[37]

Attlee was peeved but, for the moment, could do little. The imperial situation was transformed in December 1941 by Japan's attack on Pearl Harbor, making the US a full ally, and then by the fall of Singapore on 15 February 1942. This proved a turning point in the Churchill-Attlee relationship. The PM's war leadership was called into question as never before and he had to respond with a major ministerial reshuffle. He appointed Stafford Cripps – though a maverick leftist, now celebrated for his time as ambassador in Moscow – as Leader of the Commons, with a seat in the War Cabinet. He also invented the title of Deputy Prime Minister for Attlee, making official his de facto role, and appointed him Secretary of State for the Dominions. This was the Labour leader's first major departmental post. It also gave him central place in the making of imperial policy.[38]

Although Cripps and Attlee had feuded in the past, they shared a deep and informed concern about the India question. In June 1938 Attlee spent a weekend at Cripps' country house in the Cotswolds, where he and other Labour politicians met Jawaharlal Nehru, leader of the Congress party. Here they tried to move on from the failure of the Government of India Act, with its clumsy federal solution imposed from above, to the idea of a representative constituent assembly to allow Indians to devise their own constitution, followed by a transitional period to full self-government. In February 1942 Attlee and Cripps picked up the idea afresh, taking advantage of the new political dynamics. With his usual vigour Attlee chaired the War Cabinet's new India Committee, convening seven meetings over eleven days to thrash out a declaration. When their document proved too divisive for the Cabinet, Cripps salvaged the situation by offering to go out to India, taking a revised version of the declaration as his negotiating brief.

Although Cripps' mission in March–April 1942 ended in failure, the debate surrounding it reveals clearly Attlee's distinctive, historically informed attitude to Indian politics. In a memo for the Cabinet on 2 February 1942, he argued that 'the East is now asserting itself against the long dominance of the West'. The fact that Western countries were now 'driven to a belated recognition of China as an equal and of the Chinese as fellow fighters for civilisation against barbarism makes the Indian ask why he, too, cannot be master in his own house'. Yet Attlee did not see this as the end of British influence because 'the history of at least 150 years has forged close links between India and the United Kingdom', including 'acceptance by politically conscious Indians of the principles of democracy and liberty'. If Britain wanted the people of India to 'take part with us in the common struggle', it must, as far as possible, 'make them sharers in the things for which we and they are fighting'. In these assumptions about India and its British political heritage – based on the ideas of Thomas Babington Macaulay – we can see the roots of Attlee's confidence, when Prime Minister, that Empire could be transformed into Commonwealth.[39]

Aside from India, Attlee exploited his new pedestal as Deputy Prime Minister to raise questions in the dark days of 1942 about Britain's strategy, in particular its commitment to the strategic bomber offensive against Germany. In April he urged dispersion of bomber strength to offer close support to military operations in both the India-Burma theatre and the Middle East, where it seemed that the fate of the British Empire would be decided. Winston was dismissive of these 'fashionable ideas', arguing that the focus on bombing Germany was 'the only way in our power of helping Russia'.[40] Attlee returned to the charge in the summer, when it seemed that Rommel's tanks might soon break through to Cairo. On 10 July he sent a lengthy memo to the PM. This criticised the failure to move beyond the static military concepts of the last war, built around the cumbersome division – 40,000 strong, with 'an immense litter of ancillary services which almost swallow up the fighting men'. He also castigated the Air Ministry for regarding troop support as 'an illegitimate filching of its resources' because its thinking was 'dominated by the conception that the war can be won by the big bombers'. Instead, he argued that 'air forces must be integral parts of the Army and Navy and not mere lendings and scrapings grudgingly subtracted from the Air Force.'[41]

Winston's reply was testy. Although conceding some of Attlee's points, on the big issues he was defiant – pointedly reminding his deputy that 'Britain for the last twenty years was hagridden by pacifism and haunted by the craven fear of being great, while Germany was passionate about preparing for a war of revenge and world dominion.' He said he had no intention of turning the air force into 'a mere handmaid of the Army' and insisted that 'on the whole, the best chance of winning the war will be with the big bombers. It will certainly be several years before British and American forces will be capable of beating the Germans on even terms in the open field.'[42]

Their clash on strategy was predictable: Winston had consistently privileged Europe and North Africa over the Far East, and his advocacy of the bomber dated back to the Great War era. What's interesting is how Attlee conducted the argument. Having tried out his ideas on Eden – with whom he was developing a close working relationship intended to put what he called 'a brake on Winston's wild ideas'[43] – he wrote privately to the PM rather than submitting a formal Cabinet paper.

Attlee's most significant impact as Deputy PM in the coalition was to prepare the way for Labour's post-war period in power. A landmark was publication in December 1942 of the long-awaited Beveridge report on social insurance. William Beveridge, a former director of the London School of Economics, proposed that social insurance should be reorganised to ensure a national minimum income for all classes 'from the cradle to the grave'. To do this depended on three underlying and interrelated 'Assumptions': a national health service, family allowances, and the maintenance by the state of something close to full employment. Such was the national mood in the grim middle of the war that the report was a bestseller, selling over 600,000 copies in the first few weeks.[44]

Winston initially echoed warnings from the Treasury. 'A dangerous optimism is growing up about the conditions it will be possible to establish here after the war,' he told the War Cabinet on 12 January 1943, reminding them of the country's likely financial position. He said he did not wish to 'deceive the people by false hopes and airy visions of Utopia and Eldorado'.[45] Under pressure from Labour MPs, Attlee was having none of this. Eventually the two of them came up with a compromise. The coalition must not be committed to introduce legislation to reform the social services during the war, but there would be no commitment *against* such legislation.[46]

During 1943 Attlee chipped away at Winston's resistance to post-war planning. Through a Cabinet reshuffle in September after the death of Kingsley Wood, he became Lord President of the Council, the decisive position on the home front. In Cabinet on 14 October, Attlee openly objected to Churchill's delaying tactics: 'There were many subjects on which the formulation of policy could not await the end of the war' and which, furthermore, were not issues of real controversy between the political parties. At their next discussion, on 21 October, the PM instructed that 'any decisions which are needed for the supreme objects of FOOD and EMPLOYMENT in the years immediately after the war must be taken now whether they involve legislation and whether they are controversial or not.' According to Dalton, the PM – in 'a very good temper and great spirits' – said he had been 'led to see the question quite differently' after being 'jostled and beaten up by the Deputy Prime Minister', for which he professed himself 'very grateful'. Dalton was delighted by 'this remarkable change' in the PM's attitude. Afterwards he congratulated Attlee – for years an object of contempt – who said 'there had been a frightful row last week, and loud explosions from the PM' but now 'the smoke had cleared away' and Churchill himself 'had led the Tory troops through the breach which we had made in their defences'.[47]

In January 1945 Attlee even had the temerity to chide the weary PM for his casual handling of domestic business – bashing out a long letter on his own typewriter rather than using a secretary, to make sure his indictment did not leak out. While acknowledging Winston's absorption with the 'military conduct of the war', Attlee deplored his cavalier treatment of the many papers about civil affairs, on which hours of work had been devoted:

> When they do come before the Cabinet it is very exceptional for you to have read them. More and more often you have not read even the note prepared for your guidance. Often half an hour and more is wasted in explaining to you what could have been grasped by two or three minutes reading of the document. Not infrequently a phrase catches your eye which gives rise to a disquisition on an interesting point only slightly connected with the subject matter. The result is long delays and unnecessarily long Cabinet imposed on Ministers who have already done a full day's work and who will have more to deal with before they go to bed.[48]

The PM 'exploded', to quote Jock Colville, and drafted a caustic reply – only to be told by his wife and others that Attlee was quite right. So Winston dictated a curt acknowledgement, assuring Attlee, 'I shall always endeavour to profit by your counsels', and then told his staff: 'Let us think no more of Hitlee or Attler. Let us go to the movies'. Everyone in Number 10 adjourned to watch Bette Davis and Humphrey

Bogart in the soapy melodrama *Dark Victory*. The Deputy PM's letter was never mentioned again, but it is a striking expression of Attlee's 'Don't be a bloody fool' slogan.[49]

Attlee's ascent was not evident to most of the public, and there was general surprise at Labour's landslide victory in July 1945. This owed much to the national yearning for a better life after years of wartime sacrifices. Attlee and his colleagues had kept reminding people of the betrayed hopes of 1918 when, they argued, the people had won the war but the 'hard-faced' men had won the peace. And Winston played into their hands with his notorious election broadcast on 4 June, claiming that a socialist government could implement its programme only by resorting to 'some kind of Gestapo, no doubt very humanely directed in the first instance'. The 'Gestapo speech' was neatly exploited by Attlee on the radio next evening. With heavy irony he thanked the PM for helping the electorate to understand 'how great was the difference between Winston Churchill, the great leader in war of a united nation, and Mr Churchill, the Party Leader of the Conservatives'.[50]

* * *

The little man now had to operate front-of-house. That he certainly did – but not in Churchillian ways. Winston was a public presence, his successor almost a public absence. (According to one post-war joke, an empty taxi arrived at Number 10, and Attlee got out.) But whereas Winston knew how to grab and shape public opinion – as Clem once remarked, whatever he did always had 'a little touch of the buccaneer, and perhaps of the condottiere' – Attlee 'did know how to run an institutional system'.[51] As Prime Minister he usually operated behind the scenes: writing judicious memos, handling people one-on-one, and deftly manipulating committees. He allowed time for discussion ('a monologue is not a decision', he claimed to have once told Winston) before offering a brisk summing-up that was rarely challenged. ('You don't take a vote. No. Never.')[52] A highly efficient worker, Attlee would not tolerate ministers arriving at Cabinet meetings without having read the papers. His outraged memo to Winston in January 1945 came from the heart.

Once ministers had been appointed, Attlee – unlike Churchill – usually left them to get on with their business. As he famously observed of Ernest Bevin, his Foreign Secretary, 'You don't keep a dog and bark yourself; and Ernie was a very good dog.' Bevin was indeed a special case – Attlee called their relationship 'the deepest of my political life' – but his general precept was that a PM 'must always work through the Minister . . . if he's picked the right man, he should trust him. If he finds he can't, he should get rid of him.' This latitude fitted the bill in many cases because, during years in Opposition, Labour had formulated a detailed programme of nationalisation, to which Attlee was fully committed. That was the overriding agenda of the new government.[53]

What also helped immeasurably was the sea-change in British politics during the war. Winston's commitment in May 1940 to 'victory at all costs' meant total war, and this – to quote historian David Marquand – 'entailed a form of war socialism: a command economy run on egalitarian lines. The wartime state allocated raw materials, rationed most items of consumer expenditure, controlled prices, fixed profit margins, subsidised food, conscripted women and evacuated children.' By 1945 public expenditure accounted for over half of GDP, compared with just under a quarter in 1938. Equally important, 'war socialism also transformed the public culture. Pre-war heresies came in from the cold; proposals that would have been ruled out by Stanley Baldwin and Neville Chamberlain were absorbed into the conventional wisdom.'[54]

This was the unintended consequence of Churchill's war, but it had been the clear intent of Attlee's war management. He grasped the logic of war socialism and saw its potential significance for peacetime. And, as he kept telling the left, the war coalition had brought an unruly group of socialists into the heart of Whitehall, giving them experience of government and making them familiar and trusted figures for the British public. Indeed Attlee, in retirement, opined that this had probably been his most important achievement: 'to take a party intact into a coalition, keep it intact for five years, bring it out intact, and win an election with it when most people expected defeat.' He added drily, 'Not many precedents for that.'[55]

Although Attlee was ready to let his team play their own game, he did come out to bat when it mattered. Hugely important was his performance in the Commons on 6 December 1945 when Winston called a vote of censure on the new government – deploring its preoccupation, 'impelled by Socialist theory, with the formulation of long-term schemes for nationalisation' when the nation needed 'food, work and homes'. He spoke for seventy minutes, directing most of his fire at key ministers. Attlee received only a few patronising sentences near the start noting that the new PM had 'not sought in any way to embitter or inflame our proceedings . . . He does not need to grind his personal axe, and will probably be content if he can keep hold of it.'[56]

Replying, Attlee adopted a dry mocking style, poking fun at Churchill's 'quiet note of injured innocence' about how Labour's partisan government had supposedly 'driven this public-spirited Opposition' into a motion of censure. He added, 'I have not forgotten the right hon. Gentleman's broadcast at the beginning of the Election, nor have the people of this country. That was when any partisan tone was introduced.' This allusion to the Gestapo speech delighted the Labour benches. He threw in a compliment about how Churchill had 'earned, rightly, the respect of this country as a great man who inspired our fighting Forces'. But, he said, this was no longer wartime, yet Churchill did not change. That was why the Tories lost the 1945 election, because 'the prima donna held the stage.' The country, he concluded, 'does not like one-man shows.'[57]

This mocking speech was a clever way to turn Winston's record as a great war leader against him. Jim Callaghan, a new Labour MP and future PM, still remembered in 1983 how 'Attlee was absolutely devastating. We really did roar our approval', because that performance was 'something quite remarkable against Churchill's experience and his absolute control'. Even normally hostile papers declared the new PM the surprise winner of this eagerly awaited duel. And in 1951, on a list of his most notable achievements as party leader, Clem included 'Speech in the House replying to Churchill which established my debating position vis a vis him.'[58]

Attlee may not have planned his ascent in the deliberate Churchillian manner but he had definitely arrived; indeed, at the age of 62, he had done so four years earlier than his predecessor. But having reached the great battlefield, Attlee, like Winston, was having to fight on ground not of his own choosing – or imagining. In May 1940 it was the fall of France which upset all Churchill's assumptions. In August 1945 Attlee faced an equally grave existential crisis, created by the atomic bomb and Britain's near-bankrupt international position, just when the US seemed to be turning in on itself and severing what Winston called the 'special relationship'.

In November 1945, Attlee flew to Washington in an effort to disabuse Congress of its worst fears about British socialism. Although not making the same impact as Churchill – one reporter said Attlee looked and sounded like the treasurer of a children's aid society presenting his annual report – the new PM stressed to a joint session of Congress on 13 November that Labour was a 'freedom-loving' movement rooted in the ideals that had inspired Magna Carta, the Pilgrim Fathers and the Declaration of Independence.[59] During his visit he had several talks with the President about the bomb. But Truman, pressed by his advisers and by Congress, was gradually wriggling out of the understandings Churchill had reached with Roosevelt – which were looser than Winston claimed and were also unknown to much of the Washington bureaucracy. By early 1946, it was clear that the US was going to block the sharing of information and technology relating to the atomic bomb with all countries, including Britain. A bill to that effect, sponsored by Senator Brien McMahon, was working its way through Congress.

Attlee felt he had been utterly let down by the Americans. Thereafter, observed biographer Kenneth Harris, 'the essence of his leadership was to make the best of an impossible situation.'[60] Although 1945–50 was at least peacetime, this was not dissimilar to the challenge facing

Winston after the fall of France. Winston had not been cowed. Nor was Attlee after 1945. Despite the financial crisis, the 'little man' kept going with Labour's nationalisation agenda, though he left much of the detail to his ministers. He also went ahead with a British Bomb – and that he did almost alone.

This decision reflected Attlee's fears of Russia and his doubts about America. He had always been sceptical about the future of the wartime alliance with Moscow, speculating in January 1943 that the USSR 'would wish to absorb all the Slav states'.[61] And he did not share the hopes Winston invested in his personal relationship with Stalin. Attlee lacked the personality for summitry; in any case, his impressions of Stalin at Potsdam in July 1945 were not favourable – 'a pretty ruthless tyrant'. By late 1945, amid deepening tensions, Attlee had virtually abandoned the Churchillian conceit of maintaining a 'personal correspondence' with the Soviet leader. But he and Winston did see eye-to-eye on the 'iron curtain' speech in March 1946. Informed in advance of its main thrust, Attlee told Churchill, 'I am sure your Fulton speech will do good,' and he later declined to comment on a motion from over 100 Labour MPs asking him repudiate the tone and content. Instead, he simply stated that Churchill had spoken 'in an individual capacity' in a foreign country. Like Truman, Attlee found it helpful for a statesman of Winston's renown to express his own fears about Soviet policy.[62]

Deteriorating relations with the USSR undermined Attlee's initial hopes of international control of the Bomb through the UN. So he moved forward on the production of a British Bomb. Once it became clear that two of Labour's 'Big Four' – Dalton and Cripps – had serious reservations about the cost, Attlee removed them from further discussions. The formal decision was taken by a special Cabinet sub-committee (anonymously called GEN 163) which met only once, on 8 January 1947.[63] Attlee never doubted the rightness of this action. Otherwise, he said in 1959, 'we would have put ourselves entirely in the hands of the Americans' at a time (before NATO) when 'nobody could be sure' that they 'would not revert to isolationism'. Status mattered as well as security. 'For a power of our size and with our responsibilities to turn its back on the Bomb did not make sense.' Bevin put the point more sharply. 'We've got to have this thing over here whatever it costs,' he told Dalton and Cripps. 'We've got to have the bloody Union Jack flying on top of it.'[64] At a gut level, the issue was 'greatness'.

Here was Clem the patriot in full colours. Indeed, he managed Britain's Bomb like a martinet: truly Major Attlee, or perhaps like those 'ruthless' Renaissance princes he had admired as an Oxford undergraduate. He handled the project almost entirely on his own, alongside a few scientific advisers. Parliament was not even informed until May 1948, and then in a brief and anodyne statement – 'all types of modern weapons, including atomic weapons, are being developed' – which attracted little comment in the Commons or the press. The costs (over £100 million) were concealed from Parliament, to the astonishment of Churchill when he returned to the premiership in 1951. He was informed that they had been buried in 'general expenditure' voted for the Ministry of Supply. Winston continued the same 'necessary' practice of concealment and gave approval for Britain's first atomic test, which took place off the coast of Australia in October 1952.[65]

Yet the Bomb also revealed Attlee again as a *radical* patriot. He had not altered his first thought in August 1945 that atomic weapons had rendered 'out of date' strategic bases in the Middle East and Far East. He returned to the charge regularly over the next eighteen months. In March 1946, for instance, he wrote a memo stressing how airpower and the Bomb had called into question an imperial strategy conceived in the nineteenth century and based on seapower. This particularly applied to the control of the Mediterranean: central to Churchill's strategy during the Second World War. 'In the present era we must consider carefully how to make the most of our limited resources. We must not, for sentimental reasons based on the past, give hostages to fortune.' By 'limited resources' Attlee meant manpower as well as finance, because he was also under pressure from the economics ministries to accelerate the pace of demobilisation and get men back into export-earning industries. He believed the Bomb offered the hope of a more manpower-lite defence policy.[66]

But there was an outcry when Attlee brought the issue to a head in January 1947. Opposed by Bevin, senior diplomats and the three Chiefs of Staff (who threatened to resign), the PM was obliged to back down.[67] He did, though, preside over the end of Britain's ill-fated mandate in Palestine, where, by 1947, roughly 10 per cent of Britain's armed forces, 100,000 men, had been trying to keep the peace in a country the size of Wales. 'What are we getting out of it?' demanded Churchill in the Commons on 31 January. These men could be 'strengthening our depleted industry'.[68] But he supported Bevin's policy of handing the problem to the UN, which voted for partition – whereupon Attlee's government announced in December 1947 that Britain would pull out on 14 May 1948 and leave Jews and Arabs to their own devices. What few expected was that the Zionist forces would be so effective, that much of the Arab population would flee or be expelled, or that both the USA and the USSR – for different reasons – would rapidly recognise the new state of Israel. Amid the chaos and bloodshed, Labour's miscalculations seemed calamitous. But in truth, successive British governments had been unable to handle the explosive legacies of the Palestine mandate. After 1945 they blew up in Labour's face at a time when Attlee had his eyes on other crises.

The imperial issue that really mattered to Attlee was India and it was he who directed Labour's policy to end the Raj, in sharp contrast with his neglect of Palestine. His long-standing view was that Britain should be preparing India for independence within the British Empire and, as PM, he had seen the true balance sheet of what victory had cost. Winston, however, remained a diehard and, out of power, he did not have to confront the post-war economic and financial crisis. Deeper biases also played a part. Since the 1930s Labour had enjoyed close relations with the leaders of the Congress party – especially, through Cripps, with Jawaharlal Nehru – and it underestimated the potency of Jinnah and the Muslim League. Winston, by contrast, continued to despise Hindu culture, regarded Congress as wartime traitors, and extolled Muslims and Sikhs as 'martial races' on whom Britain relied for its Indian Army. He and the Tories kept close if surreptitious contacts with Jinnah, which could only encourage the Muslim leader's intransigence about a separate Islamic state.[69]

An interim government was formed in September 1946, consisting exclusively of Congress members, headed by Nehru as Prime Minister. Communal violence escalated, resulting in thousands of deaths. On Christmas Eve, Attlee summarised for the Cabinet a bleak assessment of the situation from the Viceroy, Lord Wavell. 'We are not in a position to maintain British rule in India beyond 31st March, 1948, and possibly not for so long.' Facing 'virtually civil war between Hindus and Muslims', Wavell advised a phased withdrawal over the next twelve months.[70] The PM had already decided (without consulting the full Cabinet) to replace Wavell with Admiral Lord Louis Mountbatten, a second cousin of King George VI, who had impressed Attlee as the dynamic Commander-in-Chief in Southeast Asia at the end of the war. After six weeks of backstage negotiations, a firm timetable for ending the Raj emerged – with Attlee pushing ahead despite objections from many colleagues, including Bevin.[71]

The appointment of Mountbatten and a commitment to transfer power by June 1948 were announced by the PM in the Commons on 20 February 1947. The two actions showed Major Attlee at his boldest, trying to make a virtue of necessity. He hoped that setting a firm date for the transfer to Indians of responsibility for their own security and welfare would concentrate their minds, finally nailing the belief on all sides that, whatever Britain said, it would never quit India.[72]

The ensuing debate turned into a memorable duel between Churchill and Attlee. Winston lambasted the PM for moving beyond Dominion status, ignoring commitments to protect minorities and the Untouchables, and especially failing to secure agreement between Hindus and Muslims. He considered it 'a cardinal mistake to entrust the government of India to the caste Hindu, Mr. Nehru', who was 'the most bitter enemy of any connection between India and the British Commonwealth'. Winston was particularly critical about the June 1948 deadline, asking,

'How can one suppose that the thousand-year gulf which yawns between Muslim and Hindu will be bridged in 14 months?' He also landed a telling blow about the contrast between Labour's policies on the two great imperial issues of the moment. 'There is a time limit for India, but no time limit for Palestine. I must say, that astonished me. Two bottles of powerful medicine have been prepared, but they are sent to the wrong patients.' And so Winston moved to his peroration: 'It is with deep grief I watch the clattering down of the British Empire, with all its glories and all the services it has rendered to mankind. I am sure that in the hour of our victory, now not so long ago, we had the power, or could have had the power, to make a solution of our difficulties which would have been honourable and lasting. Many have defended Britain against her foes. None can defend her against herself.'[73]

'Winston was his unique self,' noted one Tory observer, 'magnificent, restrained but imaginative' and 'toward the end, deeply moving.'[74] As with Palestine, he sought to lay all the blame on the mistakes made by the current PM and his colleagues rather than on the problems they inherited. But Attlee turned history back on his predecessor, mocking Winston as a prisoner of his own past who had taken the same line for years with 'a constancy that completely ignores the march of events'. The PM reiterated lessons he had learnt in 1929. 'Nationalist feeling runs right through all the Indian classes. That is the reason why you cannot carry on against the will of the Indian people.' Drawing himself up to his full height, the little radical patriot declared, 'We believe that we have done a great work in India. We believe that the time has come when Indians must shoulder their responsibility.' He denied that Britain was 'betraying' its mission. 'Anyone who has read the lives of the great men who have built up our rule in India and who did so much to make India united will know that all those great men looked to the fulfilment of our mission in India, and the placing of responsibility for their own lives in Indian hands.' Watching from the public gallery, Mountbatten's press secretary was impressed by Attlee's performance. 'The man burns with a hidden fire and is sustained by a certain spiritual integrity which enables him to scale the heights when the great occasion demands.'[75]

In the event, the Indian endgame descended into chaos and blood-shed, as Winston had warned. A unified country proved out of reach and, although it was possible to transfer power to two separate states, the human cost was appalling: perhaps a million deaths and 15 million people displaced. The hastily drawn borders between Pakistan and India, tilted towards the latter, proved a running sore, prompting wars in 1947–8 and 1965, and in 1971 when East Pakistan broke away from West Pakistan (a thousand miles away) to form Bangladesh. On this issue (like Palestine), one reads the documents of the mid-1940s today with a sense of utter unreality: the paper solutions composed in neat Whitehall prose seem entirely divorced from the dreadful human real-ities of an empire that had lost control. In the words of one recent Mountbatten biographer: 'No resident of Viceroy's House had enjoyed so much power – the irony being that at no point since 1857 [the Mutiny] had the British found themselves so powerless.' But Mountbatten's connection with the Crown helped counter Winston's charges of unpatriotic 'socialist scuttle' by 'coating the narrative of timely closure with royal approval' and packaging the grand narrative in 'spec-tacle and ceremony'.[76]

The 'transfer of power' was an exercise in smoke and mirrors. Yet, as Attlee chided his critics, what realistic alternatives existed in 1946–7 to make up for decades of foot-dragging and neglect? Senior Tories such as Eden, Macmillan and former Viceroy Halifax did not chal-lenge the setting of a deadline, though they deplored the ensuing haste and chaos. And although the 'old Bengal Lancer', as Eden put it, was sometimes 'alive and kicking', Winston did not turn India into a passionate crusade as he had done in the 1930s. Now in his seven-ties, he lacked the energy, knew it was too late, and was mostly absorbed by his memoirs. As on Palestine, he talked grandly of missed opportunities after the war, but was vague on specifics. For him, Nehru's last-minute decision to keep India in the Commonwealth helped sugar the pill. And Attlee in *Empire into Commonwealth* (1960), his own attempt at a positive narrative, noted with delight that 'Lord Halifax subsequently went on record' to state that without the opposition of Churchill and his friends to the Government of India Act, 'we might have got an all-India solution to the Indian problem before the Second World War.'[77]

* * *

Attlee's radical cuts in global commitments, however messy, eased Britain's financial overstretch. Equally important, the United States – after its disengagement from Europe in 1945–6 – began to provide significant assistance as concerns mounted in Washington about the communist threat. The Marshall Plan in 1947–8 and the North Atlantic Treaty of April 1949, both largely handled at the British end by Bevin, created an unprecedented Western alliance. Beneath that security umbrella, Labour maintained the pace of nationalisation – to Winston's abiding anger. The coal mines were taken over in January 1947 and the rail companies a year later, followed by electricity and gas in April and May 1949. But the flagships of the Attlee's first government in 1945–50 were the National Insurance Act of 1946 and the National Health Service (NHS), inaugurated on 5 July 1948. Although rooted in decisions of Winston's wartime coalition, both of these had been conceptually transformed. The basic principle of social insurance had shifted from selection to universality – 'the notion of flat-rate contributions and an equality of benefit for all as a bonding of a common citizenship'.[78] And the wartime concept of the NHS was radically reworked by Aneurin Bevan, who saw that it required the nationalisation of the hospitals in order to be workable. Yet the NHS also reveals the general problem with Labour's pell-mell nationalisation: the vast medical leviathan was inadequately costed. Within three years it would require the introduction of prescription charges.

At any event, Labour after 1945 'had a doctrine, a programme, and a mandate', as historian Paul Addison observed. 'But the Conservatives had none of these, and were uncertain which way to go' – whether to espouse a full-blooded policy of 'free enterprise' or a mixed economy and the welfare state. Winston liked to keep things fluid, and anyway, between 1945 and 1947, he 'took part in none of the debates over nationalisation, social insurance or the National Health Service'. Though still capable of arousing Parliament on his day, 'he had no intention of applying himself to the daily grind of Opposition' – leaving that to Eden, his impatient heir-apparent.[79] Winston loved to luxuriate in grand rhetoric. He told a Tory conference in May 1948: 'Socialism is the philosophy of failure, the creed of ignorance, and the gospel of envy'. Unless Britain got free of its 'perverse' doctrines, there could be 'no hope for recovery. This island cannot maintain its population as a great power.'[80]

Winston kept demanding an election, which the PM had to call before the following summer. When Attlee opted for 23 February 1950, the roles played by the two men contrasted markedly with those they had taken in 1945. This time the Tories avoided making Winston the centrepiece of their campaign – he was too busy with his memoirs – whereas Labour built itself around Attlee, who was driven some 1,300 miles around the country by his long-suffering wife. Winston did, however, hit the headlines with his speech about Cold War tensions in Edinburgh on 14 February, in which he called for 'another parley at the summit, if such a thing were possible'. That phrase, coming from Churchill, went around the world, but Bevin dismissed such 'stunt proposals'. The diarist Harold Nicolson also saw its essentially political point: to 'suggest talks with Stalin on the highest level inevitably makes people think, "Winston could talk to Stalin on more or less the same level. But if Attlee goes, it would be like a mouse addressing a tiger. Therefore, vote for Winston."' The PM retaliated during an election speech in Nottingham: 'Mr Churchill is a great master of words. But it is a terrible thing when a master of words becomes a slave of words. There is nothing behind these words'. He added: 'Mr Churchill is like a cock that crows and thinks it produced the dawn.'[81]

In the event, Labour continued in power after 23 February but with a majority of only five. This was now a tired government, staffed by many ministers who had been running Whitehall departments for a decade since 1940. They staggered on for another eighteen months until the election of October 1951, which returned Churchill to Number 10. During the endgame two issues stood out: Europe and Korea. Each sheds light on how Attlee and Churchill understood Great Britain's place in the world.

In May 1950 Robert Schuman, the French Foreign Minister, invited Britain to join in talks about forming a European Coal and Steel Community. The Government was still trying to complete nationalisation of the iron and steel industries, against fierce opposition from the industry and the Tories. That was one reason why it declined to go ahead. But the question of sovereignty was also fundamental. When the French set an absolute deadline of 2 June, the Cabinet followed the advice from permanent secretaries in the key departments: 'It has been our settled policy hitherto that in view of our world position and interests, we should not commit ourselves irrevocably to Europe in the political or economic sphere unless we could measure the extent and effects of the commitment.' Later the PM told the French ambassador of Britain's 'broad agreement with the conception of European unity' but insisted it was 'quite impossible for us to sign a blank cheque'. Attlee's private secretary put it more pungently: 'He felt that Britain ought not to be bossed around by a lot of Frogs.'[82]

Later, Churchill liked to claim that if Britain had joined in the talks, a better plan would 'probably' have emerged, but in fact his 'three circles' concept (see Chapter 8) imposed similar restraints on Tory Europeanism. 'When there was no longer political advantage to be gained from using "Europe" as a stick to beat the Labour Government,' observed historian Alan Bullock, 'Churchill's views were very close to Bevin's.' And to those of Attlee and Eden. Socialists or capitalists, they all saw Britain as a global power, whose interests could not be confined to Europe.[83]

What also distracted attention was the sudden North Korean invasion of the South on 25 June, news of which arrived during the Commons debate on the Schuman Plan. Although it took some years to become clear that 'the bolt-from-the-Parisian-blue in May 1950 effectively terminated Britain's leadership of postwar Europe', by contrast the fallout from the Korean War signed the death sentence for Attlee's government and 'did much to poison the internal life of the Labour party for the rest of the 1950s'.[84]

Attlee, worried about communist China's possible threat to Hong Kong, initially opted simply to move the British Far Eastern fleet. But then he shifted ground, under pressure from the ambassador in Washington, Sir Oliver Franks, who stressed the symbolic value of sending 'a token ground force'. First because 'too often in the past we have taken our time to make a decision' on a US proposal, with the result that even if Britain eventually backed the US line, it got little credit for doing so. With the Americans, Franks insisted, initial reactions always mattered. Secondly, a quick and positive offer would also signal that, after Britain's recent recovery from economic difficulties, it was no longer 'one of the queue of European countries' but 'one of two world powers outside Russia'.[85]

Despite Attlee's commitment of some land forces, Winston criticised the slowness with which the 'expeditionary force' was being assembled and despatched to Korea. Then communist China suddenly entered the war, and inept comments from Truman suggested that nuclear weapons might be used in Korea. Although these were later corrected, there was consternation in the Commons and Attlee decided he must meet the President face-to-face. Winston was greatly exercised to learn that Attlee had allowed his personal agreement with FDR at Quebec in 1943 to lapse, especially clause two – that neither country would authorise use of the bomb on third parties without the other's consent. But his scientific adviser Lord Cherwell said privately that he had always considered Quebec to be 'a provisional arrangement', and that it was most unlikely the US would have allowed Britain to 'assert a veto in perpetuity in her use of the bomb' simply on the basis of a wartime executive agreement between the two leaders.[86]

In Washington Attlee nearly extracted a joint-use agreement from the President, before White House advisers intervened, but he did receive assurances that Truman would constrain the escalating conflict with Chinese forces. Above all, the optics were important: Attlee taking the stage and dealing as an equal partner with the US President. He told journalists: 'As long as the Stars and Stripes flies in Korea, the British flag will fly beside it.'[87]

Attlee returned home to general applause. Winston told the Commons that the trip had done 'nothing but good', but asked why this was the PM's first 'direct discussion' with the President in five years. He also pressed for information about use of the Bomb, to which Attlee replied opaquely, 'I received assurances which I consider to be perfectly satisfactory.' The war was now playing havoc with Labour's finances. In January the Cabinet approved new defence estimates of £4.7 billion over three years, which pushed the share of GDP going to defence from 8 per cent, before the crisis, to 14 per cent. Hugh Gaitskell, the Chancellor, considered the mood close to 'panic' and likened it to '1940'. The second day of the Commons debate about his defence spending plans, 15 February 1951, was also the date on which nationalisation of the iron and steel industries took effect. The Tories made much of Labour's folly in wasting a fortune for a socialist hobbyhorse just when it was asking taxpayers to spend another fortune on defence.[88] Labour's attempt to combine a global foreign policy and a socialist domestic policy was economically unsustainable. Gaitskell privately noted that 'in our political and military association with America', Britain was trying to uphold a status that implied a '2 to 1 power ratio' whereas the 'real ratio' was around '7 to 1'. Although the exact impact of Korean war rearmament on Britain's economy remains a matter of debate, it was a clear cost of the 'special relationship' ideology – yet one that Attlee, like Churchill, was ready to bear.[89]

Attlee's last hurrah was the election campaign of October 1951. Although now often sounding tired and out of touch, as one journalist observed, 'his sincerity grips an audience far more than any tricks of oratory.' And he remained dismissive of Churchillian summitry: ideas that 'the whole of the destiny of mankind could be settled by a few big fellows sitting around a table smack too much of the Führer principle'. On election day, Attlee went down to honourable defeat, holding Winston's majority to only seventeen MPs. The King awarded him the Order of Merit (OM), adding to the Companion of Honour (CH) Attlee had received when the wartime coalition broke up in 1945.[90]

* * *

There was a certain symmetry about Attlee and Churchill in their final phase of political engagement, 1951–5. Both stayed on the stage too long – Winston as Prime Minister and Clem as Leader of the Opposition – but each believed he still had a mission to accomplish. The Churchillian swansong was to be a peace summit with the Americans and Soviets to help thaw the Cold War. Attlee's hope was to hold his party together in the emerging feud between Gaitskell and Bevan. Winston finally left Downing Street in April 1955, and his successor, Eden, called a snap election in June. After Labour went down to a second defeat – which right and left blamed on each other – Attlee resigned as party leader. By then Gaitskell had consolidated his position, winning the leadership with a clear majority on the first ballot. Elevated to the House of Lords, Attlee took quiet but unfeigned delight at the honours he had accrued, penning this limerick in 1956:

> Few thought he was even a starter,
> There were many who thought themselves smarter,
> But he ended PM
> CH and OM
> An earl and a knight of the garter.[91]

For twenty years from 1935, when Attlee became Labour leader, he and Winston had stood centre stage in British politics. Their partnership in 1940–5 was existentially vital: while Churchill was war leader, Attlee took care of the home front – also adroitly laying foundations for his own post-war premiership. Their political battles were fierce but rarely personal, with bouts of illness prompting get-well messages and floral bouquets. On one occasion in the early 1950s, when Winston and Clementine invited the Attlees to lunch at Chequers, the two couples played croquet afterwards on the lawn. Hard to imagine that occurring between a modern British PM and the leader of the Opposition.[92] As an orator, Churchill stood alone: listening to Attlee's 'thin and frail' voice at the Mansion House in 1947, Harold Nicolson noted that 'as a public speaker he is, compared to Winston, like a village fiddler after Paganini.' Yet there were times when Clem's quiet crispness or gentle mockery went down better than Winston's orotundity. Attlee was also 'an exceptionally gifted party leader, difficult to name a better one', in the judgment of Harold Macmillan, who succeeded Eden as Tory Prime Minister, whereas that was rarely said of Winston – repeatedly caricatured by Attlee as a 'prima donna'.[93]

When Churchill died in January 1965, Attlee was one of the pall-bearers at the state funeral. In a reflective obituary, he judged Churchill to have been 'the greatest leader in war this country has ever known'. Not because he was 'the greatest warrior' or 'strategist' but because 'he was able to solve the problem that democratic countries in total war find crucial and may find fatal: relations between the civil and military leaders.' A former soldier, Winston knew enough about war to prod the generals but he did not 'overrule' them. His Cabinet meetings were 'not good for business' but 'he kept us on our toes, partly just by being Winston, and partly because he was always throwing out ideas'. Attlee described his 'egotism' as 'monumental' – indeed unapologetically so: '"Of course I am an egotist," he said to me in the Cabinet room one day. "Where do you get if you aren't?"' But, Attlee added, 'not only did he believe in his own destiny, he believed in the destiny of Britain', and that was vital during the war. On the other hand, Attlee considered it 'a pity' that Winston did not retire in 1945. 'I had seen enough of him during the war to be sure that, unless there was a war on, he would not make much of a prime minister. What Britain required when the war was over was an architect, somebody who could build new parts into our society, and repair damage.'[94]

Attlee was, of course, holding up Winston as a mirror to himself. He was the architect who tried to repair the damage of two world wars and rebuild British society. Both men were deeply patriotic, but they differed as to what made Britain 'great'. For Winston it was the Empire, whereas

Attlee saw British imperial overstretch as an outdated burden. Despite the bloodbath in India, he was proud of bringing the Raj to what he saw as a long-overdue end and helping transform 'Empire into Commonwealth'. In 1959 he told someone who asked what he thought he would be remembered for: 'Don't know. If anything, India, possibly.'[95] At home, what mattered for him was the concept of 'social security' he had evolved when a young politician in the East End, about 'the duty of the State to act as the coordinating factor in making all individual effort work for the good of the citizens.'[96] Yet that vision was linked to a policy of state ownership which, as Winston never tired of saying, took the British Government far beyond its effective capacities into the management of huge business enterprises. Attlee never repented of nationalisation – the commitment to it in Clause Four of Labour's 1918 constitution was revoked only in 1995 by Tony Blair. This ideological rigidity was Attlee's equivalent of Churchill's imperial reverence. Neither could escape his past.

'Guardian Angel of our country's guardian':
Clementine whispers in Winston's ear after the election victory of 1951.

11

Clementine Churchill

His Most Devoted Critic

. . . September 1908, when I married and lived happily ever afterwards.

Winston S. Churchill, *My Early Life*, 1930[1]

If you will only listen a tiny bit to me, I know (barring all tragic accidents) that you will prevail & that some day, perhaps soon, perhaps not for 5 years, you will have a great & commanding position in this country . . . Just becos' I am ordinary & love you I know what is right for you & good for you in the end.

Clementine to Winston, April 1916[2]

It was 23 June 1940 – the Sunday after France surrendered. She wrote the letter. Then tore it up. But she wrote it again on Thursday 27th and pushed it under his door. 'My darling,' it began, 'I hope you will forgive me if I tell you something I feel you ought to know.' One of his entourage ('a devoted friend') had warned of 'a danger of your being generally disliked by your colleagues and subordinates because of your rough & sarcastic manner'. At meetings, she continued, 'you are supposed to be so contemptuous that presently no ideas (good or bad) will be forthcoming.' Clementine urged Winston to exercise the 'terrific power' he now enjoyed with 'urbanity, calmness and if possible Olympic calm', adding, 'I cannot bear those who served the Country

& you should not love you as well as admire and respect you – Besides you won't get the best results by irascibility & rudeness.' She signed off (with a drawing of cat), 'Please forgive your loving devoted & watchful Clemmie.'[3]

This message was no one-off. She spoke to him and wrote to him this way during most of their fifty-six years together. At the end of *My Early Life*, written in 1930, he added the deliberately puckish line about getting married in 1908 and living happily ever after. That, of course, was not the case: his was a life of *Sturm und Drang*. But the happiness and security he did enjoy was due in large measure to her. She soothed and interrogated, she encouraged and cautioned, she talked back but also talked up to him – affirming his status as pater-familias. And it cost her dear, forcing her often to compromise her Liberal principles and undermining her health. The costs of greatness were also born by their four adult children, casualties of her absorption in his self-absorption. This was especially of their only son – *his* Randolph. Only Mary was to find real happiness.

What sustained the family was her belief in him, and in his star. Its light flickered bright, but erratically, in 1914–18; in 1940 it illuminated Britain's whole struggle against Hitler. In fact, both Winston and Clementine thrived on the adrenalin of world war: it brought out the best in them and energised their sense of mission. For him these were epic struggles to preserve Britain, its Empire and all they stood for. In Clementine's case, wartime tapped what he called her 'pinko' sentiments – canteens for women factory workers in 1914–18 and aid to Russia in 1941–5 – providing her with unique opportunities to test herself and serve others.

His letters to her speak repeatedly of his love and affection. In fact, he was often singularly insensitive to her needs. Yet she accepted this most of the time because she saw in him a great historical figure. And he needed to see that in the mirror of her eyes. As one biographer observes, 'the question is not simply what she did for him but also what he could have done without her.'[4] The greatness he attained owed an immense amount to his most devoted critic. And to her continued vigilance, during his afterlife, about his image and reputation.

* * *

'Have you read my book?' That, Clemmie recalled years later, was Winston's opening gambit when he found himself sitting next to her, having arrived late at a society dinner party in March 1908.[5] When she said that she hadn't read it, he promised to send her *Lord Randolph Churchill* next morning. The book didn't materialise but Winston did, again and again. He was deeply smitten and – despite being appointed in April to his first government office – conducted a whirlwind court-ship during the spring and summer, finally popping the question at Blenheim. They were married at St Margaret's, Westminster, across the road from the Houses of Parliament, on 12 September 1908.

Things had indeed moved fast. What did he see in her? Winston – brought up in a man's world where women were expected to know their place – took a romantic view of the opposite sex, with beauty and bearing high on the list of essentials. He and Eddie Marsh, his private secretary, liked to rank a woman on whether her face could launch 'a thousand ships', a couple of hundred, or just 'a covered sampan, or small gunboat'.[6] Winston definitely wanted another Helen of Troy, and there were a few flirtations. Violet Asquith, the Prime Minister's bluestocking daughter, shared his passion for politics. They met at a dinner party in 1906 when she was nineteen and he already thirty-two. Amid the rhet-orical torrent he unleashed that evening she never forgot the line 'We are all worms. But I do believe that I am a glow-worm.' They saw a great deal of each other over the next couple of years, and Violet clearly fell deeply in love. But that never happened for Winston. Violet was argumentative and often bloody-minded. As one biographer observes, he was 'not looking for a female version of himself'.[7]

Clementine Hozier was tall and statuesque, with aquiline features. She was also animated and clever: his first letter to her declared (rather patronisingly) 'what a comfort & pleasure it was to meet a girl with so much intellectual quality & such strong reserves of noble sentiment'.[8]

There was a moral seriousness about her, rooted in a religious faith that, despite ups and downs, would always sustain her. Clementine, born in April 1885, was a decade younger than Winston. What really intrigued him in March 1908 was that, in this beautiful 22-year-old of aristocratic lineage and bearing he encountered a young woman who earned her own living. Truly a rare creature!

Clementine came from a broken home. She never knew her legal father, Sir Henry Hozier, and later concluded that she was the biological daughter of a lover of her promiscuous mother, Lady Blanche, the eldest daughter of the Earl of Airlie. After the divorce, she and her siblings lived an itinerant existence in London, Seaford and Dieppe – as Blanche indulged her bohemian tastes and dodged her creditors – before settling for a few years in Berkhamsted, north of London, where she attended the local high school for girls for three years. There she perfected her French, loved sport (she captained the cricket team), developed strong suffragette sentiments and even dreamed of going to university. Her mother and maternal grandmother firmly squashed such unladylike aspirations, moving her to London and launching her into Society. But such were the family's financial problems that Clementine did not have her own maid and had to contribute to her keep by giving French lessons and working for her cousin's dressmaking business. Many of the elegant costumes she wore to grand dinners were made or refined by her own needlework.

Perhaps Winston sensed the grit that had made a pearl. He certainly found her a sensitive listener. That first evening, and on many more, he poured out his heart. 'Write to me again,' he pleaded on 27 April. 'I am a solitary creature in the midst of crowds. Be kind to me.' There was also real physical attraction – apparently a novelty for both of them. In 1906 Clementine had been engaged and disengaged in short order to two different men, each much older than her. The experience left her humiliated, bruised and unsure of herself. But Winston was different. This time, she felt convinced, it was love. And, swept away by his eloquence and ambition, clearly she had never met anyone like him. Clementine told friends and family she had no illusions that being married to Winston would be easy, but she was sure it would be 'tremendously stimulating'.[9]

Within a month of returning from honeymoon on Lake Maggiore, Clementine was pregnant. So, in the spring of 1909 they moved out of his bachelor pad, full of toy soldiers, and into a house in up-and-coming Pimlico, not far from Parliament and Whitehall. But despite the exchanges of loving notes, signed with sketches of 'Kat' and 'Pug', married life was indeed not easy. As soon as they had their own home, Clementine established separate bedrooms. Partly because she rose early while he was a night owl, but also because she needed her own space as protection from Winston's overwhelming personality. She was highly strung, prone to temper tantrums, and they had frequent rows about his financial extravagance and about issues such as female suffrage. Clemmie was also unsettled by Winston's abiding devotion to his glamorous mother and his continued friendship with Violet, who was scathing about Clemmie ('stupid as an owl') and sceptical that the marriage would last – although she granted it might allow 'the Hozier' some 'rest at least from making her own clothes'.[10]

At the end of her pregnancy in July 1909, an exhausted Clementine left the newborn Diana to a wet-nurse and spent ten days recuperating with her sister. The next child, born in May 1911, was a baby boy, inevitably named Randolph. The arrival of a son and heir was greeted with great joy and Clemmie was able to breastfeed him. But then she had a miscarriage, followed by severe gynaecological problems, and generally found it hard to engage with her children or enjoy being a mother. Winston spent little time with them but, whenever he did, the eternal boy in him made it seem enormous fun. For mother and father, here were roots of the problems to come.

What Clementine really enjoyed was sharing in his work. Her Liberal sympathies were aroused by the welfare reforms he pushed through with Lloyd George, and in later life she spoke of these years as the happiest of her life. She fervently believed in her man and also in his cause – which was not the case when he reverted to the Tories.[11] Although she hated their move into the monumental vastness of

Admiralty House (he adored it, of course), she commented on his speech drafts, helped him overcome his lisp, and willed him on from the gallery of the House of Commons. When war broke out, she rose to the new challenges he faced. Her human antennae were usually far more sensitive than his, and she often alerted him to the way he could tread on other people's toes in his zeal and determination. She was appalled at his quixotic trip across the Channel in October 1914 to take command at Antwerp, partly because it took him away from her when she was giving birth to Sarah but mostly because she could see what damage that rush of blood to the head had done to his reputation. She also deplored his capacity to be seduced by charismatic figures – first Lloyd George and then Admiral Jackie Fisher. Clemmie was deeply involved in discussions about the Dardanelles operation and harboured grave doubts about Fisher's mental stability. On one occasion, when Winston was away for diplomatic negotiations in Paris, the Admiral told her he was actually dallying with his mistress. 'Be quiet, you silly old man,' she shouted, 'and get out.'[12]

Winston paid little heed to her warnings and was slow to see how Fisher's sudden resignation on 15 May 1916 over the faltering Dardanelles campaign left him dangerously exposed. While her husband fought for his political life, Clementine penned a frenzied letter to Asquith, begging him not to 'throw Winston overboard'. Whatever faults you see in him, she added, 'he has the supreme quality which I venture to say very few of your present or future Cabinet possess – the power, the imagination, the deadliness to fight Germany.' It was assumed at the time that she wrote the letter off her own bat, but Winston did agree she should send it – perhaps without knowing the text. In the opinion of the Asquiths, this was the letter of a 'maniac' and the conduct of a 'fishwife'. On occasions the PM read out extracts to amuse his luncheon guests.[13]

Winston's demotion was a crushing blow for both of them. His salary was cut by more than half; they had to move out of Admiralty House and rapidly find somewhere else to live. Having already been ostracised by many aristocratic relations and friends over his association with Lloyd George, they now had to endure the gleeful Tory revenge on Winston for ratting on their party a decade before. In the 1960s, Clemmie reflected that, of all the events they had lived through as a couple, nothing had been so agonising as the Dardanelles. 'When he left the Admiralty, he thought he was finished,' she told Winston's official biographer. 'I thought he would die of grief.'[14]

When Winston went off to the trenches in November 1915, she became his proxy in London – doing whatever she could to get him back into power, not just because he was her husband but also because she had no doubt he was a winner. That winter she steeled herself to schmooze with press barons, politicians, top brass and even the Asquiths, playing golf with the PM (her sporting talents proved politically valuable on many occasions) and entertaining his family for dinner and bridge. She also cultivated Lloyd George (despite considering him 'the direct descendant of Judas Iscariot'). Winston often sent anxious letters – 'I have no one but you to act for me. I shd like you to make the seeing of my friends a regular business' – but his tactlessness was unnecessary. She was working round the clock to promote his cause, while also trying to run the household on a much reduced income. The family car had to be sold to raise extra cash.

She also tried hard in her letters to make Winston learn from his mistakes. Biographer Sonia Purnell puts it well. 'Winston was forceful, impatient and loquacious. Phenomenally well briefed on a range of subjects, he also had a fierce temper and a cutting tongue' and regularly treated disagreement with his views as personally offensive. Many people therefore tried to avoid an argument. 'Often it was *only* Clementine who would point to Winston's faults; his lack of real empathy with others and tendency to bully meant that he often mistook silent acquiescence for positive support. As Clementine told him, he had to learn how to take people with him by inspiring their trust rather than cowing them into submission.' Over the years, she would have to repeat that lesson again and again.[15]

During this time of trial in 1915–16, she derived deep satisfaction from the sudden opportunity to undertake war work that drew on and expanded her own abilities. When the Ministry of Munitions was established under Lloyd George to boost war output, Clemmie was asked to join the Munition Workers Auxiliary Committee to provide canteens for the thousands of men and women who worked in the new factories. She assumed responsibility for the northeast quarter of metropolitan London. Although having no experience of such work, she plunged into it enthusiastically, glad to have an outlet for her talents and some diversion from the gnawing worries about her husband and children. She toured the area, persuading factory managers to give up sites for the canteens, and afterwards visited the canteens frequently to encourage staff (mostly volunteers), resolve problems and ensure proper standards of food, hygiene and service. Eventually she had nine canteens under her supervision, and it took considerable time to visit them now that she had given up the car. 'Without a motor it's harder to get to Enfield than to France,' she wrote him one evening, '1/4 of the day has been spent in tube, trams, train, the remainder grappling with committees.'[16]

At the end of January 1916, she was winding herself up for the big day when LG would address 2,000 factory staff. 'I am in complete charge of the arrangements & feel like a Chief Whip!' Later she wrote in jubilation, 'The whole thing went off brilliantly,' recounting how she was loaded down with praise and gifts. 'Don't tell anyone about this as it sounds vain, but I want you to know about my small success.' She also mocked LG for 'a quite undistinguished speech' and said that as they drove back into London in the dark 'he was very white shabby & tired & I felt young strong and vital and felt you out there young & strong & vital.' Having been worried about Winston going into the line, she ended the letter: 'happy & hopeful about you and your future. I know (D.V)' – *Deo volente*, 'God willing' – 'that you will come back rejuvenated & strengthened from the War & dominate all these decrepit exhausted politicians.'[17]

Perhaps the most revealing comment came in a letter sent in mid-February. 'I must tell you that from living with you & watching you for 7 years I have assimilated (in a small way) your methods & habits of work.' By this she meant getting things done quickly by driving others and herself. 'When I am in full swing I begin work at 9 a.m. & finish at 7.30 p.m. It's no using scolding me', she declared proudly, 'becos' it's all your fault – You have taught me to work outside office hours.'[18] Though she was at her best in the mornings, rather than burning the midnight oil.

Clementine's work with the munition factory canteens went on for the rest of the war, and in January 1918 she was honoured with a CBE for her services. But once Winston came back from the trenches in May 1916 – to her immense relief – and was eventually made Minister of Munitions in Lloyd George's coalition in July 1917 her priorities returned to normal: Winston and his fast-moving career reverted to top place. As before, she tried to restrain his headstrong moments – such as his insane call for the return of Admiral Fisher in March 1916 and his 'private war' against the Bolsheviks in 1919–20 – but he ignored her advice. He only heeded her pleas to stop flying after a very lucky escape from a crash landing. Deep down she yearned for the Liberal reformer she had married rather than the miniature warlord he had become. 'I would like you to be praised as a reconstructive genius as well as for a Mustard Gas fiend, a Tank juggernaut & a flying Terror,' she wrote to him a couple of weeks before the Armistice. 'Can't the men Munitions Workers build lovely garden cities & pull down slums in places like Bethnal Green, Newcastle, Glasgow, Leeds etc, & can't the women munitions workers make all the lovely furniture for them – Baby's cradles, cupboards etc . . . Do come home & arrange all this . . .'[19]

'Do come home.' Above all, she was saddened by the time he spent away from her because of his desire to be where the action was. Perhaps that explains why she failed to write to him for more than a week when he was away in France over their wedding anniversary in September 1918, at a time when she was exhausted from the canteens and another pregnancy. This earned her a rebuke for the 'completeness' and 'versatility' of her 'naughtiness' as a letter writer. The following September, when Winston was again in Paris over the anniversary, she had apparently forgotten the date until reminded by a letter from him. Her reply captured the pleasure and the pain of being married to this man of action:

> I love to feel that I am a comfort in your rather tumultuous life – My Darling, you have been the great event in mine. You took me from the straitened little by-path I was treading and took me with you into the life & colour & jostle of the high-way. But how sad it is that Time slips along so fast – Eleven years more & we shall be quite middle-aged. But I have been happier every year since we started . . . [20]

By March 1920, with Winston now Secretary of State for War and Air – so much for garden cities! – her own war work seemed a distant memory of another person: 'The Canteens – I sometimes wonder now if it was all a dream. One thing is certain, I couldn't manage them again – I began to think I had real organising ability, but it died with the War – if there was ever any! . . . This week has been occupied in taking Randolph to have his [prep] school clothes fitted. He looks such a shrimp in trousers and an Eton collar!'[21] Clementine was also overseeing the family's move into a more spacious London house (2 Sussex Square, near Hyde Park). This was needed to accommodate four children – Marigold was born in November 1918 – and also accommodate a proper artist's studio for her husband. Her letter was sent to Winston in southwest France, where he was painting and boar-hunting on the Duke of Westminster's estate.

That trip to France began a pattern of separate vacations that would continue for the rest of their marriage. They did arrange a stay in Nice in January 1921 (their first holiday since before the war) but they were there as guests of his financial benefactor Sir Ernest Cassel, and Winston was called back to London after barely a week. She decided to remain on the Riviera, staying in hotels and with various friends. Without responsibility for him or the family, she let herself relax – resuming tennis again, playing in a few amateur tournaments, and even indulging in an occasional flutter at the casinos. Noting her restlessness, Winston – now Colonial Secretary – collected her on 3 March en route by ship to a major conference in Cairo, which she greatly enjoyed. But then she came back at her own pace via Alexandria, Sicily and Naples. Biographer Sonia Purnell has sensed 'hints that she began to harbour doubts about the viability of her marriage at this point. Winston was so often engrossed in his work, but without a war there no longer seemed a need for her to help him. This was not what she had had in mind for their life together in peacetime.'[22]

Clementine returned to London on 10 April 1921, having not seen her children for more than three months. Then family came back with a vengeance. A few days later she received news that her brother Bill had shot himself in a Paris hotel room, his suicide prompted by massive gambling debts. She rushed over to France, and even persuaded Winston to come for Bill's funeral. At the end of June, bereavement hit him in turn, when his mother Lady Jennie – aged 67 but still lively, stylish and extravagant as ever – died suddenly from a haemorrhage. This followed a fall in the high heels to which she was addicted, which had caused a broken ankle, followed by gangrene and the amputation of her foot. Winston had grown less emotionally dependent on his mother over the years, but her demise left him with an enduring sense of loss. The traumatic deaths of Bill and Jennie underlined for Clemmie her accelerating sense that time was passing.

Anxious for a more enjoyable summer, Clemmie packed all four children off to Broadstairs, on the Kent seaside, with a new French nanny. The plan was for the older three to join her and Winston after a few weeks in the Scottish Highlands, as guests of the ever-hospitable Duke of Westminster on another of his estates. The children wrote to her periodically, mentioning that Marigold had been troubled by a cough and sore throat, but this was nothing new. It was only at the insistence of the hotel landlady that a doctor was finally called and Clementine notified. By then Marigold had developed a raging fever, diagnosed as septicaemia. Clemmie and Winston raced down to Broadstairs, just in time to be with her when she died on 23 August. She was not yet three. Marigold – known in the family as 'Duckadilly' – was a sweet, cheerful little child, always singing. Clemmie sang her favourite,

'I'm forever blowing bubbles', the evening before she died. Both parents were distraught – Clemmie often almost hysterical – but, characteristically, she then bottled up her grief and guilt and rarely spoke of Marigold again. After the funeral the family holidayed together, as intended, in the Highlands, before Winston moved on after two weeks to another Scottish house party, this one graced by the Prince of Wales. The shattered Clemmie was left to get Diana, Randolph and Sarah back to London for the new school term. It was only after another holiday by herself on the Riviera for a couple of months in early 1922 that she regained some degree of equilibrium.

* * *

The demise of Lloyd George's coalition in October 1922 hinted at a new dawn. With Winston having lost his seat in the Commons – where he had sat almost continuously for twenty-two years – they were able to decamp to the Riviera, renting a villa for more than six months from early December 1922 to mid-May 1923. She played tennis; he painted and wrote the first volume of his war memoirs – serialised by *The Times*, it earned him £20,000. This may well have been one of the longest periods they spent together in their marriage. There were other successful joint vacations – Florence in 1925, for instance, and Venice two years later – but separate holidays became the norm for the rest of their married life.[23]

Deeper tensions also surfaced in 1922: one political, the other domestic. The collapse of the Lloyd George coalition in October precipitated a new general election. Winston's appendectomy meant that Clemmie had to campaign for him in Dundee. She was shaken by the fierce hostility towards her husband, and by the acute poverty of Tayside, made worse by the post-war slump. Nor was she happy about his militant 'Smash the Socialists' posture. Nevertheless, she made several speeches on his behalf, usually dressed to the nines. 'Clemmie's bearing was magnificent', wrote one of Winston's friends, 'like an aristocrat going to the guillotine in a tumbril'. After defeat in Dundee, he gradually migrated towards the Tories – which for him, he said, was 'just like coming home'. But for her this was alien territory. She continued to comment on draft speeches, often usefully offering a contrary perspective, but her campaigning was done for him, not for his party, and she confined her political activities mostly to work in his own constituency, where her memory for names and faces was invaluable. According to daughter Mary, after 1924 Clementine never voted Liberal again, but 'in her heart of hearts she remained to the end of her days a rather old-fashioned radical.'[24]

The domestic tension was equally enduring. Spurred on by Winston's desire to paint and by a financial windfall from a deceased relative, they had been looking for a country property for some time, and were initially captivated by Chartwell, some twenty-five miles from London near Westerham in Kent. He never changed his mind, but she did – vehemently. The rear of the house offered spectacular vistas down a steep valley and over the Weald of Kent to the South Downs. But the front, close to a public road, was overshadowed by a steep, wooded bank which blocked out most of the afternoon sun. The Victorian interior was dark and gloomy and in serious need of extensive repair. Whereas the artist in him saw the prospects, the manager in her saw only the costs. They visited the property in July 1921 but, after she turned against it, he said little more and Clemmie assumed the matter had been dropped. In September 1922, however, he drove there with the three older children – who were predictably entranced by its Gothic interior and secret valley – and returned home to tell Clemmie, with their vocal support, that he had made an offer. After a brisk negotiation the house and eighty acres were his for £5,000.

Mary wrote in her biography of Clementine that she was 'frankly devastated' – not just by his decision but by the way he had gone behind her back. Being Winston, he was naturally confident he would win her over in time. But that never happened. Her warnings were soon vindicated: the property took eighteen months and thousands of pounds to make habitable, and its upkeep in the style he desired would prove a constant drain on their finances. According to Mary, in one of the most poignant passages of her book, 'she accepted the fait accompli, but it never acquired for her the nature of a venture shared – rather, it was an extra duty, gallantly undertaken and doggedly carried through . . . Although Chartwell was to be her principal home for the next forty years, she never became deeply attached to the place.' For Winston, however:

> Chartwell represented sheer pleasure, occupation and happiness – from the first days, when he was slaughtering laurels and building dams to later on when he was constructing walls and cottages. It became his workshop – his 'factory' – from whence poured out his books, articles and speeches, which alone kept Chartwell and the whole fabric of our family life. Here he found endless subjects to paint; here his friends and colleagues, and visitors from afar, foregathered. Here he planned his political forays, and here he retreated to relish his victories, or to lick his wounds. Chartwell never failed him, in good times and bad.[25]

Clementine buckled down to the task of making Chartwell a home. But in the spring of 1925 they were discussing the idea of letting the house for a few months a year and in late summer 1926 even he was proposing cuts including that 'No more champagne is to be bought' and 'cigars must be reduced to four a day.'[26] Domestic economies became acute in 1929–30 after Winston's finances were decimated by the Wall Street Crash, but belt-tightening was continually offset by his expensive outdoor projects, such as new pools and waterworks, a cottage for Sarah and Mary, and the building of a brick wall around the vegetable garden. Throughout the 1920s and 1930s their elegant and agreeable lifestyle was never seriously compromised, despite the fragility of their finances. All depended on Winston's health, energy and authorial talents; they lived from one book or article to the next.

All this proved a constant strain on Clemmie's highly strung nature. She needed time away to calm down and recharge her batteries. And yet, even though he often seemed to take her for granted when present, he pined for her when she was absent and knew how to play on her sense of guilt. He wrote in March 1925, when she was visiting friends on the Riviera:

> When do you think you will return, my dear one? Do not abridge yr holiday if it is doing you good – But of course I feel far safer from worry and depression when you are with me & when I can confide in yr sweet soul . . . The most precious thing I have in my life is yr love for me. I reproach myself for many shortcomings. You are a rock & I depend on you & rest on you. Come back to me therefore as soon as you can.

Although Clemmie could rise to a real crisis with stamina and resourcefulness, as her war work showed, the endless worries of the daily round – husband and children, the bills and the staff – often left her prostrate with nervous exhaustion. Winston's niece Clarissa – who later married Anthony Eden – recalled that 'Aunt Clementine was always going to bed instead of coming to lunch . . . Obviously living with Winston was quite a business'. But 'she was always conscious of her health. It was accepted within the family that she was a hypochondriac and she was definitely hysterical, no question'. Fair comment or not, Clementine would sometimes recite lines from the epitaph for an overworked governess which, she said, would serve well for her own gravestone:

> Here lies a woman who always was tired
> For she lived in a world where too much was required.[27]

In early 1935, something snapped. Lord Moyne, heir to the Guinness brewery fortune, had invited the Churchills to join him and friends on a four-month cruise to the Dutch East Indies. The official object was to catch a specimen of the fabled 'Komodo Dragon' for the London Zoo, but the desire was clearly for sun and pleasure. Winston was immersed in his politics and book writing and, in any case, he disliked being confined on a boat for weeks on end. She, however, was ready for an adventure – at least one that was safely managed. Deep down, she needed a complete break from Winston's demands and perhaps, nearing 50, she had doubts about whether he would retrieve his political career, now he was at odds with the Tory leadership over India. On 18 December 1934, after Winston's sixtieth birthday had been celebrated in style, she set off by train to Sicily where she joined Moyne's motor yacht *Rosaura*. She did not return until the end of April 1935.

The cruise took her through the Suez Canal and across the Indian Ocean to Rangoon and Singapore, on to Borneo and New Guinea. It included the east coast of Australia and the North and South Islands of New Zealand – loyal outposts of the British Empire that Winston himself never visited – before coming back via the East Indian islands of Bali and Komodo. Throughout these four months Clementine's constant companion, on board and off, was Terence Philip: a rich, suave art dealer a few years younger who was attentive and entertaining, but – unlike her husband – not demanding. 'Clementine fell romantically in love with him,' wrote Mary. 'For a brief period in her life, which for the most part was rooted in obligations, conventions and reality, she lived in a dream world of beauty and adventure. She tasted the heady elixir of admiration, and knew the pleasures of companionship in trivial doings and sayings.'[28]

There's no reason to think this was anything more than 'a classic holiday romance' which did not survive 'the return to reality' – as Mary put it – but Clementine's long absence and her frequent allusion in letters to 'Mr Philip' (soon 'Terence') clearly began to unsettle Winston. 'You have now been gone 5 weeks, and it seems a vy long time,' he wrote on 23 January. 'In another three weeks it will be half over, & we shall all be counting the days for yr return . . .' Her children took up the refrain. 'Don't forget to come home some time,' Sarah wrote on 17 February. 'Daddy is miserable and frightfully naughty without you!' His typed 'Chartwell Bulletins' were full of 'realities', especially German rearmament. 'If the Great War were resumed – for that is what it would mean, in two or three years' time or even earlier – it will be the end of the world.' While her letters, when they arrived, were full of the

'Dragon Hunt', his final Bulletin (number 11) covered Randolph's jaundice, Mary's whooping cough and Sarah's addiction to ballroom dancing ('you must deal with this situation when you come back'). He admitted, 'I have been sometimes a little depressed about politics and would like to have been comforted by you. But I feel this has been a gt experience and adventure to you, & that it has introduced a new background to yr life & a larger proportion; & so I have not grudged you your long excursion.' But, he concluded firmly, 'now I do want you back.'[29]

Quite what happened in the tropics we shall probably never know, but it remains a source of debate among Churchill biographers. Even more speculative are claims that in 1933 Winston began a four-year affair with Doris, Lady Castlerosse. This story emanated in 1985, bizarrely, from Jock Colville, who started his long career as Churchill's private secretary only in 1940, and no hard evidence has been unearthed.[30] What seems more plausible is to say that, for both Winston and Clementine, the mid-1930s were a difficult patch in their marriage, when their paths and preoccupations were more divergent than usual during their long, intimate but very supple relationship over nearly six decades. And what seems much more important is how she came back to 'reality', with a vengeance, in 1935.

It appears that the enchanted cruise gave Clemmie some much-needed perspective on her whole family life. Conscious that she and Winston had not been effective parents or even very aware of their older children, she belatedly focused on Mary, much younger than her siblings and now entering her teens. Mary lived at Chartwell and had been brought up by 'Moppet' – Clementine's cousin, Maryott White. Aware that Moppet had become, in effect, Mary's emotional mother, Clemmie decided to take her daughter on a skiing holiday, with some of her cousins, over Christmas and New Year 1935–6. This was repeated in three successive years. Until then, Mary had 'hardly ever been alone with her for any length of time'. On these holidays – during which Clemmie lost her dignity many times, until becoming quite an accomplished skier – 'I started to know my mother as a person rather than a deity' and even to 'enjoy her companionship'. Thus was forged what became a very close bond between Clementine and the daughter who later wrote her biography.[31]

The older children never enjoyed such a rapprochement. Well into their twenties, they were firmly set in their characters and their problems, above all trying to create their own identities apart from their overwhelming father and perfectionist mother.

Diana – plump, like her father, and highly strung – rushed into marriage with a handsome, wealthy South African, but the couple soon divorced. She later told her daughter that she had been desperate to create her own space 'away from all the endless talk around the Chartwell dinner table'.[32] In 1935, she married the young Tory MP Duncan Sandys and in 1936 gave her parents their first grandchild. That, for a while, proved a happier match.

Sarah, tall and elegant like her mother, also had thespian ambitions, to which her parents were strongly opposed. But, meriting her family nickname 'Mule', she successfully stood up to them. Not only did she go onto the stage but fell in love with the much older star of the show, the Jewish-American comedian Vic Oliver. After a ding-dong battle with her parents, the couple eventually eloped in 1936 and got married in New York on Christmas Eve. The marriage broke down in a couple of years. As Sarah later admitted, by marrying a man eighteen years older 'maybe I was looking for a substitute father. Indeed I have sometimes thought I was trying to marry my father'.[33] Winston adored Sarah and felt that all the three men she married during her life were unworthy of her.

Most problematic of all was Randolph, the apple of his father's eye even though they had ding-dong rows: Randolph was perhaps the only man who really stood up to his father. Determined not to shun his son, as Lord Randolph had done in the previous century, Winston spoilt him at every turn – pandering to his arrogance, paying off endless debts and turning a blind eye to his many affairs. (There's no doubt that Lady Castlerosse did sleep with one Churchill, but it wasn't Winston.) The handsome Randolph was blessed with many talents – not least being a far better off-the-cuff speaker than his father – but he lacked Winston's capacity for hard work and hard thought. Winston could not stop indulging Randolph, laying on a twenty-first birthday dinner at Claridge's to which some sixty members of the British establishment and their rising sons heard Lord Rothermere hail 'Britain's Young Man of Destiny', while Winston spoke of passing on 'the sacred lamp' of power to the next generation who, he was sure, would be equal to the task of consolidating the 'enormous Empire' that his own generation had made secure during the Great War.[34]

Clemmie's relations with Randolph were much cooler; 'right from the early days,' writes Mary, 'Randolph and she were at loggerheads.'[35] Clementine disapproved of her son's lax morals and deplored her husband's indulgence: furious rows often exploded between mother and son and between mother and father. Randolph grew adept at playing off one parent against the other. And Clemmie, like her daughters, could not escape bouts of envy about Winston's dynastic obsession with his only son.

Aside from this viscerally male bond across the generations, the politics of the 1930s created other strains between husband and wife. Clemmie backed Winston in his opposition to the India bill, and – in a rare political intervention of her own – spoke at a Tory women's meeting against moves towards Dominion status. She also shared his foreboding about the rearmament of Nazi Germany and worked energetically to make Chartwell a hospitable place for his meetings with critics of appeasement from Britain and abroad. But they were at odds over his support for Edward VIII's wish to marry 'the woman I love'. She judged that the bulk of the British people would not accept the American divorcée Wallis Simpson as their queen, and was sure Winston's opposition to Baldwin's policy on this matter would do him immense political damage. Ignoring her, he stuck to his guns and was howled down in the Commons on 7 December 1936. It was not until the coronation of George VI and Queen Elizabeth in Westminster Abbey the following May that Winston turned to Clemmie – tears in his eyes – and whispered, 'You were right; I see now the other one wouldn't have done.'[36]

The late 1930s was rough for each of them, and they spent a good deal of time apart. Asked in 1936 whether she thought Winston would ever become Prime Minister, she supposedly said, 'No, unless some great disaster were to sweep the country, and no one could wish for that.'[37]

* * *

Winston's return to the Admiralty in September 1939 not only transformed their lives; it also brought him and Clementine closer together again. They moved back into Admiralty House, allowing the sale of their apartment – Morpeth Mansions near Victoria – for much-needed cash. His £5,000 a year government salary eased the financial position and also gave them protection against creditors because of his importance to the war effort. The Office of Works converted the attic of Admiralty House into a flat for the First Lord and his wife, so Clementine did not have to worry about furnishing and running the great staterooms. She spent much time turning his office into an efficient but comfortable command centre, with red leather armchairs near the fireplace and a regularly refilled biscuit tin, plus soda siphon for his whiskies, on a small table. She also threw herself into war-related activities, raising money for the crews of minesweepers and helping run a maternity hospital in Buckinghamshire for the wives of officers.[38]

During the Cabinet crisis of May 1940, Clemmie was away from London visiting her recently bereaved sister, but she returned just in time to congratulate Winston before he went to the Palace to accept the King's commission to form a government. Her prediction in 1916 that he would 'someday' have 'a great & commanding position in this country' had been fulfilled – though it had taken much longer than 'five years'. She now supervised their move into 10 Downing Street, and threw herself into what proved *their* finest hour. She commented on his speech drafts, advocating short, everyday words. After delivering a broadcast on the radio, he would often turn to her and ask, 'How was that?' She offered endless advice, such as the letter of 27 June 1940, quoted at the start of this chapter, about his brusqueness with staff. She was also deeply unhappy with his decision to become Tory leader after Chamberlain's death in November 1940. Winston felt it essential to have control over the dominant party in both Houses of Parliament. But she argued that he was leading an all-party National Government during an unprecedented national crisis and should therefore stand above party and speak for the whole nation. During epic rows, wrote Mary, 'all her latent hostility towards the Tory Party boiled over.' She 'never altered her opinion that the step was a mistake and that it alienated much of the support which Winston received from the working classes through the vindication of his pre-war prophecies and his record as a war leader'.[39]

Clementine also accompanied Winston on visits to military units, seacoast defences and bombed-out neighbourhoods. 'Gil' Winant, the US ambassador to Britain in 1941–6, who often went along as well, did not forget the reaction of 'middle-aged women who showed great appreciation of Mrs. Churchill's coming ... the look which flashed between her and these mothers of England was something far deeper and significant than the casual newspaper accounts of social interchange.'[40] And she kept pressing Winston to let those women do their bit for the war effort, now that so many men were in the armed forces. Setting an example, she became a rooftop firewatcher in 1941 – much to his alarm – and encouraged Mary to enlist in one of new mixed anti-aircraft batteries.

As the Prime Minister's wife, Clementine received many appeals from members of the public. The predominant theme in 1940–1 was the inadequacy of the air-raid shelters in London, many of them hastily improvised during the Blitz. In December 1940 she decided to investigate in person, visiting the shelters in the underground stations unannounced with a senior female member of the Red Cross. What she saw appalled her and she documented the problems in detail: water dripping through the roofs, lice, filthy bedding and, especially, atrocious sanitation. Her comments were extremely practical and spared no detail: 'The latrines should be doubled or trebled in number. This should be easy as they are mostly only buckets ... Light should be provided over the latrines. The prevailing darkness merely hides and, of course, encourages the dirty conditions ... There should be separate latrines for little children, with low buckets and chambers [potties].'[41]

Back in 1921 Clementine had lamented that any organising ability she once possessed had 'died with the war'. Now, nearly two decades later, she reprised the role she had played with the factory canteens, but on a much larger stage. As she chivvied Government ministers or invited herself on their own inspection trips, she was exploiting her unquestioned yet unclear status as wife of the Prime Minister, as no one had done before or would do again. It was a delicate balance to strike and if she got it wrong, he would get the blame.

As biographer Sonia Purnell has remarked, Clementine was moving gingerly into the role of what Americans would call the 'First Lady'.[42] Yet this was rarely appreciated at the time: a feature article in the *Picture Post* on 23 November 1940, entitled 'The Lady of No. Ten', was unusual for singling her out, though it dwelt mostly on her, conventionally, as wife and mother. The classic 'First Lady' – at the time, and indeed until Hillary Clinton adopted a similar role – was Eleanor Roosevelt, who not only became her wheelchair-bound husband's eyes and ears in Thirties America but even had her own syndicated newspaper column, 'My Day', and spoke regularly on national radio. In October 1942 Eleanor visited the UK to see the US troops and spent a good deal of time with Clementine. After a week she noted in her diary:

> Mrs Churchill is very attractive and has a charming personality – young looking for her age. One feels that she has to assume a role because of being in public life and that the role is now a part of her, but one wonders what she is like underneath. She does a great deal of work on Russian and Chinese relief, etc, but is very careful not to voice any opinions publicly or to associate with any political organi-zations. This I felt was true of the wives of all the public officials whom I met.[43]

The two women spent a good deal of time together during Eleanor's trip; their activities included a moving visit to Canterbury and Dover, where they could see Nazi-occupied Europe in the distance across the Channel. Clemmie – herself no slouch – was at times overwhelmed by Eleanor's energy (her Secret Service codename was 'Rover') and was struck by her readiness to talk back to Winston. During a small dinner party one evening, the PM alluded to Franco's Spain. Eleanor asked him why more could not have been done in the 1930s to help the anti-fascists during the Spanish Civil War. Peeved, Winston said that people like him and Eleanor would have been the first to lose their heads if the communists had won, to which came the reply that she didn't care a bit about losing her head. He replied sternly, 'I don't want you to lose your head and neither do I want to lose mine' – whereupon Clemmie leaned across the table and said, 'I think perhaps Mrs Roosevelt is right.' Winston growled back, 'I have held certain beliefs for sixty years and I'm not going to change now.' He got up from the table, and the dinner came to an abrupt end.[44]

Clementine learnt much from Eleanor. That was evident above all in her most 'political' role – the coordination of relief aid for Russia. This nationwide fund-raising effort became a valuable diplomatic counterbalance to Winston's strategy of avoiding what he deemed a premature invasion of occupied France. By 1942, however, the pressure to 'do something' to support 'our gallant Russian allies' became intense, with mass rallies across the country for a 'Second Front'. Instead, Churchill pressed on with his 'closing the ring' strategy, gradually encircling Nazi Germany via North Africa and Italy. As compensation, weapons and supplies were sent to Russia, many of them on the dangerous Arctic convoys whose loss cost many British lives. But the moral asymmetry was stark. One Russian cartoon showed two Red Army soldiers cutting into a tin of Spam, the notorious processed luncheon meat. One says to the other, 'We're opening the second front.'

The PM had no doubt that his strategy was right, but Clementine was very unhappy. The heroic suffering of Leningrad and Stalingrad brought out all her 'pinko' sentiments. A rare reference to her in his war memoirs reads: 'My wife felt very deeply that our inability to give any military help disturbed and distressed the nation increasingly as the months went by and the German armies surged across the Steppes.' She even remonstrated with Winston at an official dinner when he decided to suspend the Arctic convoys in midsummer 1942 because of the shipping losses. Clementine was therefore both pleased and relieved when asked to become co-chair of the Red Cross 'Aid to Russia' appeal. She devoted hours to meetings, events and letter writing, taking particular trouble to thank schoolchildren who had sent their own tiny contributions. In the process she worked closely with Agnes Maisky, whose ambassador husband Ivan had been a close associate of Churchill since his anti-appeasement years. In March 1942 Winston told him, 'My own wife is completely Sovietized . . . All she ever talks about is the Soviet Red Cross, the Soviet army.' He added with a twinkle: 'Couldn't you elect her to one of your Soviets? She surely deserves it.' Such was Clemmie's energy and commitment that 'Aid to Russia' soon became known as 'Mrs Churchill's Fund'. This was the Great War canteens writ large, with huge international significance.[45]

Stalin singled out Clementine's work in a friendly message on 12 April 1943 which thanked the British people for the Aid to Russia fund and added: 'Please convey to your wife who is at the head of the fund my thanks for her untiring activities in this sphere.' When Churchill read the message on 14 April, he was 'pleased, even heartened', Maisky told Moscow. 'The paragraph devoted to Mrs. Churchill made a particularly strong impression on him. I should explain that Mrs. Churchill has a strong influence on her husband. He shares with her all the news and asks her advice on all matters.' At the end of Winston's second visit to Moscow, in October 1944, Stalin asked him to accept two 'modest presents – for Mrs Churchill a vase "Steersman on a boat," and for yourself a vase "Hunter with bow against a Bear".' The Soviet leader had a keen sense of diplomatic protocol, but also a sly sense of humour. Is it inappropriate to discern a subtext to his gift to Churchill, especially given the PM's known propensity to refer to Russia as 'Ursus Major' or 'the Bear'? And what of the present to

Clemmie – who was always trying to keep her husband on a steady course?[46]

In wartime she worked round the clock. Her first real break since the start of Winston's premiership occurred in August 1941 when he went to Newfoundland for his 'Atlantic Meeting' with FDR. She checked into a 'Nature Cure' in rural Hertfordshire where, for ten days, she had massages, osteopathy and a controlled diet, initially all-liquid, designed to give the digestive system a complete rest. The doctor there warned that she was driving herself too hard and urged that she should keep one day a week clear without any public obligations. For the next seven weeks 'Rest Day' appears punctiliously in her diary, but thereafter it disappears for good. As biographer Sonia Purnell observes drily, 'neither the Nazis nor her husband observed a six-day week.'[47]

Clementine did, however, use most of Winston's foreign trips to recharge her batteries. Sarah acted as his aide-de-camp at the Tehran and Yalta summits of the Big Three, while Mary did similar duty at Potsdam. Brought there to keep Winston in good humour, they accomplished things that no other staff members could do, such as getting him out of bed for meetings. In normal life both daughters were also 'doing their bit' for the war effort – Sarah in photographic intelligence and Mary on her anti-aircraft guns. Winston was very proud of his girls and his stereotypes about women may have shifted a little in the process. Despite growing weariness as the war progressed, Clementine also accompanied him to North America in 1943 and 1944. She did not take to FDR as much as her daughters had, particularly disliking his immediate attempt to call her 'Clemmie'. But she deepened her bond with Eleanor. All these trips left her drained, particularly over Christmas and New Year 1943–4 when she flew out to Marrakech for a month to help nurse Winston back to health from acute pneumonia. One evening she was chatting to Diana Cooper, an old friend, who raised the topic of what post-war life would be like. 'I never think of after the war,' Clementine replied calmly. 'You see, I think Winston will die when it is over ... he's seventy and I am sixty and we're putting all we have into this war, and it will take all we have.'[48]

The climax of Clementine's war was an epic tour of Russia in the spring of 1945, just as Europe was sliding from World War into Cold War. By this time, 'Mrs. Churchill's Fund' had raised over £6 million (roughly equivalent to £250 million today) and Clementine was invited by the Soviet Red Cross to come and see how it had been spent. At the end of March, Winston considered postponing her trip because of the growing tensions as the Red Army took control of Poland and Romania, but he decided to let it go ahead as 'a sign of personal good will'.[49] In the end, Clemmie was in the USSR for six weeks (2 April to 11 May). This was the first visit by the wife of a British Prime Minister (Winston being the only PM to do so) and it raised delicate protocol issues, which the Soviets resolved with great courtesy. Arriving at Moscow airport, she gave a short speech, slipping in a few sentences in Russian, about what she called 'one of the most inspiring and interesting moments of my life'. She was welcomed 'most amiably' by Foreign Minister Vyacheslav Molotov, who referred to 'present difficulties' but said 'they would pass and Anglo-Soviet friendship remain.' He and his wife hosted a 'lovely banquet' in her honour. On 8 April she was received by Stalin himself, who offered warm thanks for all her fund-raising. Afterwards he added a note to an official letter to Winston: 'I had an agreeable conversation with Mrs Churchill who made a deep impression upon me. She gave me a present from you. Allow me to express my heartfelt thanks for this present.' The gift was a fountain pen. 'My husband,' Clementine had declared, 'wishes me to express the hope that you will write him many more friendly messages with it.' Stalin accepted the pen with a smile but remarked: 'I only write with a pencil.'[50]

The PM was delighted by his wife's cordial reception in Moscow at a time of such tension between the two governments. Writing on 6 April, he told her that on the previous day Fedor Gusev, the dour Soviet ambassador, had asked for a meeting with the Foreign Secretary. Eden braced himself for another 'attack' but instead, wrote Winston,

Gusev delivered 'a message from his Government in praise of you and your work, and asking if they might offer you the Order of the Red Banner of Labour, which was of course approved'. He found this hard to square with the fraught state of diplomatic relations: 'What puzzles me is the inconsistency.'[51]

After Moscow, Clementine and her party boarded a special train to visit cities that the Aid to Russia fund had helped, starting with Leningrad ('the most beautiful city I have ever seen') and then travelling south to the Caucasus. In Stalingrad, she told Winston, 'the whole town turns out to greet us every time we go out and I am constantly amazed and moved by so much enthusiasm.' It was the same story in Rostov-on-Don, where her fund was re-equipping two large hospitals badly damaged by the Nazis. 'We were mobbed by friendly crowds. Everywhere we see smiling faces.' The fortress city of Sebastopol, however, presented 'so melancholy a spectacle . . . Before the Nazis destroyed it in their blind rage, it must have been a dream of beauty, as lovely as a poem, with its many pillared and frescoed houses.' But she was heartened by Kursk, which had found itself near the scene of the epic tank battle in July 1943: 'I was stirred to witness that in this city, whose civic chief is a woman, thousands of women have volunteered to help in its rebuilding.' Sadly 'they only had spades to clear away the rubble.'[52]

Clementine's grand tour took a full month. She returned Moscow on 5 May to find at the British Embassy a lengthy telegram from Winston – sent in code and therefore more candid than his official communications. 'You seem to have had a triumphant tour and I only wish matters would be settled between you and the Russian common people.' He told her that both Hitler and Mussolini were now dead and Germany was on the verge of surrender. But 'I need scarcely tell you that beneath these triumphs lie poisonous politics and deadly international rivalries.' He therefore urged her to 'come home after rendering the fullest compliments to your hospitable hosts.' Clemmie landed at Northolt airfield, west of London, on the morning of 12 May. The plane circled around for a while so that Winston, delayed in London, was on the tarmac ready to welcome her down the aircraft steps. On the same day he sent his 'iron curtain' telegram to President Harry Truman.[53]

The Moscow correspondent of *The Times* stated that her visit had 'provided perhaps the most notable instance of Anglo-Soviet cordiality during the war'. Although delighted by the warmth of her reception, Clementine was not oblivious to the 'poisonous politics'. She told a female MP, concerned about the fate of Polish POWs: 'When one has been in Russia, only for a few short weeks, one cannot help loving the people, and one must always separate them from their government which is mysterious and sinister, and terribly strong.'[54]

* * *

By the time Clementine arrived back in Britain, the coalition government was breaking up. And by the end of July, Winston was out of a job thanks to the Labour landslide. Although exhausted, she now had to get her mind around where and how they would live outside Downing Street. Fortunately, Diana and her husband Duncan Sandys generously vacated their flat in Westminster Gardens until renovations were completed on 28 Hyde Park Gate, a house in a quiet street near the Albert Hall. But Winston craved Chartwell, so Clemmie faced two major domestic tasks even though she considered it 'silly to have two homes just now (London & Country) because of the rations which all get eaten up in one place & becos' of servants . . . I blush to think that I who organised the Russian Fund, the kitchen in the Fulmer Maternity Hospital . . . am stumped by my own private life.' On 26 August, when she and Winston were at Chartwell ('one doesn't know where to start'), her mood was even grimmer. 'I cannot explain how it is but in our misery we seem, instead of clinging to each other, to be always having scenes. I am sure it's all my fault, but I'm finding life more than I can bear. He is so unhappy & that makes him very difficult.'[55]

Mary tried to buoy her up: 'despite all his difficultness – his overbearing – exhausting temperament – he <u>does</u> love you and <u>needs</u> you so much.' She told her mother: 'Many, many great men had wives who ran their houses beautifully and lavished care and attention on them – But they looked for love and amusement and repose elsewhere. And vice versa. You have supplied him with all these things – without surrendering your own soul or mind.' A bit of morale boosting, of course, but also true.[56]

Clemmie always felt that Winston should have rested on his laurels after 1945. She longed for a quiet retirement, but he could not survive without the adrenalin of power. Buoyed up by the Fulton speech in 1946, he stayed on as Tory leader and eyed a second term in 10 Downing Street. Hers was now a limited role. 'From helping to run the war Clementine was reduced once more to running houses,' observes biographer Sonia Purnell: 'she hovered in the background as Winston lapped up the attention.' There were a few limelight moments of her own. In June 1946 Oxford University bestowed on her an honorary degree, just as it had done to Winston in 1925. Then she had followed in the procession at his father's *alma mater*. Now, twenty-one years later, he followed her into the Sheldonian Theatre to hear the Public Orator praise the work she had done during the war and extol her as 'Guardian Angel of our country's guardian'.[57]

Her children remained a constant worry. Those early scars never really healed. The only truly successful relationship was still with Mary who, in 1947, married Christopher Soames, an ebullient Guards officer, to whom Winston immediately warmed. After he resigned from the Army, she deftly suggested that the newlyweds should move into Chartwell Farm and Christopher take over the management of the estate. He grew ever closer to Winston – playing cards, listening to his stories and introducing him to horse racing – winning over Clemmie by his boisterous charm.

The biggest problem remained Randolph. In 1941–2 he served in the desert with reckless bravery, in between drunken rants in Cairo. Later he was involved in special operations with Tito's Partisans in the Balkans. His 1939 marriage to Pamela Digby seems like a transactional affair – as Mary noted in her diary, 'Randolph wanted a son' before he went to war and 'Pam wanted glitter & fun'[58] – and it soon broke down. But Randolph was furious to learn of her passionate affair with Roosevelt's special emissary Averell Harriman, blaming his parents for encouraging it in order to promote the 'special relationship'. Encounters with his father often degenerated into blazing rows. After one 'battle royal' Clementine feared Winston might have a seizure. But despite the constant fireworks, he wanted Randolph at his side. 'I think the greatest misfortune in R's life is that he is Papa's son,' Mary confided to her diary. 'Papa has spoilt and indulged him ... R is his blind spot.' According to 'young Winston', Randolph 'found it impossible ever to forgive his parents.'[59]

The relentless demands of husband and children took an increasing toll on Clemmie. As in the 1930s, she needed plenty of breaks by herself, while Winston went off to warmer climes to paint and write his memoirs. She was at his side again to fight the election campaign in 1951, when he was finally returned to power. But she derived no pleasure of her own. 'Nothing,' said Mary, 'had changed the conviction she held in 1945, namely, that Winston should have retired at the end of the war.' And she felt 'a constant, gnawing anxiety' about his health.[60] In June 1953 he suffered a stroke during a state dinner, which left him partially paralysed for several weeks. The whole business, hushed up with the connivance of the press barons, was quietly managed by Christopher and the ever-loyal Jock Colville, who had returned for another spell as private secretary.

The stroke was a turning point. Thereafter, Clemmie had recurrent rows with him about calling it a day, which were then dispelled by billets-doux between 'Pug' and 'Cat'. Now almost 70, she was afflicted with neuritis, often wearing a support collar in private, and went away regularly for treatment and rest. But there were also highlights, notably in December 1953 when Clemmie received the Nobel Prize in Literature on Winston's behalf. (He was at a summit in Bermuda with President Eisenhower.) As observed by Mary, who accompanied her mother: 'if she came to Stockholm as a substitute, she was quickly accepted and acclaimed in her own right.' Hosted by the King and

Queen, she read out Winston's acceptance speech and was lauded by the Swedish press for her elegance and approachability. 'The success of the visit,' wrote the British ambassador to the Foreign Office, 'derived in great measure from the charm, dignity and graciousness of Lady Churchill herself and of Mrs. Soames.' Clemmie never forgot how, at the banquet that evening, the band and student choir serenaded her with 'My darling Clementine'.[61]

It took another sixteen months to prise Winston out of the premiership. Finally, on 5 April 1955 – four days after her seventieth birthday and the morning after the Queen had dined at Number 10 – his second premiership came to an end. He hung on as an MP for nearly a decade, despite growing rumbles from his constituency association and tactful pressure from Clemmie and Christopher. First elected as the century dawned, he hated to let go of his last remaining role in political life. But finally he announced that he would not stand again and in July 1964 the Commons unanimously passed a vote of thanks for his 'outstanding services to this House and to the nation'. Ever vigilant, Clemmie had complained to Christopher about an earlier draft of the resolution, which she called 'mangy'. Duly chastised, the drafters came up with something that accorded better with Clemmie's sense of what Sir Winston Churchill deserved. The final version expressed 'unbounded admiration for his services to Parliament, the nation and the world' and above all, for 'his inspiration of the British people when they stood alone, and his leadership until victory was won'.[62]

To the end of her life, in fact, Clemmie kept acting as 'Guardian Angel of our country's guardian'. The most ruthless example was her destruction of Graham Sutherland's portrait of Winston, commissioned by both Houses of Parliament for his eightieth birthday in 1954. Although he and Clemmie had taken a liking to the artist, both were shocked by the final product which he famously described, with studied ambiguity, as 'a remarkable example of modern art'. Privately, he used words like 'filthy' and 'malignant'.[63] 'I look like a down-and-out drunk who has been picked out of the gutter in the Strand,' he told his private secretary Anthony Montague Browne, and shouted at his solicitor, 'I won't go down in history like that.' Biographer Roy Jenkins commented that 'his dislike, which passed the bounds of rationality, was based partly on the ground that it made him look old and spent, which it did, and partly that it showed his face as cruel and coarse, which it was not.'[64]

'I wanted to paint him with a kind of four-square look,' Sutherland told Lord Moran, 'to picture Churchill as a rock.' In the end, however, the eyes that mattered were those of the sitter. The commission had stipulated that he be portrayed in his usual dark parliamentary attire – a black morning coat, waistcoat and striped trousers, adorned with a spotted bow tie – whereas Winston had wanted a heroic portrait, resplendent in the blue, red and white of his robes as a Knight of the Garter. As the art historian Kenneth Clark told Mary, her father had 'come to accept an image of himself, which had become an international symbol, & this Graham had completely disregarded'.[65]

For a year or so the Sutherland was secreted in the basement of Chartwell, until one day Clemmie, 'very much exercised,' asked her secretary, Grace Hamblin, 'So now, what do you suggest?' Put on the spot, Grace offered to dispose of the painting. She and her brother took it by van to his house, lit a bonfire in the back garden, and threw the canvas and frame on the flames. Next morning Grace told Clemmie what she had done, but nothing was disclosed until after the latter's death.[66]

During Winston's final illness in the New Year of 1965 the guardian angel remained at his side – preternaturally calm, holding his right hand as he breathed his last on 24 January. She stood in Westminster Hall for a period on each day of the lying in state, watching as long lines of mourners, some 320,000 in number, paid their respects, like a silent river flowing along the carpeted floor. And her lifetime of poise and elegance was on display again all through the bitterly cold day of the state funeral, when the Queen – against all precedent – awaited the arrival of her greatest commoner in St Paul's Cathedral. The congregation included President de Gaulle, and Attlee was one of the pallbearers. Now 82 and ailing, Clem needed the help of two soldiers when he stumbled on the cathedral steps, but he was deter-mined to discharge his duty to Winston. Afterwards, the coffin was taken by boat up the Thames, as massive cranes dipped in homage, and then carried by train to the family plot at Bladon. There, just outside Blenheim Palace where he had been born, Winston was buried in the twilight next to his father. That evening, back in London, Clemmie watched some of the highlights of the day on television. As she went to bed, she turned at the door and said, 'You know, Mary, it wasn't a funeral – it was a Triumph.'[67]

* * *

Mission accomplished, Clementine moved quickly to shed some of her burdens. Although she had a right to live in Chartwell for the rest of her days, she handed the house over straight away to the National Trust, asking that it be displayed as in its heyday between the world wars. She also sold up in Hyde Park and moved into something smaller and more manageable nearby. These decisions reflected her usual prudence but were also, surely, an attempt to begin a new life without Winston. She was deeply gratified in May 1965 – just after her eightieth birthday – when, on the recommendation of the Labour PM Harold Wilson, she received a life peerage. Baroness Spencer-Churchill of Chartwell took her seat as a cross-bencher, attached to no party. This astonished some; but not family and friends, who knew her 'pinko' roots.

Despite this flurry of independence, Clemmie was bound – willingly – to Winston in death as well as life. She derived great pleasure in seeing Chartwell open to the public from June 1966, with Grace Hamblin as its first administrator. And she was closely involved in the development of Churchill College, Cambridge, the national memorial to Winston and repository of his papers. Clemmie enjoyed her peri-odic visits to see the building works and meet the Fellows, students and staff. She also played a conspicuous, if ceremonial, part in the events in 1974 to mark the centenary of Winston's birth. After the family commemoration service at Bladon church, her wheelchair was pushed to the grave where she laid some flowers and whispered to Winston, 'I hope I shall not be long now.' A regular churchgoer again, as in her youth, she accepted her mortality and talked practically about her own funeral. One evening in her last year, she told Mary, 'I do miss Papa so – really more than I did just after he died.' She passed away suddenly but peacefully on 12 December 1977, aged 92.[68]

'From the day she married him until his death fifty-seven years later,' wrote Mary, 'Winston dominated her whole life; and once this priority had been established, her children, personal pleasures, friends and outside interests competed for what was left.' Asked once by her solicitor how her husband was able to juggle so many different interests – from politics to writing, from painting pictures to building walls – she replied, 'Winston never did anything he didn't want to do, and left someone else to clear up the mess afterwards.'[69] That 'someone' was usually her. She always retained her individuality – acting as his most devoted critic and maintaining the New Liberalism of her early days – but never developed a career or a life of her own. Nor did she want to. Indeed, she seems to have felt it was Winston who gave her the courage, confidence and opportunity to be the public figure she became in the Great War and, even more, during his finest hour. Yet he clearly needed her in equal measure. They energised and solaced each other.

At their wedding in St Margaret's, Westminster, in 1908, Winston's former headmaster at Harrow – now Dean of Manchester – had given the address. 'There must be in the statesman's life,' he told the young couple, 'many times when he depends upon the love, the insight, the penetrating sympathy and devotion of his wife. The influence which the wives of our statesmen have exercised for good upon their husbands' lives is an unwritten chapter of English history . . .' Those words were read again by her grandson Winston S. Churchill at Clementine's memorial service in Westminster Abbey seventy years later.[70]

The casualties of their partnership in greatness were their three older children. Why none found real fulfilment and happiness is, like all human life, a deep mystery. But the priority given by Clementine to Winston was surely a factor. The main exception was Mary – benefiting as the youngest from the painful lessons learnt too late by her mother and her siblings. The dutiful daughter became her mother's biographer, publishing that 'unwritten chapter' in 1979 and belatedly making the world aware of how much Winston's greatness depended on Clementine.

'The great artist of a great history' in his studio at Chartwell, 1947. Photographed by Hans Wild for *Life* magazine's serialisation of his memoirs.

12

Winston Churchill
Mirroring Himself

Winston . . . when I hear you talk I really wonder you didn't go into politics. You might have done a lot to help. You might even have made a name for yourself.

Lord Randolph Churchill, 'The Dream', November 1947[1]

I consider that it will be found much better by all parties to leave the past to history, especially since I propose to write that history myself.

Winston S. Churchill, 23 January 1948[2]

One day in November 1947, when Sarah was dining at Chartwell with Winston and Randolph, she posed her father a question. If you had the power, who would you bring to the table to join us? She expected him to name some famous historical personage such as Caesar or Napoleon. Instead, he said very simply: 'Oh, my father, of course.' Winston then told his son and daughter something that had happened not long before in his artist's studio in the cottage down the hill. At their urging, he had the story typed up and it was published in January 1966, on the first anniversary of his funeral.[3]

Winston had been sent a portrait of his father, painted in 1886, when he became Chancellor. The canvas was badly torn, and though 'very shy of painting human faces' he thought he would try to make a copy, intently studying the portrait and its reverse image in the mirror behind him. Deeply absorbed, probably on a dark winter's evening, Winston suddenly felt 'an odd sensation'. He looked round and there, sitting in the red leather upright armchair and fiddling with a cigarette, was Lord Randolph, looking bright and jaunty, 'just as I had seen him in his prime, and as I had read about him in his brief year of triumph'.

'Papa!'

His father, who had died in 1895, wanted to know what year it was. When told '1947', he exclaimed, 'So more than fifty years have passed. A lot must have happened'.

'It has indeed, Papa.'

'Tell me about it.'

Lord Randolph was glad to learn that the monarchy, the Turf Club and the Church of England were still going strong, but shocked that the country now had a socialist government. Winston tried to reassure him: 'You know, Papa, though stupid, they are quite respectable, and increasingly bourgeois'. The conversation moved on to other strange developments such as female suffrage and the loss of India – 'He gave a groan' – and there were some sideswipes about Winston's lack of potential – 'Bottom of the school! . . . Wrote me stilted letters.'

Asked what he did for living, Winston said, 'I write books and articles for the Press.'

'Ah, a reporter. There is nothing discreditable in that.'

What most distressed Lord Randolph was news of Europe's two great wars. 'Is there still a Tsar?'

'Yes, but he is not a Romanoff. It's another family. He is much more powerful, and much more despotic.'

'What of Germany? What of France?'

'They are both shattered. Their only hope is to rise together.'

Lord Randolph struggled to take in such startling information. 'But wars like these must have cost a million lives. They must have been as bloody as the American Civil War.'

'Papa, in each of them about thirty million men were killed in battle. In the last one seven million were murdered in cold blood, mainly by the Germans. They made human slaughter-pens like the Chicago stockyards. Europe is a ruin. Many of her cities have been blown to pieces by bombs. Ten capitals in Eastern Europe are in Russian hands. They are Communists now, you know – Karl Marx and all that. It may well be that an even worse war is drawing near.'

His father seemed stunned. He fumbled with his matchbox for some time and then said:

'Winston, you have told me a terrible tale. I would never have believed that such things could happen. I am glad I did not live to see them. As I listened to you unfolding these fearful facts you seemed to know a great deal about them. I never expected that you would develop so far and so fully. Of course, you are too old now to think about such things, but when I hear you talk I really wonder you didn't go into politics. You might have done a lot to help. You might even have made a name for yourself.'

'He gave me a benignant smile. He then took the match to light his cigarette and struck it. There was a tiny flash. He vanished.'[4]

The story became known in the family as 'The Dream'. Maybe Winston had nodded off during a November evening. Or perhaps this was a piece of creative writing, like *My Early Life*. But what he said expressed some deep personal truths. A septuagenarian who still measured himself against his unknown father. A father for whom his son's greatness would remain forever unknown.

* * *

'Be not afraid of greatness: some are born great, some achieve great-ness, and some have greatness thrust upon them.' Those words were addressed to Malvolio – the puffed-up steward in Shakespeare's *Twelfth Night* – but they may be fairly applied to Winston Churchill.

'Be not afraid of greatness'. Far from it: he yearned all his life to be great. 'He is ambitious and he is calculating,' wrote the journalist G.W. Steevens in 1899, 'yet he is not cold – and that saves him.' In similar vein, the socialist Beatrice Webb damned Churchill as 'restless, egotistical, bumptious, shallow-minded and reactionary', but also acknowledged 'a certain personal magnetism' and 'great pluck'. In his own Ruritanian-style novel *Savrola* (1900), many biographers have discerned more than a touch of autobiography. 'Ambition was the motive force, and he was powerless to resist it,' we are told of the eponymous hero. And then, from Winston himself in 1906, comes that unforgettable outburst to the young Violet Asquith: 'We are all worms. But I do believe that I am a glow-worm.'[5]

'Some are born great.' Yes, and no. His birthplace was the monumental palace built by his ancestor John Churchill, first Duke of Marlborough. But his own father was a younger son, not the bearer of the title, and Lord Randolph's meteoric rise and disastrous fall were always in the minds of those who watched his son climbing the ladder. So the Churchill name gave Winston a leg up, but he had to 'achieve greatness' through his own exertions. And, haunted by Lord Randolph's death at only 45, he was convinced that time was not on his side.

A young man in a hurry, he tried various shortcuts. The subaltern on a grey horse, deliberately courting danger and attention on the Northwest Frontier of India – like his hero, Napoleon, on the bridge at Arcole. The young officer leading his troop of lancers into a mass of 'Dervishes' on the Nile at Omdurman. The prisoner of the Boers who escaped captivity in Pretoria and crossed 300 miles of enemy territory back to his own lines. All these daring exploits written up as a war journalist and best-selling author, because Winston learned early, and for life, that worms need words in order to glow. He was equally sure that the only way to guarantee their radiance was to kindle them himself.

And so, when Winston entered the House of Commons in 1901, he was already a celebrity. After crossing the floor to join the Liberals in March 1904, he gained his first ministerial post little more than a year later. But although he then made a new name for himself as a social reformer, it was at the Admiralty that he found his métier while nearly losing his head: one might liken 1914–15 to Lord Randolph's *annus mirabilis et horribilis* of 1886. First, Winston tried to win renown in battle – this time by taking control at Antwerp – and then he sought to redeem his fortunes by becoming the grand strategist of victory in the forcing of the Dardanelles. When these hopes turned to ashes on the Gallipoli peninsula, Winston glimpsed his next opening as a great commander – perhaps leading the conquest of German East Africa and bringing new glory to the British Empire. Or else as a general commanding a brigade on the Western Front, from which he could soon rise to a more elevated station. These visions dissolved within a few weeks in December 1915, as Asquith disowned him for fear of parliamentary criticism.[6]

'From that moment Churchill aspired not to advance his military career, but to rebuild his political one.'[7] Henceforth the route to the top – if it still existed – would have to run through Westminster and Whitehall. The ministerial patronage of Lloyd George proved vital – likewise that of Stanley Baldwin in 1924 after Winston 're-ratted' to the Tories amid the challenges from Bolshevism abroad and socialism at home. Yet 'greatness' still proved elusive. Although Home Secretary at the age of 35, in 1910, it was not until 1924, aged nearly 50, that he became Chancellor of the Exchequer; Lord Randolph had been 37. And then the ladder seemed to disappear. Labour's victory in 1929 and the possibility that Neville Chamberlain might win the Tory leadership left him thinking dark thoughts about starting a new life in Canada. In the end he decided to hang on in politics, casting around for a great cause through which to force himself on the Tory Establishment. India and Edward VIII both proved toxically counter-productive, though his warnings about the German threat gradually earned him new respect. Even so, had his life ended in 1939, it might well have been seen, to quote Robert Rhodes James, as a 'political failure' and a 'personal tragedy' – showing that 'great abilities and industry cannot, in themselves, secure political success' and leaving observers puzzled that 'a mind so fertile and a character so many-faceted should have proved incapable of full development.'[8]

Instead, 1939 marked not death but resurrection. The war he had long predicted finally broke out, and this time Winston was not made sole scapegoat for disaster on the flanks. On the contrary, the Norway debacle proved his final slippery stepping stone to the job he craved. In May 1940 Labour refused to come into coalition with Chamberlain – unlike the Tories and Asquith in 1915 – opening the way for a new Prime Minister. So, did Churchill have greatness 'thrust upon him' when Lord Halifax opted out? Or did he 'seize' greatness in what he supposedly called 'the only time in my life when I have kept my mouth shut'?[9] We shall never know: the 'great silence' in the Cabinet Room on 9 May will remain mute.

There is, however, no doubt that when Churchill reached Number 10, he grabbed the opportunity with both hands. In his memoirs this became the culmination of a lifetime 'walking with destiny', so that his whole past 'had been but a preparation for this hour and for this trial'.[10] He also said, concerning 'men and women of first-class quality', that 'perhaps seventy per cent of all they have to give is expended on fights which have no other object than to get to their preferred battle-field'.[11] That was certainly true for him, finally entering Number 10 at the age of 65.

But then the man who had spent his life planning his rise to the premiership, had to change gear and learn the arts of improvisation. This was one of his greatest achievements. France collapsed within weeks of his becoming Prime Minister, making this war entirely different from 1914–18. After June 1940, Britain had no major European allies and Winston had to work with the two emerging superpowers, increasingly as their junior partner. Summitry became his way to play at the top table, exploiting his greater geographical mobility, compared with Roosevelt and Stalin, in order to act as would-be broker. Or, as Uncle Joe nicely put it: as the 'Holy Ghost' flying around within the 'Trinity'.[12]

Yet personal diplomacy, however dynamic, could not compensate for lack of hard power. Churchill stuck to the grand strategy he drafted after Pearl Harbor. He was probably right to oppose an invasion of occupied France until Britain and America had built up overwhelming resources and gained control of the Atlantic, but this meant that, if Stalin ousted Hitler, the Red Army was likely to dominate Eastern

Europe after the war. Such was in part the price of victory. Churchill's tenacious determination in 1940–2 to prioritise Britain's position in Mediterranean also left its Asian empire gravely exposed when Japan entered the fray. The crisis of early 1942 undermined British power and prestige in India and made Australians ask whether they should turn to America, not Britain, as protector.

And so Churchill's declamation in November 1942 that he had 'not become the King's First Minister in order to preside over the liquidation of the British Empire' rang increasingly hollow. This was an empire already over-extended and the crisis of 1941–2 sounded its death knell. More honest was Winston's admission to the Commons in January 1942:

> There never has been a moment, there could never have been a moment, when Great Britain or the British Empire, single-handed, could fight Germany and Italy, could wage the Battle of Britain, the Battle of the Atlantic and the Battle of the Middle East – and at the same time stand thoroughly prepared in Burma, the Malay Peninsula, and generally in the Far East against the impact of a vast military empire like Japan, with more than 70 mobile divisions, the third navy in the world, a great air force and the thrust of 80 or 90 millions of hardy, warlike Asiatics.[13]

Neville Chamberlain, the apostle of appeasement, could not have put it better. Instead of condemning Churchill's bombast about empire, however, we might marvel at what he did achieve when dealt that awful hand in 1940 – how much he made from so little for so long.

Most of his life Churchill imagined himself as a great soldier or a great warlord. Less familiar is his ambition to be a great peacemaker, captured in that sad lament after being 'kicked out' in 1945: 'I wanted to do the peace as well.'[14] Hence his passion, when back at Number 10 in 1951–5, for another 'parley at the summit' to thaw the Cold War. When reflecting on 1914–18, he had been appalled at modern warfare: scant chance for personal glory, vast carnage of civilians as well as combatants and the appliance of science to create weapons of mass destruction. From 1945, nuclear weapons made the horror of another war immeasurably worse. Of course, by the early 1950s Winston wanted to 'stay in the pub until closing time', but talk of another summit was not just a convenient excuse: that dream of being a great peacemaker was rooted in his chivalric sentiments.

* * *

Churchill certainly drew heavily on his past experience and intellectual capital during his long political career. He was also a man of phenomenal energy, setting out an eye-catching grand project whenever he was appointed to a new ministry while doing a double duty as the writer of 'books and articles' – as he casually told his father in 'The Dream'. That was how he made his living.

Despite being largely self-made, however, he also learned from others. Whatever men's need for admiring women, as Virginia Woolf complained, they also compare themselves with other men – feeling their own self either enlarged or diminished in the looking-glass of comparison. This was always true of Winston, especially in times of turmoil on the rough edges between peace and war. What, then, did he learn of greatness from his 'great contemporaries'? And how did they rate him?

As 'The Dream' suggests, Winston could never escape his father – on whose birthday, 24 January, he eventually died in 1965. But in adulthood he did come to terms with Papa, creating a biographical image that endowed Lord Randolph with a principled consistency lacking in real life while also allowing Winston go one better by taking his principles to a more appropriate party. *Lord Randolph Churchill* was published in January 1906, just before Winston was elected MP for Manchester North West in the Liberal landslide.

The author-politician was launched, but he needed a mentor. The role became manifest in the person of David Lloyd George, a decade senior in age and much more than that in political wisdom. Often working in tandem, they set the tone of New Liberalism in Westminster – promoting bold programmes of social reform, decrying naval rearmament in the

Dreadnought crisis of 1908–9 and leading the crusade against the House of Lords, many of whose members were Winston's own relatives. But the two men were not always of one mind – on female suffrage, for instance, or Bolshevism – and LG was also a better listener, less prone to keep on talking. He also displayed a tactical cunning that his younger colleague lacked. No wonder he was the senior partner in what Winston sometimes bitterly called a master-servant relationship. But that was not the last word. During the 1930s LG was an appeaser – he lacked Winston's physical courage and was terrified by the prospect of bombing – and in 1940, Churchill was profoundly right and Lloyd George profoundly wrong. Just before D-Day, LG – recalling the line of Lord Acton, the august Victorian scholar, 'I never had any contemporaries' – told his wife, 'I regard Winston as my only contemporary.'[15]

Winston's relations with Neville Chamberlain were rooted in a clash of political dynasties, though Neville's father, 'Radical Joe', was extremely helpful when Winston was researching *Lord Randolph Churchill*. Winston and Neville were thrown together in the Baldwin government of 1924–9, as respectively Chancellor of the Exchequer and Minister of Health. Both were strategic thinkers, bursting with ambition, and for a while they made common cause, for instance on the Pensions Act of 1925. But with two such egos, turf fights were inevitable and in any case Neville was more of a details man whereas Winston inclined to the big picture, convinced that successful govern-ments must always be putting 'some large issue or measure before the country, or to be engaged in some struggle which holds the public mind'.[16] Up to a point Neville agreed, and he saw Winston as 'a real man of genius', but he became increasingly irritated by that constant urge for 'the large and preferably the novel idea' of the sort that 'is capable of representation by the broadest brush'.[17]

During the 1930s, Winston's search for a great cause, depicted in lurid colours, did not bring him to Number 10. On the contrary, it took him deeper into the wilderness as he kept tilting at apparent political windmills. Ironically, Chamberlain – now Prime Minister – seems to have picked up too much from Churchill about the political value of a 'broad splash of paint'. And Neville's 'accuracy of drawing' deserted him completely in September 1938 when he tried his hand at summit diplomacy. Whereas Winston, so often accused of lacking judgment, got it right on the issue that really mattered.

Right about Hitler – or more exactly about Hitler's Germany. Churchill's view of foreign leaders was entangled with his evaluation of their countries. And in the case of Germany and France, that evaluation started young when, at the age of nine, he saw the Strasbourg monument in Paris draped in black and thought 'distinctly' that he wanted the French to regain their lost provinces.[18] In his romantic mind the real France was always draped in the bright colours of liberty and glory and personified in the genius of Napoleon (whose biography he longed to write). Whereas Germany – from his first visit in 1906 to see its military manoeuvres – seemed a grotesque juggernaut, geared for ruthless expansion. The Great War confirmed that verdict. Thereafter, fearful that 1918–19 was an armistice not a peace, he was alert for signs of revanchism.

From this perspective, Hitler was not so much an agent, more a vehicle for Germany's malevolent militarism. Winston showed little interest in the social roots of Nazism. And, unlike Chamberlain, he dd not speculate much on Hitler's mental state. His historically informed imagination focused on the German war machine, legatee of 1870 and 1914, and specifically on the new threat it might pose to Britain's island nation through airpower, which was capable of leaping the English Channel – Shakespeare's 'moat defensive'. Yet he assumed right up to May 1940 that France would take care of the Western Front: his mantra 'Thank God for the French Army' implied that Britain need do little in that department. He attributed the German breakthrough on the Meuse to the complacent rigidity of the French high command rather than the audacious brilliance of Hitler's strategy. And his determination to fight on after Dunkirk owed little to any psychoanalysis of the Führer, much more to his own sense of history: the immense challenge of a Channel crossing viewed through the lens of 1588 and 1803.

As the war progressed, Churchill did become more vituperative about Hitler. Broadcasting on the evening of Barbarossa, he spoke of 'a monster of wickedness, insatiable in his lust for blood and plunder'. But his emphasis was still on that 'vast military machine' of 'heel-clicking, dandified Prussian officers' and the 'brutish masses of the Hun soldiery'.[19] Side references later in the war – such as 'a squalid caucus boss and butcher', or the half-joking remark that Hitler should be finished off on an 'electric chair' as used for 'gangsters' in the US – suggest that Winston saw the Führer as a kind of monstrous Al Capone. Certainly, he would allow no comparison with the Great Napoleon. In November 1944 he stood in reverent silence in Paris, gazing at the Emperor's tomb, but showed not the slightest curiosity the following July when poking around the ruins of Hitler's bunker in Berlin.[20]

By contrast, he always thought of Mussolini as a great man, truly *Il Duce*. This opinion dated from the years after 1918 when the Fascist leader seemed a bulwark against the 'Red Tide' sweeping across Europe. Winston's attitude was also affected by his Gibbonian fascination with the Roman empire, itself a model for the *Pax Britannica*. But he also had no doubt that Italy, even since unification, could not hold a candle as a great power to post-Bismarck Germany. Hence his otherwise bizarre comment in 1938 that it was 'perhaps, just as well for the world that Signor Mussolini was not born a German'.[21]

During the 1930s – keen to keep the two dictators apart – he tried to avoid antagonising Mussolini over Abyssinia and the Spanish Civil War. And in 1940, when Italy became an overt enemy, he targeted it as the weakest link in the Axis. He saw victory in the Mediterranean as vital if Britain's position in North Africa were to be held, but also as the first step to liberating Europe as a whole. After Alamein, Churchill let rip about how 'one man alone' had brought Italy to defeat, blaming 'the hyena in his nature' and his 'mad dreams of imperial glory'. But in 1945 he was indignant that *Il Duce*'s last public appearance was to be hung, upside down, from a girder in a Milan service station, and his memoirs paid tribute to all Mussolini had done to raise up Italy from post-1918 anarchy. His 'fatal mistake', Churchill claimed, was made in June 1940 by failing to understand 'the strength of Britain' and its 'long-enduring qualities of Island resistance and sea-power'.[22]

Churchill tended to see what he wanted to see. This was even more the case when he looked across the Atlantic. Fascination with the United States came almost as a birth right, but that did not preclude a keen sense of rivalry in the 1920s with American seapower. Again, the German threat helped him sort out priorities during the 1930s. It brought to the forefront of his mind once more that romanticised image of the 'English-speaking peoples', bonded by culture, language and ancestry. And, despite ideological doubts about the New Deal, his conviction that courage was 'the first of human qualities' predisposed him to the wheelchair President, even before FDR threw his weight behind Britain in the summer of 1940.[23]

For the rest of the war Churchill worked on these two 'special relationships' – with Roosevelt and with the United States. Both relationships reflected wartime realities but were also products of his creative imagination. The real warmth Churchill felt personally for Roosevelt was not reciprocated. The America he romanticised was anglophone and anglophile, glossing over its ethnic and sectional tensions. And his view of FDR played down the President's innate suspicion of the British Empire and the priority he increasingly gave to Stalin. After 1945, FDR's Cold War successors – Truman and Eisenhower – shared FDR's focus on the superpower relationship and his conception of Britain as very much the junior partner.

Churchill considered Stalin to be a great leader like Roosevelt, but for very different reasons. Although he put his earlier suspicions of the Soviet regime on the back burner because of the German threat, they did not cool down and he never forgot that Stalin had cosied up to Hitler in 1939–41. But, mostly, he chose to take a positive view of Moscow's foreign policy, believing that it would follow what seemed to him Russia's obvious 'national interest' and cooperate against Nazi Germany. Buoyed up by his correspondence with Roosevelt, he hoped he could also develop some kind of epistolary relationship with the

Kremlin recluse. And finally, in August 1942, things became personal. As a result of his three days in Moscow he derived a lasting conviction that, as he put it later, 'there are two forces to be reckoned with in Russia: (a) Stalin himself, personally cordial to me, (b) Stalin in council, a grim thing behind him, which we and he have to reckon with.'[24]

The nature of that 'grim thing' was never clear – the Soviet Politburo, perhaps, or the Red Army marshals? Of course, nowadays, any idea that Stalin might have been in thrall to others sounds ridiculous. But this trope enabled Winston, after 1945, to play his double-agent role as both cold warrior and potential icebreaker: warning of the 'iron curtain' coming down across Europe yet talking up possible 'parleys' at the 'summit'. These were the lessons he drew from the war, seen through the looking-glass while facing Roosevelt and Stalin.

Charles de Gaulle was simpler. There Winston glimpsed almost a mirror image of himself: both bred as soldiers, revelling in the nation's past military glories and believing that 'greatness', *grandeur*, was essential for a people's identity and pride. Yet their wartime relationship was intrinsically unequal. Although in June 1940 de Gaulle had been thrown on Churchill's charity – an infuriating dent to his ego – he insisted at every turn on France's status as a great power, however ridiculous that appeared. One thinks of Winston's exclamation of baffled wonder during the Casablanca conference: 'His country has given up fighting, he himself is a refugee, and if we turn him down he's finished. Well, just look at him! Look at him! He might be Stalin, with 200 divisions behind his words.'[25] Gaullian tactics were perhaps in Churchill's mind during his own jousts at the summit with the Bigger Two.

As for the General, he rarely forgot a hurt – especially when inflicted by the old enemy – and in January 1963 he paid Britain back with interest when vetoing its application to join the European Economic Community. Yet the grudge was not personal. These words from his memoirs, used as an epigraph to the present book, sum up his judgment: 'Winston Churchill appeared to me, from one end of the drama to the other, as the great champion of a great enterprise and the great artist of a great history.'[26] Churchill might have said the same about de Gaulle, even though he did not consider the French leader to be in the same league as Roosevelt or Stalin. Certainly he felt that the world would have been a poorer place without *Le Grand Charles*.

That, however, could not be said of the Mahatma. Churchill viewed Mohandas Gandhi with anger and contempt. In his racial hierarchy Hindus occupied a much lowlier place than India's 'martial races' – the Sikhs and Muslims – and Gandhi was personally regarded as a conman: the fake 'fakir' who had abandoned masculine, 'civilised' attire in order to seduce the masses. De Gaulle was in many ways an adversary, but he did play the same game as Winston, both being men of power. Gandhi, by contrast, exploited the power of powerlessness in performances of political theatre against which Churchillian methods were virtually helpless. After Amritsar in 1919, Winston knew that brute force was no answer. Yet he was determined to hang on to the Raj, seen through rose-tinted spectacles since his days there in the late 1890s, and he spoke of the British Empire as his 'alpha and omega'. He goal as war leader was preserving that empire, not just saving Britain. 'The man who defied Hitler and proclaimed the virtues of Liberty was the same man who was nauseated by Mahatma Gandhi,' writes biographer Andrew Roberts. His 'obstinacy and bull-headedness' were 'equally on display over India in the 1930s and the Nazis in 1940'.[27]

And so, on the personal and the political level, Churchill could never have conceded to Gandhi the appellation 'great'. Yet that is now how the Mahatma is perceived across much of the world: a pioneer of non-violent protest, in the vanguard of post-colonialism. Winston, though fascinated by technological innovation, was spiritually a child of the Victorian age. Indeed, Clement Attlee pondered whether the many-layered Churchill had much of the twentieth century about him.

Attlee, from a comfortable professional family and educated at a minor public school, imbibed many of the patriotic, imperial values that inspired Winston. He would also have agreed with young Churchill's remark in 1901: 'I see little glory in an Empire which can rule the waves and is unable to flush its sewers.'[28] But whereas

Winston's commitment to social reform was a passing phase of his New Liberalism, leaving behind a residue of benevolent paternalism, Attlee's youthful encounter with London's East End turned his world upside down for ever. Although he fought for King and Country in 1914–18 and was fully committed to war against Nazi Germany, his real mission was to build a socialist society at home and turn Empire into Commonwealth. Here were totally different conceptions of what made a country great.

Clem was never a Churchill intimate like Lloyd George – but their relationship was long and often intense. 'Little Attlee' was leader of the Labour Party for two decades (1935–55) and he served as Deputy PM in Winston's wartime coalition. During that time, he managed much of the Home Front and quietly used 'war socialism' as the basis for something deeper and more permanent when he became premier himself. Winston could see what was going on but he lacked the time and energy to stop it. Attlee was also one of the few who talked back to Winston – but quietly and on paper, so as to avoid open rows and public criticism of the Prime Minister. These were virtues that Churchill respected: hence his remark that Attlee was 'an admirable character', even though 'not one with whom it is agreeable to dine'. Clem's obituary of Winston was certainly not uncritical, but it concluded that, 'by any reckoning, Churchill was one of the greatest men that history records.'[29]

Winston, of course, was always determined to be one of the recorders. He started early, dramatising his youthful exploits on the frontiers of empire in newspaper articles and breathless best-sellers. But the books that really counted were six volumes of memoir-cum-history about each of the two world wars. The first series, *The World Crisis*, began as a defence of the Dardanelles operation. Drawing on a wide range of documents, as historian Christopher Bell has observed, Churchill laid the foundations of 'an alternative history of the campaign, constructed from a mixture of truths, half-truths and dubious assertions' and intended to 'convince the public that the Dardanelles was actually a brilliant concept that had come close to success.'[30] Later volumes defended his strategy in 1916–18, especially the idea of avoiding further suicidal offensives like the Somme until the Americans entered the line in massive strength. But Winston's innate historical curiosity turned the project into something far broader than self-defence, including volumes that addressed the war's aftermath and even the early months on the Eastern Front. Little wonder that Balfour dubbed *The World Crisis* 'Winston's brilliant Autobiography, disguised as a history of the universe'.[31]

The memoirs of 1939–45 were actually completed during his second premiership, but by then he had learnt how to manage a research 'syndicate' whose members knew how to dig out the material and write the drafts to lay before his editorial eye and pen. The results were not always elegant – too many undigested documents, not what de Gaulle would dignify as *une oeuvre* – but they were a tribute to that massive capacity, in his prime, for hard work on multiple fronts. The aim, again, was to lay out his own case. 'I do not describe it as history, for that belongs to another generation,' he wrote in the preface to Volume I, calling his work 'a contribution to history which will be of service to the future'.[32] But the richness of the documentation – at a time when official archives were shut tight – plus the vigour and colour of his best prose made it likely that his 'contribution' would greatly influence subsequent generations, not least by putting him at the centre of the whole world war. Few readers ploughed through all those two million words, but many got the gist through mass worldwide serialisation in newspapers and magazines. Even now, it seems natural to follow the phases and phrases by which his six volumes structured events: 'The Gathering Storm', 'Their Finest Hour', 'The Grand Alliance', 'The Hinge of Fate', 'Closing the Ring', 'Triumph and Tragedy'. As historian J.H. Plumb remarked in 1969, we still 'move down the broad avenues which he drove through war's confusion and complexity'.[33] And with Winston in the forefront – because his words, not just his deeds, had become mirrors of greatness.

Nevertheless, Churchill could not command history for ever. On 18 June 1940, as France surrendered, he urged Parliament and people to 'brace ourselves to our duties and so bear ourselves that, if the British

Empire and its Commonwealth last for a thousand years, men will still say "This was their finest hour".[34] But that was the language of inspirational exhortation not factual description. Like all empires, Britain's could not avoid decline. In fact, what's surprising is not its fall but its rise. From the seventeenth century to the twentieth Britain was able to capitalise on the security of its island position, at a time when the continent of Europe was wracked by a succession of ruinous land wars. And in an age of seapower, the country's substantial navy gave it security against invasion and the capacity to protect and project Britain's global trade. A combination of seapower and slavepower helped generate the capital and raw materials to fuel Britain's precocious industrial revolution. By 1860, a country with only 2 per cent of the global population was producing half the world's iron and steel and accounting for 40 per cent of world trade in manufactured goods. It had the highest GDP in the world and its people, despite vast inequalities of wealth, enjoyed the highest average per capita income. This was clearly not a position that could be sustained indefinitely, once other powers industrialised and extended their domains. Of particular importance were the two great continent-wide empires: Russia and the United States, plus Germany, whose two bids for European hegemony were eventually defeated only at the cost of Britain's global power. The change in the country's relative position was evident during Churchill's lifetime. When he was born in 1874, Britain produced nearly a quarter of the world's manufactures; but only a tenth when his chancellorship ended in 1929 and little more than one-twentieth at the time of his death in 1965.[35]

Not only was the *Pax Britannica* inevitably ephemeral, it was also less substantial than it seemed, even at the zenith of British power. It is customary nowadays to picture the Empire as a possession: those tracts of land coloured pink on old maps. Yet it was always in flux, commercial as much as colonial, its geographical focus shifting over time without any firm guiding idea.[36] What's more, for a country that was small in both territory and population, holding onto empire depended to a significant degree on bluff and bribery, credibility and acquiescence – because there was never sufficient raw force. Nowhere was this truer than in the case of the Raj, whose population was over 250 million in 1881 and nearly 390 million in 1941 (the comparable figures for the UK were 35 million and nearly 50 million). When numbers began to count, especially in wartime, the days of Britain's imperial leverage were numbered.

In fact, Britain's empire lasted only another quarter century after Churchill became Prime Minister. Public preoccupation with 1940 as our 'finest hour' encourages the feeling that it's been all downhill since then. Perhaps it has been, but that's not a healthy attitude for a country or a productive national self-image. Nor, let it be said, is it truly Churchillian. Though prone to nostalgia, Winston was a man who, in his prime, grasped the future with both hands and showed an unexpected gift for improvisation; who, when France collapsed in 1940, immediately saw the importance of America and Russia, reaching out with passionate intensity to their leaders. And a man who, after the defeat of the Third Reich, astonished the world by calling on France and Germany to make peace and forge a united Europe. In November 1942, when the Torch landings lost momentum, he exclaimed that North Africa should be 'a spring-board and not a sofa'.[37] One might say the same about Britain's Churchillian heritage – rather than being an excuse to sink into nostalgia, it should be a jumping-off point for the future. A celebration of the man's timeless spirit, rather than his now dated worldview. A spur to maximise the country's assets in soft as well as hard power, instead of pretending it still possesses the clout of today's global giants.

That's why it has been useful to see Churchill through the eyes of his contemporaries, especially those whom *he* would not have called 'great' because they saw the world quite differently from him. Gandhi and Attlee are two examples, both fundamentally at odds with him about politics and society and reflecting attitudes to social hierarchy and imperial rule that accorded more closely with the trends of the later twentieth century. But most interesting, perhaps, in our own day is his wife. From the start, Clementine glimpsed the sacrifices that would be entailed by marriage to Winston. Even though she did manage to keep 'a room of her own', her blue-stocking tendencies, suffragette passions and Liberal values all had to be kept under wraps because her 'life's work' was to support an egotistical genius. Yet their marriage did not prove a one-way street. His status opened doors, otherwise locked, through which she could exploit her talents – such as the Great War canteens for munitions workers, when she learnt to drive herself and others in what she proudly saw as a Churchillian mode. Even more striking was her leadership of the 'Aid for Russia' appeal in 1942–5, which also provided an outlet for her guilt about his failure to mount a second front. Yet her most important work took place behind the scenes – listening supportively to his anxieties and plans and offering sensitive criticism, especially about the need to persuade not cajole.

Winston wouldn't have considered Clementine to be a 'great contemporary' – his view of women was highly traditional – but what she did was essential to his greatness. The casualties in this joint project were their children, as is so often the case for political orphans. Clementine was not naturally maternal, and she warmed to the role of mother only with her youngest, Mary, when the others were already badly scarred. The biggest casualty was Randolph. As Winston's highly talented only son, bearing the name that mattered, he was indulged beyond reason, probably in compensation for Lord Randolph's coldness and contempt. Winston tolerated his own son's arrogance, paid off his debts and turned a blind eye to his boorish manners and loose morals.

And yet there was a sticking point. Winston alluded to it, with chilling candour, in 1931, when Randolph was twenty – talking to him about the 'battle of life' as they walked around the lawn at Chartwell. 'My father died when I was exactly your age,' Winston said, putting his arm around the young man. 'This left the political arena clear for me. I do not know how I should have fared in politics had he lived on.' The message was clear: the world was big enough for only one Churchill. And Randolph understood. As he told his father in 1947, 'it's very hard for two generations to carry the same flag simultaneously!'[38]

Perhaps that's why Winston made Lord Randolph disappear from 'The Dream' – before he discovered just how far his son had eclipsed him.

And perhaps why he published no sequel to *Great Contemporaries*: lack of time and energy aside, there was – quite simply – no need. The mirrors had served their purpose. He had led his country through its greatest modern crisis. He had seen off one of the world's most bestial dictatorships. And he had written himself into history in ways that neither Roosevelt nor Stalin – the war's two great victors – ever did. He might have echoed Lord Acton: 'I never had any contemporaries.'

Yet, despite his prodigious energy and remarkable achievements, Churchill was a man of his time. And, a century and a half after his birth, I believe that is how we should see and understand him.

Acknowledgements

This book started life during Covid lockdown but, like all worthwhile projects, developed a life of its own. I am very grateful to my agent, Natasha Fairweather, and my publishers in London and New York, Arabella Pike of HarperCollins and Brian Distelberg of Basic Books, for helping me to conceptualise and revise my approach. When I needed to cut the draft significantly, comments from Brian's colleague Brandon Proia proved invaluable. My warm thanks to project editor Katy Archer and copy-editor Steve Gove for their care in turning text into book. Amanda Russell helped me source the illustrations. The index was compiled by Mark Wells.

The book reflects many conversations over the years with colleagues and friends who share my interest in the Second World War and its legacies – notably Warren Kimball, David Woolner, Vladimir Pechatnov and Kristina Spohr. Allen Packwood, Director of the Churchill Archives in Cambridge – another long-standing supporter – generously read and commented on the whole draft. The chapter on Gandhi benefited from early discussions with Nazmul Sultan. Thanks to Russell Barnes of Clearstory Productions and the films we have made together, I have been able to see and imagine history in very different ways. I also recall with appreciation some 'eminent Churchillians' of the academic world who passed away before their time: Paul Addison, Alex Danchev and John Ramsden. Conversations with Lady Mary Soames were memorable both for their content and her personality.

As usual, I am indebted to my 'local libraries', especially the Cambridge University Library, but also the Seeley Historical Library and the Library of Christ's College. The College has been my intellectual base for four decades and I am immensely grateful to colleagues from a wide variety of disciplines for their company, interest and conversation amid such beautiful surroundings. My fellow historians of today – Harriet Lyon, Helen Pfeifer and Purba Hossain – study very different periods from me but that has made our regular Quartet meetings particularly stimulating.

Quotations from the the speeches, works and writings of Winston S. Churchill are reproduced with permission of Curtis Brown, London, on behalf of the Estate of Winston S. Churchill, © the Estate of Winston S. Churchill. Quotations from 'The Dream' and the papers of Lady Clementine Spencer Churchill are used by permission of The Master, Fellows and Scholars of Churchill College, Cambridge.

Over the years I've had the opportunity to write about a wide diversity of topics, but Winston Churchill has been a hardy perennial – viewed and reviewed in the changing mirror of our times. As a child, I visited his family home at Chartwell soon after it was opened to the public in 1966 because my parents, Leslie and Marian Reynolds, were keen Churchillians. My first book, published in 1981, about Britain and America, 1937–41, was dedicated to them and to my American wife, Margaret Ray Reynolds – 'My Three Rs' as I called them. Leslie and Marian have passed on, but Margaret has been a constant presence and support, as we puzzle over what has happened to our two countries across the last half-century. Nowadays my writing is also embedded in another Reynolds family – that of son Jim, his wife Emma and their three young children: Jake, Toby and Isla. So, this book, looking at Churchill from the perspective of the 2020s, is dedicated to my new 'Three Rs' in the hope that it will help them – in years to come – to understand a little more about Grandpa and the hall of historical mirrors it has been his privilege and pleasure to explore.

David Reynolds
June 2023

Illustration credits

Abbreviations

Addison	Paul Addison, *Churchill on the Home Front, 1900–1950* (London, 1993)
Alanbrooke	Lord Alanbrooke, *War Diaries, 1939–1945*, ed. Alex Danchev and Daniel Todman (London, 2001)
AMB	Anthony Montague Browne, *Long Sunset* (London, 1995)
APP	American Presidency Project: https://www.presidency.ucsb.edu/documents
ATLE	Clement Attlee Papers (CAC)
CAB	Cabinet Office papers (TNA)
CAC	Churchill Archives Centre, Churchill College, Cambridge
CD	*The Churchill Documents*, compiled by Randolph S. Churchill, Martin Gilbert and Larry Arnn (23 vols, Boston, MA and Hillsdale, MI, 1966–2019)
CE	Michael Wolff, ed., *The Collected Essays of Sir Winston Churchill* (4 vols, Bristol, 1976)
CHAR	Chartwell Papers (CAC)
CHUR	Churchill Papers (CAC)
COS	Chiefs of Staff (UK)
C-R	Warren F. Kimball, ed., *Churchill and Roosevelt: The Complete Correspondence* (3 vols, Princeton, 1984)

CS   *Winston S. Churchill: His Complete Speeches, 1897–1963*,
                ed. Robert Rhodes James (8 vols, New York, 1974)
CSCT   Clementine Churchill Papers (CAC)
CWMG   *Collected Works of Mahatma Gandhi* (New Delhi,
                1956–94), maintained on
                https://www.gandhiheritageportal.org/
Dalton   *The Political Diary of Hugh Dalton, 1918–40, 1945–60*,
                ed. Ben Pimlott (London, 1986)
Dalton WW2   *The Second World War Diary of Hugh Dalton, 1940–45*,
                ed. Ben Pimlott (London, 1986)
FDRL   Franklin Delano Roosevelt Library, Hyde Park, NY
FO   Foreign Office papers (TNA)
Fringes   John Colville, *The Fringes of Power: Downing Street
                Diaries, 1939–1955* (London, 1985)
FRUS   Department of State, *Foreign Relations of the United
                States* (multiple volumes, Washington DC)
GC   WSC, *Great Contemporaries*, ed. James W. Muller
                (Wilmington, DE, 2012)
HC Debs   House of Commons, Debates
HJ   *Historical Journal*
In Command   David Reynolds, *In Command of History: Churchill
                Fighting and Writing the Second World War* (London,
                2004)
JCH   *Journal of Contemporary History*
Jenkins   Roy Jenkins, *Churchill* (London, 2001)
Kersaudy   François Kersaudy, *Churchill and de Gaulle* (London,
                1981)
Kremlin Letters David Reynolds and Vladmir Pechatnov, eds, *The
                Kremlin Letters: Stalin's Wartime Correspondence with
                Churchill and Roosevelt* (New Haven, CT, 2018)
LRC   WSC, *Lord Randolph Churchill* (London, 1907 –
                single volume edn)
MEL   WSC, *My Early Life* (London, 1930)

Moran 1968	Lord Moran, *Winston Churchill: The Struggle for Survival, 1940–1965* (London, 1968)
Moran 2002	Lord Moran, *Churchill at War, 1940–1945* (London, 2002)
Moran 2006	Lord Moran, *Churchill: The Struggle for Survival, 1946–60* (London, 2006)
NC	Neville Chamberlain papers, Birmingham University Library
Nicolson	Harold Nicolson, *Diaries and Letters, 1930–1962*, ed. Nigel Nicolson (3 vols, London, 1966–8)
OB	*Winston S. Churchill* (8 vols, London, 1966–88) – the official biography by Randolph S. Churchill (vols 1–2) and Martin Gilbert (vols 3–8)
PREM	Prime Minister's papers (TNA)
Roberts	Andrew Roberts, *Churchill: Walking with Destiny* (London, 2018)
Rose	Norman Rose, *Churchill: An Unruly Life* (London, 1994)
RRJ	Robert Rhodes James, *Churchill: A Study in Failure, 1900–1939* (London, 1973 pbk)
Rzheshevsky	Oleg A. Rzheshevsky, *War and Diplomacy: The Making of the Grand Alliance – Documents from Stalin's Archive* (Amsterdam, 1996)
Soames	Mary Soames, *Clementine Churchill* (2nd edn, London, 2002)
Speaking	Mary Soames, ed., *Speaking for Themselves: The Personal Letters of Winston and Clementine Churchill* (London, 1998)
SWW	WSC, *The Second World War* (6 vols, London, 1948–54)
TNA	The National Archives, Kew, Surrey, England
TWC	WSC, *The World Crisis* (6 vols, London, 1923–31)
VBC	Violet Bonham Carter, *Winston Churchill As I Knew Him* (London, 1965)

WM	War Cabinet Minutes (CAB)
WO	War Office papers (TNA)
WP	War Cabinet Papers (CAB)
WSC	Winston Spencer Churchill

Notes

Introduction

1. See the essays in Allen Packwood, ed., *The Cambridge Companion to Churchill* (Cambridge, 2023), esp. 1–27, 396–400.
2. *GC*, preface. 'There were wonderful giants of old' was a school song from his *alma mater*, Harrow.
3. Moran 2006, 220, 2 Dec. 1953.
4. Virginia Woolf, *A Room of One's Own* (1929; London, 2020), 28.
5. *The Complete War Memoirs of Charles de Gaulle*, trans. Jonathan Griffin and Richard Howard (New York, 1998), 58.
6. AMB, 302–3.
7. William Shakespeare, *Twelfth Night*, Act 2, Scene 5.
8. *GC*, 65.

1 Lord Randolph Churchill

1. Letter of 11 Jan. 1899, CD 2:1002.
2. VBC, 27.
3. *MEL*, 76.
4. Medical notes in CD 1:542–4, 547.
5. He told his private secretary in the early 1950s, 'You know my father died of Locomotorataxia, the child of syphilis,' AMB, 122. This was also his mother's understanding: see Rose, 19, 350.
6. RSC to WSC, 9 Aug. 1893, CD 1:390–1; Roberts, 27.
7. OB 1:242. In *MEL*, 73, Winston said he graduated eighth out of 150.
8. Addison, 9; Roberts, 76, 79.
9. *MEL*, 76.
10. Quoted in Paul Johnson, *Churchill* (New York, 2009), 26.
11. *MEL*, 25.
12. *MEL*, 27, 37; Roberts, 14, 16.

13. *MEL*, 29–31.

14. *MEL*, 123.

15. *MEL*, 125.

16. Roberts, 23, 24 (letters); CD 1:295 ('Mummy'). For a more sympathetic appraisal of the maternal Jennie, see David Lough, ed., *Darling Winston: Forty Years of Letters between Winston Churchill and His Mother* (London, 2018).

17. *MEL*, 19, 52–3.

18. *MEL*, 76, 167.

19. *MEL*, 60.

20. David Cannadine, 'Churchill and the Pitfalls of Family Piety', in Robert Blake and William Roger Louis, eds, *Churchill* (Oxford, 1993), 10.

21. Rose, 21.

22. OB 1:179.

23. Charles Eade, ed., *Churchill by his Contemporaries* (London, 1955), 3.

24. CD 2:835.

25. CD 2:774–80; *MEL*, 136–9.

26. CD 2:792–3, 839.

27. CD 2:811–12, 839, 854–5.

28. CD 2:913, 922–3.

29. *MEL*, 182.

30. CD 2:978, 979, 981; see also WSC, *The River War* (2 vols, London, 1899).

31. CD 2:974 and n2.

32. *MEL*, 225.

33. WSC, *The River War*, 364.

34. Quotations from CD 2:1002 ('trees'), 971 and 997 (Kitchener); Roberts, 62 ('Hints').

35. OB 1:451–3.

36. J.B. Atkins, *Incidents and Reflections* (London, 1947), 122, 123, 125.

37. *MEL*, 271.

38. CD 2:1204, 1218–19, 1223, 1225.

39. A phrase from Jenkins, 22.

40. CD 2:751.

41. HC Debs, 13 May 1901, vol 93, cols 1562–79, quoting esp. from 1574–5.

42. HC Debs, 13 May 1901, 93:1571–2.

43. HC Debs, 13 May 1901, 93:1565–6, 1568.

44. *MEL*, 382–3; Addison, 19.

45. CD 2:698.

46. CD 3:168.

47. Quotations from CD 3:174, 183.

48. CD 3:243.

49. CD 3:310, 323.

50. OB 2:77.

51. HC Debs, 29 Mar. 1904, 132:1022–5; CD 3:325–6.

52. HC Debs, 22 Apr. 1904, 133:1001.

53. OB 2:80.

54. CD 3:436, letter of 15 Aug. 1902.

55. OB 2:133–5.

56. George C. Brodrick, *The Oxford Magazine*, 30 Jan. 1895, 179.

57. Lord Rosebery, *Lord Randolph Churchill* (London, 1906), 3; see also Rosebery to WSC, 15 Jan. 1906, OB 2:141.

58. RRJ, 19–20.

59. *LRC*, x.

60. *LRC*, 471; R.F. Foster, *Lord Randolph Churchill: A Political Life* (Oxford, 1981), 270, 349, 375, 395.

61. R.E. Quinault, 'Lord Randolph Churchill and Tory Democracy, 1880–1885', *HJ*, 22 (1979), 141–3; Robert Rhodes James, *Lord Randolph Churchill* (London, 1986 edn), 213 ('Tory Democracy'); cf. *LRC*, 375–7.

62. For example, *LRC*, 235, 245, 274, 520.

63. *LRC*, 220 ('a man arose'), 238–9.

64. *LRC*, 627, 822–3.

65. *LRC*, 569.

66. Fabian Ware, 'Conservative Opportunists and Liberal Imperialists', *The Nineteenth Century* (March 1907), 406, 408.

67. CS 1:552: Speech in Manchester, 11 Jan. 1906.

68. OB 2:143; William Scawen Blunt, 'Randolph Churchill: A Personal Recollection', *The Nineteenth Century* (March 1906), 401.

69. OB 2: 142–3.

70. WSC to Lord James, 18 Jan. 1906, quoted in Foster, *Lord Randolph Churchill*, 386.

71. VBC, 27.

2 David Lloyd George

1. David Lloyd George to William George, 23 Mar. 1916, quoted in William George, *My Brother and I* (London, 1958), 253.6

2. Lord Boothby, *Recollections of A Rebel* (London, 1978), 52.

3. Richard Toye, *Lloyd George and Churchill: Rivals for Greatness* (London, 2007), 1, quoting Stanley Baldwin in Jan. 1937.

4. VBC, 161.

5. Letter of 23 Dec. 1901, CD 3:104.
6. VBC, 161.
7. Boothby, *Recollections*, 52.
8. For background, see Toye, *Lloyd George and Churchill*.
9. *MEL*, 380.
10. Letter of 23 Dec. 1901, CD 3:104.
11. CD 3:390.
12. Hopwood to Elgin, 27 Dec. 1907, CD 4:729–30; cf. Ronald Hyam, 'Churchill and Empire', in Blake and Louis, eds, *Churchill*, 168.
13. CS 1:681, speech at Manchester, 18 Oct. 1906.
14. CS 1:671–7, speech at Glasgow, 11 Oct. 1906.
15. Diary, 12 Feb. 1908, in Lucy Masterman, *C.F.G. Masterman: A Biography* (London, 1927), 97–8.
16. OB 2:296.
17. See WSC memo, July 1908, CD 4:827–31.
18. WSC to Asquith, 26 and 29 Dec. 1908, CD 4:860–1, 862–4.
19. Toye, *Lloyd George and Churchill*, 51–5; Addison, 69. See also Allen Packwood, 'A Tale of Two Statesmen: Churchill and Napoleon', *Finest Hour*, no. 157 (Winter 2012–13), 14–20.
20. John Grigg, *Lloyd George: The People's Champion, 1902–1911* (London, 1978), 222–5.
21. Speeches of 25 June 1907 and 7 May 1908, CS 1:807 and 1040–1.
22. Bentley B. Gilbert, *Lloyd George: A Political Life. The Architect of Change, 1863–1912* (London, 1987), 354 ('excitable'); Grigg, *People's Champion*, 66–7.
23. OB 2:363–5.
24. Cabinet paper, 25 Oct. 1910, CHAR 12/1/5.
25. Addison, 128.
26. WSC to Asquith, 3 Jan. 1911, CD 4:1032–3; see also 1240–4.
27. Quoted in RRJ, 49–50; Masterman, *C.F.G. Masterman*, 184.
28. Addison, 140–51; Grigg, *People's Champion*, 291–3; Masterman, *C.F.G. Masterman*, 208 ('thrashing').
29. See Grigg, *People's Champion*, 294–303.
30. Toye, *Lloyd George and Churchill*, 81–2; CD 5:1473, quoting WSC letter of 18 Dec. 1911.
31. Asquith to WSC, 1 Apr. 1912, CD 5:1483.
32. *Speaking*, 26; letter written c. 1885, in Kenneth O. Morgan, ed., *Lloyd George Family Letters* (Cardiff, 1973), 13–14.
33. John Campbell, *If Love Were All: The Story of Frances Stevenson and David Lloyd George* (London, 2006), 43; John Grigg, *Lloyd George: From Peace to War, 1912–16* (London, 1997 pbk), 79.

34. T.G. Otte, *Statesman of Europe: A Life of Sir Edward Grey* (London, 2020), 409–15.
35. CD 4:1116, 1120.
36. Memo of 13 Aug. 1911, largely printed in WSC, *The World Crisis, 1911–14* (London, 1923), 60–4.
37. OB 2:528.
38. Gilbert, *Lloyd George*, 454–9; Jenkins, 201, 205.
39. VBC, 237.
40. Toye, *Lloyd George and Churchill*, 91–3, 102–3.
41. This paragraph draws on documents in CD 5:1818–73, quoting notes of 16 Dec. 1913, 1833.
42. Grigg, *Lloyd George: From Peace to War*, 134–7.
43. LG to WSC, 27 Jan. 1914, CD 5:156; see also Toye, *Lloyd George and Churchill*, 102–13.
44. Speech of 17 Mar. 1914, HC Debs, vol. 60.
45. Simon to Asquith [Jan. 1914], CD 5:1859.
46. Addison, 168–71.
47. Arthur J. Marder, *From the Dreadnought to Scapa Flow*, vol. 2 (London, 1965), 85.
48. CD 6:163, 165–6, 176–8, quoting Asquith to Venetia Stanley, 7 Oct. 1914, 177–8.
49. OB 3:126, 129.
50. A.J.P. Taylor, ed., *Lloyd George: A Diary by Frances Stevenson* (London, 1971), 10.
51. OB 3:154, 187.
52. WSC to Asquith, 29 Dec. 1914, CD 6:343–5.
53. Barry Gough, *Churchill and Fisher: Titans at the Admiralty* (Barnsley, 2017), 510.
54. See CD 6:337–43, 350–6 for memos by Hankey, 28 Dec. 1914 and LG, 31 Dec. 1914.
55. CD 6:558–9.
56. VBC, 360–1.
57. Gough, *Churchill and Fisher*, 385 (emphasis in original).
58. CD 7:898, 921, 925–6.
59. OB 3:473.
60. Taylor, ed., *Stevenson Diary*, 52, entry for 19 May 1915.
61. Grigg, *Lloyd George: From Peace to War*, 256.
62. Toye, *Lloyd George and Churchill*, 148.
63. Letters of 18 and 21 Dec. 1915, in *Speaking*, 137, 139.
64. OB 3:712–15.

65. HC Debs, 7 Mar. 1916, 80: 1420–30, quoting col. 1426.

66. OB 3:722, 725, 733.

67. OB 3:387–8.

68. HC Debs, 23 May 1916, 82:2009–27, quoting cols 2012, 2027.

69. David Lloyd George, *War Memoirs*, vol. 3 (London, 1934), 1068; OB 3:823.

70. WSC to CSC, 28 Jan. 1916, OB 3:823.

71. Quotations from William George, *My Brother and I* , 253 ('horse-power'); Roberts, 167 ('barrister'); *New York Times*, 31 Oct. 1971 (Johnson).

72. Since this was a secret session, there was no official record of the speech. The argument is summarised in WSC, *The World Crisis, 1916–18* (London, 1927), 253–4.

73. WSC, *World Crisis, 1916–18*, 255.

74. Taylor, ed., *Stevenson Diary*, 158, 19 May 1917.

75. Quotations from OB 4:33.

76. WSC to Sinclair, 29 Dec. 1917, OB 4:62–3.

77. OB 4:158.

78. Taylor, ed., *Stevenson Diary*, 5 Mar. 1919, 169 (emphasis in original).

79. HC Debs, 3 Mar. 1919, 113:85–6.

80. HC Debs, 3 Mar. 1919, 113:69; 'The Bolshevist Menace', 11 Apr. 1919, CS 3:2770–4, quoting 2773 and 2771.

81. OB 4:229–30.

82. WSC to LG, draft, 17 Feb. 1919, CD 8:544.

83. OB 4:277–8.

84. OB 4:332, 333, 335.

85. OB 4:355–6.

86. HC Debs 10 Feb. 1920, vol 125:34–46, esp. cols 40–46.

87. OB 4:417–18.

88. CD 9:1237–46, quoting 1240 and 1246; CS 3:3027.

89. CD 9:1319; Taylor, ed., *Stevenson Diary*, 210, 26 Apr. 1921.

90. CD 10:1712–13.

91. 'Election Memories', first published in Sep. 1931, in WSC, *Thoughts and Adventures*, ed. James W. Muller (London, 2009 edn), 226.

92. Speeches of 4 and 25 Mar. 1922, quoted from CS 3:3236, 3233 and 3281.

93. Speech of 3 Jan. 1920, quoted from CS 3:2921.

94. Addison, 201.

95. Colin Cross, ed., *Life with Lloyd George: The Diary of A.J. Sylvester, 1931–1945* (London, 1975), 281, 3 Oct. 1940.

96. Taylor, ed., *Stevenson Diary*, 328.

3 Neville Chamberlain

1. WSC to Baldwin, 6 June 1927, CHAR 18/64.
2. Chamberlain diary, 19 Apr. 1928, in Graham Smith, *Burying Caesar: Churchill, Chamberlain and the Battle for the Tory Party* (London, 1999), 41.
3. *SWW* 1, 388–9; Clementine's proof annotations on CHUR 4/131/94.
4. Smith, *Burying Caesar*, 9–10.
5. *GC*, 65, 70.
6. *GC*, 74–6.
7. OB 5:694.
8. WSC to Rowan, 19 July 1947, CD 22:741.
9. David Dilks, *Neville Chamberlain, vol. I: Pioneering and Reform, 1869–1929* (London, 1984), 398.
10. Drafts and revisions at CHUR 4/76/54–6, 282–8. All but a single sentence of this passage was cut from the published text of Churchill's memoirs: see *SWW* 1:19.
11. P.J. Grigg, *Prejudice and Judgment* (London, 1948), 174.
12. Speech of 10 Mar. 1928 in Stanley Baldwin, *This Torch of Freedom: Speeches and Addresses* (London, 1935), 308.
13. CHUR 4/76A/54; Dutton, *Neville Chamberlain*, 14.
14. Keith Feiling, *The Life of Neville Chamberlain* (London, 1946), 129, 459–62; OB 5:68. See also Addison, 237–8; Cab 64 (24) 2 and 6, 26 Nov. 1924, CAB 23/49.
15. OB 5, chs 4 and 7, quoting 114.
16. Dilks, *Neville Chamberlain*, vol. I, 431, 441.
17. Dutton, *Neville Chamberlain*, 34, 43.
18. OB 5:245–6.
19. WSC to Baldwin, 6 June 1927 CHAR 18/64/3–13.
20. WSC to Baldwin, 6 June 1927, CHAR 18/64/9–10, and exchanges with Chamberlain, 10–11 June, folios 38–40.
21. Addison, 278.
22. Quoting Addison, 277, 278.
23. OB 5:277, 280.
24. Chamberlain to Irwin, 12 Aug. 1928, in OB 5:296; Chamberlain diary, 28 Mar. 1928, in Feiling, *Chamberlain*, 147; CAB 23/57/264 and /273.
25. Chamberlain to Irwin, 12 Aug. 1928, in OB 5:297; Chamberlain diary, 19 Apr. 1928, in Smith, *Burying Caesar*, 41.
26. Winston to Clementine, 27 Aug. 1929, in OB 5:344–5.
27. John Barnes and David Nicholson, eds, *The Empire at Bay: The Leo Amery Diaries, 1929–1945* (London, 1988), 146; OB 5:365.

28. Kenneth Young, ed., *The Diaries of Sir Robert Bruce Lockhart, 1915-1938* (London, 1973), 186, entry for 20 Sep. 1931.

29. Quoting from Roberts, 50, 364-5.

30. Roberts, 50, 364-5; OB 5:741 (Baldwin).

31. OB 5:663, 675, 685-7, quoting Baldwin, 687.

32. R.A.C. Parker, *Churchill and Appeasement* (London, 2000), 80-5.

33. *SWW* 1:141.

34. Roberts, 398-9.

35. Erik Goldstein, 'Neville Chamberlain, the British official mind and the Munich Crisis', *Diplomacy and Statecraft*, 10 (1999), 278.

36. Eden to PM, 18 Jan. 1938, draft, FO 371/21526, A2127.

37. HC Debs, 14 Mar. 1938, 333:93-100, esp. 95, 100.

38. HC Debs, 24 Mar. 1938, 333:1399-1413.

39. *News Chronicle*, 15 Sep. 1938, 1.

40. Cab 38 (38) 1, 14 Sep. 1938, CAB 23/95/39-40.

41. Neville to Ida, 11 Sep. 1938, NC 18/1/1068.

42. So claimed Neville to Ida, 3 Sep. 1938, NC 18/1/1066.

43. Neville to Ida, 19 Sep. 1938, NC 18/1/1069; see also Cab 38 (38) 1, 14 Sep. 1938, CAB 23/95/35.

44. Hilda to Neville, 16 Sep. 1938, NC 18/2/1091, and Neville to Ida, 19 Sep. 1938, NC 18/1/1069.

45. Cab 39 (38), 17 Sep. 1938, CAB 23/95; Sir Thomas Inskip, notes, 17 Sep. 1938, INKP 1 (CAC).

46. Cab 43 (38), 25 Sep. 1938, CAB 23/95/198-200.

47. Neville to Hilda, 2 Oct. 1938, NC 18/1/1070.

48. Nicolson, 1:370.

49. Neville to Hilda, 2 Oct. 1938, NC 18/1/1070. The speech is in HC Debs 339:5-26, quoting from col. 13.

50. Lord Home, *The Way the Wind Blows* (London, 1978), 65; *Daily Mirror*, 1 Oct. 1938, 1, 14.

51. Parker, *Churchill and Appeasement*, 175.

52. Quotations from CAB 23/94, fo. 296 (Chamberlain); John Harvey, ed., *The Diplomatic Diaries of Oliver Harvey, 1937-1940* (London, 1970), 15 Sep. 1938, 180; Nicolson, 1:371.

53. HC Debs 5 Oct. 1938, 339:360-73, esp. cols 360, 361, 365-6, 369.

54. HC Debs 6 Oct. 1938, 339:544-54, esp. cols 545, 551; WSC to Chamberlain, 5 Oct. 1938, and Chamberlain to WSC, 6 Oct. 1938, NC 7/9/38 and /39.

55. Letters of 8 and 15 Oct. 1939, NC 18/1/1124 (Winston), 18/1/1125 ('loathe').

56. Letter of 11 Dec. 1939, in CD 14:497.

57. 'The Naval Memoirs of Admiral J.H. Godfrey', TS. (1965), vol. 5, 63, 111–12, and vol. 7, 225–6 (CAC); CD 14:1134.

58. Godfrey, 'Memoirs', 5:63; Nicolson, 1:37.

59. Gabriel Gorodetsky, ed., *The Maisky Diaries* (London, 2015), 270–1; HC Debs, 11 Apr. 1940, 359:746–7.

60. Neville to Ida, 13 Apr. 1940, NC 18/1/1150.

61. HC Debs, 8 May 1940, 360: 1263–6, 1283; Nicolson, 1:78–9.

62. For a detailed discussion of the evidence, see Roberts, 501–9.

63. OB 5:687.

64. James Stuart, *Within the Fringe: An Autobiography* (London, 1967), 87; Neville Chamberlain to Archbishop of Canterbury, 14 Oct. 1940, in Feiling, *Chamberlain*, 455.

65. HC Debs, 12 Nov. 1940, 365:1617–19. See also Roberts, 616–17, 661.

4 Adolf Hitler

1. Max Domarus, *Hitler, Speeches and Proclamations, 1932–1945* (Würzburg, 1997), 2062.

2. *TWC: The Aftermath* (London, 1929), 457.

3. *SWW* 2:42–3.

4. See the epigraphs to this book.

5. *SWW* 1:65–6; OB 5:447–8. For a similar line in Mar. 1949, see OB 8:464.

6. OB 2:225, 196.

7. Craig, 'Churchill and Germany', in Blake and Louis, eds, *Churchill*, 21.

8. Johnson, 'Churchill and France', in Blake and Louis, eds, *Churchill*, 43–5; OB 6:73.

9. TWC: *The Aftermath*, 439, 456–7.

10. TWC: *The Aftermath*, 451, 457.

11. HC Debs, 13 May 1932, 255:2352.

12. HC Debs, 23 Nov. 1932, 272:87, 89–90.

13. HC Debs, 23 Mar. 1933, 276: 538–52, quoting cols 539, 542–3.

14. HC Debs, 285:1193, 7 Feb. 1934.

15. HC Debs, 28 Nov. 1934, 295:857–72, quoting from cols 858–60, 866–7.

16. Basil Collier, *The Defence of the United Kingdom* (London, 1957), 528; OB 5:673–4; R. J. Overy, 'German Air Strength 1933 to 1939: A Note', *HJ*, 27 (1984), 465–71, esp. note 5.

17. *SWW* 1:180.

18. Harold Macmillan, *Winds of Change, 1914–1939* (London, 1966), 575.

19. HC Debs, 28 Nov. 1934, 295:861, 862.

20. N.J. Crowson, *Facing Fascism: The Conservative Party and the European Dictators, 1935–1940* (London, 1995), 158–63; CE 1:402.

21. Donald Cameron Watt, 'Churchill and Appeasement', in Blake and Louis, eds, *Churchill*, 204.

22. Brian Bond, *Liddell Hart: A Study of His Military Thought* (London, 1976), 67, 85.

23. HC Debs, 7 Nov. 1933, 281:139, 140, 142; 23 Mar. 1933, 276:552 ('Don Quixote').

24. HC Debs, 333: 99–100, 14 Mar. 1938.

25. Statement on 28 July 1936, quoted in *SWW* 1:179.

26. *SWW* 1:56 and errata slip after 610.

27. HC Debs, 332:246, 22 Feb. 1938.

28. Ernest R. May, *Strange Victory: Hitler's Conquest of France* (New York, 2000), 314–22; CD 15:638–40.

29. CE 1: 424–5 and 394–5.

30. *SWW* 1:459.

31. CHUR 4/104/56–7, 82–3.

32. On this, see Allen Packwood, *How Churchill Waged War: The Most Challenging Decisions of the Second World War* (Barnsley, 2018), ch. 1.

33. Richard Toye, *The Roar of the Lion: The Untold Story of Churchill's World War II Speeches* (Oxford, 2013), 41–2.

34. Churchill to Chamberlain, 10 May 1940, NC 7/9/80.

35. Chamberlain diary, 15 May 1940, NC 2/24A; Halifax diary, 25 May 1940, Hickleton Papers (Borthwick Institute, York), A 7.8.4.

36. CAB 65/13, confidential annexes, WM (40) 139/1, 140, 141/1, 142, 145/1. For further detail see David Reynolds, *From World War to Cold War: Churchill, Roosevelt and the International History of the 1940s* (Oxford, 2006), 75–98.

37. Quotations from Chamberlain diary, 26 May 1940, NC 2/24A, and from CAB 65/13/180, 187.

38. Thomas Munch-Petersen, '"Common Sense Not Bravado": The Butler-Prytz Interview of 17 June 1940', *Scandia*, 52 (1986), 73–114, quoting from 74.

39. John Lukacs, *Five Days in London, May 1940* (New Haven, 1999), 126, 136, 187–90.

40. Dalton WW2, 26, 28 May 1940.

41. Halifax diary, 27 May 1940.

42. Dalton WW2, 26–9, 28 May 1940.

43. Notes of interview with Ismay, 11 July 1946 and Ismay to Sherwood, 23 July 1946, Robert E. Sherwood papers (Houghton Library, Harvard University), folders 1891 and 415.

44. HC Debs, 18 June 1940, 362:60–1.

45. *SWW* 2:81, 144, 231.

46. CAB 66/7, COS paper WP (40) 168 (emphasis in original).

47. HC Debs, 18 June 1940, 362:59–60.

48. CAB 66/11, WP (40) 362, para. 214.

49. David Stafford, 'The Detonator Concept: British Strategy, SOE and European Resistance after the Fall of France', *JCH*, 10 (1975), 185–217, quoting 202. See also CD 15:559.

50. CAB 66/11, WP (40) 352, 3 Sep. 1940.

51. Dalton WW2, 28.

52. CAB 65/13/326–8, WM 176 (40) 5 CA, 22 June 1940.

53. James Leutze, ed., *The London Observer: The Journal of General Raymond E. Lee* (London, 1971), 12; Toye, *Roar of the Lion,* 62.

54. HC Debs, 4 July 1940, 362: 1049–51.

55. Toye, *Roar of the Lion*, 63.

56. *Fringes*, 185, 4 July 1940.

57. *SWW* 1:211.

58. Ian Kershaw, *Hitler 1936–1945: Nemesis* (London, 2000), 276.

59. *SWW* 2:34–5.

60. Quotations from Kershaw, *Hitler*, 293, 298.

61. Nicholas Stargardt, *The German War: A Nation under Arms* (London, 2015), 100–03.

62. Kershaw, *Hitler*, 300–3.

63. Domarus, *Hitler, Speeches and Proclamations, 1932–1945*, 2062.

64. Quoted in *Fringes*, 200, 24 July 1940.

65. Andrew Roberts, 'The Holy Fox': A Life of Lord Halifax* (London, 1991), 249–50; Lord Birkenhead, *Halifax: The Life of Lord Halifax* (London 1965), 460.

66. Kershaw, *Hitler*, 302, 307–8; *Fringes*, 195; CAB 66/7, WP (40) 168.

67. Kershaw, *Hitler*, 305, 335, also xv–xviii (emphasis in original).

68. HC Debs, 12 Nov. 1940, 365:1619.

69. Broadcast of 22 June 1941, in CS 6:6428-9.

70. *Hitler's Table Talk: Hitler's Conversations recorded by Martin Bormann*, trans. Norman Cameron and R.H. Stevens (Oxford, 1988), 72, 186–8, 18 July 1941 and 7 Jan. 1942; Christa Schroeder, *He Was My Chief: The Memoirs of Hitler's Secretary*, trans. Geoffrey Brooks (Barnsley, 2009), 55.

71. *Hitler's Table Talk*, 8, 587, 624, 11–12 July and 22 July 1941, 9 Aug. 1942.

72. CAB 65/19, WM 66 (41) 5 CA and CAB 65/24, WM 120 (41) 5 CA.

73. Cabinet Secretary's notes of WM (42) 86th meeting, 6 July 1942, CAB 195/1; see also David Reynolds, *The Long Shadow: The Great War and the Twentieth Century* (London, 2013), 289–98.

74. *The Testament of Adolf Hitler*, trans. R.H. Stevens (London, 1961), 4 Feb., 2 Apr. 1945, 32–5, 107.
75. HC Debs 27 Feb. 1945, 408:1276–7. Similarly, in *SWW* 1:vii.
76. *TWC, The Aftermath*, 457.
77. 'The Tragedy of Europe', 19 Sep. 1946, in CD22:458–60.
78. Moran 2002, 330–4, 16 July 1945; OB 8:61.

5 Benito Mussolini

1. 'Memorandum on Sea-Power, 1939', 27 Mar. 1939, PREM 1/345.
2. Discorso alla Camera dei Fasci e delle Corporazioni, 2 dicembre 1942, http://bibliotecafascista.blogspot.com/2012/03/discorso-alla-camera-2-dicembre-1942.html
3. 'Dictators on Dynamite', *Collier's Magazine*, 3 Sep. 1938, in CE 1:413–14. Churchill's original title was 'The Dictators at the Cross-Roads' – see CHAR 8/620/71–91.
4. Letter dated 6 Apr. 1897, in CD 2:749.
5. WSC to CSC, 25 Mar. 1926, in *Speaking*, 298.
6. Moran 2002, 334, 16 July 1945.
7. *MEL*, 9–10.
8. Churchill to Grey, 5 Mar. 1915, CHAR 26/2/96.
9. *TWC, 1915*, 331; *TWC, 1916–1918*, 341.
10. WSC to CSC, 5 Sep. 1923, in *Speaking*, 275.
11. Quotations from Richard Lamb, *Mussolini and the British* (London, 1997), 87–9. See also OB 5:142 and CAB 23/52, Cab 1 (26) 4, 19 Jan. 1926.
12. CSC to WSC, 20 and 25 Mar. 1926, and WSC to CSC, 28 Mar. 1926, in *Speaking*, 295, 297, 298.
13. OB 5:226.
14. Lamb, *Mussolini and the British*, 105; Denis Mack Smith, *Mussolini* (London, 1983), 211, 214–15.
15. MacGregor Knox, *To the Threshold of Power 1922/33: Origins and Dynamics of the Fascist and National Socialist Dictatorships* (Cambridge, 2007), 325.
16. For text see Cmd. 4880, *Joint Resolution of the Stresa Conference, 14 April 1935* (London, 1935).
17. Renzo de Felice, *Mussolini il duce: vol. 3/1, Gli anni del consenso, 1929-1936* (Turin, 1996), 608.
18. Zara Steiner, *The Triumph of the Dark: European International History, 1933-1939* (Oxford, 2007), 126.
19. HC Debs, 2 May 1935, 301:602, 611.
20. CE 1:343–4.
21. WSC to Austen Chamberlain, 1 Oct. 1935, CHAR 2/237/83.

22. CS 6:5672–4, quoting 5673.

23. HC Debs, 24 Oct. 1935, 305:357–68.

24. HC Debs, 24 Oct. 1935, 305:368.

25. Steiner, *Triumph of the Dark*, esp. 156–7, 187–8, 193–4; Ian Kershaw, *Hitler 1936–1945* (London, 2000), 25–6.

26. 'The Spanish Tragedy', *Evening Standard*, 10 Aug. 1936, in WSC, *Step by Step, 1936–1939* (London, 1947 edn), 39–40. Bela Kun led the short-lived Hungarian Soviet Republic in 1919.

27. HC Debs, 14 Apr. 1937, 322:1063; *The Times* [London], 28 Apr. 1937, 17.

28. HC Debs, 14 Apr. 1937, 322:1069.

29. John Harvey, ed., *The Diplomatic Diaries of Oliver Harvey, 1937–1940* (London, 1970), 48, 22 Sep. 1937.

30. *Facing the Dictators* was the title of vol. 1 of Eden's memoirs (1965). A.J.P. Taylor sneered that 'Eden did not face the dictators; he pulled faces at them.' *English History, 1914–1945* (London, 1970 pbk), 754.

31. HC Debs 5 Nov. 1936, 317:282–3, 316–17.

32. See articles of 17 Feb. 1938 and 30 Jan. 1939 in *Step by Step*, 205, 309, 312.

33. *Step by Step*, 229, 332–5.

34. Lamb, *Mussolini and the British*, 244–5, 248–50, 265.

35. Notes, 3 Apr. 1938, in CD 13:979.

36. WSC, 'Mussolini's Choice', 13 Apr. 1939, in *Step by Step*, 333.

37. WSC to Chamberlain, 27 Mar. 1939, enclosing memo dated 25 Mar., PREM 1/345.

38. On the background, see Christopher M. Bell, *Churchill and Seapower* (Oxford, 2013), 155.

39. Quotations from 'Memorandum on Sea-Power', para. 2, and 'Let the Tyrant Criminals Bomb!', *Collier's*, 14 Jan. 1939, in CE 1:423–4.

40. CAB 66/3, WP (40) 135, 21 Nov. 1939, para. 4.

41. *SWW* 1:107–8. The exchange is in PREM 4/19/5.

42. Galeazzo Ciano, *Diary, 1937–1943*, ed. Renzo de Felice (London, 2002 edn), 271, 315, 356, entries for 2 Sep. 1939, 23 Jan. and 29 May 1940.

43. John Gooch, *Mussolini's War: Fascist Italy from Triumph to Collapse, 1935–1943* (London, 2020), 108, 160–1; Mack Smith, *Mussolini*, 294, 297–8.

44. CD 15:1284–8.

45. Harold Nicolson, *Diaries and Letters, 1939–1945* (London, 1967), 131, entry for 23 Dec. 1940.

46. CAB 80/14, annexe to COS (40) 521.

47. Telegram of 11 Aug. 1940, CD 15:645–7; Correlli Barnett, *Engage the Enemy More Closely: The Royal Navy in the Second World War* (London, 2000), 213.

48. Gooch, *Mussolini's War*, 164; Mack Smith, *Mussolini*, 303–4.

49. *SWW* 3:152; *In Command*, 231–6.

50. HC Debs, 7 May 1941, 371:994.

51. *'Chips': The Diaries of Sir Henry Channon*, ed. Robert Rhodes James (London, 1993), 307, 6 June 1941; Kevin Jefferys, *The Churchill Coalition and Wartime Politics, 1940–1945* (Manchester, 1995), 86–8.

52. A.W. Martin and Patsy Hardy, eds, *Dark and Hurrying Days: Menzies' 1941 Diary* (Canberra, 1993), 65–6, 118–19, 163–4; see also *In Command*, 245–6.

53. Alan Watt, *The Evolution of Australian Foreign Policy, 1938–1965* (Cambridge, 1968), 24–5.

54. *In Command*, 246–8.

55. WSC to Dill, 13 May 1941, CD 16:660–1. For the other documents see WO 216/5.

56. Cecil King, *With Malice Toward None: A War Diary*, ed. William Armstrong (London, 1970), 140.

57. Churchill, minutes, 25 and 29 Aug. 1941, PREM 3/163/3.

58. Defence Commt (Operations) DC(O) (41) 65/1 and DC(O) (41) 66/1, 17 and 20 Oct. 1941, in CAB 69/2 and CAB 69/8.

59. *SWW* 3:551.

60. See *In Command*, 264–7, and Bell, *Churchill and Seapower*, 240–53.

61. *SWW* 4:81.

62. *SWW* 4:43; notes in CHUR 4/255, quoting respectively fos 123–4 and 118.

63. CHUR 4/255/124.

64. Quotations from David Day, *John Curtin: A Life* (Sydney, 1999), 438–9, 444.

65. *SWW* 4:343–4.

66. Horst Boog et al, *Germany and the Second World War*, volume 6 (Oxford, 2001), 706–10, 718–20, 740; Gooch, *Mussolini's War*, 314; Lamb, *Mussolini and the British*, 303.

67. Mack Smith, *Mussolini*, 330–5, 360.

68. Moran 2002, 85; John Harvey, ed., *The War Diaries of Oliver Harvey, 1941–1945* (London, 1978), 165.

69. HC Debs, 27 Jan. 1942, 377:598; H.R. Trevor-Roper, ed., *Hitler's Table Talk 1941–1944* (Oxford, 1988), 573–4

70. Ian Jacob, diary, 8 Aug. 1942, JACB 1/17 (CAC).

71. WSC to CSC, 9 Aug. 1942, in *Speaking*, 467.

72. WSC to War Cabinet, 21 Aug. 1942, Reflex 177, CHAR 20/87/68.

73. Notes of 30 Mar. 1948, CHUR 4/20B/366–7.

74. Statistics from Niall Barr, *Pendulum of War: The Three Battles of El Alamein* (London, 2005), 404, 408.

75. James K. Sadkovich, 'Understanding Defeat: Reappraising Italy's Role in the Second World War', *JCH*, 24 (1989), 45–6.

76. CS 6:6692–5 and 6710–15; see also draft in CHAR 9/189/131.

77. Speech of 2 Dec. 1942, http://bibliotecafascista.blogspot.com/2012/03/discorso-alla-camera-2-dicembre-1942.html

78. Mack Smith, *Mussolini*, 339.

79. *SWW* 6:640–1.

80. *SWW* 5:48.

6 Franklin D. Roosevelt

1. FDR to WSC, 30 Jan. 1942, *C–R* 1:337.

2. Speaking to his American publishers at Chartwell. Quoted in *Life*, 16 Nov. 1953, 92.

3. Alanbrooke, 1 Apr. 1945, 680; similarly in CSC to WSC, 23 Nov. 1943, in *Speaking*, 486.

4. WSC's terminology – see *Fringes*, 24 Feb. 1945, 564.

5. *GC*, 211.

6. Author's conversation with Lady Soames, 4 Mar. 2004.

7. Message of 8 Dec. 1941, *C–R*, 1:283.

8. CD 1: 134, 147.

9. CS 3:2613-16; Martin Gilbert, *Churchill and America* (New York, 2005), 77.

10. *SWW* 1:345; Michael Beschloss, *Kennedy and Roosevelt: The Uneasy Alliance* (New York, 1980), 200, 230, citing Kennedy's unpublished memoirs.

11. CE 1:232; OB 8:358.

12. CD 11:1033; CSC to WSC, 14 Nov. 1928, in *Speaking*, 332.

13. Gilbert, *Churchill and America*, 111–12, 123.

14. Patrick Renshaw, *Franklin D. Roosevelt* (London, 2004), 67.

15. Gilbert, *Churchill and America*, 111.

16. *C–R*, 1:23 (inscription).

17. 'While the World Watches', *Collier's*, 29 Dec. 1934, reprinted with revisions as 'Roosevelt from Afar' in *GC*, 358–68, 483–5.

18. Roosevelt, Annual Message, 4 Jan. 1939 (APP); David Reynolds, *From Munich to Pearl Harbor: Roosevelt's America and the Origins of the Second World War* (Chicago, 2001), 50–3.

19. Domarus, *Hitler, Speeches and Proclamations, 1932–1945*, 1449.

20. Sir Arthur Willert, memo, 25–26 Mar. 1939, 2, Willert papers (Sterling Library, Yale University), 14/61; FDR to Roger Merriman, 15 Feb. 1939, PSF 46: Britain (FDRL).

21. FDR to WSC, 11 Sep. 1939, *C-R* 1:24.
22. 'To End War', *Collier's*, 29 June 1935, in CE 1:351-2.
23. Quoting from WSC to Marshall Diston, 3 Oct. 1937, and to Lord Linlithgow, 3 Nov. 1937, in OB 5:871, 886.
24. Harold Ickes, diary, vol. 31, 4380, 12 May 1940 (Library of Congress, Washington DC).
25. Kennedy to FDR, 20 July and 2 Nov. 1939, PSF 53: GB, Kennedy (FDRL).
26. Anglo-French Supreme War Council, SWC 39/40, 13th meeting, 31 May 1940, 12, CAB 99/3; Charles de Gaulle, *Complete War Memoirs* (New York, 1998), 104.
27. HC Debs, 20 Aug. 1940, 364:1171.
28. WSC to FDR, 20 May 1940, in *C-R* 1:40.
29. WSC to Halifax, 24 June 1940, FO 371/24240, A3582/131/45.
30. Quotations in this paragraph from David Reynolds, *The Creation of the Anglo-American Alliance, 1937-1941* (London, 1981), 112, 127.
31. CAB 65/10, WM 310 (40) 5, 27 Dec. 1940.
32. CAB 65/10, WM 299 (40) 4, 2 Dec. 1940.
33. *C-R*, 1:87-111, quoting 109.
34. *SWW* 2:501.
35. Press conference, no. 702, 17 Dec. 1940; Morgenthau diary, 337:135, 9 Dec. 1940 (both FDRL).
36. Quotations from Reynolds, *Creation of the Anglo-American Alliance*, 159, 167, 171.
37. HC Debs. 12 Mar. 1941, 369:1292.
38. WSC to Eden, 2 May 1941, PREM 3/469, 350; *C-R* 1:181-2.
39. WSC to Dominion PMs, 3 Aug. 1941, FO 371/26151, A6944/18/45; Robert E. Sherwood, *Roosevelt and Hopkins* (New York, 1948), 350-1.
40. Geoffrey C. Ward, ed., *Closest Companion* (New York, 1995), 141; Roberts, *Churchill*, 677.
41. WSC to Queen Elizabeth, 3 Aug. 1941, PREM 3/485/6/16
42. FDR press conference, no. 795, 2 Jan. 1942, 3 (FDRL); John Barnes and David Nicholson, eds, *The Empire at Bay: The Leo Amery Diaries, 1929-1945* (London, 1988), 788.
43. CAB 65/19, 19 Aug. 1941, WM 84 (41) 1, confidential annex.
44. Alanbrooke, 209.
45. *C-R* 1:283-4.
46. Sherwood, *Roosevelt and Hopkins*, 442.
47. The papers, as given to FDR, are in *C-R* 1:294-308.
48. Part 3, '1943', *C-R* 1:301-4.
49. *SWW* 3:584-5; cf. *In Command*, 267-70.

50. Messages of 30 Jan., 18 Feb. and 18 Mar. 1942, in *C–R* 1:337, 362–3, 420–2.
51. *SWW* 4:343–4.
52. *SWW* 4:338.
53. *C–R* 1:420.
54. *C–R* 1:400–04, 446–9.
55. Letter of 3 Apr. 1942, *C–R* 1:441 (emphasis in original).
56. Message of 12 Apr. 1942, in *C–R* 1:448; Alanbrooke, 248–9.
57. Quoted in Mark A. Stoler, *Allies and Adversaries: The Joint Chiefs of Staff, the Grand Alliance, and U.S. Strategy in World War II* (Chapel Hill, NC, 2000), 76.
58. Rick Atkinson, *An Army at Dawn: The War in North Africa, 1942–1943* (New York, 2002), 16.
59. Larry I. Bland, ed., *George C. Marshall: Interviews and Reminiscences for Forrest C. Pogue* (Lexington, VA, 1991), 622.
60. CHUR 4/287, fos 83, 97–9.
61. For fuller discussion see *In Command*, 374–5.
62. C–R 2:501.
63. *SWW* 5:193; CHUR 4/313/5.
64. CAB 79/66/151–4, COS 254 (43) 4; David Dilks, ed., *The Diaries of Sir Alexander Cadogan OM, 1938–1945* (London, 1971), 26 Oct. 1943, 570.
65. Message of 17 Oct. 1943, in *C–R* 2: 541; COS 254 (43) 4.
66. *FRUS, Cairo and Tehran*, 489–90.
67. WSC to Cadogan, 19 Apr. 1944, PREM 4/197/2.
68. *C–R* 3: 139, 162.
69. WSC–Stalin conversation, 30 Nov. 1943, CAB 66/45, WP (44) 9; Michael Howard, *The Mediterranean Strategy in the Second World War* (London, 1968), 57.
70. Alanbrooke, 29 Feb. 1944, 527; Moran 2002, 230, 23 Sep. 1944.
71. C–R 3:222, 225–9; Alanbrooke, 564, 30 June 1944.
72. C–R 3:217–19.
73. WSC to Wilson, 10 Feb. 1944, CHAR 20/156; Alanbrooke, 558, 14 June 1944.
74. *In Command*, 393–5, 445–6.
75. Omar N. Bradley, *A Soldier's Story* (New York, 1951), 368–9; Roland G. Ruppenthal, *Logistical Support of the Armies*, volume 1 (Washington DC, 1953), 481–8.
76. WSC to CSC, 17 Aug. 1944, in *Speaking*, 501.
77. Jenkins, 757.
78. Quotations from Gilbert, *Churchill and America*, 321–2.

79. CD 20:2035, 2082, 727.

80. Alanbrooke, 544, 7 May 1944.

81. Moran 2002, 99–100, 24 Jan. 1943, 99–100; Barry Phipps, 'Churchill, Art and Politics', in Allen Packwood, ed., *The Cambridge Companion to Churchill* (Cambridge, 2023), 157.

82. Sarah Churchill, *A Thread in the Tapestry* (London, 1967), 62–3.

83. Morgenthau Presidential Diaries, 5:1093, 15 May 1942 (FDRL).

84. Lord Avon [Anthony Eden], *The Reckoning* (London, 1965), 424; Moran 2002, 224, 20 Sept 44.

85. WSC to Eden, 4 Mar. 1944, CD 19:1966.

86. Marian Holmes, diary, 2 Feb. 1945, quoted in Gilbert, *Churchill and America*, 327; Avon, *Reckoning*, 512, diary 4 Feb. 1945; Halifax to WSC, 15 Apr. 1945, CHAR 20/214.

87. Message of 17 Mar. 1945, *C–R* 3:574; OB 7:1254.

88. *CS* 7:6823-7; WSC to Richard Law, 16 Feb. 1944, PREM 4/27/10.

89. *C–R* 3:394, 398–9; *FRUS, Malta and Yalta*, 5 Feb. 1945, 628.

90. Quotations from the 17 April 1945 speech come from HC Debs, vol. 409.

7 Josef Stalin

1. Stalin, conversation with Milovan Djilas, 5 June 1944, https://digitalarchive.wilsoncenter.org/document/219903

2. Dalton WW2, 836n.

3. Avon, *Reckoning*, 514.

4. For Lloyd George, see *The Maisky Diaries: Red Ambassador to the Court of St James's, 1932–1943*, ed. Gabriel Gorodetsky (London, 2015), 170. See also Nicolson, 1:394, 3 Apr. 1939.

5. Printed in WSC, *Into Battle* (London, 1941), quoting 131.

6. Gabriel Gorodetsky, *Grand Delusion: Stalin and the German Invasion of Russia* (New Haven, 1999), 37; WSC to Stalin, 25 June 1940, CD 15:417–18.

7. *SWW* 3:331-2.

8. Messages of 25 and 28 July 1941, in *Kremlin Letters*, 30–1; *War Diaries of Oliver Harvey*, 24.

9. Messages of 3 and 13 Sep. 1941, *Kremlin Letters*, 40–1, 45–6.

10. CD 16:1368–70.

11. WSC to Stalin, 4 Nov. 1941, Stalin to WSC, 8 Nov. and to Maisky, 19 Nov. in *Kremlin Letters*, 64–70.

12. WSC to Stalin, 21 Nov. 1941, and Stalin messages of 23 and 30 Nov. in *Kremlin Letters*, 71–4.

13. Eden to Halifax, 22 Jan. 1942, FO 954/29A/361; Eden memo, 28 Jan. 1942, WP (42) 48, CAB 66/21, para. 8.

14. Eden memo, 28 Jan. 1942, para. 4, WP (42) 48, CAB 66/21.

15. *Maisky Diaries*, 418; *C-R* 1:394.

16. Oleg A. Rzheshevsky, *War and Diplomacy: The Making of the Grand Alliance - Documents from Stalin's Archive* (Amsterdam, 1996), 121 (henceforth Rzheshevsky).

17. See Rzheshevsky, 121-3, 138-9.

18. *C-R* 1:490.

19. Steven M. Miner, *Between Churchill and Stalin: The Soviet Union, Great Britain, and the Origins of the Grand Alliance* (Chapel Hill, NC, 1988), 246-51 stresses the American impact.

20. Rzheshevsky, 174-5, 177, 224.

21. *FRUS* 1942, 3:577; Rzheshevsky, 205-6.

22. Rzeshevsky, 204, 210-11, 218-20; *C-R* 1:504.

23. Rzheshevsky, 269, 274, 281-2, 298-9.

24. Message of 9 July 1942, *Kremlin Letters*, 124-7, quoting 125.

25. Stalin to WSC, 23 July 1942, *Kremlin Letters,* 129; *Maisky Diaries*, 454 (ellipses in original).

26. Avon, *Reckoning*, 338.

27. *Maisky Diaries*, 456-7; *Kremlin Letters*, 132-4.

28. OB 7:217.

29. Ian Jacob diary, 14 Aug. 1942, Jacob papers JACB 1/17 (CAC).

30. The British minutes of the conversation are in CAB 127/23. Quotations from CHUR 4/279/245 (bombing) and Moran 2002, 67, 12 Aug. 1942 ('glow').

31. *With Prejudice: The War Memoirs of Marshal of the Royal Air Force Lord Tedder GCB* (London, 1966), 330-1; *Cadogan, Diaries*, 471. For the 'home truths', see CHUR 4/279/157 and /203.

32. See *Kremlin Letters*, 141-2, 144-5, and the British record of the 13 August meeting in CAB 127/23.

33. Moran 2002, 68-9, 13 Aug. 1942, 68-9; Cadogan, *Diaries*, 471. On the interpreters, see Jacob diary, 13 Aug. 1942, JACB 1/17.

34. Churchill to War Cabinet, 14 Aug. 1942, PREM 3/76A/9.

35. Churchill to Stalin, 14 Aug. 1942, *Kremlin Letters*, 145.

36. Moran 2002, 70, 72, 14 Aug. 1942.

37. Clark Kerr diary, FO 800/300/138-45.

38. *SWW* 4:446; A.H. Birse, *Memoirs of an Interpreter* (London, 1967), 97-105, quoting 101.

39. *SWW* 4:445-9; see also Birse's notes in PREM 3/76A/12/35-7, and Birse, *Memoirs*, 103. For Maisky's advice, see *Maisky Diaries*, 458-9, 461.

40. *C-R* 1: 571; *Kremlin Letters*, 148, 611. The Russian word '*dusha*' could be a translation from English of either 'soul' or 'heart' - the latter sounding

more Churchillian – but either way it connotes 'the essence of a person'. After meeting Putin on 16 June 2001, Bush told reporters: 'I was able to get a sense of his soul, a man deeply committed to his country and the best interests of his country': https://www.presidency.ucsb.edu/documents/ the-presidents-news-conference-with-president-vladimir-putin-russia-kranj

41. Stephen Kotkin, *Stalin: Paradoxes of Power, 1878–1928* (London, 2014), 736.

42. *SWW* 4:448.

43. *C–R* 1:637, 643.

44. Churchill to Eden, 27 Oct. 1942, FO 954/25B.

45. *Kremlin Letters*, 178–80.

46. As related by WSC to Maisky on 8 Feb. 1943: see *Maisky Diaries*, 481–2.

47. Stalin to FDR and WSC, 30 Jan. 1943, Map Room papers, box 8 (FDRL).

48. *Maisky Diaries*, 477, 7 Feb. 1943.

49. See CD 18:686–7 and 690.

50. *C–R* 2:191.

51. *Kremlin Letters*, 237–8.

52. *SWW* 4: 679–80; memo of Maisky visit, 23 Apr. 1943, FO 954/19B/487–9; *Maisky Diaries*, 508–9. See also Lawrence Rees, *World War Two Behind Closed Doors: Stalin, the Nazis and the West* (London, 2008), 51–5; Anna M. Cienciala, Natalia Lebdeva and Wojciech Materski, eds, *Katyn: A Crime without Punishment* (New Haven, 2007).

53. WSC to Clark Kerr, 2 May 1943, CD 18:1177.

54. *Kremlin Letters*, 54–9; WSC to Roosevelt, 26 May 1943, and FDR's revisions to Marshall's draft, both in MR box 8 (FDRL).

55. Stalin to Roosevelt and Churchill, 11 June 1943, MR box 8.

56. *Kremlin Letters*, 267–72; WSC to Clark Kerr, 26 June 1943, PREM 3/333/5/ 252–3.2.

57. WSC to Clark Kerr, 29 June 1943, PREM 3/333/5/245.

58. *C–R* 2:278–9, 285, 290; *Kremlin Letters*, 275–6.

59. Churchill to King George VI, 11 Aug. 1943, CD 18:2237–8.

60. Martin J. Sherwin, *A World Destroyed: The Atomic Bomb and the Grand Alliance* (New York, 1977), 85, 89 ('only two'); *Kremlin Letters*, 295.

61. See *Kremlin Letters*, esp. 279–80, 313.

62. From Moran 2002, 173–5, 30 Nov. 194.

63. CD 19:1271, 1534; HC Debs, 22 Feb. 1944, 397:696–7.

64. WSC to Eden, 1 April 1944, FO 954/26B.

65. C–S 6 June and S–C 11 June 1944, CHAR 20/166/15 and 76.

66. *C–R* 3:295–6; *Kremlin Letters*, 459–63.

67. *Kremlin Letters*, 468–71.

68. The typescript of Birse's record, with Cabinet Office amendments, is in FO 800/302/227–35.

69. For a colourful account of the meeting, dictated six years later, see *SWW* 6:199 and CHUR 4/356/152.

70. Eden–Molotov meeting, 10 Oct. 1944, PREM 3/434/2. On the 11th, they settled on 80:20 for the USSR in Bulgaria and Romania, in return for conceding the British demand for 50:50 in Yugoslavia.

71. *SWW* 6:204; cf. *In Command*, 460.

72. Jonathan Rose, *The Literary Churchill: Author, Reader, Actor* (London, 2014), 384.

73. W. Averell Harriman and Elie Abel, *Special Envoy to Churchill and Stalin* (New York, 1975), 362.

74. WSC to JS, 20 Oct. 1944, CHAR 20/173/62; Moran 2002, 247, 16 Oct. 1944.

75. WSC to War Cabinet, 17 Oct. 1944, CHAR 20/181/8–9.

76. Thomas M. Campbell and Edward R. Stettinius, eds, *The Diaries of Edward R. Stettinius, Jr., 1943–1946* (New York, 1975), 214, 11 Jan. 1945; *Fringes*, 555; *FRUS, Malta and Yalta*, plenary, 6 Feb. 1945, 668-9.

77. See David Reynolds, *Summits: Six Meetings That Shaped the 20th Century* (London, 2007), ch. 3.

78. George McJimsey, ed., *Documentary History of the Franklin D. Roosevelt Presidency*, vol. 14 (New York, 2003), 631–3, 638–9.

79. Dalton WW2, 836, 23 Feb. 1945; *Fringes*, 562; HC Debs, 408:1283–4, 27 Feb. 1945.

80. Reynolds, *Summits*, 138–9.

81. *C–R* 3:547–51, 564–6, 587–9, 613.

82. *C–R* 3:630.

83. See Moran 2002, 304 and 306, 27 Apr. and 20 May 1945.

84. The term used by FDR's Chief of Staff: William D. Leahy, *I Was There* (New York, 1950), 315–16.

85. Report by the Joint Planning Staff, 'Operation "Unthinkable"', 22 May 1945, CAB 120/691.

86. Alanbrooke, 693, 24 May 1945; PM to COS, 9 June, CAB 120/691.

87. Cadogan, *Diaries*, 778.

88. *SWW* 6:583; Truman to WSC, 30 July 1945, in G.W. Sand, ed., *Defending the West: The Truman-Churchill Correspondence, 1945–1960* (Westport, CT, 2004), 142.

89. McLuer to WSC, 3 Oct. 1945, and WSC to Truman, 8 Nov. 1945, CHUR 2/230/350 and 166–7.

90. *New York Times*, 14 Mar. 1946, 1 and 4.

91. William Taubman, *Stalin's American Policy: From Entente to Détente to Cold War* (New York, 1982), 141–4; David Holloway, *Stalin and the Bomb* (London, 1994), 168–71.

92. Moran 2006, 22, 27 June 1946; Bracken to Beaverbrook, 16 Oct. 1946, Beaverbrook papers, C/56 (House of Lords Record Office).

93. Speech at MIT, 31 Mar. 1949, https://winstonchurchill.org/resources/ speeches/1946-1963-elder-statesman/mit-mid-century-convocation/

94. Montgomery to WSC, 21 Jan. 1947 and WSC to Stalin, 3 Feb. 1947, CHUR 2/143/95 and 100.

95. *CS* 8:7944, 8282, 8296–7; see also John W. Young, *Winston Churchill's Last Campaign* (Oxford, 1996).

96. *Fringes*, 650, 655; Young, *Churchill's Last Campaign*, 130.

97. HC Debs 515: 897, 11 May 1953,

98. *CS* 8:8604; also CHUR 5/56A/156.

99. WSC to Eisenhower, 16 Apr. 1956, CHUR 2/217, 98–9; AMB, 158.

100. Moran 1966, 801, entry for 6 Dec. 1959. (Not published in the 2006 edition.)

8 Charles de Gaulle

1. Alain Peyrefitte, *C'était de Gaulle: La France redevient la France* (Paris, 1994), 24 Jan. 1963, 370.

2. CHUR 4/300/532.

3. Charles de Gaulle, *Mémoires de Guerre* (Paris, 2000 edn), 5. See also Sudhir Hazareesingh, *In the Shadow of the General: Modern France and the Myth of de Gaulle* (Oxford, 2012), 43.

4. On the relationship, see François Kersaudy, *Churchill and de Gaulle* (London, 1981); Douglas Johnson, 'Churchill and France', in Blake and Louis, eds, *Churchill*, 41–55; François Bédarida, 'Winston Churchill's Image of France and the French', *Historical Research*, 74 (2001), 95–105.

5. 'France and Europe', speech at Metz, 14 July 1946, CD 22:404–5.

6. Kersaudy, 30–1, OB 2:225, 196; CD 22:405.

7. Kersaudy, 75.

8. Henri Amouroux, *Le 18 Juin 1940* (Paris, 1990 edn), 327.

9. OB 7:855–6.

10. Discussed in chapter 4.

11. Kersaudy, 84–6.

12. Julian Jackson, *A Certain Idea: The Life of Charles de Gaulle* (London, 2018), 179.

13. Record of meeting on 30 Sep. 1942, 6, PREM 3/120/6; Nicolson, 138, 20 Jan. 1941.
14. Jackson, *A Certain Idea*, 179; WSC to Eden, 30 May 1942, PREM 3/120/7.
15. John Colville, *Footprints in Time* (London, 1976), 113–15; Kersaudy, 154–60.
16. Pierre Billotte, *Le temps des armes* (Paris, 1972), 187; WSC to Eden, 5 Nov. 1942, PREM 4/27/1.
17. Jackson, *A Certain Idea*, 206–8.
18. Jean Lacouture, *De Gaulle: The Rebel, 1890–1944* (New York, 1990), 397.
19. Harvey, *War Diaries*, 192–3.
20. Text in CHAR 9/156, esp. fos 257–9. Bordeaux was where the French government capitulated in June 1940.
21. Kersaudy, 230.
22. Jackson, *A Certain Idea*, 251.
23. Moran 2002, 97, 22 Jan. 1943.
24. WSC to Attlee and Eden, 21 May 1943, FO 371/36047.
25. Avon, *Reckoning*, 397–8; memos dated 13 July 1943, by Eden and WSC, PREM 3/181/8.
26. As told later to the British ambassador in Washington – see Halifax, diary, 12 May 1943, Hickleton papers, A 7.8.12.
27. Harold Macmillan, *War Diaries: Politics and War in the Mediterranean, January 1943–May 1945* (New York, 1984), 101, 122, 1 and 14 June 1943.
28. Jackson, *A Certain Idea*, 301–2, 314.
29. WSC to FDR, 1 June 1944, *C–R*, 3.156.
30. Record of WSC–de Gaulle conversation, 4 June 1944, CAB 66/50, WP (44) 297; de Gaulle, *Mémoires*, 487–8. See also OB 7:789–90, and Jackson, *A Certain Idea*, 310–14.
31. *In Command*, 412–13.
32. Jackson, *A Certain Idea*, 325–9.
33. Kersaudy, 369–71, 375–6.
34. According to de Gaulle, *Complete War Memoirs*, 727–8.
35. Robert Dallek, *Franklin Roosevelt and American Foreign Policy, 1932–1945* (New York, 1979), 611, n. 37; Richard Law, memo of conversation with FDR, 22 Dec. 1944, FO 371/44595, AN 154.
36. De Gaulle, *Complete War Memoirs*, 760.
37. WSC to Eden, 25 Nov. 1944, PREM 4/30/8.
38. De Gaulle, *Complete War Memoirs*, 225.
39. British minutes of plenary session on 7 Feb. 1945, 3, copy in PREM 3/51/4.

40. *FRUS*: *The Conferences at Malta and Yalta, 1945* (Washington DC, 1955), 628.

41. Jean Lacouture, *De Gaulle: The Ruler, 1945–1970* (New York, 1992), 124.

42. WSC to de Gaulle, 12 Sep. and de Gaulle to WSC, 17 Sep. 1948, CHUR 4/22, fos 227–44.

43. CD22:458–60.

44. WSC to de Gaulle, 26 Nov. 1946, CHUR 2/30; Sandys, note of talk with de Gaulle, 13 Dec. 1946, CHUR 2/20A.

45. CD 22:1188–9.

46. WSC, note for the Cabinet, 29 Nov. 1951, C (51) 32, CAB 129/48. 'Commonwealths' was in the paper.

47. Michael Charlton, *The Price of Victory* (London, 1983), 190, 195, 307; also Simon Burgess and Geoffrey Edwards, 'The Six plus One: British policy-making and the question of European economic integration, 1955', *International Affairs*, 64 (1988), esp. 407, 413.

48. Wm. Roger Louis and Roger Owen, eds, *Suez 1956: The Crisis and its Consequences* (Oxford, 1989), 336–7.

49. N. Piers Ludlow, *Dealing with Britain: The Six and the First UK Application to the EEC* (Cambridge, 1997), 32.

50. Harold Macmillan, *At the End of the Day, 1961–1963* (London, 1973), 365.

51. Jackson, *A Certain Idea*, 584–5, 588–9.

52. Stephen George, *An Awkward Partner: Britain in the European Community* (Oxford, 1998).

53. Richard Davis, 'The Geometry of Churchill's "Three Majestic Circles": Keystone of British Foreign Policy or *trompe l'œil*?' in Mélanie Torrent and Claire Sanderson, eds, *La puissance britannique en question: Diplomatie et politique étrangère au 20e siècle* (Brussels, 2013), 79–92.

54. Moran 2002, 98, 22 Jan. 1943; Alistair Horne, *Macmillan, 1957–1986* (London, 1989), 319.

55. John Ramsden, *Man of the Century: Winston Churchill and his Legend since 1945* (London, 2002), 3, 280.

56. *SWW* 2:189; Lacouture, *De Gaulle: The Rebel*, 200.

57. See *In Command*, esp. 329–32, 411–13, 453–4.

58. CHUR 4/311/52 and 107–8; CHUR 4/362/267.

59. CHUR 4/300/532; SWW 4: 611.

60. Lacouture, *De Gaulle: The Ruler*, 154–8.

61. Cyrus Sulzberger, *The Last of the Giants* (New York, 1970), 8; similarly Louis Terrenoire, *De Gaulle, 1947–1954: Pourquoi l'Echec?* (Paris, 1981), 198.

62. De Gaulle, *Complete War Memoirs*, 58.

63. See Kersaudy, 64, 120, 426.

64. *GC*, 290–1.
65. *GC*, 291.
66. As recalled by the diplomat Sir Antony Acland, British Library, 8 June 2004.

9 Mohandas K. Gandhi

1. David Arnold, *Gandhi: Profiles in Power* (London, 2001), 147.
2. Speech at Epping, 23 Feb. 1931, CS 5:4985.
3. Judith M. Brown, *Gandhi: Prisoner of Hope* (London, 1989), 1.
4. Speech, 26 July 1897, in CS 1:28
5. Nazmul S. Sultan, 'Moral Empire and the Global Meaning of Gandhi's Anti-Imperialism', *Review of Politics*, 84 (2022), 545–69.
6. Ronald Hyam, *Elgin and Churchill at the Colonial Office, 1905–1908: The Watershed of the Empire-Commonwealth* (London, 1908), 418–19.
7. HC Debs, 28 Feb. 1906, 152:1231–44.
8. 'Interview with Churchill', in CWMG 6:257–8, doc. 286; Birla to WSC, 23 Sep. 1935, CHAR 2/240B/185–6.
9. WSC to Selborne, 2 Jan. 1908, quoted in Toye, *Churchill's Empire*, 111.
10. Ramachandra Guha, *Gandhi: The Years that Changed the World, 1914–1948* (London, 2018), 4–5, 86–7.
11. Gandhi to Viceroy, 29 Apr. 1918, CWMG 14:377–8, doc. 257.
12. HC Debs, 8 July 1920, 131: 1719–33, esp. cols 1725, 1729–30.
13. WSC to Montagu, 8 Oct. 1921, CD 10:1644–5; Toye, *Churchill's Empire*, 154, 172.
14. Conference of Ministers, 9 Feb. 1922, CAB 23/39/141.
15. Sunil Khilnani, *The Idea of India* (London, 1998 pbk), 164.
16. Letter to Lord Irwin, quoted in Keith Middlemas and John Barnes, *Baldwin: A Biography* (London, 1969), 536; WSC draft in CHUR 4/76A/256–7; Birkenhead, *Halifa*, 206 (quoting Birkenhead).
17. R.J. Moore, *The Crisis of Indian Unity, 1917–1940* (Oxford, 1974), 41.
18. *Daily Mail*, 16 Nov. 1929, in OB 5:355–7.
19. Arnold, *Gandhi*, 147–51.
20. OB 5:369.
21. OB 5:375–7, quoting 377.
22. Birkenhead, *Halifax*, 294–8.
23. Speech at Epping, 23 Feb. 1931, CS 5:4985.
24. Jonathan Hyslop, 'Gandhi 1869–1915: The transnational emergence of a public figure', in Judith M. Brown and Anthony Parel, eds, *The Cambridge Companion to Gandhi* (Cambridge, 2011), 48–9.
25. CS 5:4971; Addison, 313–14.
26. CS 5:4985.

27. Middlemas and Barnes, *Baldwin*, 581; Dalton WW2, 128, 18 Dec. 1940.

28. WSC to Baldwin, 24 Sep. 1930, in OB 5:368.

29. Roberts, 342; cf. Roberts, *'Holy Fox'*, 41, and Jenkins, 436.

30. *Speaking*, 354; see also OB 5:367, 369.

31. Middlemas and Barnes, *Baldwin*, 588–90.

32. Roberts, *'Holy Fox'*, 40.

33. Guha, *Gandhi*, 382.

34. HC Debs, 12 Mar. 1931, 249:1417–26.

35. Hugh Martin, quoted in RRJ, 261.

36. HC Debs, 12 Mar. 1931, 249:1448–67.

37. OB 5:416.

38. RRJ, 267.

39. Warren Dockter, *Churchill and the Islamic World* (London, 2015), 212–13; OB 5: 603.

40. Middlemas and Barnes, *Baldwin*, 712,

41. E.g. WSC to Mira Slade, 21 Sep. 1934, CHAR 2/225/23.

42. Birla to Gandhi, 25 Aug. 1935, CD 12:1243–5; Toye, *Churchill's Empire*, 187–8.

43. Birla to WSC, 23 Sep. 1935, CHAR 2/240B/185–6.

44. Guha, *Gandhi*, 526, 529.

45. J.C. Smuts, 'Gandhi's Political Method', in Sarvepalli Radhakrishnan, ed., *Mahatma Gandhi: Essays and Reflections on his Life and Work* (London, 1939), esp. 282–5.

46. Guha, *Gandhi*, 579–80, 586; for Gandhi's statement see CWMG 70:290 (doc. 335).

47. 'A Baffling Situation' in *Harijan*, 6 April 1940; CWMG 71:388, doc. 371; for Jinnah's speech, 22 Mar. 1940, see http://www.columbia.edu/itc/mealac/pritchett/00islamlinks/txt_jinnah_lahore_1940.html

48. WM 30 (40) 4, 2 Feb. 1940, CAB 65/5.

49. Gandhi to Linlithgow, 26 May 1940; 'How to Combat Hitlerism', *Harijan*, 22 June 1940; 'To Every Briton', *Harijan*, 6 July 1940, in CWMG 72:100–1, 187–9, 229–31, docs 128, 249, 281,

50. Quotations from CD 15:397, 506–8, 529, 589.

51. Guha, *Gandhi*, 628–38; Gandhi to Hitler, 24 Dec. 1940, CWMG 73:255–7, doc. 307.

52. Guha, *Gandhi*, 671–3; Moran 2002, 61, 7 Aug. 1942.

53. *Amery Diaries*, 9 Sep. 1942, 832; HC Debs, 10 Sep. 1942, 383:302–4.

54. Messages to FDR and Chiang, 13 and 26 Aug. 1942, *C-R* 1:563; CHAR 20/79A/55–6.

55. Yasmin Khan, *The Raj at War: A People's History of India's Second World War* (London, 2013), 183 ('millenarian'); Sugata Bose and Ayesha Jalal, *Modern South Asia: History, Culture, Political Economy* (London, 1997), 160 ('uprising'); Brown, *Gandhi*, 339 ('viability').

56. See Ayesha Jalal, *The Sole Spokesman: Jinnah, the Muslim League and the Demand for Pakistan* (Cambridge, 1985), ch. 3.

57. CAB 65/33, WM 25 (43) 1, 7 Feb. 1943, *Amery Diaries*, 872, 7 Feb. 1943.

58. CD 18:429; see also 440, 503, 523–4 and *Amery Diaries*, 875, 1 Mar. 1943.

59. CD 18:494, 509.

60. 'Notes, India', for 30 Mar. 1943, CHAR 9/191A/1–12, quoting fos 5, 7, 8 and 10.

61. Gandhi, in his turn, coupled Hitler and Churchill together as apostles of violence: Brown, *Gandhi*, 317.

62. Wavell, diary, 9 Feb. 1944, quoted in Khan, *The Raj at War*, 213. Chapter 15 of this book offers a judicious appraisal of the famine debate.

63. CAB 66/41, WP (43) 435 (Wavell) and WP (43) 445 (WSC); CAB 65/36, WM 136 CA, 7 Oct. 1943.

64. Quotations from *Amery Diaries*, 905–6. See also Brown, *Gandhi*, 343.

65. *Amery Diaries*, 982; WSC to Wavell, 27 May 1944, CHAR /20/165/43.

66. WSC to CSC, 1 Feb. 1945, in *Speaking*, 512; *Fringes*, 563, 23 Feb. 1945; *The Art of the Possible: The Memoirs of Lord Butler* (Harmondsworth, 1973 pbk), 112.

67. Guha, *Gandhi*, 755–6; *Amery Diaries*, 1045 note.

68. Gandhi to WSC, 17 July 1944, in CWMG 77:391–2, doc. 278, and also appendix 20, 478; WSC to Viceroy, 1 Nov. 1944, CHAR 20/174/33.

69. Speech of 5 Oct. 1946, CD 20, esp. 476–7.

70. Toye, *Churchill's Empire*, 273–5; Moran 2006, 349, 3 Feb. 1955.

71. CWMG 87:187, doc. 174; Arnold, *Gandhi*, 222.

72. A theme emphasised in Khilnani, *Idea of India*, e.g. 27, 31, 73, 125, 201–2.

73. Sumit Sarkar, *Modern India, 1885–1947* (Basingstoke, 1989), 437.

74. Judith M. Brown, *Modern India: The Origins of an Asian Democracy* (Oxford, 1985), 337. See also Yasmin Khan, 'Performing Peace: Gandhi's assassination as a critical moment in the consolidation of the Nehruvian state', *Modern Asian Studies*, 45 (2011), 57–80.

75. David Hardiman, 'Gandhi's global legacy', in Brown and Parel, *Cambridge Companion to Gandhi*, 254.

76. Speech of 18 July 1946, in CD 22:408; Guha, *Gandhi*, 888–9, 892.

77. *SWW* 4:660–1; cf. CHUR 4/57/112–15, and CHUR 4/298/22, 23 ('furore').

78. *SWW* 4:196; CHUR 4/264/183.

79. Roberts, 342.

80. Quotations from Brown, *Gandhi*, 387.
81. Faisal Devji, *The Impossible Indian: Gandhi and the Temptation of Violence* (London, 2012), 174–5.

10 Clement Attlee

1. Kenneth Harris, *Attlee* (London, 1982), 244.
2. 'Lord Attlee, the Gallipoli Poet', *Guardian*, 22 Apr. 1963, 22.
3. Clifford's recollections (1987) in CD 22:222–3.
4. Robert Crowcroft, *Attlee's War: World War II and the Making of a Labour Leader* (London, 2011), 10.
5. Roberts, 293–4.
6. Quotations from Harris, *Attlee*, 13–15.
7. C.R. Attlee, *As It Happened* (London, 1954), 18.
8. Addison, 53–4.
9. Attlee, *As It Happened*, 21. See also Jon Cruddas, 'Attlee, the ILP and the Romantic Tradition', Attlee Memorial Lecture, 4 Nov. 2011.
10. Attlee, *As It Happened*, 35.
11. Clem to Tom, 2 Apr. 1918, in John Bew, *Citizen Clem: A Biography of Attlee* (London, 2016), 90; note [1918], Attlee papers, ATLE 1/18 (CAC).
12. C.R. Attlee, *The Social Worker* (London, 1920), ch. 1, quoting respectively 21, 24 and 18.
13. CHAR 9/66B/121.
14. Leo McKinstry, *Attlee and Churchill: Allies in War, Adversaries in Peace* (London, 2019), 97.
15. HC Debs, 15 June 1925, 185:85–7, 89–90.
16. Harris, *Attlee*, 5–7.
17. HC Debs, 2 Dec. 1931, 260:1118–31, esp. cols 1120–1, 1125–7.
18. Attlee, *As It Happened*, 74.
19. McKinstry, *Attlee and Churchill*, 115.
20. HC Debs, 7 Nov. 1933, 281:145–7; OB 5:456; Harris, *Attlee*, 116.
21. McKinstry, *Attlee and Churchill*, 127–9.
22. Harris, *Attlee*, 98, 119; Dalton, 196, 26 Nov. 1935.
23. Harris, *Attlee*, 136–7.
24. Bew, *Citizen Clem*, 202–4, 217–18.
25. Moran 1968, 269.
26. McKinstry, *Attlee and Churchill*, 153–4; https://www.theguardian.com/world/2018/nov/20/clement-attlee-child-refugee-paul-willer-fled-nazis-1939

27. HC Debs, 5 Oct. 1938, 339:359–73 (also OB 5:996–1001); *Clem Attlee: The Granada Historical Records Interview* (London, 1967), 17.

28. HC Debs, 3 Oct. 1938, 399:50–66, esp. cols. 51–2, 59.

29. Francis Beckett, *Clem Attlee: Labour's Great Reformer* (London, 2015), 213.

30. Attlee to WSC, 1 July 1939, CHAR 8/628/22.

31. McKinstry, *Attlee and Churchill*, 177–8.

32. HC Debs, 7 May 1940, 360:1086–94.

33. *Attlee: The Granada Historical Records Interview*, 20. He made the same point less pungently in his memoirs: see Attlee, *As It Happened*, 140.

34. Beckett, *Clem Attlee*, 471–2.

35. WSC to Eden, 24 May 1941, PREM 4/100/5.

36. CAB 66/18 WP (41) 203, docs 15 and 18; McKinstry, *Attlee and Churchill*, 268–70.

37. Toye, *Churchill's Empire*, 213–14; HC Debs 9 Sep. 1941, 374:68–9.

38. On the power dynamics behind the reshuffle, see McKinstry, *Attlee and Churchill*, 287–96.

39. CAB 66/21, WP (42) 59, 2 Feb. 1942, paras 1–5, 10.

40. M139/2, 16 Apr. 1942, CHAR 20/67; see also OB 7:92.

41. Attlee to WSC, 10 July 1941, PREM 3/499/9; Harris, *Attlee*, 199–200, 585–7.

42. WSC to Attlee, 29 July 1942, PREM 3/499/9.

43. Harris, *Attlee*, 208.

44. Addison, 365–9.

45. CAB 66/33, WP (43) 18, 12 Jan. 1943.

46. Attlee to WSC, no date, Attlee papers ATLE 2/2 (CAC).

47. CAB 65/40, WM (43) 140 CA, 14 Oct. 1943; CAB 65/36, WM 144 (43) 1, 21 Oct. 1943; Dalton WW2, 655–7, 21 Oct. 1943.

48. ATLE 2/2, fos 16–21, quoting fo. 18.

49. Harris, *Attlee*, 242–4; *Fringes*, 554–5, 20–21 Jan. 1945. WSC's reply is in ATLE 2/2, fo. 22.

50. McKinstry, *Attlee and Churchill*, 411–15.

51. HC Debs, 17 Apr. 1935, 300:1861; Crowcroft, *Attlee's War*, 231 – a central theme of his book.

52. Williams, *A Prime Minister Remembers*, 82.

53. Quoting Harris, *Attlee*, 268, and Williams, *A Prime Minister Remembers*, 150 and 84.

54. David Marquand, 'Labour's own Captain Mainwaring', *New Statesman*, 2 Sep. 2016, 41.

55. Harris, *Attlee*, 567.

56. HC Debs 6 Dec. 1945, 416:2530–51, quoting cols 2530–1.

57. HC Debs 6 Dec. 1945, 416:2551–65, quoting cols 2551–2, 2564–5.

58. McKinstry, *Attlee and Churchill*, 459 (Callaghan); Bew, *Citizen Clem*, 291–2; Attlee note [1951] in ATLE 1/5, fo. 4. The censure debate is not mentioned in the official Churchill biography: see OB 7:173.

59. Bew, *Citizen Clem*, 382.

60. Harris, *Attlee*, 286.

61. Dalton WW2, 544, 5 Jan. 1943; cf. Harris, *Attlee*, 210.

62. Williams, *A Prime Minister Remembers*, 71 (Potsdam); David Reynolds, *From World War to Cold War* (Oxford, 2006), 261–2.

63. CAB 130/16, GEN 163/1, 8 Jan. 1947.

64. Harris, *Attlee*, 288; Peter Hennessy, *Cabinets and the Bomb* (Oxford, 2007), 48.

65. Hennessy, *Cabinets and the Bomb*, 69–70, 77–86.

66. CAB 131/2, DO (46) 27, Attlee memo of 2 Mar. 1946.

67. Alan Bullock, *Ernest Bevin: Foreign Secretary, 1945-1951* (London, 1984), 348–54; Raymond Smith and John Zametica, 'The Cold Warrior: Clement Attlee Reconsidered, 1945-7', *International Affairs*, 61 (1985), 247–51.

68. HC Debs, 31 Jan. 1947, 432:1333–50.

69. Nicholas Owen, 'The Conservative Party and Indian Independence, 1945–1947', *Historical Journal*, 46 (2003), esp. 416–17.

70. CAB 29/15, CP (46) 456, 24 Dec. 1946.

71. Harris, *Attlee*, 378; Philip Ziegler, *Mountbatten* (London, 1985), 353–6.

72. HC Debs, 6 Mar. 1947, 434:768.

73. HC Debs, 6 Mar. 1947, 434:663–78.

74. Sir Robert Cary, quoted in Toye, *Churchill's Empire*, 272.

75. HC Debs, 6 Mar. 1947, 434:763–72; Harris, *Attlee*, 381.

76. Adrian Smith, *Mountbatten, Cold War and Empire, 1945-79* (London, 2023), ch. 1, quoting 28, 30. For a vehement critique of the last Viceroy, see Andrew Roberts, *Eminent Churchillians* (London, 1995), ch. 2, 'Lord Mountbatten and the Perils of Adrenalin'.

77. Robert Rhodes James, *Anthony Eden* (London, 1986), 321 (Lancer); Earl Attlee, *Empire into Commonwealth* (London, 1961), 35–6; cf. Earl of Halifax, *Fulness of Days* (London, 1957), 125–6.

78. Hennessy, *Never Again*, 128.

79. Quotations from Addison, 388, 390–1.

80. CD 22:1068.

81. CD 22:1650; Bullock, *Bevin*, 755; Nicolson 3:186; McKinstry, *Attlee and Churchill*, 525.

82. CAB 129/40, CP (30) 120; CAB 128/17, CM 34 (50) 1; Attlee to Bevin, 7 June 1950, PREM 8/1428; Sir David Hunt, quoted in McKinstry, *Attlee and Churchill*, 534.

83. Quoting Bullock, *Bevin*, 784–7.

84. Hennessy, *Never Again*, 390, 416.

85. Franks to PM, 15 and 23 July 1950, PREM 8/1405, pt. I; see also Alex Danchev, *Oliver Franks: Founding Father* (Oxford, 1993), 125–8.

86. CD 22: 1958–62.

87. Harris, *Attlee*, 465.

88. HC Debs, 14 Dec. 1950, 482:1350–1464, quoting cols 1357, 1363; Philip M. Williamson, *Hugh Gaitskell* (Oxford, 1982), 169.

89. Williamson, *Gaitskell*, 195.

90. McKinstry, *Attlee and Churchill*, 567–9, quoting *Daily Herald*, 22 Oct. 1951.

91. Harris, *Attlee*, 545.

92. AMB, 120,

93. Nicolson 3:113, 10 Nov. 1947; Harris, *Attlee*, 532 (Macmillan).

94. 'The Churchill I Knew', in *Churchill by his Contemporaries:* (London, 1965), 14–35.

95. Harris, *Attlee*, 553.

96. Attlee, *The Social Worker*, 18.

11 Clementine Churchill

1. The last lines of *MEL*, 385.

2. CSC to WSC, 6 Apr. 1916, in *Speaking*, 198.

3. Letter of 27 June 1940 in Soames, 325–6.

4. Sonia Purnell, *First Lady: The Life and Wars of Clementine Churchill* (London, 2016), 2. See also her essay 'The Influence of Clementine Churchill', in Allen Packwood, ed., *The Cambridge Companion to Winston Churchill* (Cambridge, 2023).

5. Roberts, *Churchill*, 118, 1013.

6. Christopher Hassall, *Edward Marsh: A Biography* (London, 1959), 131.

7. Quotations from VBC, 15–16, and Purnell, *First Lady*, 34.

8. WSC to CSC, 16 Apr. 1908, in *Speaking*, 7.

9. Quotations from *Speaking*, 9, and Purnell, *First Lady*, 33.

10. Mark Bonham Carter and Mark Pottle, eds, *The Life and Letters of Violet Bonham Carter*, vol.1 (London, 1996), 162.

11. Soames, 96–7.

12. Barry Gough, *Churchill and Fisher: Titans at the Admiralty* (London, 2017), 354.

13. Soames, 141–2.
14. OB 3:473.
15. Quoting CSC to WSC, 30 Dec. 1915, and WSC to CSC, 19 Jan. 1916, in *Speaking*, 142, 156; Purnell, *First Lady*, 89–90.
16. Soames, 148–9, 156.
17. CSC to WSC, 27 Jan. and 4 Feb. 1916, in *Speaking*, 162–3, 167–8.
18. CSC to WSC, 16 Feb. 1916, CHAR 1/118A/72.
19. CSC to WSC, 29 Oct. 1918, in *Speaking*, 216–17.
20. WSC to CSC, 15 Sep. 1918, and CSC to WSC, 14 Sep. 1919, in *Speaking*, 214–15, 220–1; also Purnell, *First Lady*, 112, 122.
21. CSC to WSC, 31 Mar. 1920, CHAR 1/135/2–3.
22. Purnell, *First Lady*, 127.
23. Purnell, *First Lady*, 145; Soames, 289.
24. Quotations from OB 4:878 ('guillotine'), and Soames, 238–9.
25. Soames, 249.
26. WSC to CSC, 17 Apr. 1924 and [late summer] 1926, in *Speaking*, 281, 301–2.
27. WSC to CSC, 15 Mar. 1925, in *Speaking*, 291–2; Purnell, *First Lady*, 175–7.
28. Soames, 299.
29. Quotations from *Speaking*, 376, 391, 198, and Soames, 295 [Sarah].
30. For different views on Terence Philip and Lady Castlerosse, see Purnell, *First Lady*, 185–9; Roberts, 383–7; Warren Dockter and Richard Toye, 'Who Commanded History? Sir John Colville, Churchillian Networks, and the 'Castlerosse Affair', *JCH*, 54 (2019), 401–19.
31. Soames, 278–9.
32. Quotation from Josh Ireland, *Churchill & Son* (London, 2021), 151.
33. Sarah Churchill, *Keep on Dancing: An Autobiography* (London, 1981) 56–7.
34. OB 5:435; Purnell, *First Lady*, 180–1; Ireland, *Churchill and Son*, 102–4.
35. Soames, 270.
36. Soames, 301–6.
37. John G. Winant, *A Letter from Grosvenor Square: An Account of a Stewardship* (London, 1947), 98.
38. Purnell, *First Lady*, 210–11.
39. Soames, 336.
40. Winant, *Letter from Grosvenor Square*, 46.
41. Soames, 334; CSCT 3/3/24–5.
42. Purnell, *First Lady*, 1–7.
43. 'Diary of Trip to Great Britain', 30 Oct. 1942, Eleanor Roosevelt papers, box 2963 (FDRL).

44. Eleanor Roosevelt trip diary, 27 Oct. 1942; Purnell, *First Lady*, 268–75.
45. *SWW* 3:421; *Maisky* Diaries, 421, 450; Soames, 360–3.
46. Quotations from *Kremlin Letters*, 232, 488.
47. Soames, *Clementine Churchill*, 344; Purnell, *First Lady*, 260.
48. Lady Diana Cooper, *Trumpets from the Steep* (London, 1960), 182.
49. WSC to Eden, 25 Mar. 1945, FO 954/26C/591.
50. Soames, 405–6; *Kremlin Letters*, 577–8.
51. WSC to CSC, 6 Apr. 1945, CSCT 2/34/44–5.
52. Soames, 408–11.
53. WSC to CSC, 5 May 1945, in *Speaking*, 530; WSC to Truman, 12 May 1945, CAB 120/186).
54. 'Mrs Churchill Home. Memorable Tour in Russia', *The Times*, 14 May 1945, copy in CSCT 3/48/79; CSC to Rathbone, 23 May 1945, in Soames, 413.
55. Mary to CSC, 14 and 26 Aug. 1945, in Soames, 428–9.
56. Mary to CSC, 13 Oct. 1945, Soames, 439.
57. Purnell, *First Lady*, 326–7; Soames, 444.
58. Emma Soames, ed., *Mary Churchill's War: The Wartime Diaries of Churchill's Youngest Daughter* (London, 2021), 164, 24 Sep. 1942.
59. Diary, 25 Mar. 1942, in *Mary Churchill's War*, 127; Winston S. Churchill II, *His Father's Son*, 202.
60. Soames, *Clementine Churchill*, 470.
61. Soames, 481; R.B. Stevens to Eden, 14 Dec. 1953, copy in CSCT 3/90, 102.
62. Soames, 524–9.
63. Moran 1968, 652.
64. AMB, 171; Roberts, 946 [solicitor]; Jenkins, 890.
65. Moran 1968, 652; Clark to Mary, 10 Aug. 1978 in Soames, 551.
66. Soames, 550–1; Purnell, *First Lady*, 341.
67. Soames, 545.
68. Quotations from Soames, 565.
69. Soames, 265–6.
70. Soames, 573.

12 Winston Churchill

1. 'The Dream', CE 4:511.
2. HC Debs, 23 Jan. 1948, 446:557.
3. OB 8:364.
4. 'The Dream', CE 4:504–11.
5. RRJ, 18; VBC, 16.

6. OB 3, ch. 19 esp. 598, 605–6, 611.

7. OB 3:617.

8. RRJ, 445–6.

9. Gerald Pawle, *The War and Colonel Warden* (London, 1963), 53.

10. *SWW* 1:526–7.

11. *GC*, 65.

12. Harriman and Abel, *Special Envoy*, 362.

13. HC Debs, 27 Jan. 1942, 377:601–2.

14. OB 8:126.

15. A.J.P. Taylor, ed., *Lloyd George: A Diary by Frances Stevenson* (London, 1971), 328; *Selections from the Correspondence of the First Lord Acton*, volume 1, ed. J.V. Figgis and R.V. Laurence (London, 1917), x.

16. WSC to Baldwin, 6 June 1927 CHAR 18/64/3–13.

17. Chamberlain to Irwin, 12 Aug. 1928, OB 5:297.

18. See above, ch. 8. In 'The Dream', 510, Winston had his father recall that story.

19. Broadcast of 22 June 1941, in CS3:6428–9.

20. HC Debs 28 Sep. 1944, 403:481; notes for WM 86 (42), 6 July 1942, CAB 195/1; OB 5:1120.

21. CE 1:413–14.

22. CS 6:6712–13; *SWW* 5:48.

23. *GC*, 211.

24. CD 18:686–7 and 690.

25. Moran 2002, 97, 22 Jan. 1943.

26. De Gaulle, *Complete War Memoirs*, 58.

27. *Maisky Diaries*, 353, 7 May 1941; Roberts, 977.

28. OB CV 2/1:104.

29. Harris, *Attlee*, 244; *Churchill by his Contemporaries*, 35.

30. Christopher M. Bell, *Churchill and the Dardanelles* (Oxford, 2017), 368–9.

31. Blanche E.C. Dugdale, *Arthur James Balfour* (2 vols, London, 1936), 2:337; see also Robin Prior, *Churchill's 'World Crisis' as History* (London, 1983).

32. *SWW* 1:vi.

33. J.H. Plumb, 'The Historian', in A.J.P. Taylor et al, *Churchill: Four Faces and the Man* (London, 1969), 149.

34. HC Debs, 18 June 1940, 362:60–1.

35. David Reynolds, *Britannia Overruled: British Policy and World Power* (London, 2000), ch. 1, esp. 11–12.

36. John Darwin, *Unfinished Empire: The Global Expansion of Britain* (London, 2012), xi–xiv.

37. PM to Gen. Noel Holmes, 23 Nov. 1942, CHAR 20/67/9.

38. Winston S. Churchill II, *His Father's Son: The Life of Randolph Churchill* (London, 1996), 86–7; Randolph to WSC, 7 Feb. 1947, CHUR 1/42/171–5.

Index